Bertolt Brecht
Centenary Essays

D1344631

GERMAN MONITOR No. 41
General Editor: Ian Wallace

Bertolt Brecht
Centenary Essays

Edited by

Steve Giles
and Rodney Livingstone

Amsterdam - Atlanta, GA 1998

∞ The paper on which this book is printed meets the requirements of "ISO 9706:1994, Information and documentation - Paper for documents - Requirements for permanence".

ISBN: 90-420-0319-7 (bound)
ISBN: 90-420-0309-X (paper)
©Editions Rodopi B.V., Amsterdam - Atlanta, GA 1998
Printed in The Netherlands

Table of Contents

Preface

The publication of this collection of essays marks the centenary of Brecht's birth on 10 February 1898. It appears ten years after the publication of the initial volumes in the new Brecht edition, the *Große kommentierte Berliner und Frankfurter Ausgabe*,[1] and is the first major collection of essays on Brecht to take full account of that new edition. The essays were commissioned from scholars and critics around the world, and cover six main areas: biographical controversies; neglected theoretical writings; the semiotics of Brechtian theatre; new readings of classic texts; Brecht and the GDR; and contemporary appropriations of Brecht's work.

In the wake of German unification and the collapse of Stalinist regimes in Eastern and Central Europe, it has often been suggested that the writings of a committed Marxist such as Brecht are of no relevance to our post-historical, post-modern age. In Brecht's case, moreover, political hostility has been buttressed by excoriating attacks on his personal and professional credentials, notably in John Fuegi's *The Life and Lies of Bertolt Brecht*.[2] Although many of Fuegi's more lurid and grossly inaccurate accusations have been given short shrift by Brecht scholarship,[3] the issues which Fuegi raises concerning collaboration or exploitation of Brecht's female co-workers cannot be ignored. The essays by Kuhn and Preece confront precisely these issues from the perspectives of biography, memoir, and fictionalised accounts of Brecht's dealings with others. As Kuhn indicates, such apparently straightforward matters in fact raise a host of theoretical questions concerning authorship and textuality. The essays by Giles and Livingstone focus therefore on neglected theoretical writings, while Ujma considers his relationship with Ernst Bloch, but all three essays question the nature of Brecht's Marxism and his understanding of modernity. This is a central theme in Giles' commentary on *Der Dreigroschenprozeß*, Brecht's most sustained and sophisticated theoretical essay. The dialogical and dialectical aspect of Brecht's writing, underlined by Livingstone in his discussion of *Me*-ti, is also crucial in Vaßen's analysis of Brecht's city poetry, as is its reception by Walter Benjamin.

The five essays at the heart of the collection deal with Brechtian theatre. White and Rokem focus their attention on the sign systems and spatial configurations that are characteristic of epic theatre, whilst Roche rethinks

Brecht's relationship to the European comic tradition. Moss and Holmes both concentrate on *Leben des Galilei*, taking up the thematics of decentring addressed by Rokem, but also reviewing the play's contemporary relevance in the light of recent critical debates on the viability of Enlightenment reason and Marxist politics.

Brecht's uneasy relationship with GDR writers and cultural politics is explored in the next three essays. Thomaneck compares Brecht and Anna Seghers' very different conceptions of law and justice in the context of socialist reconstruction after 1945, whilst Davies and Parker analyse the contradictory nature of Brecht's relationship with the cultural and political hierarchies of the GDR. The question of Brecht's standing and reception in the GDR after his death in 1956 plays an important role in Rechtien's discussion of his impact on Christa Wolf's work in the 1960s and 1980s, as does his understanding of science and socialism.

Like Brecht, Christa Wolf has been the subject of vitriolic attacks in recent years during the debates provoked by the publication in 1990 of *Was bleibt*. The theoretical dimension of those debates provides the framework for Herhoffer's reconsideration of Brecht's *Lehrstücke* in terms of the controversial concept of *Gesinnungsästhetik*. Herhoffer shows that even these texts, commonly taken to be the most didactic of Brecht's works, retain a flexibility and dynamic openness which transcend the narrow confines of their ostensible politics, and it is the dialectical and deconstructive tenor of Brecht's plays which, as Weber demonstrates, has been of particular interest to contemporary American playwrights. Mumford, finally, discusses the most radical of recent critiques and appropriations of Brecht in her exploration of materialist feminists' engagement with gestic acting, Marxism and gender, and performance theory.

Warmest thanks are due to the contributors for their prompt delivery of manuscripts, to the Universities of Nottingham and Southampton for their generous financial support, and to Keith Harris for his word-processing wizardry.

Steve Giles
University of Nottingham
October 1997

Rodney Livingstone
University of Southampton

[1] Bertolt Brecht, *Werke. Große kommentierte Berliner und Frankfurter Ausgabe*, Hg. W. Hecht, J. Knopf, W. Mittenzwei, K-D. Müller (Berlin, Aufbau/ Frankfurt aM, Suhrkamp, 1988-), cited throughout this collection in the abbreviated form *BFA*, followed by the relevant volume and page numbers.

[2.] John Fuegi, *The Life and Lies of Bertolt Brecht* (London, HarperCollins, 1994), published in the USA as *Brecht and Company. Sex, Politics, and the Making of Modern Drama* (New York, Grove Press, 1994).

[3.] See for example J. Willett, J. K. Lyon, S. Mews, H. Ch. Norregaard, 'A Brechtbuster Goes Bust: Scholarly Mistakes, Misquotes, and Malpractices in John Fuegi's *Brecht and Company*', *The Brecht Yearbook*, 20 (1995), 258-367. Fuegi's own credentials have not been enhanced by his refusal to engage in public debate with his critics, nor by the ruling of a Paris court that his book defames Brecht's daughter, Barbara Brecht-Schall.

TOM KUHN

Bertolt Brecht and Notions of Collaboration

'Nenne doch nicht so genau deinen Namen'
(*Mann ist Mann, BFA*, 2, 210)

Amongst the literary artists of the twentieth century Brecht stands out as quite extraordinarily inclined to seek the creative input of others. Friends and enemies, sexual partners and professional associates, philosophers, musicians, visual artists and other writers, practitioners from film and theatre, and, finally, audiences and publics wherever he encountered them: all may be said to have made a significant contribution to the oeuvre. Brecht's collaborations are, moreover, rather different from most modern artistic partnerships. For a start, it seems that the inclination to share and exchange was there already in even his earliest literary excursions, and that it persisted unabated, through a thousand variations of circumstance, until the end of his creative life. It anticipated (and survived) all manner of theories and belated justifications. It was not just a short-lived experiment, like that, for example, of the French Surrealists, proceeding from a particular theory of artistic production in the modern world. Secondly, for Brecht there is not just one artistic partner, nor even a series of 'significant others', there are multiple, continuous and synchronous friendships and partnerships of almost every imaginable shape and hue. The first task of this essay is therefore, very simply, to hold fast to the extraordinary extent and variety of collaborative relationships at the centre of Brecht's artistic project.

Beyond that my purpose is to attempt to expound and confront some of the ideas about how such relationships functioned, and about what they may mean for readers of Brecht. I am not concerned with establishing new facts, although a sort of typology of collaborations may emerge from my remarks. The cases I mention feature only as examples.[1] Nor am I particularly concerned with the issues of attribution, acknowledgement and copyright, important though these are. Briefly: bourgeois aesthetics and bourgeois law - even in its 'socialist' versions - tend to identify the author as originator and as singular. This practice provided the conditions for contemporary accusations of plagiarism and for the squabbles over rights with Kurt Weill. After Brecht's death it enabled the Brecht heirs easily to assert the family rights over those of the various 'Mitarbeiter'. But it is worth pointing out that this was not entirely Brecht's fault. Brecht himself was reasonably concerned to credit his collaborators. A large number of manuscripts and publications name several authors. The original issues of the *Versuche* sometimes acknowledge a number of names equally. It is the later re-issues and editions which have tended to demote the others to 'Mitarbeiter' in small print, or to exclude them altogether. Over time, as the name of Brecht came to represent more and, above all, as direct control over publications slipped out of his hands, the practice of installing the single (male) author reasserted itself. It is worth remarking also that, for all the talk about Brecht supposedly trampling over the rights of others, there are also some clear counter-examples, the most prominent being where Brecht tangled with the film industry.[2] There are, even today, legal and above all ethical arguments for acknowledging the contribution of all the co-workers in the various processes of artistic creation around Brecht. More central for me, however, is the idea that naming the authors in their plurality may confer a new interpretative freedom upon the modern reader.

There are pitfalls in any attempt to draw the strands together. Brecht's collaborations are so varied that it is difficult to arrive at generalisations. What is more, talk of collaborative or collective creativity must entail at least passing consideration of general theories of authorship. We may have learnt to be wary of referring to the authorial personality or consciousness to validate textual 'meaning'. On the other hand, it would be perverse to deny that a knowledge of biography - in modern times an almost unavoidable knowledge of biography - and of the circumstances of the genesis of a work of art, must make a difference. As Brecht himself remarked, even just the rumour of the author's radical convictions may have a profound effect on the reception of the work (*BFA*, 21, 485). Approaching Brecht, it is not a question of permitting biography to enter our readings; rather, since biography is already there, what are we to do with it? I simply seek to use this conjunction of life (or lives) and work to open (and not to close) channels of interpretation and enquiry.

Issues of authorship have become crucial to our understanding of Brecht for a number of other reasons besides the real extent and centrality in his creative life of self-conscious collaboration. Firstly, one of the most familiar ways, both of reading the work and of accounting for the general phenomenon of multiple authorship, appears to have collapsed: ideas of socialist collectivity need not stand or fall with really existing socialism, nevertheless it is time to reexamine some of the associated vocabulary and assumptions. Secondly, the scandals of Brecht the plagiarist (which had its origins in the 1920s and was loudly proclaimed by the Nazis) and the shameless exploiter of women (which had honourable feminist beginnings) have recently been reasserted with such fever that one might wonder whether Brecht himself had written anything at all worth reading.[3] Thirdly, a new edition of Brecht's works, the *Große kommentierte Berliner und Frankfurter Ausgabe*, is nearing completion.[4] Multi- and disputed authorship clearly have consequences for the practice of establishing critical editions. The appearance of a new attempt to do justice to Brecht's practices invites comment. Finally, collaboration might nowadays be styled a 'postmodern' meeting of discourses, replacing ideas of the unique inspiration of the subject which dominated images of the artist from the eighteenth century through to modernism. Yet Brecht and those who worked with him themselves reflected quite extensively on authorship and intellectual property. Does this make of Brecht and his collaborators prophets of the postmodern?

As I have suggested, the collaborative habit established itself very early in Brecht's life, namely within the circle of close friends in Augsburg in his last school years and at the beginning of his time in Munich. As far as we can reconstruct the dynamics of this fluctuating group (Pfanzelt, Neher, Münsterer, Bezold and the rest) Brecht was dominant, but they all exchanged poems and diary sketches, offered suggestions and material, and re-wrote each others' work.[5]

Brecht's practices at this stage, and later too, might be comprehended in terms of a psychological case-history. We probably even know enough about his biography (his physical frailty, his relationship with his mother and so on) tentatively to reconstruct this and to trace patterns of dependence and the search for approval and reprobation.[6] What might first have appeared as a willingness to listen and share we might now explain as a lack of self-reliance, or else as an inclination to dominate. There are obvious problems with this. The many spirited stylisations which these young men both committed to paper (some in semi-autobiographical genres) and essayed to live out (in dress, mannerism and conversation) make it more or less impossible to distinguish securely between a fictional and a real. The name 'Bert Brecht' already refers, both in early literary texts and in theoretical reflections, to something other than just a self; and other people's names and nicknames contain, in these early works, a similarly ambiguous gesture of both the assertion and the denial of the individual. The psychological-biographical approach to the works, which treats literature as a revelation of personality, can turn out to be perilously circular. Besides, we have simply too little evidence to decide between two conflicting narratives: did Brecht have a talent for seeking out creative friends whose gifts he could exploit, or did he, crucially, encourage a creative effervescence amongst the friends he already had? We may choose to see him, here and later too, as an 'enabler' as much as an 'exploiter'. Finally, Brecht himself appears to have been becoming increasingly aware of the value for his own creativity and literary career of the protean spontaneities he could derive from these relationships. The stylisations of himself and his friends (as the poet Brecht and his charmed and gifted circle) became a premise for further creative processes.

Collaboration and Authorship

Whether or not Brecht was consciously in control, and whatever the real psychology behind these sorts of strategy, the circumstance of multiple authorship and of mutually improvised stylisation leaves traces in the works themselves. These are more interesting than biographical speculation, for they begin to upset the conventional image of the relationship between artist and artwork, and they give the awkward early texts their radical, modern edge. In the 'Lieder zur Klampfe' the 'author' and his collaborators and 'friends' are placed as fictional figures inside the text. The poems are presented as the chatter of their multiple fictionalised voices. Their shifting perspectives and opinions may in part be traced to their collaborative origin. *Baal* itself, many of the scenes and songs and dialogues of which seem to have originated in conversations and improvisations with the friends, begins to emerge as an open fragment which achieves itself in an exchange of collaborative performance and composition. The creative processes involved appear like a kind of slow-motion jazz improvisation; and the resultant compositions are essentially a 'performance literature', conceived not only in, but also for a particular context and public. This is one reason why the later formalised theatre versions and attempts to establish a purely textual coherence for *Baal* are, as Brecht himself recognised, essentially unsatisfactory.[7]

Even before the 1920s Brecht's literature had begun to appear as a process of provocation and riposte, a dialogue, and a site of competing discourses. Here already there were many Brechts, or many voices that present themselves to us as 'Brecht'. And it was here that literature was first experienced as productive within a community, and even productive of a community. Is it too much to suggest that this experience of a model of friendly group collaboration stayed with Brecht? Notions of a productive society of partners, governed by Brecht's very individual morphing of fraternité, 'Freundlichkeit', become a central topos of the later work.

It is striking also how early Brecht began to develop a quite consciously impersonal and anti-romantic attitude towards authorship. Some would see this still (in perhaps Freudian terms) as a mask behind which Brecht could shelter his vulnerable ego. I should prefer to see it as a polemical and iconoclastic gesture which gradually, through the odd admixtures of political ideology and the real experience of a culture industry, developed into a more coherently anti-bourgeois attitude to artistic creation and intellectual property. This may clearly provide an important intellectual framework for practices of multiple authorship. (It will also make it impossible to keep the issues of collaboration entirely separate from those of citation, textual borrowing and plagiarism.)

Especially in the years 1929 to 1931, in the context of the *Lehrstück* experiments, in a period of an ever more focussed Marxist politicisation, and against the background of the legal wrangles with the Nero-Film company about the filming of the *Dreigroschenoper*, Brecht's theoretical reflections become more coherently radical and less carelessly polemical. He voices a deep mistrust both of 'the individual' and of 'expression' (e.g. *BFA*, 21, 201); and in their place he begins to develop notions of 'collectivity' (320) - and 'production' (488). Ideas of influence or quotation, and of translation, adaptation, and so too of original authorship (and original meaning) begin to crumble into a wash of commodified cultural material unrecognisable to the humanist tradition.[8] Brecht's own contemporary practices of borrowing, of collective teamwork, and of self-adaptation - his whole handling of material in, for example, the texts of the *Lehrstücke* - gesture towards a practical realisation of these ideas for the progressive artist working within a still bourgeois society. The inclinations and friendly collaborations of his youth have been theorised, and the theory itself now provided the stimulus for further experiments in collective authorship.

On the one hand, the work of art becomes, in this theory, something apart from its author or producer, which may be marketed as a commodity (*BFA*, 21, 485-488; 22.1, 257). On the other hand, the nature of the modern world is such that the single individual's take on it is anyway unlikely to be interesting. One of the 'Herr Keuner' stories nicely sums up the shortcomings of the conventional image of originality and singular authorship:

> ... ohne jede Hilfe, nur mit dem kümmerlichen Material, das ein einzelner auf seinen Armen herbeischaffen kann, errichten sie ihre Hütten! Größere Gebäude kennen sie nicht, als solche, die ein einziger zu bauen imstande ist! (*BFA*, 18, 18).

Teamwork was now rationalised as an almost necessary part of the modern scientific method. Brecht was becoming convinced that the creative act had become a creative process, a dialectical continuum, and that the idea of an isolated and original invention had lost its importance.

The Benjaminian image of the 'author as producer' has of course a very clear context in European modernism, as do the notions of assemblage or montage to which Brecht repeatedly appeals. Other elements of this Brechtian theory are clearly amenable to Marxist theorisation: the dialectical relationships between author, artwork and tradition, and the collective production of art within a societal nexus. However, some of the ideas Brecht was developing in this period may just as well be taken to gesture far beyond his immediate intellectual context, towards, for example, Roland Barthes's theories of 'the death of the author' (Barthes briefly invokes Brecht in his famous essay of 1968).[9] I shall come back to these wider conceptual ramifications. First, however, I should like to return to the practices of collaboration themselves.

There is a photograph of 1927 which purports to show Brecht at work. In fact it presents a room full of people: Brecht stands somewhat aloof in front of a bookcase, the boxer Paul Samson-Körner is playing the piano, three other men (who have not all been reliably identified) sit round a table with Elisabeth Hauptmann, who is typing.[10] The scene is ironically 'staged', as Brecht himself explained, and yet it perhaps presents us with a jokey version of a 'Zusammenarbeit' to which Brecht genuinely aspired (see *BFA*, 21, 207).

One after the other, his close associates have commented on Brecht's habit, so unusual in a literary artist, of surrounding himself with friends and conversation partners, even, or perhaps especially, when he was working. He appears to have retained an extraordinary ability to attract talented people and to encourage them to unfold their talents in the service of a collective project. Some of the collaborators may well have been bullied and dominated by Brecht. There may have been a serious disjunction between the theory and the practice of fraternal collectivity. Others, however, like Eisler, Korsch or Dudow, were strong-minded, independent individuals, confident in their own areas of competence. Most of the accounts suggest that Brecht's was the organising intelligence, but that everybody participated very willingly, and that, if the work was demanding or there was a certain personal price to pay, they were nonetheless content that it was worth it. Lion Feuchtwanger remarked,

> Brecht fraß viel Leben, ... er war herrisch und stolz und forderte von seinen Freunden geduldige Mitarbeit. Aber er war ohne jede Hoffart und Prahlerei und gab selber neidlos, großmütig, in Fülle. Er gab mehr, als er verlangte. Das Wort Solidarität hat durch ihn neuen Sinn bekommen.[11]

It is a perilous task to attempt to disentangle the dynamics of Brecht's working teams. There are only a few instances where we can say with any confidence who contributed what to which work. For the rest, we can only imagine how projects were conceived collectively, in discussion, how the various participants undertook research and contributed material, how texts were shared and exchanged and improved, and, not least, how people were delegated to solicit publishers and theatres, and to seek out new specialists for specific tasks. Although some of the partnerships, such as that with Eisler, were partnerships of equals, the day-to-day practices of the team sometimes seem analogous to those of a Renaissance painter's studio - with apprentices seeking out models, sketching preliminary studies, and, later, painting in the wash of the sky while the 'master' refines the detail. A further image of this activity is provided by the presentation of 'scientific' teamwork and experiment in Galileo's laboratory in Brecht's own later drama.[12]

The most intriguing point is that most of the texts themselves were not generated in lonely isolation, but in the group and in debate. The typescripts (there are very few manuscripts) reveal tantalisingly little information about their genesis. We can be quite certain anyway that the scriptor was only one of the authors. Very often typescripts have annotations or corrections in more than one hand, and very often we have more than one typescript. Even if we cannot establish a hierarchy of drafts, or distinguish the 'authorised' from the 'unauthorised', these details give us a little insight into aspects of the collective generation of texts, and of the transmission of text through appropriation, often translation, adaptation, and revision.

Such self-consciously experimental processes flourished above all in the avant-garde scene of Berlin. The experience of exile, from 1933 onwards, led, as in many other areas of Brecht's life and literature, to a curtailment of the aspirations for collaborative work. No longer surrounded by sympathetic associates, Brecht found himself for much of the 1930s on the rural southern coast of the Danish island of Fyn, amongst foreigners. Moreover, the seriousness of the immediate political task seemed to demand some reductions. The period of untrammeled collaborative experiments with other artists, with audiences and with the new media, the period of the *Lehrstücke* and of *Kuhle Wampe*, was definitely over. In fact, however, Brecht managed to establish quite a circle even here. Letters, the journal and accounts by others all suggest that there were extended conversations almost every evening with such close friends as Hanns Eisler, Walter Benjamin, Karl Korsch, Fritz Sternberg, and the women in Brecht's life: alongside Helene Weigel, Margarete Steffin and Ruth Berlau. The last of these has commented on Brecht's apparent need to talk in order to formulate clearly: simply, 'Brecht dachte besser, wenn er sprach'. For that he needed people to talk with. Of the later years at the Berliner Ensemble Käthe Rülicke-Weiler makes a very similar point: 'Was entstand, entstand im Gespräch.'[13]

Insofar as the object of these conversations was to write plays, in other words to compose more conversations, these work practices make an obvious sort of sense. Perhaps the voices, opinions and inflections of others helped Brecht to people his plays and to create his dialogues. But it goes much further than this. For a start, Brecht was not only writing plays. Interestingly, several of his most important writings in theory and prose are substantially in dialogue or in direct speech: *Der Messingkauf, Flüchtlingsgespräche, Das Buch der Wendungen*. The shorter theoretical essays tend to set up an argument as though they were establishing a debating position, and inviting response. Taken together the many fragments can seem like many voices and perspectives, congruent and sympathetic, but far from a resolved and unified monologue. This is, if you like, the dialectical method even in

its pre-Hegelian sense. Indeed, we may comprehend Brecht's general fondness for
fragmentary, impersonal, narrated and dialogue forms in terms of his ideas and
experience of authorship, and of the artwork in modern society. These are ideas we
can apply even to the poetry. I have already mentioned the voices of the early poems.
Brecht came to conceive of poetry as quite the reverse of the self-expressive lyric
monologue of tradition; instead it was to be a dialogue in a social context.
Consequently, the preferred forms are appeals, pleas, songs in praise, epitaphs and
exhortations; and the poems themselves are full of the names and voices of friends,
associates, authorities and models. We cannot say that individual texts were a direct
product of a particular collaboration, but we can say that this whole literary project
was designed - perhaps above all in exile - to conjure or create a dialogic
community.

Art and literature are often thought of as a dialogue with the self. To some
extent Brecht simply (but radically) externalises this notion. The self would be for
him, at best, capable only of monotonous reiteration. So Brecht seeks debate with
others, and makes art a product of the confrontation. And although we might suspect
that at least some of Brecht's associates presented him, not with counters to, but
merely with extensions of, the self, Rülicke-Weiler remembers how little time he had
for those who could only agree with him, or whose responses were predictable:
'Mich interessiert nicht, was ein Mensch mit sich, sondern was er mit anderen
kämpft' (*The Brecht Yearbook 19*, 178). After all, 'die Widersprüche sind die
Hoffnungen' (*BFA*, 21, 448). So fragments and gestures and principles of the
exchanges with such key friends as Korsch, Steffin, Eisler and Benjamin lodge
themselves in every turn of Brecht's contradictory texts. In this sense, it would be
futile to seek to unweave the contributions, or to apportion authorship. There is a
much more fundamental and intimate connection between the practices and ideals of
collaboration and the uniquely purposeful dialogic communication which we
recognise in Brecht's literature.

Brecht's female collaborators

A great deal has been made especially of the part which Brecht's female
collaborators (a problematic 'category') played in the creation of the work. It is quite
clear, for example, that Elisabeth Hauptmann, despite the perhaps playfully revealing
evidence of that 1927 photograph, was far more than a secretary. She, like the
others, commented on and contributed to re-drafts, researched new projects, and
mediated the foreign literatures, especially the English, American and Far Eastern,
which increasingly found their way into Brecht's work in the 1920s. In particular,

she furnished the original 'books' for *Die Dreigroschenoper* and *Happy End* (now normally ascribed to her), translated virtually the whole text of what was to become *Der Jasager* (from Arthur Waley's English version of a Taniko Nô-play) and of *Die Ausnahme und die Regel* (from a French version of an old Chinese play).[14] In the exile period Margarete Steffin and Ruth Berlau took similar, though less indispensable, roles.[15] Although I have suggested that it is neither possible nor desirable, except for legal-financial reasons (and it's a little late for that), to apportion precise shares in the authorship of Brecht's works, it is abundantly clear that these women, and Hauptmann in particular, have received too little acknowledgement for their very extensive involvement. Some of the works could not have come about without them, and Brecht could never have appeared so prolific without their contribution. And in all this activity, Brecht seems to have been the undisputed boss, rather than the pugnacious colleague he appears in some other collaborative relationships (with men).

Yet these three women had lives of their own, and creative talents and aspirations in their own right. So did they subjugate themselves, and why? Their lives and their writings were, until recently, more or less ignored by a critical establishment for whom they were doubly stigmatised, as committed Communists and as women. That they have now become available only complicates the puzzle. Some of their literary works are very similar in style to pieces we think of as Brecht's. There are poems and stories which we would now certainly ascribe to Hauptmann or Steffin which have previously been ascribed, perhaps not even unreasonably, to Brecht. According to one account, this stylistic self-effacement, which has parallels in other aspects of their lives, can be explained in terms of the immense and dictatorial influence, whether conscious or not, which Brecht exerted over his female companions and assistants.[16] Since Brecht's biography is shot through with instances of personal mistreatment and (at least) sexual betrayal, it is easy to construct these relationships in terms of exploitation - whether (here again there are two contradictory models) by the sexually potent and creative genius, or by the uncreative inadequate desperate to compensate. Alternatively, some would insist that Hauptmann, Steffin and Berlau quite willingly submitted, either out of love for the man, or out of loyalty to the anti-fascist cause, or else in sober recognition of the commercial fact that the Brecht imprint would ensure a wider dissemination for their work than they could hope for without it.[17]

All these relationships and collaborations carry with them the fraught baggage of discourse between the sexes, and it is probably vain to pretend to unravel them finally. It must be said, however, that any combination of the above theses depends on a pretty damning assessment of the women's own self-awareness. We apportion more respect to all sides of these relationships if we recognise at least the possibility of collaborative cross-pollination, rather than exploitative dominance. There is certainly one very clear case of a mutual development of a literary language of images and forms, which was productive for both sides of the partnership: in the sonnets which Brecht and Steffin exchanged in the 1930s.[18] We might, in any case, pause to remember that Brecht and his partners and family were striving to overcome just those social conventions and constructions by which we may now be tempted to judge them. Interpersonal relationships in the modern world are portrayed in Brecht's works as conditioned by capitalist economics. Love especially is distorted and destroyed. All the same, right across the Europe of the 1920s and 30s, left-wing writers tended to see some often ill-defined manifestation of love as inseparable from their politics. To some (such as Antonio Gramsci or Rosa Luxemburg) it was the instrument of revolution; to others a more limited but still potentially enormously productive confrontation with the unknown, an extension to a whole class, maybe to humanity, of what they felt for their friends. For Brecht and Steffin, their relationship was perhaps an emblem of such sexualised politics. In any case - although these emotions are liable to seem to us irretrievably lost in the utopian romanticism of the past - if we are going to get involved in biography, it seems reasonable to take more seriously these people's sense that they were participating in new relationships for a new age, and in an important project of love and friendship. Brecht himself, predictably perhaps, warns us against having fixed images of people and relationships, and exhorts us to set up changeable models, with a presumption of a higher good (*BFA*, 22, 10). For Brecht, and perhaps for the women too, the love and friendship which were invested here provided a very model of committed collaborative productivity.

It is questionable also whether isolated narratives stereotyping women as the victims of horrible males can offer us anything very constructive.[19] The pattern of sexual and cultural relations according to which we might understand Brecht's relationships with creative women is more than familiar. It may be more appropriate to see Brecht's partners as the victims, not of one demonised man, but of male cultural and social history. In this context, yes of course, they submitted themselves to a male economy of authorship and literary creativity, and they suppressed their femininity in favour of a man's cause. But set against that generalised history, the case of Brecht and his female co-workers can appear in an even dimly positive light: he did value and support them, and, sometimes against the odds, he helped them through to a sort of expression and fulfilment which, hobbled as it might seem from our own perspective, was still more than many of their contemporaries could imagine.

Finally, one might ask whether we need to read the texts themselves as irretrievably marked by traces of male exploitation or victimisation. If we do, we perhaps pass up the opportunity for approaches more productive and pertinent to our own situation. Some feminist writers have found themselves able to make use of Brechtian theory in order to move, as it were, beyond the man Brecht, and as a part of a feminist project. The theory of *Gestus*, despite its apparent origin with this devil Brecht, invites us after all to consider not only the performer and the spectator in their historical specificity, but also the author.[20] Following this sort of lead, we might conclude that the task of the critic of these collaborative relationships would not be to rail against patriarchal history, nor just resentfully and belatedly to apportion credit to all the various collaborators, but to develop a concept of collaborative authorship, even a collaborative aesthetic, which would support our efforts to overcome the persistent romantic myths of (male) artistic creativity.

Theatre and Productivity

Brecht's creative life, unlike that of some dramatists, did not start out from the practicalities of working for the theatre, but it is clear that his conception of collective or collaborative artistic projects was very soon sharpened as much by this experience as by his engagement with socialist ideology. The theatre is virtually always an essentially collaborative site. This is almost a commonplace. The dramatist is absolutely dependent upon the cooperation of others in the preparation of a play in production. Firstly, there is the need to work together with those responsible for the non-textual elements of production. Secondly, re-writes in the course of rehearsals are a frequent feature of theatre work - as the participants find out what 'works', in response to the needs of actors and in reaction to reception by an audience. According to Elisabeth Hauptmann, 'erst bei der Inszenierung wurde meistens die endgültige Form eines Stückes erarbeitet'.[21] Thirdly, commercial and institutional considerations tend to have a far greater influence on drama (and, even more, film) than they do on the other literary arts; these interests too demand a less individualist approach and a division of responsibilities. Despite the bitter tone of some of Brecht's remarks in the *Dreigroschenprozeß* (e.g. *BFA*, 21, 478-479), these were generally speaking practical exigencies to which he joyfully responded. He experienced collective negotiation with competent professionals and with the institutions of the bourgeois culture industry, not as a limitation on his artistic freedom, but as a necessary challenge against which the creative writer might battle out his own forms. The resistance and the contradictions could become productive.

It might not normally be appropriate to describe the relationship between a writer-director and an actor as collaborative, but there is considerable evidence that Brecht's dealings with a smallish band of trusted individuals was one of mutual exchange in the conception and creation of a role. The greatest of these was his wife

Helene Weigel. Several roles, most prominently that of Mutter Courage, were not just conceived with Weigel in mind, but were developed with her (compare *Brechts Lai-tu*, 86). One might even go further. Brecht's extremely high opinion of Weigel's acting skills is well documented, and yet, contrary to one's expectation of a 'Brechtian' actress, contemporary accounts and photographic and film evidence reveal her to have been a very emotional performer, more inclined to empathy than to distance. Is it not possible that Brecht's conception of acting as a sort of codified reported action made most theatrical sense in close confrontation with an acting practice which inclined to almost the opposite?[22]

Throughout his creative life Brecht also sought close collaboration with a number of designers and scenographers, foremost amongst whom was Caspar Neher, his onetime schoolfriend. Neher's first contribution to a work was to sketch the characters while Brecht and others were still working on early drafts, thus providing the team with images for discussion, which then fed back into their own conceptions. It is a contribution to the development of ambience and of character which is not easy to quantify. The next stages too amounted to far more than mere stage design. Both Neher and Karl von Appen worked with constant sketches of the actors' groupings and movements, creating performance shapes which were central to Brecht's rehearsal methods; and these sketches could provoke textual as well as directorial changes. When it came to blocking a scene in detail, Egon Monk reports that Brecht was quite simply unable to proceed if Neher happened to be absent.[23] Building the imagery of the stage became as much part of the rehearsal process as was the development of the performances of the actors (*BFA*, 22:1, 229-234). Again, however, there are wider ramifications. The idea of a philosophy which refunctioned the theatre in its social relations demanded the development of a new stage aesthetic. If we imagine that a sort of evolutionary symbiosis of text, visual imagery and performance was already a part of Brechtian practice at the time of the *Lehrstücke*, then we may begin to have an idea of its significance. The *Lehrstücke* rejected traditional theatre architecture and the conventional spatial relations between 'stage action', musical 'accompaniment' and 'audience'. Indeed all these words are misnomers: the distinctions between the elements were transformed or dissolved, the hierarchies replaced by dialectical collaborations. Brecht's whole doctrine of the 'Trennung der Elemente' (*BFA*, 24, 79) might be understood in terms of a dialogue of independent, equal partners.

We do not have room here for a proper consideration of Brecht's dealings with the non-literary arts. However, it would be odd not to mention Brecht's many and important collaborations with composers. These relationships involved sometimes tense negotiations, as Brecht sought to avoid the conventional unequal division of roles, by which one art-form appropriates the other (most often the composer dominates his librettist). Again, especially after the unexpected (and to Brecht deeply suspicious) success of *Die Dreigroschenoper*, Brecht sought to re-function the conventional relationships. The greatest successes in this field were achieved in the close friendship with Eisler, which spanned from their work on *Die Maßnahme* in 1930 until Brecht's death. Together they strove to achieve a dialectical relationship between text and music, in which each depended for its full effect on the other. Berlau gives a glimpse of how closely they worked together on, for example, *Die Rundköpfe_und die Spitzköpfe* and *Furcht und Elend des III. Reiches (Brechts Lai-tu*, 98-99). The suggestion is that Eisler contributed to the whole conception of the work, rather than merely providing the music. From the late 1920s the musical element was anyway essential to Brecht's image of the theatre. He derived his theatrical (and theoretical) ideas to a significant extent from musical forms and experiments. This is particularly obvious in the development of forms borrowed from oratorio and semi-staged opera for the *Lehrstücke*, some of which were given their first performances at avant-garde music festivals rather than in the context of the theatre. Of course these images of new musical-theatrical forms also influenced things like the spatial relations between stage and public.

We can take these ideas further. The dialectical methods of Marxist theory, for which Brecht showed such an enormous fondness, encouraged a relativisation of the traditional relations, not only between the various elements of the theatrical event, but, all importantly, between writer (or artistic collective) and public. What I have so far been inclined to call 'the work' could perhaps even be held, not to be the simple product of even plural authors, but to emerge in a process of exchange with an audience or readership. A note in the programme of the *Badener Lehrstück* at its premiere in 1929 even hinted that the categories of audience and reception might be redundant, since all should 'participate' (*BFA*, 24, 90). So the text or work was required to remain flexible - to which end, in his later reflections on the *Lehrstück* form, Brecht recommended elements of free improvisation and augmentation (*BFA*, 22:1, 351-352). In one famous instance the stages of a process of 'audience participation' were fixed and recorded: when the pupils of the Karl Marx-Schule criticised (and modified) *Der Jasager* (*BFA*, 24, 92-95). This may represent a considerable amplification of ideas of collaboration and teamwork.

In the first place, notwithstanding the political, social edge they acquire in Brecht's practice, these ideas belong again very securely in the context of modernism. Mallarmé, for example, had already demanded that the audience 'produce' the book. And in the early twentieth century theories of musical practice were according the performers an ever larger part in the completion of the composition. Indeed it is in such conceptions of a bourgeois pedagogic music-practice that Brecht's *Lehrstück* theory has one of its origins. For Brecht, however, the work is not so much simply to be 'completed' by the public (the concept of completion is at odds with his image of literary processes which resist closure); rather, the written work is the grain of provocation which initiates what Barthes might call 'le texte', or, in Brecht's apparently more rationalist, humanist terms: debate and 'pedagogy'. Brecht attempted to encourage these processes by offering provocative, provisional and changeable pieces, which would be endlessly re-fashioned in dialogue with their audiences and with reality. So the text is the very reverse of singular and auctorial.

At this point it would be very easy to erode distinctions and plunge into an undifferentiated intertextuality. On the other hand, and despite efforts to claim his work for the 'postmodern', it seems to me that Brecht himself was far from doing this. It is a move which is difficult to reconcile with other ways in which his texts function. Brecht's theories of artistic production and of the artwork in society are modern; his practices of appropriating and re-fashioning foreign textual materials are radical; his dramatic characters are socially conditioned pseudo-subjects who have no 'means of expression' of their own, but rather a 'gestische Sprache' which is completely informed by ideology. Nevertheless, it is perhaps in the nature of his comprehension of the political that Brecht's understanding of his own *poetic* language should remain that of a realist.[24] So let us stop short, and simply hold onto the idea that, in Brecht's case, it is the straightforward facts of multiple authorship and of endlessly changeable texts which help to liberate us from reductive and author-centred readings. The author, or the authors play a part, but it is no longer such a rigidly privileged part, since, although his life, or their lives are inscribed in the text, they are not the authoritative origin of it.

The relation to Brecht's ideas of pedagogy is quite close. Teaching, in Brecht's sense, needs no text, or not a final one: it is not a question of the establishment and transmission of authority, but rather a process which, initiated in dialogue, then continues in the work of the pupils: a pedagogic metatext. In this sense we are fortunate that the reception of Brecht's work has not depended on monolithic critical exegesis, since, as much as the critics, the theatres have executed the work, in both East and West. This has, in an odd way, helped to ensure that the 'many Brechts', in ever renewed collaborations, have outlived the 'one Brecht'.

Four Conclusions

Several of the members of Brecht's collaborative teams survived fascism, exile and the war to re-group in the new socialist GDR, where they were joined by a host of younger newcomers, Benno Besson, Peter Palitzsch, Käthe Rülicke-Weiler and so on. To most this must have seemed, at least at the outset, the great opportunity to take up the collective experiments of the 1920s, and to take a step nearer to the realisation of the fraternal pedagogic project. The early onset of Brecht's frustration with the Berliner Ensemble team is, however, well-documented. He is said to have complained that he had no pupils, merely employees. In comparison with the relative *Narrenfreiheit* of the Weimar Republic and the isolated independence of exile, the collective of East Berlin had to function in a context of defensive and rigid institutions and hierarchies. Stalinism created conditions inimical to the fragmentary and jostling impulses, the improvisatory and dialogic exchanges of Brecht's best practices. He found himself no longer in irreverent combat with his 'literary field', but increasingly defined and shackled by a politicised culture industry and a critical establishment which required his theatre and his works to be a monolith. His poetry now, when he retreated to Buckow, was less a dialogue than it had ever been. The botched achievement of the socialist republic was the backdrop against which fraternal collaboration foundered.

I have suggested that it was nevertheless, to some extent, the saving of Brecht that his work became the plaything of at least two cultural establishments in competition. That debate may not have been the most fruitful, but at least it was debate. What are we to expect of unification? The new 'authorised version' of the monumental *Große kommentierte Ausgabe*, combining the voices of Berlin and Frankfurt, seemed at its (pre-unification) launch to be itself an extraordinary achievement of collaboration. Now it begins to look like a one-way takeover and an impoverishment. Besides, the edition has done little or nothing (except grudgingly, in the notes) to restore the 'Mitarbeiter' to full collaborator status. Bourgeois scholarship, modern editorial practice, and their fateful companion, the book market, still make little attempt to deal with multiple authorship and changeable texts. The competing versions and the plural Brechts survive, but they survive better, for the time being at least, outside Germany and outside Europe, out of the hands, for the most part, of editors and their like, and in the work of theatres and readers.

All the phenomena I have attempted to describe can of course be dealt with by a simple turn to pre-modern conceptions of authorship, or by thinking, as Michel Foucault would have us do, in terms of 'author-functions' rather than personal, historical authors. Foucault's critique of the convention of authorship has demonstrated how we tend to rely upon 'the author': for example to account for unevenness or disunity in terms of evolution or outside influence; and to neutralise contradictions, in the conviction that there must be an unconscious or conscious level at which all can be resolved.[25] It is easy to think of examples of just this sort of approach to the work of Brecht. I am well aware that in this essay I have adumbrated something like a contextualised four-phase biographical development (Augsburg-Berlin-exile-Berlin) which simply appeals to 'teams' instead of to a single author.

Such approaches can all be disturbed (and the contradictions kept alive) if we take seriously the ideas of collaboration and multiple authorship I have outlined. To give a very simple example, we tend to think of Brecht as the humanist educator with a conscious programme; but the idea that the singular author to any substantial degree controlledly directs these processes (whether we call them a pedagogy or not) begins now to look distinctly shaky.

I have nonetheless sought to retain a reasonably strong image of a contextualised, plural yet personal authorship (rather than an 'author-function'), in order not to evade the particular and historical interest of this case and this oeuvre. Even if, as time goes by and one socialist vision fades, we may be less inclined to invest in the ethical and political life of the real author, we will remain concerned to comprehend the changing terms of cultural production, and to weigh cultural production against human cost. These are issues and equations of interest in the case of Brecht. What I hope I have also suggested is how we may seek to interrogate the historical, not in search of sociological documents, but in order to discover another set of possibilities for reading and using the work in our own present. The potential of a recognition of the plural signature of 'Brecht' is that it helps to create a text, in dialogic exchange between past and present, in which our own voices may become once again more audible.

---

1.   My reflections are dependent on the work of, amongst others, the scholars acknowledged in the notes. I have undertaken substantive research myself only into the friendships of Brecht's youth (see below). The patterns and imbalances of published research must be, to a certain extent, reproduced in this essay. One might generalise: the emphasis thus far has been on music, on women, and on individual relationships taken in isolation; there has been too little work on the other arts, on men, and on teamwork.

2.   The filming of the *Dreigroschenoper* provoked forceful reflections by Brecht on the subjects of copyright, intellectual property and the artwork as commodity (*BFA*, 21, 448-514, and compare below). The Hollywood film *Hangmen Also Die* provides a further example.

3.   See especially John Fuegi, *The Life and Lies of Bertolt Brecht* (London, Camden House 1994).

4.   Bertolt Brecht, *Große kommentierte Berliner und Frankfurter Ausgabe,* edited by W. Hecht, J. Knopf, W. Mittenzwei, K-D. Müller (Frankfurt a.M.: Suhrkamp 1988-). References to Brecht's work in this edition, abbreviated *BFA*, are by volume and page number only.

5.   For a detailed account of these relationships, see Hanns Otto Münsterer, *The Young Brecht,* ed. Tom Kuhn and Karen Leeder (London, Libris, 1992) - a translation of Münsterer's *Bert Brecht: Erinnerungen aus den Jahren 1917-22* (Zürich, Arche, 1963), with additional material; and Tom Kuhn, '"Ja, damals waren wir Dichter"': Hanns Otto Münsterer, Bertolt Brecht and the dynamics of literary friendship', in: *The Brecht Yearbook, 21* (1996), 49-66.

6. As Carl Pietzcker has done, *'Ich kommandiere mein Herz'. Brechts Herzneurose: ein Schlüssel zu seinem Leben und Schreiben* (Würzburg, Königshausen & Neumann, 1988).

7. Brecht's later fascination with jazz as a mode of composition appropriate to the technological age is documented, e.g. *BFA*, 21, 301.

8. Elisabeth Hauptmann is inclined to count the contents of his library amongst his 'Mitarbeiter', *Julia ohne Romeo: Geschichten, Stücke, Aufsätze, Erinnerungen,* ed. Rosemarie Eggert and Rosemarie Hill (Berlin and Weimar, Aufbau, 1977), p.185. This unhelpfully bursts the bounds of the category of 'collaboration'.

9. See also Steve Giles, 'Post/Structuralist Brecht? Representation and Subjectivity in *Der Dreigroschenprozeß*', in *The Brecht Yearbook 17: The Other Brecht I (*1992), 147-164, for a further exposition. Claudette Sartiliot sets Brecht in an even more ambitious modernist and postmodern context, *Citation and Modernity: Derrida, Joyce, Brecht* (Norman and London, University of Oklahoma Press, 1993).

10. The picture was published as one of a series of 'artists at work' in the Berlin magazine *Uhu*. It has been often reproduced, e.g. in Ernst and Renate Schumacher, *Leben Brechts in Wort und Bild* (Berlin, Henschel, 1979), plate 178.

11. Quoted from *Julia ohne Romeo*, p.237. There are remarks by others who, especially later, felt they had been 'used' (perhaps most notably Marieluise Fleißer), but, given the number of collaborators, they remain comparatively few. Contrast, e.g. Ludwig Berger, 'Die Lust an der Kooperation', *Theater Heute*, 8 (1967), 27.

12. Thanks go to Darko Suvin for suggesting the analogy with the artist's studio. The picture of such activity in *Leben des Galilei* is of course again ironic (the 'plagiarism' of the telescope, and so on) and far from unambivalent.

13. Ruth Berlau, *Brechts Lai-tu: Erinnerungen und Notate*, ed. Hans Bunge (Berlin, Eulenspiegel 1987), p.115; Rülicke-Weiler in interview with Hartmut Reiber, *The Brecht Yearbook 19: Focus: Margarete Steffin* (1994), 177.

14. Compare John Willett, 'Bacon ohne Shakespeare? - The Problem of Mitarbeit', in *The Brecht Yearbook 12. Brecht: Women and Politics* (1983), 121-137; Astrid Horst, *Prima inter pares: Elisabeth Hauptmann, die Mitarbeiterin Bertolt Brechts* (Würzburg, Königshausen und Neumann, 1992); and Paula Hanssen, 'Brecht's and Elisabeth Hauptmann's Chinese Poems', in *The Brecht Yearbook 19*, 187-201. For the small anthology of Elisabeth Hauptmann's own writings *Julia ohne Romeo,* see note 6. For Ruth Berlau's assessment of Hauptmann's importance, see *Brechts Lai-tu*, p.69.

15. For Berlau, as well as *Brechts Lai-tu* (note 10) we also have an anthology of stories, *Jedes Tier kann es. Erzählungen* (Mannheim, Persona, 1989), from the Danish: *Ethvert dyr kan det* (Copenhagen, 1940). Steffin's own writings have only recently appeared, as *Konfutse versteht nichts von Frauen: Nachgelassene Texte*, ed. Inge Gellert (Berlin, Rowohlt 1991); the case of Steffin is extensively debated in *The Brecht Yearbook 19*, especially the essays by Simone Barck, Stefan Hauck and Wolfgang Jeske.

16. E.g. Pietzcker, p.85.

17. Compare Rülicke-Weiler, in *The Brecht Yearbook 19*, 179-180. Werner Hecht has a wonderfully unironic version of the selfless service of the 'dritte Sache', *Brecht: Vielseitige Betrachtungen* (Berlin, Henschel, 1978), p.150.

18. This poetic correspondence has been analysed by Stefan Hauck, in *The Brecht Yearbook 19*, 91-117. He reveals the extent to which even that traditional male monologue, the love poem, became for Brecht a dialogue with the sexual partner.

19. This approach has been given short shrift by Sabine Kebir, in her *Ein akzeptabler Mann? Streit um Brechts Partnerbeziehungen* (Berlin, Der Morgen, 1987).

20. Compare Elin Diamond, 'Brechtian Theory/Feminist Theory: Towards a Gestic Feminist Criticism', *The Drama Review* XXXII, 1 (1988), 82-91.

21. *Julia ohne Romeo*, p.187. This betrays an unduly traditional image of the work, since in theatrical practice and in Brechtian theory there is no 'endgültige Form', the text remains provisional.

22. Compare the work with Charles Laughton described in 'Aufbau einer Rolle. Laughtons Galilei', in *BFA*, 25,.

23. The processes are described, with many illustrations, by John Willett in *Caspar Neher: Brecht's Designer* (London, Arts Council Touring Exhibition Catalogue, 1986), see e.g. p.109, and by Ruth Berlau in *Brechts Lai-tu*, p.212. See also Christopher Baugh, 'Brecht and Stage Design', in *The Cambridge Companion to Brecht*, ed. Peter Thomson and Glendyr Sacks (Cambridge, Cambridge University Press, 1994), pp.235-253.

24. Claudette Sartiliot, *op.cit.*, disagrees fundamentally. She draws illuminating comparisons with Bakhtin, Barthes and Derrida, amongst others. However, she appears to fail to distinguish between Brecht's characters' language (which is socially constructed) and the language of Brecht's literature (which is able to reveal that social construction). Perhaps Brecht's inclination to model his theories of art on a relatively narrow understanding of industrial production tended to downvalue poetic language as a simple 'raw material'.

25. Michel Foucault, 'What is an author?' (1969), English in *Language, Counter-Memory, Practice: Selected Essays and Interviews,* ed. Donald Bouchard (Ithaca, NY, Cornell University Press, 1977).

JULIAN PREECE

The Many Faces of B.B. in Fiction and Memoir:
From Fleisser and Feuchtwanger to Canetti and Weiss

Few, if any, German cultural figures of this century have served as real-life models for as many fictional and dramatic characters as Bertolt Brecht. Only Sigmund Freud and Franz Kafka could possibly rival him for the interest shown by playwrights and novelists. From impassioned, Expressionist revolutionary who forsakes art for social action in the Munich Soviet of 1918/1919 (*1918*, Lion Feuchtwanger, originally to be entitled *Thomas Brecht*)[1] and ballad-singing Marxist technocrat (*Erfolg*, Feuchtwanger) to the exiled standard bearer of an imperilled civilisation (*Die Ästhetik des Widerstands*, Peter Weiss); from exploitative womaniser (*Avantgarde*, Marieluise Fleisser; *Loving Brecht*, Elaine Feinstein), vain, self-seeking star who embodies the corrupt spirit of the Weimar age (*Die Fackel im Ohr*, Elias Canetti), brash opportunist (*Tales from Hollywood*, Christopher Hampton), to seasoned survivor caught in the cross-fire of art and politics in post-war East Berlin (*Die Plebejer proben den Aufstand*, Günter Grass), he has been assigned a great many roles.[2]

In addition to these fictional accounts which treat Brecht as a literary figure is the abundance of memoirs written by friends, associates, and collaborators, often dedicated solely to his memory. All attest to his dominating, yet magnetic personality.[3] The sketches and images which emerge from the memoirs complement the fictions: those from the early period focus on his personality, while those after 1933 turn generally to more intellectual and political themes. The boundaries between fact and fiction blur in both genres: a confessional memoir by a close friend is written in the third person (*Tage mit Bertolt Brecht*, Arnolt Bronnen); another primarily autobiographical confession pretends in every way to be fiction (*Avantgarde*); a three-volume autobiography slots Brecht into a symbolic (and thus ultimately fictional) structure (*Die Fackel im Ohr*); a similarly panoramic memoir makes Brecht into a 'station' on a personal progress through political pitfalls in exile (*Das Exil im Exil*, Hans Sahl); another into an example of a powerful critical spirit in the authoritarian GDR (*Ein Deutscher auf Widerruf*, Hans Mayer); and an entirely fictional account pretends to be autobiography (*Loving Brecht*).[4] Benno Besson delivers a theatrical history of the GDR by relating his involvement with Brecht himself in East Berlin, the

Berliner Ensemble after Brecht's death, and finally his career as an international director of Brecht's plays.[5] Weiss chooses the form of a depersonalised mock autobiography, the collective memoir of the German workers' movement and resistance to Fascism. The most rounded portrait, however, Feuchtwanger's Kaspar Pröckl in *Erfolg*, is also the most fictionalised. While the memoirs in the main contribute to the mythicisation of Brecht's memory, helping to shape our 'image' of him today, in fiction he becomes more a figure from contemporary mythology: his name signifies more than any other in German or even European culture the writer who associated his work with political commitment and struggle.

The 'Young Brecht' of course boasts a legend all to himself.[6] Bronnen, Carl Zuckmayer, and Grete Fischer all encountered him with lute or guitar in hand, as depicted by Feuchtwanger and later Feinstein.[7] Fischer perhaps wrote a greater truth than she realised, when she recalled how 'Er wirkte wie ein Vorläufer des Popsängers von heute, von der Lederjacke bis zur Klampfen' (*Dienstboten*, 246). According to Zuckmayer when Brecht picked up his instrument, 'alles hockte um ihn her, wie in einem magischen Bann geschlagen,' (*Als wär's ein Stück von mir*, 375). Hans Otto Münsterer remembers 'die Faszination [...] die von ihm ausging' and confesses 'ich jedenfalls hatte den Angelhaken vom ersten Augenblick an verschluckt und wäre für Brecht durchs Feuer gegangen'.[8] He describes the unusual dynamic at work in Brecht's relationships:

> Es war eben das Wunder von Geist und Charme, wie es nur wenigen Menschen beschieden ist, ein Glück für Männer und Frauen. Daß das Zusammentreffen mit dem Genius gleichzeitig auch ein Fluch ist, läßt sich natürlich nicht leugnen; die Maße sind anders, ohne Leid wird es nie gehen (*Bert Brecht*, 130).

This corresponds to the crushing experience of emotional manipulation depicted by Fleisser, who like Brecht's other lovers who left testimonies, remained on friendly terms with him despite his sometimes devastating behaviour. Their lack of bitterness is remarkable and their loyalty reciprocated. Ruth Berlau fell in love instantly and justifies his every action from 1934 to his death.[9] Like Fleisser, Paula Banholzer had to free herself from his overweening influence: 'Brecht hat mich beherrscht, er hat mich fasziniert, zu jeder Zeit. Aber er hat auch alle seiner Freunde beherrscht. Brecht war immer eine dominierende Figur'.[10] Brecht's superiority over other mortals takes on mythic proportions for Bronnen; he was 'wie ein Fürst, der inkognito unter seinen Untertanen weilt; ein Wissender unter den Unwissenden' (*Tage mit Bertolt Brecht*, 80). The jealousies and antagonisms are those usually found in a love affair. Both

Marianne Zoff and Caspar Neher are rivals and the friendship ends when Brecht meets Helene Weigel. Fritz Sternberg's first reaction is more self-assured, yet even he, some years Brecht's senior, was captivated.[11] He recognises how Brecht uses their friendship: Sternberg visits him, never the other way around, in order for Brecht to pick his brains and exploit his reading. Twenty years later, exiled in New York, Sternberg performs a personal favour and for the first time earns Brecht's gratitude: 'Es war, glaube ich, das erstemal in diesen zwanzig Jahren, daß Brecht sich bei mir bedankte' (*Der Dichter und die Ratio*, 56). Zuckmayer confirms the general impression:

> Brecht war in vieler Hinsicht gefährlich, wie vermutlich jedes Genie. Er wollte keine Bewunderer oder Jünger, aber Mitarbeiter, die sich ihm zu- und damit unterordneten. Er hatte bei aller scheinbaren Konzilianz ein starkes Machtbedürfnis, nämlich nach geistiger Macht, die nicht kommandiert, aber leitet (*Als wär's ein Stück von mir*, 321).

Only Canetti, writing some fifty years after his encounter with the young poet and playwright, strikes a more negative note, as he fails to fall under the spell and cannot see how the negative qualities he observes are redeemed in any way. He describes him too as 'herrschsüchtig' (*Die Fackel im Ohr*, 260), a man who uses people for his own ends 'ohne ihnen zu verfallen' (255), thus evading personal commitment to them. He employs a rather more demeaning image to characterise Brecht's hold over others: 'ein Schüler, der seine erste Zigarre raucht und andere, denen er Mut machen will, um sich versammelt' (260). Canetti's Brecht is, however, more important as a symbolic figure in the scheme of his narrative, which deserves to be placed half-way between memoir and fiction for that reason. This also opens up one significant distinction between the fictional and autobiographical treatments of Brecht: whereas in autobiography he is remembered with warmth and admiration, in novels and plays he is more often assigned the role of villain.

The language and imagery in these reminiscences are astoundingly consistent: words like magic, fascination, domination, enthralment, genius, superiority, power, manipulation recur. The later accounts, fewer in number, are more sober. Eric Bentley realises, however, how Brecht carefully crafted 'his own image in the minds of his admirers'.[12] Max Frisch paints a completely different picture of Brecht the intellectual, the teacher and explainer who loves discussion, contradiction, and challenge in argument.[13] While Frisch is unmoved by his politics, he is convinced he is in the presence of a superior mind and recognises the magnetism of his personality, though for different reasons than those who knew him in the 1920s: 'Die Faszination, die Brecht immer wieder hat, schreibe ich vor allem dem Umstand zu, daß hier ein Leben wirklich vom

Denken aus gelebt wird' (*Tagebücher*, 254). This Brecht is patient, rather shy, good-natured, cerebal, and eternally curious, above all marked by a desire to learn and to review his assumptions from first principles:

> Auch sonst hat Brecht dieses Ernsthaft-Bereitwillige, das keine Schmeichelei ist und auch keine duldet, das Überpersönlich-Bescheidene eines Weisen, der an jedem lernt, der über seinen Weg geht, nicht von ihm, aber an ihm (260).

Mayer writes too of 'die Güte' and highlights his intellectual playfulness in discussion which had to lead to practical conclusions 'die notwendig waren und nützlich, wollte man richtig handeln unter den gegebenen Umständen' (*Ein Deutscher auf Widerruf*, 149).[14] Mayer heroises his subject, however, believing him to have a political power almost equal to that of the GDR authorities:

> Die Mitglieder eines Politbüros mochten kommen und gehen, sie hatten Macht auf Widerruf, wie sich stets wieder zeigen sollte. Brecht war, als Bürger dieses Staates, eine Macht ohne Widerruf, und das sollte man sich gesagt sein lassen (144).

Mayer wants to dispel the 'legend' that Brecht identified with Ulbricht's regime by documenting his critical opposition. In so doing he lends weight to the equally potent counter-legend of Brecht's influence over political decisions, supporting in particular the proposition that had Brecht lived another six months, the wave of arrests which resulted in sentences for Harich, Janka, Just and others, which followed the Hungarian Uprising in October in 1956, would not have occurred.[15]

Fleisser's fictional alter ego, Cilly Ostermeier, has a rather different perspective, though the man she describes is easily recognisable from the memoirs of other friends and lovers from the 1920s. Her entire dilemma is contained in the first sentence: 'Es war nicht ganz heraus, war sie seine Mitarbeiterin, Freundin, Geliebte oder wurde sie seine Frau?' (*Avantgarde*, 117). She uses imagery of consumption and submission, writing of his 'Verschleiß an Menschen' (117); 'der Mann saugte sie auf' (118); 'Der Mann war eine Potenz, er brach sie sofort'; 'Mit Worten schwang er die Peitsche' (120); he is a 'Dompteur' (119). In her play *Tiefseefisch*, which contains her first portrait in the form of the impressario of a 'Dichtfabrik', the authoritarian Brecht figure is convinced of his own superiority: 'Vergessen Sie nie, daß ich meinen Freunden voraus bin, daß mein Instinkt weiter nach vorne faßt' (*Tiefseefisch*, 341). Ostermeier's self-worth becomes entirely dependent on what 'der Mann' thinks of her: if she does not survive the confrontation 'war sie es eben nicht wert' (*Avantgarde*, 117); 'ohne ihn war sie gar nichts' (118). She has to give up her independent life, her doctorate, in order to help him when he needs her; as a dramatist he tells her what subjects to choose, summons her back to Berlin, directs her play in his own way without prior discussion. He makes clear what the terms of their relationship are at the outset: 'Es ging zuvor um die Sache. Der Mensch war so wichtig nicht, der Mensch ließ sich ersetzen' (120). A personal relationship involving mutual fidelity and long-term commitment is a bourgeois invention; because it introduces notions of ownership it is a capitalist intrusion into the private sphere. Kaspar Pröckl in *Erfolg* holds similar views.

The central figure of *Avantgarde*, however, is not Brecht, who is not mentioned by name, but Ostermeier, whose experiences are based also on those of Elisabeth Hauptmann. The story concentrates on the preconditions of female success in a man's world, and the social and emotional pain of writing and publishing as a woman from a provincial, petty-bourgeois background. 'Der Mann', however, helps Ostermeier in her career, which she acknowledges, and does not gain her trust with promises he does not keep. Rather, she realises he is emotionally hardened, scarred by previous affairs, and determined not to become entangled in a conventional relationship because of past experiences. Ostermeier gains some self-respect at the end of the story and frees herself from him, summing up his behaviour with an apparent paradox which characterises other portraits too: 'Der Mann war ein Wesen besonderer Art. Im Endziel suchte er den Menschen zu helfen. In der Handhabung war er ein Menschenverächter' (132).

Fleisser's story contains quite remarkably similar insights to the entirely fictional novel published by Feinstein, based on material provided by John Fuegi.[16] Frieda Bloom, her central figure and first-person narrator, who seems to be modelled in part on Fleisser, is quite enthralled from the first, even though the Brecht she yields to possesses all the faults adumbrated so thoroughly by the novelist's source. Unlike the emotive Fuegi, who misrepresents Fleisser's testimony, Feinstein allows Brecht to grow in stature and to earn Bloom's respect. Twenty years after their affair his mourning for Margarete Steffin cancels past misdeeds. Feinstein evidently does not believe very strongly in Fuegi's twin thesis of emotional tyranny and literary theft, as what looks at the outset to be a fictional illustration of his 'research' turns into a far more powerful and moving narrative.

Like Fleisser, Feuchtwanger preferred a fictional presentation to memoir, though for rather different reasons. There are other real-life models in *Erfolg*, a social realist novel which depicts the years in Munich straddling the Inflation and the 'Bierkellerputsch' of 1923 as if from the perspective of the year 2000. Feuchtwanger portrays key figures from the Bavarian elites in politics, the judiciary, industry, and culture; Kaspar Pröckl is one of half-a-dozen of the most prominent on the grounds of his particular world view, Marxism, which, as an automobile engineer, he combines with a faith in technology. Once more a distinction is made between the personal and the political, but the two are closely linked. Pröckl's politics (his initials could stand for 'Kommunistische Partei') derive from an emotional need to understand the world and his role in it: 'Nicht Mitgefühl mit den Unterdrückten oder derlei Sentimentalitäten hatten ihn hingeführt, bewahre' (*Erfolg*, 396). His beliefs constitute both an expression of his personality and an emotional prop. Pröckl is attractive to women, despite his apparently unprepossessing appearance, and has a complicated private life. His 'unrasiertes, hageres Gesicht' (51) is complemented by his tattered leather jacket which he never seems to remove; he is described as 'anstrengend, fanatisch, unmanierlich' (151) by the heroine Johanna Krain, and frequently displays 'seine finstere, despotische Art' (365), which 'verlangte viel und gab nichts' (357). He is instrumental in conversation with others by guiding them to talk about their own affairs in order to glean information while revealing nothing about himself. Once he begins to sing 'seine zotigen, proletarischen Verse' 'mit schriller Stimme, häßlich, unverkennbar mundartlich' (246), the portrait is unmistakable and it is by no means wholly flattering.

Feuchtwanger is less than fair in terms of politics too. Since one of Pröckl's partners in debate is the authorial alter ego, the bourgeois writer, Jacques Tüverlin, the author is always going to have the last word. Pröckl's difficulties with his essay, 'Über die Funktion der Kunst im marxistischen Staat', border on the comic; and he lets his ideology come before his friendship with Martin Krüger, the gaoled Museum director, with fatal consequences for Krüger. After resigning angrily from his position in the 'Bayrische Kraftfahrzeugwerke' he undergoes a crisis which reaches its climax with the discovery of his irrational alter ego, the mad artist Fritz Eugen Brendel (whose name recalls Bertolt Eugen Brecht) in a lunatic asylum. Pröckl's crisis is then resolved with a typically contradictory decision to run a car factory in the Soviet Union for his former employers. Pröckl represents one of several individual attitudes in a panoramic novel which includes an array of representative characters and perspectives. Unlike Canetti, Grass, and Weiss, who published after Brecht's death, Feuchtwanger obviously cannot use his name. What is remarkable from our present perspective, particularly in view of subsequent fictional versions of Brecht, is that he should choose to model one of his key figures on a comparatively little known thirty-year-old poet and playwright, his friend and collaborator.

As a rule the writer of fiction is not concerned primarily to enhance understanding of the raw subject matter but selects a figure or a constellation of figures from the past (or the present in Feuchtwanger's case) in order to develop a contemporary theme or illuminate the past from an original angle. Grass knew that by basing *Die Plebejer proben den Aufstand*, set at the time of the Uprising of 17 June 1953 in the GDR, on Brecht's work with the Berliner Ensemble he ensured maximum critical impact. Had he chosen a motif from classical mythology, say, or from a more remote part of German or European history, his point would have been harder to get across. In order to demonstrate his thesis that writers cannot influence political events in the crude manner demanded by some 'committed' writers at the beginning of the 1960s, he chooses to pit Brecht's pen against the might of the Soviet tanks used to put down the uprising.

Brecht's name was as good as synonymous with the perennial twentieth-century theme of 'the writer and politics' and the play was universally deemed to be an attack on Brecht's alleged hypocrisy in rehearsing a play on class struggle and revolution, (Shakespeare's *Coriolanus*), while refusing to join the ranks of the workers in the real revolution taking place on the streets outside. Yet *Die Plebejer* is not really about Brecht at all, as Grass stated shortly afterwards: 'Ich habe genausogut mich gemeint'.[17] Grass was on the point of launching himself on a public career as an independent electoral campaigner for the SPD. He intended to lend his reputation as a novelist to the progressive cause of Social Democracy, twenty years after the defeat of National Socialism. The play helped him formulate his understanding of his own role:

> Aus der Arbeit an *Die Plebejer proben den Aufstand* ergab sich für mich jedenfalls die Erkenntnis, daß da ein Graben ist: Auf der einen Seite steht der Schriftsteller und Künstler, der die revolutionären Forderungen zu Papier bringt, auf der anderen ist die Realität, die sich fluchwürdigerweise anders verhält, als es der Künstler will (*Gespräche*, 188).

This insight has little or no relevance to Brecht's career in the GDR. The wisdom that the play demonstrates is that a playwright's true place is in the theatre; if he joins the barricades then it is only as an ordinary citizen. For Grass this is an uncomfortable truth and the theme of another, greater work a decade and a half later, *Das Treffen in Telgte*. For critics during the Cold War it constituted a venomous attack on a cultural icon of the Left. They either applauded or condemned it accordingly. After 1965 Grass became persona non grata in the GDR and his credentials with the West German Left lay in tatters.[18] Yet 'der Chef' in fact comes over rather more positively, as he speaks good sense, and is proved right in the course of the action. He earns a place in the pantheon of Grass characters who veer between melancholic resignation and revolutionary utopianism.[19] He does in the end lend his name to a note of protest, the authorities cut and edit his message, and publish a sanitised version which gives the impression that he supported their measures. Grass wants to say that it is wrong to expect, as the delegates from the Stalinallee do, that a man of letters, however renowned, can make a difference on the basis of his literary reputation in the world outside the theatre. Whether the play helps us understand the real Brecht in June 1953 is another matter entirely.

Canetti uses the name Brecht in a similar way in *Die Fackel im Ohr*, the second of three volumes of his autobiography spanning his first thirty-two years up to emigration and exile in the wake of the 'Anschluß' in 1938. As well as charting the development of an individual creative personality, Canetti weaves an interpretation of the times which preceded National Socialism into his narrative. The way characters behave, their attitudes, morality, and values, are reflected in what happens on the stage of world politics. During his sojourn in Berlin Canetti witnesses the prelude to the Nazi takeover. He sees *Die Dreigroschenoper* ('der genauste Ausdruck dieses Berlin', *Die Fackel im Ohr*, 285) to be the apotheosis of the corrupt values (fame, egomania, self-centredness, money, and cynicism) which Brecht also embodies himself. Rather than an attack on gangster capitalism, police complicity in crime, and a satire on bourgeois happy ends, Canetti believes it to celebrate its subjects, claiming that it 'alles verherrlicht, was man sonst schamvoll versteckt' (286).

Canetti's high-minded and rigourously moral estimation of an author's responsibility to society is set out clearly in 'Der Beruf des Dichters'.[20] This rigorous morality informs his damning assessment of Brecht, who, contrary to popular expectations, flouts his social and moral responsiblity, in short his responsibility to his art, on all points. Canetti makes 'Brecht' stand for all the showbiz razzmatazz of artistic Berlin in the late 1920s, epitomising all that is false, self-seeking, pretentious, and hypocritical in a cultural milieu which permitted Nazism to take root. The first thing he notices about Brecht is his 'proletarische Verkleidung' (253). More reprehensible is the value he places on money and material possessions, in particular the car he won himself for writing a succesful advertising jingle. For Canetti this is quite simply intellectual prostitution inspired by cynicism of the highest order. He sees Brecht treat people as material objects too: 'unter seinem Blick fühlte man sich wie ein Wertgegenstand, der keiner war, und er, der Pfandleiher, mit seinen stechenden schwarzen Augen, schätzte einen ab' (254). Brecht delights in exercising power over others, which is anathema to the future author of *Masse und Macht*; his facial appearance also seems to contradict Canetti's central theme of life-giving and life-enhancing personal transformation dependent on constant personal growth and change: 'unglaublich schien, daß er erst dreißig war, er sah nicht aus, als wäre er früh gealtert, sondern als wäre er immer alt gewesen' (254).

Brecht embodies a panoply of negative traits, chiefly manipulativeness and a devotion to money, as few others do, on the author's path in the direction of enlightenment. The autobiography is both a literary antidote to the values espoused by Brecht, which favour the inert, the material, and the non-human, and a demonstration of life in all its forms and varieties, meaning above all a capacity for renewal, metamorphosis, and receptiveness to new people and to new ideas. The unassuming Isaac Babel acts as a foil to Brecht in this section, 'Das Gedränge der Namen', because he is interested in everything and everyone around him.

As an anti-example Brecht has a place in the development of the autobiographical hero; as a real figure encountered at an important historical moment, he has wider symbolic significance as a representative of a corrupt culture. Canetti certainly sets out to debunk the myth of Weimar Berlin, and there is some originality in the way that he does this; his jibes at Brecht, however, whose heroic myth he also wants to challenge, appear somewhat cheap, even secondhand. Yet to read this autobiography as a memoir by dipping into it for reminiscences of famous figures is the wrong way to read it: anyone who does so with regard to Brecht will be disappointed by the familiar reproaches. Canetti takes Brecht the cultural and political symbol and subverts it; his portrayal is of little worth in contributing to factual knowledge. That Canetti gives Brecht such prominence signals once more the resonance of his name in the cross-over field of culture and politics. No matter that there are many other writers and artists who come off little better in Canetti's estimation, no matter that Brecht's perhaps irritating persona at this time contrasted to his tribulations in exile, with which Canetti would have been familiar. It is Brecht who stands out, who has a chapter to himself, and who earns his full ire.

Canetti's autobiography belongs to that clutch of books in German, which include *Doktor Faustus* and *Jahrestage*, which give an interpretation to a panoramic sweep of German twentieth-century history. Another such novel is *Die Ästhetik des Widerstands*, which makes arguably the greatest epic use of Brecht. Weiss coincidentally begins his novel where Canetti breaks off, in 1937, covering the next eight years in three volumes of densely packed prose. The second part of volume two ('das Herzstück des Gesamtunternehmens')[21], which Brecht dominates, is set in Stockholm between August 1939 and April 1940. It begins with the announcement of the Molotov-Ribbentrop Pact which throws the exiled communist resistance into complete turmoil, turning their world on its head and shattering their hopes, as the official Communist line is now friendly to National Socialist Germany. This comes after apparent Soviet betrayal of the heroic struggle in Spain and the first news of the Show Trials in Moscow. Understanding and assimilating this information and its consequences in the months ahead is the main theme of the section.

Once more, two themes come to the fore in association with Brecht: 'der Zusammenstoß zwischen Literatur und Politik' (*Die Ästhetik des Widerstands*, vol.2, 168); and the relationship between the personal and the political, the individual and the collective struggle. The nameless narrator provides few character details on Brecht but those we are given suggest a somewhat unsympathetic personality. He is 'kalt' and 'listig', takes little notice of the young narrator, despite his dedicated efforts on the 'Engelbrekt' project, and regards himself almost haughtily as the 'primus inter pares' in the collective. In the final impressive episode depicting his hurried flight to Finland, he appears supremely selfish:

> Der Gedanke, was aus uns andern und all den Internierten, den in der Illegalität Lebenden werden sollte, war belanglos. Erwogen wurde jetzt nur, was Brecht auf die Reise mitnehmen konnte (312).

Brecht, however, is not trying to save himself since 'es ging um sein Werk' (310), which has 'eine allgemeingültige, politische Bedeutung' because it derives from 'das kollektive Wissen' (168). Brecht must flee to safety because 'sich auch hier nun die Barbarei hermache über die Literatur' (316) and because barbarism has notched up so many victories over his contemporaries:

> ein Überlebender war er, schrecklich in seiner Nähe die Stille um Toller, Ossietzky und Tucholsky, und um Mühsam, den sie erdrosselt, aufgehängt hatten im Klosett in Oranienburg (317).

Brecht escapes with his manuscripts and books ('unsere Verbündeten im Kampf gegen die feindlichen Gewalten', 315) by the skin of his teeth. The meaning of his stumble, which closes the second volume, as he clambers abroad the vessel which will take him to a temporary haven in Finland, has nothing to do with his personal frailty, however: as an image it shows how a whole civilisation, progressive Western literature as represented in his library, is tottering on its feet.

'Literature and politics' have a completely different meaning for Weiss than for Grass. The idea that Brecht may seek to influence events directly in any way is now absurd. Yet artistic activity, in this case 'eine dramatische Epik zu entwerfen, die den Widersprüchen und Vieldeutigkeiten der Geschehnisse gerecht werden könnte', is considered in every respect to be 'den politischen Vorgängen ebenbürtig' (177). As the Germans prepare to invade Poland Brecht starts work on a Swedish theme for a potentially Swedish audience. The collective fails in its attempt to write a play based on the fifteenth-century revolutionary hero, Engelbrekt, despite meticulous research and dogged effort. This failure is instructive for two reasons: the narrator learns from it, afterwards wishing to become 'ein Chronist, der gemeinsames Denken wiedergab' (306), the ultimate result of which is *Die. Ästhetik des Widerstands* itself; and the insurmountable difficulties in finding historical material which will deal adequately with the present demonstrate how fissured and imperilled the present is.

There is some sense in seeing the novel as a mammoth essay on the power of reason and the plight of the Enlightenment at the moment the most atavistic, irrationalist forces threatened to bury European civilisation for good, since 'Erst wenn sich das Truggebilde von der Vernunft durchdringen ließe, könnte es niedergerissen werden' (171). After the heroism of Hercules depicted in the Pergamon Frieze which opens the novel, the narrator is thrown into the brutal reality of history and experiences ever greater difficulty in establishing heroes and villains, good and evil, black and white values. These difficulties reach their climax now in this section, which directly precedes the real and awful resistance inside Nazi Germany, the subject of the third and last volume.

The narrative switches repeatedly between the description of the background to Engelbrekt and the present, drawing numerous parallels which seem to demonstrate nothing except how hopeless it is to draw parallels. The only valid similarity seems to be that the powerless and dispossessed have no influence over events and little hope of understanding them. Brecht's answer to this helplessness is to make it a theme of the play they are writing, in a manner which is paralleled once more in the way the novel itself is written:

> Wir müßten versuchen, sagte Brecht, unsere jetzige Beklommenheit auf die Auseinandersetzung mit den damaligen Gegebenheiten zu übertragen, dergestalt, daß wir unsere Niederlage, unsre begrenzte Sicht, unser unaufhörliches Raten in die Schilderung einbeziehen (219).

The narrator does this in a highly revealing sentence in the middle of a passage devoted to the misuse of clerical power in fourteenth-century Sweden. The Church in the guise of Saint Birgitta attempts to quell popular unrest by means of a vision of Christ's suffering on the cross designed to distract attention from material troubles. The text suddenly switches to the present and such is the gravity of the news, its unexpectedness, and the inability of the narrator to assimilate it that the grammar too is pulled out of joint in the form of a rhetorical anacoluthon:

> Beim Eindringen der deutschen Truppen in Polen, bei ihrem rasend schnellen Vormarsch dachten wir uns die gräßliche und prophetische Ansprache, die von der Zerfetzung des Menschen handelte, und von der Anteilnahme daran, ich selbst, so schrie uns die Beseßne zu, schloß ihm mit meinen Fingern den Mund, und schloß ihm die Augen, doch seine steif gewordenen Arme konnte ich, als er von den Balken genommen worden war, nicht beugen, und seine Knie ließen sich, wie ich auch drückte, nicht strecken (187).

The textual dislocation mirrors not only Christ's plight on the cross; it encapsulates the physical and intellectual helplessness of the narrator and his comrades. It is Brecht who leads the way to survival.

The material of Brecht's life is the stuff of contemporary myth, offering a heady mix of sex and politics; his biography sweeps us past the Munich Revolution, Weimar Berlin and the Golden Twenties, the rise of the Nazis and communist opposition, exile in Europe and the USA, McCarthyism, and finally conflict in the newly founded German Democratic Republic. For all these periods in Brecht's life there are fictional narratives or dramatisations. The reasons for including a character clearly based on him (Feuchtwanger, Grass), even bearing his name (Canetti, Weiss), have nothing to do with his person, so to speak, but with the significance of his name to the authors' contemporaries. Broadly speaking there are two strands in both the literary and autobiographical material: the personal Brecht, philanderer, always controlling friend and manipulating lover who takes what he wants and needs from others, inspiring, perhaps strangely, comradeship rather than bitterness in them; and Brecht the committed writer turned activist, the poet who in his last years seemed to have signed up with the commissars.

There may be charges that can be laid against him, which provide material for memoirs and fictional treatment alike and which may affect how we judge if not his work, then his role in history and his present reputation: that he had unequal relationships, that his partners suffered emotionally and materially because of his domineering actions, and that the way he conducted his personal affairs contradicted his principles, or at least what people wanted to believe his principles were. This last charge, which is the most powerful of all, extends to other fields, his finances, for instance, or his choice of an Austrian passport during his last years in the GDR. It has a resonance because it is often felt that individuals campaigning for a better world in the name of socialism should lead saintly lives. While it is impossible to disentangle the personal from the political completely, even in the case of a man who lent little importance to the individual or private sphere in his work, it is ultimately the political Brecht who demands attention in this context for his role in four works by major authors who take German twentieth-century history, or an aspect of it, as their theme (Feuchtwanger, Grass, Canetti, and Weiss). He now appears more as a figure from contemporary political and cultural mythology; the 'real' Brecht is generally left far behind. *Die Ästhetik des Widerstands* moves as far as possible from a personal portrait and thereby honours Brecht's place in cultural and political history most fittingly.

---

[1] *Thomas Brecht* became the first *Thomas Wendt* (1919) before Feuchtwanger settled on his final title, *Neunzehnhundertachtzehn*. Lion Feuchtwanger, *Gesammelte Werke*, vol. 11, *Stücke in Proza* (Amsterdam, Querido Verlag, 1936), pp. 157-286. The theme is strikingly similar to that developed by Günter Grass forty years later.

[2] Peter Weiss, *Die Ästhetik des Widerstands*, (Frankfurt aM, Suhrkamp, 1975/78/81); Marieluise Fleisser, *Tiefseefisch*, in *Gesammelte Werke*, vol 1, Hg. Günther Rühle (Frankfurt aM, Suhrkamp, 1972), pp.289-356; and *Avantgarde*, vol.3, pp.117-68; Elaine Feinstein, *Loving Brecht* (London, Hodder and Stoughton, 1993); Elias Canetti, *Die Fackel im Ohr* (Frankfurt aM, Fischer, 1981); Christopher Hampton, *Tales from Hollywood* (London and Boston, Faber and Faber, 1983); Günter Grass, *Die Plebejer proben den Aufstand*, in *Werkausgabe in zehn Bänden*, Hg. Volker Neuhaus (Darmstadt and Neuwied, Luchterhand, 1987), vol.8, *Theaterspiele*.

[3] *Brecht as They Knew Him* (Berlin, Seven Seas, 1974) has contributions from 32 friends and collaborators.

[4] Arnolt Bronnen, *Tage mit Bertolt Brecht. Geschichte einer unvollendeten Freundschaft* (Vienna and Munich, Kurt Desch, 1960); Hans Sahl, 'Schwierigkeiten im Verkehr mit dem Dichter Bert Brecht', in *Das Exil im Exil. Memoiren eines Moralisten II* (Hamburg, Luchterhand, 1990), pp.171-74; Hans Mayer, 'Brecht', in *Ein Deutscher auf Widerruf. Erinnerungen* (Frankfurt aM, Suhrkamp, 1984), vol.2, pp.141-56.

[5] Benno Besson, *Jahre mit Brecht*, Hg. Christa Neubert-Herwig (Willisau, Switzerland, Theaterkultur-Verlag, 1990).

[6] This is why Tom Kuhn and Karen J. Leeder choose the phrase as the title of their English edition of Münsterer's memoir: Hanns Otto Münsterer, *The Young Brecht*, translated and introduced by Tom Kuhn and Karen J. Leeder, (London, Libris, 1992).

[7] Carl Zuckmayer, *Als wär's ein Stück von mir. Erinnerungen* (Frankfurt aM, Fischer, 1969); Grete Fischer, *Dienstboten, Brecht and andere. Zeitgenossen in Prag, Berlin und London* (Olten and Freiburg in Breisgau, Walter-Verlag, 1966).

[8] Hans Otto Münsterer, *Bert Brecht. Erinnerungen aus den Jahren 1917-1922* (Zurich, Verlag der Arche, 1963), p.26.

13. Max Frisch, 'Brecht', *Tagebücher 1946-1949: 1966-1971* (Frankfurt aM, Suhrkamp, 1978), pp.253-60.

14. See also Hans Mayer, *Erinnerung an Brecht* (Frankfurt aM, Suhrkamp, 1996).

15. See Paul O'Doherty, 'Hans Mayers späte Abrechnung mit der DDR', in *The New Germany. Literature and Society after Unification*, ed. Osman Durrani, Colin Good, and Kevin Hilliard (Sheffield, Sheffield Academic Press, 1995), pp.412-26.

16. She thanks Fuegi 'for the use of his forthcoming book, *Brecht and Co: An Archaeology of Voices*'.

17. Günter Grass, *Werkausgabe*, vol.10, *Gespräche*, p.49.

18. See Jochen Wittmann, 'The GDR and Günter Grass: East German Reception of the Literary Works and Public Persona' in *German Literature at a Time of Change 1989-1990. German Unity and German Identity in Literary Perspective*, ed. Arthur Williams, Stuart Parkes, and Roland Smith (Bern, Lang, 1991), pp.273-84.

19. See Dieter Stolz, *Vom privaten Motivkomplex zum poetischen Weltentwurf. Konstanten und Entwicklungen im literarischen Werk von Günter Grass (1956-1986)* (Würzburg, Königshausen and Neumann, 1994), pp.226-39.

20. In *Gewissen der Worte. Essays* (Frankfurt aM, Fischer, 1981), pp.179-90.

21. According to Jost Hermand, 'Der Über-Vater Brecht. Brecht in der *Ästhetik des Widerstands*', in *Brecht 83. Brecht und Marxismus. Dokumentation. Protokoll der Brecht-Tage 1983* (Berlin, Henschel, 1983), pp.190-202 (p.190).

CHRISTINA UJMA

'Der strenge und der schwärmende Ton'
Notes on Bloch and Brecht in the Twenties and Thirties
(Translated by Jonathan Long)

There are shelfloads of secondary literature on both Bloch and Brecht, and it is thus astonishing that hardly any attention has been paid to the relationship between two such well-known and popular authors. After emigrating to the West in 1961, Bloch was regarded by GDR Germanists as *persona non grata*, as someone whose name was henceforth unmentionable, and so the Bloch-Brecht relationship was ruled out as an object of research. Even Werner Mittenzwei's biography of Brecht, published in 1987, is no real exception, though Bloch is at least mentioned. In the research literature devoted to Bloch in the West, on the other hand, the emphasis was for years placed on his late works *Das Prinzip Hoffnung* and *Das Experimentum Mundi*. Bloch's most intensive relationship with Brecht, however, existed in the twenties and thirties, during the Weimar Republic and the early years of exile, and so West German research has yielded equally little. Although Hans-Thies Lehmann's article[1] and Gudrun Klatts's treatise *Vom Umgang mit der Moderne*[2] represent praiseworthy exceptions, significant aspects of the relationship between Bloch and Brecht have remained unexamined. This, presumably, will soon change because new documents have become available – primarily letters by Bloch to his wife, and fragments of other correspondence – which prove that during the Weimar Republic Bloch and Brecht held very similar views, and entertained a closer friendship than had hitherto been assumed.[3] These documents will throw new light on the biographies of both writers, but the interpretive possibilities of published texts in which Bloch analyses and comments on Brecht's work are in fact far from exhausted. In his extensive output for the literary reviews of the Weimar Republic and in *Erbschaft dieser Zeit* (1935), Bloch tried to decipher the signature of his age by analysing the cultural phenomena of the late twenties and early thirties, and so it was only natural that he should have concerned himself with Brecht, who had become highly successful towards the end of the Weimar Republic. Bloch's essays show that he reviewed the work of his friend with commitment, but also sometimes with a critical eye, and that the two authors' attitudes towards contemporary and modern art were in certain respects fundamentally at odds, despite their numerous common interests.

The documents of the friendship are distributed somewhat irregularly, and apart from a few exceptions they are to be found amongst Bloch's writings. This is due partly to Bloch's aforementioned work for the literary reviews of the Weimar Republic, and partly to the fact that in his later years he was often asked about both his pre-war days, and his contact with other intellectuals and artists of the Weimar Republic. In one of these interviews, Bloch speaks of his first meeting with Brecht, an encounter which was thoroughly typical of the intellectual culture of the Weimar Republic. The Berlin intelligentsia of the time used to meet in bars and cafés, and in a theatre bar Bloch met Brecht who was then regarded as an up-and-coming talent and who had come to Bloch's attention through his story of piracy 'Bargan läßt es sein', published in the *Neues Merkur* in 1921.[4] Bloch did not give the date of this meeting, but it presumably took place during Brecht's 'mißlungene Eroberung Berlins' in 1921-2.[5] Neither of them kept a record of their next meeting, but documents prove that they were both co-founders of the *Gruppe 1925*, a left-wing writers' organisation[6] which also included Döblin, Musil, Werfel, Holitscher, Toller, and Klabund, among others.[7]

The 'Dreigroschenoper'

Bloch and Brecht met frequently during the Weimar Republic, and moved in the same circles of committed left-wing artists. Their names crop up in connection with a planned periodical *Krise und Kritik*, a project on which their mutual friend Walter Benjamin also collaborated.[8] Bloch was fascinated by the *Dreigroschenoper* project. Karola Bloch reports in her memoirs that Bloch went along to rehearsals for the *Dreigroschenoper*, which numerous Berlin writers and artists of the time also attended.[9]

The *Dreigroschenoper*, first performed in August 1928, represented a breakthrough for Brecht and turned him into a literary success almost overnight. It was greatly admired not only by a wide audience but also by Bloch. Bloch was a close friend of the other creator of the *Dreigroschenoper*, Kurt Weill. He was interested in the theory of music not only through his friendship with the conductor Otto Klemperer, which went back to before the First World War: he also concerns himself with a philosophy of music in the longest chapter (170 pages) of his very first work, *Geist der Utopie*. His interest in the philosophy of music meant that he was also a regular contributor to the music periodical *Anbruch*, which was based in Vienna and appeared from 1929 under the editorship of Adorno. Adorno had begun his editorship with a polemical and programmatic editorial in which he postulated that *Anbruch* was once again to become an organ of the fight against reactionary music, and a forum for the avantgarde.[10] It was here that Bloch published his first journalistic discussion of Brecht, namely the article 'Das Lied der Seeräuber-Jenny in der *Dreigroschenoper*', which bears a greeting to Kurt Weill and Lotte Lenya as its epigraph.

Bloch's contribution is very unusual because he discusses not the entire *Dreigroschenoper*, but merely a single song which is itself highly incongruous because it is about a person who does not appear in the play at all. The 'Lied der Seeräuber-Jenny', the famous song about the young dishwasher who dreams up a pirate ship with eight white sails and fifty canon on board to come and rescue her from her miserable existence and put to death the inhabitants of the town on her orders, is performed by Polly at her wedding. Bloch particularly likes the anarchic element concealed within a little ditty whose actual performance is so harmless and soulfully sentimental: 'Ein neuer Volksmond bricht durch die Schmachtfetzen am Dienstmädchen- und Ansichtskartenhimmel',[11] and the music unites funeral march, jazz and chanson:

> [...] die Musik ist gleichfalls zwischen Bar als Kathedrale, Kathedrale als Bar ununterscheidbar. Blumen wachsen aus dem faulsten Operettenzauber, aus Kitzelchansons von 1900, aus der Herrlichkeit amerikanischer Jazzfabrikate, mit der Hand nachgemacht, vorgemacht. ('Das Lied')

For Bloch, ancient myths of freedom, and Biblical allusions concerning the lowly that shall be exalted, are combined in the melody and text of this song. He sees the appearance of an image of the Redeemer, the Messiah, and finds a mixture of religious and messianic motifs, tinged with a trace of Pietism and Salvation Army, and enriched with a good measure of blasphemy:

> Im Weill-Brecht-Land macht sich aber nicht nur die Frömmigkeit gemein, sondern die Blasphemie rechtgläubig. *Der himmlische Bräutigam erscheint der Schubertschen Nonne, die hier Seeräuber-Jenny ist, und das Hoppla ist so apokalyptisch wie man nur will.* ('Das Lied')

The close of the *Dreigroschenoper* is likewise placed by Bloch within this context: the king's mounted messenger, who saves Mackie Messer from execution, provides a fairytale, Fidelio-like ending, and it is only logical that the play should end with a chorale – though as Bloch objects, it would have been more consistent with 'revolutionary logic' if, at the close, the 'ship with eight sails and fifty canon on board' had brought about the happy ending.

Bloch accounts for the success of the *Dreigroschenoper* – which came as a surprise to all concerned –, and the fact that upright citizens went in their droves to see a revolutionary play, in terms of its 'boozy joviality', but stresses that the 'Lied der Seeräuber-Jenny', in contrast to the rest of the play, did not deserve this misguided applause. All in all, Bloch locates the subversive character of the *Dreigroschenoper* in the fact that the music of the slums, and elements of revue and pulp fiction, are combined with quite anomalous contents. He describes Jenny's song as a 'cantata for our time': 'Ihr Lied gehört in die Wochen vor Weihnachten. Echte Adventstimmungen, den Anforderungen des neuzeitlichen Geschmackes entsprechend' ('Das Lied'). An aspect of the 'Lied der Seeräuber-Jenny' to which Bloch draws special attention is the fact that the subversive nature of the feminine is particularly in evidence here. In fact, a third of the article deals with this theme. Bloch sees in the smile of the 'Seeräuber-Jenny' a sign of witch-like mystery: 'Haben nicht Flintenweiber, Petroleusen zu allen Zeiten die Revolution begleitet und paßt nicht dem Weib die Räuberbraut vorzüglich auf den Leib [...]'. The subversive feminine smile was often linked to the red peril, and a direct path leads from the smile of the 'Seeräuber-Jenny'

> zum Rebellensymbol der Paradiesschlange, mit der Eva sich so gut versteht... die Paradiesschlange ist die Raupe der Göttin Vernunft. Und die 'Seele' nicht zu vergessen, die allemal weiblich ist, das Mädchen Psyche im entsetzlichen Vaterhaus der Welt. ('Das Lied')

Here, Bloch is not so much following Brecht as developing his own programm which he formulated the same year, 1929, in the essay 'Viele Kammern im Welthaus'. Here, he conjures up images of the 'Falltüren in der Welt',[12] the 'Orte, an denen die gewohnte Wirklichkeit ihren Boden verliert' ('Kammern'), and hence all phenomena which burst the bounds of prevalent *ratio*, the things which interrupt the habitual order, amongst which he numbers the Dionysian, the mystical, love, and femininity. He is concerned with the mysteries of the beginning and the helplessness of philosophy and *ratio* in the face of the secrets of existence, and of the numinous. He calls for '*ein[en] Katalog des Ausgelassenen, jener Inhalte, die im männlichen, bürgerlichen, kirchlichen Begriffssystem keinen Platz haben*' ('Kammern'). The plenitude of the disparate and particular, Bloch argues, can no longer be subsumed under a concept of the general; it can no longer be integrated within a hierarchy, tending by its very nature to undermine any system. Following Bachofen, the feminine, in this and other essays of the time, stands for the vital principle, that which is fecund and chaotic, whereas the masculine stands for systematic rigidity. This mode of thought is in no way untypical of the time; on the contrary, it had its origins in turn of the century discourse.

In his interpretation of the 'Lied der Seeräuber-Jenny' as a figure for the feminine subversive, then, Bloch forges a link with his own thought. Brecht could hardly have approved of this interpretation which, in addition, tears the song from its context and overestimates its importance. On the other hand, those socially critical tendencies which *do* exist in the play culminate in the 'Lied der Seeräuber-Jenny', as Mittenzwei agrees.[13] Be that is it may; it is highly unlikely that Brecht agreed with Bloch's positive evaluation of the feminine. On the contrary, violence is unleashed uninhibitedly against women time after time in his early plays, the most famous example being *Baal*, with whom, as Reinhard Baumgart says, Brecht thoroughly identified.[14] In Brecht's writings on contemporary literature, the feminine is likewise defined as weak and negative, as opposed to the strong and positive masculine. In a polemic of 1926, Brecht accuses contemporary literature of being too feminine. The novels of Thomas Mann are named in this connection:

> Zweierlei Damen
>
> In meinen Augen ist es ein Vorteil der nordischen Literatur, daß man einfach schon durch die Lektüre herausbringen kann, ob das Buch von einem Mann oder einer Frau geschrieben ist. Ist es nicht angenehm, daß man, wenn man nach der Lektüre von *Jerusalem* und den *Buddenbrooks* feststellt, diese Bücher seien von Frauen geschrieben, bei *Jerusalem* recht behält und bei *Buddenbrooks* nicht? Die Geschlechtsbestimmung des Verfassers ist in Deutschland nur durch Beilegen einer Photographie möglich. Wenden wir uns den Kriminalromanen zu.[15]

There is in any case no successor to the Seeräuber-Jenny, that anarchic and subversive woman, in Brecht's later work. This is a likely reason for the fact that Bloch was to extol the 'Lied der Seeräuber-Jenny' repeatedly throughout his life and to recommend it as an anthem for ceremonial occasions, analogous to a national anthem.[16]

Weill's and Brecht's *Dreigroschenoper* is likewise feted in Bloch's *Erbschaft dieser Zeit*, first published in 1935. Here, the 'Lied der Seeräuber-Jenny' is once again praised and this time Bloch is less sceptical about the socially critical function of the text as a whole. It is precisely Weill's use of the popular song and elements of operetta which Bloch regards as subversive in the positive sense, and as considerably more effective than avantgarde music. He interprets the *Dreigroschenoper* overall as a parable of the society of the Weimar Republic:

Die *Dreigroschenoper* konnte auch an dies Lumpenhafte sich, kraft der gärenden Zeit, besonders genau anschließen: ihre Bettler und Gauner sind nicht mehr solche der Opera buffa, gar des Lumpenballs, gar der Wohltätigkeit, sondern der zersetzenden Gesellschaft in Person. Daher, o falsche Freunde, diese Töne, daher Brechts höhnische Süße, geschärfte Leichtigkeit noch einmal, daher die Weisen Mackie Messers und dieser Tiger Brown. [...] Der Versuch der *Dreigroschenoper* hat die schlechteste Musik in den Dienst der heute fortgeschrittensten gestellt; und sie zeigt sich gefährlich. Aus der Hure im bürgerlichen Straßendienst wurde ein anarchische Schmugglerin, wenigstens eine anarchistische.[17]

Revue Forms

For Bloch, the intermingling of revue with serious music attempted by the *Dreigroschenoper* is exemplary. In the essay 'Mangel an Opernstoffen' of 1930,[18] he again discusses the situation of modern serious music, which he regards as less advanced than modern literature and painting. In contrast to the eighteenth and nineteenth centuries, when opera was the art-form of the ascendant bourgeoisie, there is nowadays a lack of suitable subject-matter; it is no longer evident what operas should be about. Bloch stresses that not only the subject-matter but also the musical language has, in part, become stale. At a time when traditional thematic and musical forms are exhausted but no new development is in the offing, Kurt Weill is the only one amongst younger composers who has successfully revitalised older forms. Bloch states this both in *Erbschaft dieser Zeit* and in the essay 'Mangel an Opernstoffen'. Weill, he maintains, has successfully developed a forward-looking musical form by reverting to epic and lyrical forms with the 'Lied' as musical object.[19] Furthermore, the revue form adopted in the two Brecht-Weill collaborations *Die Dreigroschenoper* and *Aufstieg und Fall der Stadt Mahagonny* is, with its anarchic disorderliness, the form commensurate with the times, but also the form in which past and future meet.

Bloch's assessment of the revue as both in keeping with the times and pointing to the future is thoroughly in accord with his philosophical programme of those years. In the essay 'Die Zauberflöte und Symbole von Heute', which appeared in *Anbruch* in 1930, Bloch ascribes to Mozart's masterpiece an 'anarchic surrealism', stating that the 'Singspiel' was a revue with the resources of the seventeenth century. He even goes so far as to place it in the company of the *Dreigroschenoper*.[20] In so doing, he both asserts the current relevance of *Die Zauberflöte* and simultaneously furnishes the revue with an honourable history. The revue was the new form of entertainment of the Weimar Republic, and Bloch detected the revue form in many places. For instance, he entitled his review of Walter Benjamin's work *Einbahnstraße* 'Revueform in der

Philosophie'. In 1928, when this essay first appeared in the *Vossische Zeitung*, Bloch was very critical of these revue forms and Benjamin's experiment in surrealistic montage. In the modified version which was published in 1935 in *Erbschaft dieser Zeit*, on the other hand, he is full of praise for the revue form, believing that it could bring about a renewal of philosophy. Bloch had something similar in mind in his discussion of Wagner. In the essay 'Die Rettung Wagners durch Karl May',[21] he suggests that Wagnerian forms, which have become shallow and whose revolutionary musical function was lost in the suffocating sensuousness of the late nineteenth century, could be changed by means of Karl May, i.e. by means of tawdriness and kitsch, in order to make them once more recognisable.

> Wie verstehen große Werke kaum mehr anders als märchenhaft mit Kolportagenschein, und Fidelio wurde die Orientierungssäule jeder Kolportage, von der Dreigroschenoper, der des Königs nicht fehlt, bis zur Geburt der Metaphysik aus der Geist der Kolportage. Mehr als ein Weg aber führt von der Räuberbraut zur Wagnerschen Schwüle, von den Traumverschlingungen der alten Kolportage, [...] von der Haddedhins, bei denen Karl May gleichfalls nicht war, zu den Germanen des Rings, von der Silberbüchse Winnetous zu Nothung und seinem Kampf gegen den weißen Vater, vom Traum-Orient zur Kitsch-Edda: diese Wege müßten auch umgekehrt gegangen, Wagner ganz auf sein Seeräuberschiff gebracht werden, mit acht Segeln, fünfzig Kanonen an Bord...[22]

Here, the *Dreigroschenoper*, and the 'Lied der Seeräuber-Jenny' which is alluded to at the end, attain exemplary status – that much is clear. Bloch's hoped-for 'Geburt der Metaphysik aus dem Geist der Kolportage' was not to materialise, at least not in Brecht's subsequent work, because from 1929-30 the latter turned to the restrained, objective form of the didactic play (*Lehrstück*), whose appeal is greatly limited. Bloch's hymns of praise to the *Dreigroschenoper*, then, celebrate the Brecht of yesterday, which may well be Bloch's way of expressing criticism of his friend's most recent artistic development.

Frictions

Alongside positive comments on the *Dreigroschenoper*, Bloch already notes in his 1930 essay 'Die Zauberflöte und Symbole von Heute' that Brecht is too objective and sober.[23] In *Erbschaft dieser Zeit*, Bloch argues along two different lines: the aforementioned positive discussion of the *Dreigroschenoper* is included, and the *Aufstieg und Fall der Stadt Mahagonny* is likewise acclaimed.[24] On the whole, however, Bloch takes up a highly critical stance towards New Objectivity, not only in *Erbschaft dieser Zeit*, but also earlier: in his articles for the review section of the *Frankfurter Zeitung* he found little that was positive in this literary trend which took over from Expressionism. Bloch felt a strong affinity for the Expressionist period; in *Geist der Utopie*, after all, he had produced a philosophy of Expressionism. Whilst he saw Expressionism as the art of the rebellious subject, New Objectivity entailed the positive affirmation of alienation.

Brecht's *Lehrstücke*, in which Bloch discerns a meld of objectivity and montage, find an echo in *Erbschaft dieser Zeit*. Brecht is held up as conclusive proof that montage is not merely a product of bourgeois decay, but can also be productive for the class-conscious left (*Erbschaft*, 226-7). Primarily, however, acclaim is reserved for what Bloch later terms the 'anarchic and late gothic' elements of Brecht's work. Bloch does contrast Brecht's objectivity from 'bürgerlich-neusachliche Banalität', calls him a 'Leninist der Schaubühne', and praises the political achievement of the *Lehrstücke* as experiments which turn the stage into a laboratory, but all in all he cannot summon up much enthusiam for them. He describes the pedagogical impetus behind them, but to characterise the lack of aesthetic appeal entailed in the concept of the *Lehrstück* as a communist didactic experimentation machine is not exactly positive (*Erbschaft*, 246-7). Brecht's anarchism and the adventurous romanticism which had so pleased Bloch in 'Bargan läßt es sein' have faded. The *Lehrstücke*, writes Bloch, offer the audience not an evening of theatre, but an evening of theory.

Here, Bloch remains tentative in his criticism of the dryness and aesthetic shortcomings of the *Lehrstücke*. In the essay 'Ein Leninist der Schaubühne', published in 1936, he makes his point more clearly: 'Once the goal of a classless society has been attained, there will no longer be much to learn from plays like this',[25] but there will still be plenty to learn from the *Dreigroschenoper* and *Mahagonny*. In the essay 'Das Problem des Expressionismus nochmals', dating from 1940, it is again only Brecht's early work whose positive points Bloch stresses (*Erbschaft*, 276). Although he was also involved with those of Brecht's plays which Bloch criticises, such as *Der Jasager*, Kurt Weill emerges in a more positive light (*Erbschaft*, 237). Bloch once again acknowledges Weill's musical achievements as a composer in the *Dreigroschenoper*. Close examination of the articles on the *Dreigroschenoper* and *Aufstieg und Fall der Stadt Mahagonny* reveals that Bloch's praise is directed slightly more towards Weill than towards Brecht.

At the famous Writers' Congress in the Defence of Culture, which took place in Paris in June 1935, the ever greater divergence in Bloch's and Brecht's positions suddenly became apparent. Here writers and intellectuals from all over the world met to discuss intellectual strategies for the defeat of fascism. Bloch and Brecht were amongst them. In his contribution to the discussion, Brecht strongly attacked the politics of the Popular Front, whose strategy it was to operate a common policy with the anti-fascist movements of the bourgeoisie, and to orient themselves not towards the struggle against capitalism, but towards the defence of humanism and the struggle against fascist barbarism. Brecht, on the other hand, insists on the analysis of capitalism:

> Viele von uns Schriftstellern, welche die Greuel des Faschismus erfahren und darüber entsetzt sind, haben diese Lehre noch nicht verstanden, haben die Wurzel der Roheit, die sie entsetzt, noch nicht entdeckt. Es besteht immerfort bei ihnen die Gefahr, daß sie die Grausamkeiten des Faschismus als unnötige Grausamkeiten betrachten. Sie halten an den Eigentumsverhältnissen fest, weil sie glauben, daß zu ihrer Verteidigung die Grausamkeiten des Faschismus nicht nötig sind [...]. Diejenigen unserer Freunde, welche über die Grausamkeiten des Faschismus ebenso entsetzt sind wie wir, aber die Eigentumsverhältnisse aufrecht erhalten wollen [...] können den Kampf gegen die so sehr überhandnehmende Barbarei nicht kräftig und nicht lang genug führen, weil sie nicht die gesellschaftlichen Zustände angeben und herbeiführen helfen können, in denen die Barbarei überflüssig wäre.[26]

Bloch, who was so concerned with modern culture and the Popular Front, could hardly have sympathised with Brecht's conference paper with its peremptory demand that the discussion be about not culture or barbarism but the property relations, since fascism could otherwise be neither combatted nor analysed.[27]

Bloch's paper was entitled 'Dichtung und sozialistische Gegenstände'. Its theme was the current relevance of modern art and the relationship between the artistic avant-garde and left-wing politics:[28]

> Vor dreißig Jahren war noch Klingklang überall, besang Dehmel den 'Arbeitsmann', brannten Dichter in den Sozialismus durch wie in ein Abenteuer. Damals hatte die Materie noch Weinlaub im Haar, das Diesseits war nicht nackt wie eine Tatsache, sondern 'nackt wie das Leben', von Fidusmenschen bewohnt, von jener Sonne beschienen, die das Wochenende des dionysischen Kleinbürgers geworden ist. Heute dagegen werden andere Papiere verlangt, die Revolution verachtet die graeculi, die tänzerischen, die träumerischen, die schönen Propheten, hat die römische Kälte.[29]

Whilst Brecht insisted on an analysis of capitalism and ignores the question of art, Bloch begins with a nostalgic glance backwards at the exemplary unity of a life-reforming subculture and socialism at the turn of the century and the *Jugendstil* period. In comparison with this synthesis, Bloch continued, contemporary communist political culture and its cultural politics had retained hardly any positive features. Again he speaks of 'Dunkelmänner des Intellekts' who repulse poetry and art with political plans and excessive sobriety. A forceful plea for pluralism of the imagination is foremost in Bloch's paper. 'In der Kunst gibt es keine Generallinie': with this quotation from Stalin he attempts to lend added weight to his demand for pluralism, a necessary but unsuccessful appeal.[30] For it was precisely this conference which marked a decisive change in the relationship between the communist movement and the artistic avant-garde: the final rift between communists and surrealists. André Breton's invitation was retracted, an event which put an end the struggle to unite poetic and political revolution which had occupied him for so many years.[31] The conclusion of Breton's paper, which was not delivered by him personally, contains demands which are very close to Bloch's concerns; this applies not only to the imagination, but also to the life-reforming impetus: '"Die Welt verändern", hat Marx gesagt, "das Leben ändern", sagte Rimbaud, uns verschmelzen beide Sprüche zu einem einzigen Schlachtruf.'[32]

Eulenspiegeleien?

Bloch's speech, and the interpretation of art and culture which it puts forward, could hardly be more distanced from Brecht's speech. Two comments by Brecht about the oppositions which emerged during the conference exist in the form of two letters which follow on from a controversial discussion between Bloch and Brecht at the congress.

In the letter, dated by Brecht 'July 1935', he urges Bloch to be more objective.[33] The object of his criticism is *Erbschaft dieser Zeit*, which Brecht describes as the 'Eulenspiegeleien eines großen Herrn' and accuses their author of 'regelwidriges Benehmen als Philosoph'.[34] The tone of this letter is forcedly comic, but it is highly reproachful and advises the author of *Erbschaft dieser Zeit* – who not only concerns himself with montage as an art form but also wishes to be a montage himself[35] – to turn his attention in future to his own subject, philosophy:

> Aber in vollem Ernst (auch das obige ist nicht nur Spaß): Es könnte eine große Sache sein, wenn Sie sich die Philosophie vornähmen und untersuchten, wo das abendländische Berufsdenken absackt, weil es auf Anpassung an nicht mehr haltbare ökonomische, politische Zustände ausgeht. Es muß da ganz große verödete Felder geben, höchst interessante Problemschrumpfungen.[36]

This letter has given rise to several interpretations. Lehmann has linked Brecht's reaction with that of Benjamin,[37] but precisely those passages in which Bloch does what Brecht suggests in the above letter and engages with philosophy, undertaking an ideological-critical stroll through the history of philosophy and giving it a dressing-down with an almost Brechtian peremptoriness, meet with Benjamin's disapproval.[38] The strong points of the work which Benjamin underlines in his letter to Kracauer are the 'Versuch über den ungleichzeitigen Widerspruch' and the 'Abschnitt über Märchen und Mythos',[39] hardly the passages of which Brecht would have approved, especially since Bloch postulates that the left should not allow myth to become the preserve of the right, but should rather make full use of it for its own political ends. It is probably rather the case that Bloch's and Brecht's ideas about art had developed along widely divergent lines; and Brecht was also presumably not exactly overjoyed at the lukewarm reception of the *Lehrstück* style in *Erbschaft dieser Zeit*.

Dolf Sternberger pinpointed very precisely the differences between Bloch and Brecht in an article dating from 1960, and it seems to me that his comments are applicable not only to the late work of the two authors:

> Diese Grundidee Blochs, die er lebenslänglich verfolgt hat, ist freilich derjenigen Brechts ganz unähnlich – trozt aller Koinzidenz des ideologischen Bekenntnisses. Brecht ist Moralist, Bloch ist Utopist. Bloch hofft auf Erlösung, Brecht pocht auf Bewährung. Der Philosoph bedenkt die letzten Dinge, der Dichter die nächsten. Der Ton ist wie vertauscht: dem Poeten eignet der strenge, dem Denker der schwärmende.[40]

Brecht's attempt to banish him from the realm of art was not permitted to go unchallenged by Bloch, who pointed out in his reply to Brecht that the schoolmasterly style of academic philosophers did not lend itself to an adequate analysis of the present, whereas the use of modernistic, literary forms facilitated insights which could not be gained any other way:

> Es wachsen dadurch der Erkenntnis neue Formen zum Zweck der Durchdringung oder auch Beachtung kleiner, abseitiger, irritierender Gegenstände zu, deren Gewicht bei durchgehends würdiger Methode gar nicht wägbar ist. Aber vielleicht meinen wir ganz Verschiedenes, und ich wäre Ihnen dankbar, wenn Sie mir numerieren würden, was denn Ihnen (der Behandlung, dem Stoff, nach?) dem Guten im Weg steht. Das wäre zugleich eine Fortsetzung unseres Gesprächs, das Problem der nicht ausgekreisten, sondern endlich fachkundig besetzten und besiegten 'Wärme' ('Irratio') betreffend.[41]

Bloch is very willing to enter into dialogue with Brecht, and in spite of the latter's harsh criticisms and the manifest differences in their positions he is unwilling to break off the discussion. He thus closes with a request that contentious issues be discussed by letter.

In his reply, which was in all probability never sent, Brecht avoids discussing aesthetic questions, taking as his starting point instead Bloch's criticism of the cold objectivity of contemporary culture. He isolates a quotation from Bloch's Paris speech concerning the 'frigidification' of existence, which Bloch happily and extensively denounces, analysing it as an effect of capitalism. Fascism, for the Bloch of *Erbschaft dieser Zeit*, is primarily the rebellion of misled people against coldness, objectivity, modernity itself. Brecht points out that capitalism, which installed objectivity in the first place, can also do otherwise, and in its fascist culture offers warmth and a sense of national community but works nevertheless with merciless coldness. He concludes his letter with the following words: 'Wir haben die Güte verlacht, die Humanität durch den Kakao gezogen. Das war *vor* der Niederlage. Jetzt stoßen wir ein Geheul aus und betteln um Demokratie als Almosen.'[42]

It is hardly surprising that Brecht never sent the letter. Agreement about how to evaluate coldness and warmth, objectivity and *irratio* seems unattainable. At the time, Bloch was involved in similar controversies with Adorno and Benjamin.[43] It is not the case, however, that Bloch shifted his position to any great extent. He was rather continuing his own programme, begun in the Weimar Republic, of developing an antithetical alternative to the sobriety of the Weimar Republic, to the culture of coldness and rationality, of reification and alienation. In opposition to the ostensibly classicistic New Subjectivity, Bloch time and again conjures up that which is anarchic, warm, anti-bourgeois and sometimes even organic. The essay 'Herbst, Sumpf, Heide und Sezession' (1932) plays off the coolly rational art of New Objectivity against the *Jugendstil*, praising the latter's ornamental, dreamlike art which feeds off fairytale, myth and nature.[44] Parts of this essay, especially the aforementioned nostalgic backward glance at the exemplary unity between left-wing subcuture, bohemianism and politics, were incorporated in the speech Bloch gave at the Paris Congress in Defence of Culture. In their dispute over warmth and coldness, Bloch and Brecht revivified an old controversy concerning the modern world, namely what attitude to take towards its coldness and objectification. They moved within traditional fields of opposition: if Bloch conjures up the ornamental *Jugendstil* in an era characterised by the unadorned functionalism of New Objectivist architecture; if he summons femininity and the Dionysian alongside fairytale and myth as those forces which resist cold objectification, then he stands in Romantic opposition to the modern world. Brecht's coolly objective, emphatically analytic bent marks the opposite pole. Helmut Lethen situates him within the tradition of iron modernity ['eisige Moderne']:

> Brechts Kälte-Szenarien bilden ein Environment, in dem Trennungsfähigkeit geübt werden soll. Wenn Brecht Lernprozesse darstellt, dann in einem Raum, dessen

dominierende Qualität die Kälte ist [...]. Selbstbestimmtes Subjekt wird nur, wer gelernt hat, eine Wegstrecke durch den Kälteraum zurückzulegen, ohne sich von Räumen symbiotischer Wärme ablenken zu lassen.[45]

The dominant influence which the rhetoric employed by both thinkers had on the critique of modernity can be traced back to its very beginnings;[46] moreover, it characterises this critique even today, having recently cropped up in the postmodern engagement with modernity.[47] It has already been frequently pointed out – most recently by Cornelia Klinger – that those positions which stand on the side of warmth and subjectivity are not necessarily anti-modern, but are rather an integral part of modernity itself.[48] The resurgence of these dualisms, as Lethen remarks, is always to be understood as a symptom of social crisis:

Aber immer wenn das Projekt Moderne in eine kritische Phase tritt, spalten sich die Diskurse. Es entmischen sich die verschiedenen Schattierungen des Lebens: als Schatten eines Wärme-Kults tritt der Kälte-Kult auf den Plan. Der Ideologie der Intimität, den Subkulturen der Wärme antwortet das Pathos der Distanz und das funktionalistische Lob der Entfremdung.[49]

The relationship between intoxication and sobriety, warmth and coldness, rationality and irrationality not only forms the leitmotif of Bloch's aesthetic thought, but also informs the political passages of *Erbschaft dieser Zeit*. In general, it is the Romantic challenges to capitalism which interest Bloch, and which he regards, despite protestations to the contrary, as the truly important issue. This circumstance brought him the justified reputation as the representative of a romantic strain within Marxist thought.

Bloch's and Brecht's drifting apart is indeed paradoxical in that it happened at a time when both turned to Marxism – with quite different results –, where they found themselves united in opposition to the narrow-minded limitations imposed upon art from the side of orthodoxy. In contrast to Brecht, who felt that he was one of those personally under attack in the Expressionism debate, but who wanted nothing to do with Expressionism and confided his anger only to friends and to the drawer of his writing desk, Bloch repeatedly entered into the journalistic debate. Bloch defended Expressionism as a subject-centred, humane artistic trend, which, in contrast to Realism and Objectivity, possessed real fire and authenticity.

Bloch had no desire to perceive the exonerating elements of the cult of coldness, and spent the rest of his life looking for the 'strain of warmth' in Marxism, for it was only *warmth* which he found in his view stayed on course and was pregnant with hope. Despite the recrudescence of their friendship in the GDR (of all places), Bloch and Brecht stood on opposite sides of this fundamental aesthetic divide, in which there was to be no reconciliation right up to Brecht's death. Even into old age, Bloch had little positive to say about Brecht's *Lehrstücke* or his later work, but plenty about the *Dreigroschenoper* and *Aufstieg und Fall der Stadt Mahagonny*.

---

[1]   Hans-Thies Lehmann, "'Sie werden lachen: es muß systematisch vorgegangen werden"': Brecht und Bloch – ein Hinweis', in *Ernst Bloch: Sonderband Text + Kritik*, ed. Arnold (Munich, text+kritik, 1985).

[2]   Gudrun Klatt, *Vom Umgang mit der Moderne: Ästhetische Konzepe der dreißiger Jahre: Lifschitz, Lukacs, Lunatscharski, Bloch, Benjamin* (Berlin, 1984), pp. 174-8.

[3]   See Erdmut Wizisla, 'Ernst Bloch und Bertolt Brecht: neue Dokumente ihrer Beziehung', in *Bloch Almanach*, 10 (1990), ed. Karlheinz Weigand, 87-105; and Anna Czajika, 'Rettung Brechts durch Bloch', in *The Other Brecht/Der andere Brecht: Brecht-Jahrbuch* 18 (1993). 121-3.

[4]   See *Tagträume vom aufrechten Gang: Sechs Interviews mit Ernst Bloch*, ed. Arno Münster (Frankfurt, 1977), p. 55.

[5]   See Werner Mittenzwei, *Das Leben des Bertolt Brecht oder der Umgang mit Welträtseln* (Frankfurt, 1987), vol I, pp. 154-83.

[6]   See N.N., "'Gruppe 1925": Zur Abendveranstaltung des Berliner Senders am 17 August', in *Der deutsche Rundfunk* 33 (1926).

[7]   On Brecht's activities in the *Gruppe 1925*, see Mittenzwei, pp. 228-232.

[8]   See Wizisla, pp. 90-1.

[9]   See Gottfried Wagner, *Weill und Brecht: Das musikalische Zeittheater* (Munich, 1977), p. 230.

[10]   See Heinz Steinert, *Adorno in Wien: Über die (Un-)Möglichkeit von Kunst, Kultur und Befreiung* (Frankfurt, 1993), p. 152.

[11]   'Das Lied der Seeräuber-Jenny in der *Dreigroschenoper*', *Anbruch* (1929), 125-7. Henceforth cited in the text as 'Das Lied'.

[12]   'Viele Kammern im Welthaus', *Frankfurter Zeitung*, 15 February 1929. Henceforth cited in the text as 'Kammern'.

[13]   Mittenzwei, pp. 282-3.

14. Reinhart Baumgart, *Selbstvergessenheit: Drei Wege zum Werk: Thomas Mann, Franz Kafka, Bertolt Brecht* (Vienna, 1990), pp. 82-95.

15. Brecht, 'Kehren wir zum Kriminalroman zurück', in *BFA*, 21, p. 128.

16. See *Tagträume vom aufrechten Gang*, p. 55.

17. Bloch, *Erbschaft dieser Zeit* (Zürich, 1935), p. 172.

18. *Die literarische Welt*, 6 (1930), no.31.

19. 'Der Mangel an Opernstoffen'.

20. 'Die Zauberflöte als Symbol von Heute', *Anbruch* 12 (1930).

21. *Anbruch* 11 (1929), Heft 1.

22. 'Rettung Wagners' *Anbruch* 11, p. 8.

23. 'Die Zauberflöte und Symbole von Heute', *Anbruch* 11.

24. See also 'Der Mangel an Opernstoffen'.

25. Reprinted in *Erbschaft dieser Zeit*, p. 254.

26. *Paris 1935. Erster Internationaler Schriftstellerkongress zur Verteidigung der Kultur: Reden und Dokumente*, Akademie der Wissenschaften der DDR (Berlin, 1982), p. 140.

27. See *Paris 1935*, pp. 138-41.

28. Ernst Bloch's 'Dichtung und sozialistische Gegenstände' first appeared in *Mitteilungen der deutschen Freiheitsbibliothek* (Paris: 5, 1935). It is reprinted unchanged in *Paris 1935*, and in *Zur Tradition der deutschen sozialistischen Literatur: Eine Auswahl von Dokumenten 1926-1935* (Berlin and Weimar, 1979). Subsequent references to Bloch's text will be to the latter edition.

29. 'Dichtung und sozialistische Gegenstände', p. 885.

30. 'Dichtung und sozialistische Gegenstände', p. 887.

31. See Elisabeth Lenk, *Der springende Narziß: André Bretons poetischer Materialismus* (Munich, 1971).

32. *Paris 1935*, p. 309.

33. Bertolt Brecht, *Briefe*, vol. I, ed. Günter Glaeser (Frankfurt, 1981), p. 255.

34. Brecht, *Briefe* I, p. 255..

[35.] On Bloch's concept of montage, see Klatt, pp. 176-8; and Christina Ujma, *Ernst Blochs Konstruktion der Moderne aus Messianismus und Marxismus: Erörterungen von Lukacs und Benjamin* (Stuttgart, 1995), pp. 245-53.

[36.] Brecht, *Briefe* I, p. 256.

[37.] See Lehmann; also Florian Vaßen, "'krumme Wege" und "schräger Querschnitt'': Ernst Blochs literarisch-philosophische Schreibweise in *Erbschaft dieser Zeit'*, in *Text+Kritik Ernst Bloch*, p. 132.

[38.] See Benjamin's letter to Kracauer of 15 January 1935, in Walter Benjamin, *Briefe an Siegfried Kracauer, mit vier Briefen von Siegfried Kracauer an Walter Benjamin* (Marbacher Schriften 27, Marbach, 1987).

[39.] See Benjamin's letter to Kracauer of 15 January 1935. On the numerous interpretations of Benjamin's famous letter on *Erbschaft dieser Zeit*, see C. Ujma, 'Walter Benjamin zum 100. Geburtstag: Lumpensammler, Blochs Benjaminische Sicht des Surrealismus', *Bloch Almanach,* 12 (1992), 65-100.

[40.] Dolf Sternberger, 'Vergiß das beste nicht!', in *Materialien zu Ernst Blochs 'Das Prinzip Hoffnung'*, ed. B. Schmidt (Frankfurt, Suhrkamp, 1977), pp. 148-9.

[41.] Bloch, letter to Brecht of 6 August 1935. Full text printed in Wizisla, 'Ernst Bloch and Bertolt Brecht', 93.

[42.] Brecht, *Briefe*, I p. 258.

[43.] See Christina Ujma, 'Walter Benjamin zum 100. Geburtstag'.

[44.] 'Herbst, Sumpf, Heide, Sezession', in *Frankfurter Allgemeine Zeitung*, 21 September 1932.

[45.] Lethen, 'Lob der Kälte: Ein Motiv historischer Avantgarden', in *Die unvollendete Vernunft: Moderne versus Postmoderne*, ed. D. Kamper and W van Reijen (Frankfurt, 1987), pp. 290-1.

[46.] See Lethen, 'Lob der Kälte'; and Manfred Frank, *Kaltes Herz, Unendliche Fahrt, neue Mythologie: Motiv-Untersuchungen zur Pathogenese der Moderne* (Frankfurt, 1989).

[47.] See Lethen, 'Von Geheimagenten und Virtuosen. Peter Sloterdijks Schulbeispiele des Zynismus aus der Literatur der Weimarer Republik', in *Peter Sloterdijks 'Kritik der zynischen Vernunft'*, ed. Otto Kallscheuer et al. (Frankfurt, 1987).

[48.] Cornelia Klinger, *Flucht, Trost, Revolte: Die Moderne und ihre ästhetischen Gegenwelten* (Munich, 1985).

[49.] Lethen, 'Lob der Kälte', p. 283.

STEVE GILES

Marxist Aesthetics and Cultural Modernity in *Der Dreigroschenprozeß*

In October 1930, Brecht sued the Nero film company for allegedly infringing his authorial rights in their production of his most successful play to date, *Die Dreigroschenoper*. Although Brecht lost the subsequent court case,[1] the experiences which he garnered through his confrontation with the Nero film company afforded him new insight into the nature of cultural production in contemporary capitalist society. In the course of 1931, Brecht wrote a detailed analysis of his legal dispute and its aesthetic and sociological ramifications, published in early 1932 as *Der Dreigroschenprozeß*.[2] This text has been relatively neglected by Brecht scholars, partly as it has never been translated into English in its entirety.[3] Its neglect in no way reflects its significance, however, either in Brecht's work or in the context of modern critical theory. It has been described as 'ein Meisterwerk angewandter Dialektik',[4] and as such is, I would argue, Brecht's most sustained and sophisticated theoretical essay, surpassing in this respect such classics as the *Messingkauf* dialogues and the *Kleines Organon für das Theater*. *DGP* is one of the major exemplars of Marxist aesthetic theory in the Twentieth Century, comparable in insight and originality to Walter Benjamin's *Das Kunstwerk im Zeitalter seiner technischen Reproduzierbarkeit*.[5]

My aim in this paper is to consider Brecht's theory of modern culture as articulated in *DGP* by focussing on four main areas of interest: (i) the nature and viability of traditional and/or bourgeois art and aesthetics; (ii) the condition of art under contemporary capitalism; (iii) the impact of technology on art and its social relations; (iv) the effects of film on artistic reception and production. I conclude by appraising Brecht's overall construction of post/modernity at this crucial juncture in his career.

Bourgeois Aesthetics and Traditional Art

Brecht's account of traditional art forms in *DGP* centres on the bourgeois novel. Whereas other Marxist theorists have characterised this genre according to its realistic or naturalistic pretensions – one thinks of Lukács's classic essay 'Erzählen oder Beschreiben', written some five years after *DGP* [6] – Brecht assesses bourgeois narrative forms in terms of the coherence rather than the correspondence theory of truth. Such texts may well project a world, Brecht concedes, but the latter's consistency with reality is purely internal: 'Innerhalb dieser Welt stimmen dann alle Einzelheiten natürlich genau, die, aus dem Zusammenhang gerissen, den "Details" der Realität gegenüber keinen Augenblick waschecht wirken können.' (*DGP*, 465)   The bourgeois novel's internal coherence derives simply from the world-view of its 'creator' or author, which suffuses the novel and masks its empirical falsehood. (*DGP*, 465)   This symbiotic relationship between author and textual world also sustains the notion that an art-work is the appropriate expression of a personality, a notion which Brecht attributes in turn to bourgeois ideology. (*DGP*, 485)

Brecht also gives a more general account of bourgeois aesthetics, arguing that its typical categories are fate, inwardness, transfiguration and, crucially, the (eternally) human. (*DGP*, 477)   Indeed, he continues, it is precisely the belief in the (eternally) human which underpins bourgeois aesthetics' founding idea, namely that art is an inviolable phenomenon which is societally autonomous and thus able to manifest itself in any place and at any time. Brecht links aesthetic autonomy to Kantian disinterestedness, sardonically observing that although art's utility is reputed to be very great, it is seldom made explicit. This, he suggests, is because one of art's most valued predicates is a certain uselessness, art's utility consisting in the fact that it contains something 'das sich der gemeinen Nutzung entzieht und ohne Interesse geliebt wird. Etwas lieben zu können ohne Interesse gilt als Blüte des menschlichen Geistes.' (*DGP*, 507)

Now Brecht changes tack, and notes that for bourgeois aesthetics, the making of art is rooted in human beings' innate drive to express themselves. Brecht takes this assertion to be tautological – the human equivalent of the definition of fish as creatures that swim. At the same time, rather more significantly, he indicates that the concept of art adumbrated by bourgeois aesthetics corresponds with many other ideas constitutive of the Aristotelian-medieval world picture. (*DGP*, 507) While as a historical statement Brecht's claim is tendentious and anachronistic, it is evident that he associates bourgeois aesthetics, centred on autonomy, disinterestedness, expressivity and the eternally human, with a pre-Copernican world-view. As Brecht's arguments elsewhere in *DGP* make clear, this superannuated world-view is to be supplanted, via the processes of contemporary capitalist modernisation, by a properly radical Marxist aesthetic which will, if necessary, forsake the categories of Art and Humanity altogether.

Although Brecht implies that his account of bourgeois aesthetics encompasses a broad sweep of European cultural history stretching as far back as the Middle Ages, or even Ancient Greece, he deals in fact with developments in aesthetic theory which emerge from the late eighteenth century onwards.   Like Benjamin in the *Kunstwerk* essay, Brecht wishes to theorise the specificity of contemporary art, and he therefore attempts to develop a historical model which captures essential features of art that are said to pertain both to modern and pre-modern cultures. I would suggest, however, that like Benjamin, Brecht is in fact articulating a crisis in post-Enlightenment and post-Romantic aesthetic theory and practice. Although, as Brecht implies, the modern aesthetic tradition is rooted in the Renaissance, the crisis which he seeks to address must be construed in the more historically specific terms which he develops when characterising the situation of art under contemporary capitalism.

Art under Capitalism

Brecht investigates the condition of art under capitalism at two distinct but interrelated levels. On the one hand, he addresses capitalism's dehumanising and reifying impact, while on the other he analyses the implications for art of its subjection to capitalist market relations and commodification. In Brecht's view, as we have noted, the founding category of bourgeois aesthetics is the (eternally) human. Now he argues that capitalism is in the process of consigning to oblivion the anthropocentric notion that 'Man' is the measure of all things (*DGP*, 477), thereby destroying the ideological construct of 'der Mensch' ('Man'). (*DGP*, 509) Individual needs, Brecht informs us, are being reconstituted on a mass basis and are being automatised. (*DGP*, 477) Contemporary capitalism is thus destroying the humanistic basis of the bourgeois novel as outlined earlier, together with the latter's introspective psychology.[7] Prevailing conceptions of aesthetic value may still invoke the criterion of expressivity, but, as far as Brecht is concerned, art-works whose value resides in the fact that they embody the unique expression of a specific personality are no longer viable. (*DGP*, 509)

The expressive theory of art had assumed that the author's individual experiences were the touchstone of reality. (*DGP*, 465) This position is no longer tenable because under capitalism, Brecht argues, reality as such ('Die eigentliche Realität') has become functional and human relationships have become reified. As a result, mimetic/illusionist and expressive theories of art are rendered obsolete. This is because photographic reproductions of 'reality' cannot depict those abstract and functional relations which now constitute social reality, just as reality in total is no longer accessible to (individual) experience:

> Die Lage wird dadurch so kompliziert, daß weniger denn je eine einfache "Wiedergabe der Realität" etwas über die Realität aussagt. Eine Fotografie der Kruppwerke oder der AEG ergibt beinahe nichts über diese Institute. Die eigentliche Realität ist in die Funktionale gerutscht. Die Verdinglichung der menschlichen Beziehungen, also etwa die Fabrik, gibt die letzteren nicht mehr heraus. Es ist also tatsächlich "etwas

aufzubauen", etwas "Künstliches", "Gestelltes". Es ist also ebenso tatsächlich Kunst nötig. Aber der alte Begriff der Kunst, vom Erlebnis her, fällt eben aus. Denn auch wer von der Realität nur das von ihr Erlebbare gibt, gibt sie selbst nicht wieder. Sie ist längst nicht mehr im Totalen erlebbar. Wer die dunklen Assoziationen, die anonymen Gefühle gibt, die sie erzeugt, gibt sie selbst nicht wieder. (*DGP*, 469)

This epistemological and ontological crisis in bourgeois aesthetics is exacerbated by the art-work's situation in the capitalist market-place, as exemplified especially by the commodity character of film. The starting point of Brecht's discussion of artistic commodification is the debate concerning film's status as art, but, unlike other critics and theorists, Brecht refuses to be drawn into otiose discussions on the relative aesthetic merits of enjoyable films as opposed to edifying art. (*DGP*, 467) Instead, he implies that the classification of cultural products as art has always had a commercial basis. The significance of film is that it provides the opportunity to distribute artistic products on a new and massive scale, albeit on the basis of an enormous turnover of capital. (*DGP*, 468) This restructuring of the forces and relations of artistic production has led, however, to further anguished debate concerning the aesthetic consequences of film's commodity status.

Brecht identifies two main positions in this debate, both of which he rejects. First, he rehearses the argument that film's commodity character has absolutely no detrimental effects on its artistic integrity. On this viewpoint, films are commodities, but only on an incidental basis. While the commodity form is needed in order to bring films into circulation, art's task is to liberate film from this corrupting and degenerate situation: 'Der ("schlimme") Warencharakter des Filmwerks wird durch Kunst aufgehoben.' (*DGP*, 475) Brecht takes this argument to be absurd because of its utterly naive response to the transformative power of commodification. Secondly, he considers the claim that film is so drastically commodified that it must be excluded from the realm of art altogether, so that the ethereal status of art may be preserved: 'Der Kunstcharakter der andern Kunstgattungen wird durch den ("schlimmen") Prozeß im Film nicht berührt.' (*DGP*, 475) Brecht's riposte is to accuse those advocating this position of socio-economic blindness:

> Aber nur wer die Augen schließt vor der ungeheuerlichen Gewalt jenes revolutionären Prozesses, der alle Dinge dieser Welt in die Warenzirkulation reißt, ohne jede Ausnahme und ohne jede Verzögerung, kann annehmen, daß Kunstwerke irgendeiner Gattung sich hier ausschließen könnten. (*DGP*, 474)

In fact, he concludes, the truly profound meaning of this process is that it links all things and all people to one another, and thus coincides with the process of communication itself. At the same time, his overall response to the impact of artistic commodification is rather more ambivalent, particularly when he analyses art's position in the capitalist market place.

Brecht's central claim is that capitalist market relations shatter the integrity of the art-work by splitting it up into its component parts. He contends that as soon as a literary product is marketed, its unity decays. Whereas artistic unity had once been grounded in the identity between creator and work or plot and meaning, now the work may be given one or more new authors, new meanings, and even a new form. (*DGP*, 485, 488) In fact, Brecht concludes, there is no significant difference between the market's assault on artistic unity, and the recycling of disused motor cars:

> Diese Demontierung von Kunstwerken scheint zunächst denselben Gesetzen des Marktes nach zu geschehen, wie die von unbrauchbar gewordenen Autos, mit denen man nicht mehr fahren kann und die man also in ihre kleinere Einheiten (Eisen, Lederpolster, Lampen usw.) zerlegt und so verkauft. (*DGP*, 488)

Furthermore, because art is a form of human communication – Brecht punningly uses the term 'Verkehr' (traffic) – it is conditioned by those factors that generally determine communication. As a result, Brecht concludes, contemporary capitalism is in the process of revolutionising the traditional concept of art in four ways. His first point is that as soon as an art-work is invented, it is separated from its inventor, marketed, and thus turned into a commodity. He observes, secondly, that any originality of plot derives not from some innate intellectual thesis incorporated in the art-work, but from the needs of the market. Thirdly, he contends that an art-work can be dismantled into its composite parts, some of which may be removed according to economic or political criteria. And finally, he asserts, an art-work's language is separable from its dimensions of mime and gesture. (*DGP*, 488-9)

Although much of what Brecht has to say here is determined by the specific features of film production and adaptation, his argument does contain wider implications. For instance, his first three claims could easily apply to artistic media such as theatre or opera, or indeed to the process of cultural appropriation in general, whether carried out by critics and scholars or by Departments of National Heritage. At the same time, he implies that key propositions in bourgeois or idealist aesthetics have been rendered untenable by capitalist market forces. These forces have disintegrated the symbiotic union of author and work presupposed by the expressive theory of art; replaced organic form with mechanical 'unity'; and transformed authors from creators into producers. (*DGP*, 466) Brecht's overall conclusion is succinctly expressed as follows: 'Ist der Begriff Kunstwerk nicht mehr zu halten für das Ding, das entsteht, wenn ein Kunstwerk zur Ware verwandelt ist, dann müssen wir vorsichtig und behutsam, aber unerschrocken diesen Begriff weglassen'. (*DGP*, 508)

Art, Technology, and Progress

Brecht's understanding of the relationship between art and technology centres on his concept of an apparatus ('Apparat'). He maintains that the utilisation of apparatuses characterises not just film production, but artistic production in general. This latter claim is expounded in the concluding section of *DGP*, 'Über die Veranstaltung soziologischer Experimente', where Brecht restates his case for a radical reconceptualisation of art that dispenses with the categories of traditional aesthetics. In Brecht's view, traditional theories of art tried to conceive of what is 'purely human' or 'purely artistic' without reference to apparatuses, but in so doing ignored the fact that all human activity involves apparatuses, a notion which Brecht supports by citing the definition of man as *homo faber* ('das werkzeugschaffende Tier'). (*DGP*, 512)

While at a superficial level Brecht's argument is convincing, what he means by an apparatus, particularly in the artistic context, remains rather vague. The term 'Apparat' is sometimes used in *DGP* to mean either apparatus or equipment in general, or a cine camera, whilst in other of Brecht's early theoretical writings, the term often refers to political or institutional apparatuses. Brecht also uses the term apparatus in *DGP* in order to refer to any device or contrivance that might be used in artistic production, in which case it would presumably encompass pieces of flint at one end of the spectrum, and highly sophisticated film technology at the other. Such an assertion would be true, if somewhat trivial, and it is only when Brecht considers the significance of contemporary reproductive technologies that his argument becomes more compelling.

The development of the film industry in particular involves a qualitative transformation in the nature of artistic production. The old forms of cultural transmission – Brecht mentions written texts such as novels – are being superseded by a new type of artistic production which is highly technologised, and therefore regularly redefined by technological advance. (*DGP*, 464) This upheaval affects not only film, but also photography, and Brecht's fundamental ambivalence towards technological 'progress' is well exemplified in his account of contemporary improvements to cameras: 'Man kann als Beispiel für technischen Fortschritt, der eigentlich ein Wegschritt ist, die Vervollkommnung der Fotografenapparate nehmen.' (*DGP*, 480)   New cameras are far more light-sensitive than the old models that were used to make daguerrotypes, and so can be worked with under almost any lighting conditions. But, Brecht continues, the portraits produced by new cameras are vastly inferior to those produced by old-style cameras. The reason for this inferiority is that the longer exposure times required by old-fashioned cameras made it possible to preserve and absorb more facial expressions on the photographic plate. At the same time, Brecht maintains that it does not therefore follow that the new cameras are worse than the old ones.   These new cameras might, for example, inaugurate a new type of photography that dissects or dismantles the human face instead of epitomising it: the key point for Brecht is that the emergence of new technology entails giving art new functions. (*DGP*, 480-81)

The theoretical basis of Brecht's discussion is clarified when he considers the proposition that a film could be formally progressive, but regressive as regards its content. He cites Marx's celebrated – and implicitly Hegelian – view of the relationship between form and content: 'In Wirklichkeit nämlich existiert gar kein Unterschied zwischen Form und Inhalt und gilt auch hier, was Marx über die Form sagt: sie sei nur so weit gut, als sie die Form ihres Inhaltes sei.' (*DGP*, 480)   It is important, though, to note that Brecht does not flesh out the symbiotic relationship between form and content in expressive terms; in fact, he expounds on it with reference to the impact of technology on established art forms.   Not only, he implies, are changes in artistic form brought about by technological developments: it is also imperative that 'progressive' art be abreast of such developments and reconstitute itself in response to them.

Brecht's fellow artists and intellectuals, however, adopt an attitude to technological developments which, he argues, is at best ambivalent and at worst regressive. Film directors, for example, are quite incapable of realising the potential of film technology because they hang on to outmoded aesthetic theories and practices. They attempt to produce artefacts which are true to nature, but they construe truth to nature in terms of life as portrayed on stage. As a result, they strive when filming to conceal the supposed shortcomings of their camera equipment, defining a shortcoming as any feature of the camera which undermines the 'truth to nature' of their depictions. Brecht finds this approach absurd. The typical film director, he suggests, does not grasp the potential of his medium, being 'meilenweit von jeder Ahnung entfernt, gerade diese Mängel seines Apparates könnten Vorzüge sein, denn dies würde eine Umfunktionierung des Films voraussetzen.' (*DGP*, 481)   Furthermore, Brecht maintains, those artists and intellectuals who wish to hang on to traditional aesthetic categories are compelled to adopt the view that art retains an authentic core which is free from the influences of modern industry, and remains quite untouched by new modes of cultural transmission such as radio, film, and book clubs. (*DGP*, 466) On this view, only art's inauthentic parts are technologised and commodified, but this is a view which Brecht decisively rejects. Brecht insists that art *in its entirety* is commodified, and influenced by new technologies. (*DGP*, 467)   Moreover, those apparatuses associated with film in particular make it possible to transcend the old type of art, 'der alten untechnischen, mit dem Religiösen verknüpften, "ausstrahlenden" "Kunst".'[8] (*DGP*, 466)

Accordingly, in *DGP* Brecht proposes a new type of radical art which he locates at the intersection of two axes: cognitive and functional. The cognitive dimension involves a non-mimetic and abstract realism capable of reconstructing and mediating those modes of social reality expounded in the Krupp/AEG passage cited earlier:

> Es ist also tatsächlich "etwas aufzubauen", etwas "Künstliches", "Gestelltes". Es ist also tatsächlich Kunst nötig ... aber wir reden, so redend, von einer Kunst mit ganz anderer Funktion im gesellschaftlichen Leben, nämlich der, Wirklichkeit zu geben. (*DGP*, 469)

Art's cognitive role is bound up with its pedagogical refunctioning, which entails not only a multiplication of the means of artistic representation, but also their frequent change. (*DGP*, 466) This latter point is exemplified when Brecht explains that his aim in filming *Die Dreigroschenoper* had been to shatter his original work, yet simultaneously retain its societal function - namely its attack on bourgeois ideoology - within a new apparatus. As things were, his original work was indeed shattered, but according to commercial criteria. (*DGP*, 485) Nevertheless, Brecht continually associates this radical, refunctioned art with the progressive potential of film, though he does concede that film's progressive potential has seldom been realised in practice. (*DGP*, 477-8)

The Impact of Film on Artistic Production and Reception

One of the most striking features of *DGP* is its relative lack of attention to questions of artistic reception. This is unexpected, not only because of the relative prominence of this issue in Brecht's writings on theatre, but also in view of his foregrounding of film's progressive potential. When Brecht does consider aesthetic response to film in *DGP*, it tends to figure in his discussion as a secondary issue; indeed, he first refers to film reception in *DGP* in the course of his analysis of film production. He observes that, just as anybody who watches films comes to read stories differently, so too the writer of stories - who also watches films - comes to write differently. Writers are thus dependent on film not simply because their works may provide the basis for film scripts, but more fundamentally because film transforms the very nature of writing and artistic representation. This transformation is primarily due to the idiosyncrasies of film technology, so much so that even those writers who do not themselves employ film technology seek to incorporate its dynamics in their work:

> Die Verwendung von Instrumenten bringt auch den Romanschreiber, der sie selbst nicht verwendet, dazu, das, was die Instrumente können, ebenfalls können zu wollen, das, was sie zeigen (oder zeigen könnten), zu jener Realität zu rechnen, die seinen Stoff ausmacht, vor allem aber seiner eigenen Haltung beim Schreiben den Charakter des Instrumentebenützens zu verleihen. (*DGP*, 464)

In other words, literary production has been profoundly and ineluctably technologised, with the result that older modes of cultural transmission are being radically altered or even superseded. (*DGP*, 464) Brecht maintains that the new cultural apparatuses such as film can be used to transcend the outdated untechnological and anti-technological type of art outlined earlier.

Brecht clarifies the nature of film's innovative potential by contrasting film with the bourgeois novel and bourgeois drama. Unlike the bourgeois novel, Brecht argues, film cannot project a world whose coherence is guaranteed by the subjectivity of its author. What film can do, he suggests, is provide detailed, useful, applied knowledge about human action. This brings Brecht to the nature of drama. Whereas motivation in bourgeois drama is, in Brecht's opinion, rooted in the depths of its characters' inner lives, film adopts a functional and external perspective. In film, people are (stereo)types who take on specific attitudes in the particular situations which they encounter. Moreover, their inner lives constitute neither the causes nor the primary result of their actions, so that the dialectic of self and action embodied in bourgeois drama is lacking.[9] (*DGP*, 465) Film's primary need, he continues, is external action rather introspective psychology: the *Vonaußensehen* of non-Aristotelian theatre rather than the empathetic identification characteristic of its bourgeois counterpart, and his argument reaches a pithy anti-humanist conclusion with the words: 'Tritt der Mensch als Objekt auf, werden die Kausalzusammenhänge entscheidend.' (*DGP*, 478)

Brecht exemplifies cinematic externalism with reference to the Russian film *Der Weg ins Leben*, whose thematic focus prompted the spectator to establish causal connections between the behavioural patterns of its various characters. (*DGP*, 477) There is a clear parallel between Brecht's understanding of film reception and Benjamin's account of reception-in-distraction in the

Kunstwerk essay, according to which the new mode of aesthetic response associated particularly with film develops in the audience the attitude of an expert examiner. It is, however, important to note that Brecht did not share – in *DGP* at any rate – the view that the development of film response is technologically driven. Instead, Brecht characterises audience reaction to films in more general political and socio-economic terms. It may well be that certain types of progressive film can generate the new type of reception extolled by Benjamin, but Brecht asserts nevertheless that in the context of the capitalist opposition between work and recreation, watching films for recreational purposes turns the film viewer into an idler and exploiter. (*DGP*, 475-6)

Brecht's positive evaluation of film is, paradoxically, both utopian and anachronistic. It is anachronistic in the sense that his assessment of cinematic externalism and objectivism seems to be based on the representational conventions typical of silent movies, while its utopian dimension turns on the fact that Brecht adheres to a radical aesthetic which was culturally marginal both in Weimar Germany and in the Soviet Union. He also concedes that, for a while at any rate, novelists and dramatists may be able to write more 'filmically' than those involved in actually making films, because novelists and dramatists are less dependent on means of production than are film writers. Nevertheless, he emphasises the fact that filmic means of production are thoroughly saturated by capital ('durchkapitalisiert') (*DGP*, 465), so that not only film writers but intellectual workers in general ('Kopfarbeiter') are being subjected to a process of proletarianisation. (*DGP*, 466) What Brecht has in mind is, of course, the drastic shift in the socio-economic position of cultural producers – be they journalists, broadcasters, or script-writers – entailed by the irresistible rise of new technologies hand in hand with new media. As long as they neither own nor control their means of production, Brecht's 'Kopfarbeiter' are no more and no less than their labour power:

> Die Abwanderung der Produktionsmittel vom Produzierenden bedeutet die Proletarisierung des Produzierenden, wie der Handarbeiter hat hier der Kopfarbeiter im Produktionsprozeß nur mehr seine nackte Arbeitskraft einzusetzen, seine Arbeitskraft aber, das ist er selber, er ist nichts außer dem. (*DGP*, 466)

Idealist notions of authorship grounded in individual creativity are being further undermined by the fact that the economic and technological imperatives of film require collective production, a development which Brecht welcomes because of its radical potential, though in view of Brecht's own experience of collective production in the filming of *Die Dreigroschenoper* (*DGP*, 479), such optimism seems to be somewhat inappropriate. The notion that only individuals can produce unique and special artefacts is dismissed by Brecht as capitalist ideology (*DGP*, 478-9), and his argument forms an intriguing pendant to Benjamin's connection of secularisation and authenticity in the *Kunstwerk* essay. There, Benjamin had claimed that as the cult-value of images is secularised, so the basis of their uniqueness is redefined. Instead of being a property of cult images, uniqueness becomes an attribute either of the maker of images, or of the latter's skill in image making. The secularisation of art thus involves cult-value being displaced by the value of authorial authenticity.

The implication of Brecht's argument, on the other hand, is that the film industry is now destroying even that secularised mode of authenticity. This is why Brecht takes film to signify a revolutionary new stage in the development of cultural modernity, transforming artistic composition and apprehension as well as relocating intellectual workers within the emergent forces and relations of contemporary cultural production. It is therefore misleading to suggest, as Inez Müller does, that Brecht's attitude to the new technological media was fundamentally positive.[10] At the same time, Müller does qualify this claim in a different context when she observes that Brecht and Benjamin distinguished between the technological potential of the new media and the economic interests of the capitalist film industry. Brecht's potentially optimistic approach to the relationship between new technology and socio-economic power is forcefully indicated in the following passage: 'Die Technik, die hier siegt und nichts anderes zu können scheint, als den Profit einiger Saurier und damit die Barbarei zu ermöglichen, wird, in die rechten Hände gelangt, durchaus anderes können. Es ist unsere Aufgabe, ihr in die richtigen Hände zu helfen.' (*DGP*, 509)[11]

The Postmodern Condition?

We saw earlier that in *DGP*, Brecht relates the propositions of bourgeois aesthetics to the Aristotelian-medieval world view. He contends that capitalism has rendered these propositions obsolete, and in so doing he invokes an understanding of modernity which at first sight seems to be fairly straightforward. The interventions of modern technology in the production process have downgraded Man, and compounded the decentring of Humanity brought about by the Copernican Revolution that shattered the Aristotelian-medieval world picture. As Brecht wrote in the 1931 version of *Mann ist Mann*,

> Die Technik greift ein. Am Schraubstock und am laufenden Band ist der große Mensch und der kleine Mensch schon der Statur nach betrachtet gleich. ... Was sagt Kopernikus? Was dreht sich? Die Erde dreht sich. Die Erde, also der Mensch. Nach Kopernikus. Also daß der Mensch nicht in der Mitte steht. Jetzt schauen Sie sich das

einmal an. Das soll in der Mitte stehen? Historisch ist das. Der Mensch ist gar nichts! Die moderne Wissenschaft hat nachgewiesen, daß alles relativ ist.[12]

At the same time, Brecht's specification of modernity is both ambiguous and ambivalent.

Brecht's ambivalence is implicit in his reaction to capitalism's spectacular success in colonizing the supposedly autonomous domain of culture, a process which enthralls him to such a degree that he appears to celebrate precisely those socio-economic forces which otherwise alienate cultural producers:

> In diesem Sinne ist die Umschmelzung geistiger Werte in Waren (Kunstwerke, Verträge, Prozesse sind Waren) ein fortschrittlicher Prozeß und man kann ihm nur zustimmen, vorausgesetzt, daß der Fortschritt als Fortschreiten gedacht wird, nicht als Fortgeschrittenheit, daß also die Phase der Ware als durch weiteres Fortschreiten überwindbar angesehen wird. Die kapitalistische Produktionsweise zertrümmert die bürgerliche Ideologie. (*DGP*, 508-9)

The ambiguities in Brecht's account of modernity relate to his characterisation of its socio-temporal structure. On the one hand, he construes the Aristotelian-medieval/post-Copernican axis as the historical origin of and guiding metaphor for the rise of modernity. On the other hand, in the extract from *Mann ist Mann* above, he invokes the paradigm shift in post-Copernican science inaugurated by Einstein's theory of relativity. At one level, therefore, modernity appears to be coextensive with the rise of industrial capitalism and modern science, but Brecht also refers us to a radical break within modernity and thus implicitly questions whether we have now moved into the phase of post-modernity. The spectre of postmodernism beckons, yet here too we may observe a final and crucial difference between Benjamin and Brecht. Whereas in the *Kunstwerk* essay, Benjamin seeks to establish a properly post-modernist aesthetic, in *DGP* Brecht is already moving in the direction of a reconstructed but abstract critical realism which will, if necessary, eschew the artistic practices of modernism altogether.[13]

[1.]   For further discussion see Steve Giles, 'In for a *Threepenny*, in for a Pound: Brecht's *Beule* Suit', in Steve Giles, *Bertolt Brecht and Critical Theory. Marxism, Modernity and the 'Threepenny' Lawsuit* (Bern, Lang, 1997).

[2.]   Bertolt Brecht, *Der Dreigroschenprozeß. Ein soziologisches Experiment*, in Bertolt Brecht, *BFA*, 21, pp.448-514, cited henceforth as *DGP*.

[3.]   Several pages of *DGP* are translated in *Brecht on Theatre. The Development of an Aesthetic*, ed. J. Willett (London, Methuen, 1978), pp.47-50. The most helpful German commentary on *DGP* remains Dieter Wöhrle, 'Bertolt Brechts "Dreigroschenprozeß" - Selbstverständigung durch Ideologiezertrümmerung', *Sprachkunst*, 11 (1980), 40-62.

4. *Bertolt Brecht. Epoche - Werk - Wirkung*, Hg. K-D. Müller (München, Beck, 1985), p.172.

5.   Walter Benjamin, *Gesammelte Schriften*, Hg. R.Tiedemann und H.Schweppenhäuser, I:2, (Frankfurt aM, Suhrkamp, 1979-), pp.472-508. For detailed discussion of *DGP* in relation to the *Kunstwerk* essay, see Steve Giles, '*Vorsprung durch Technik*? Aesthetic Modernity in *Der Dreigroschenprozeß* and the *Kunstwerk* Essay', in Giles, *Bertolt Brecht and Critical Theory*.

6.   Georg Lukács, 'Erzählen oder Beschreiben? Zur Diskussion über Naturalismus und Formalismus', in *Seminar: Literatur und Kunstsoziologie*, Hg. Peter Bürger (Frankfurt aM, Suhrkamp, 1978), pp.72-115.

7.   Brecht's German is ambiguous at this point - 'Er' (*DGP*, 477) could refer either to film or to capitalism. He suggests that 'it' is anti-humanist by virtue of its focus on processes and external action. This could refer to filmic representation, or to capitalism and the behaviourist psychology which Brecht takes to be commensurate with it.

8.   Brecht's specification of the old type of art bears an uncanny resemblance to Benjamin's terms of reference in the *Kunstwerk* essay, right down to the category of aura ('radiating' art). Similar observations are made by Rolf Tiedemann, 'Die Kunst in anderer Leute Köpfe zu denken. Brecht – kommentiert von Walter Benjamin', in Walter Benjamin, *Versuche über Brecht*, Hg. Rolf Tiedemann (Frankfurt aM, Suhrkamp, 1978), pp.175-210 (p.193); Peter Bürger, 'Kunstsoziologische Aspekte der Brecht-Benjamin-Adorno-Debatte der 30er Jahre', in *Seminar: Literatur und Kunstsoziologie*, pp.11-20 (pp.13-14); and Inez Müller, *Walter Benjamin und Bertolt Brecht. Ansätze zu einer dialektischen Ästhetik in den dreißiger Jahren* (St. Ingbert, Röhrig, 1993), pp.166-7. This aspect of the Brecht/Benjamin relationship is also considered in Giles, '*Vorsprung durch Technik*'.

9.   For further discussion in relation to Hegelian dramatic theory, see Steve Giles, *The Problem of Action in Modern European Drama* (Stuttgart, Heinz, 1981).

10. Müller, *Walter Benjamin und Bertolt Brecht*, pp.108, 147.

11. Brecht's reference to the Jurassic landscape of the contemporary mass media presumably implies that Murdoch and his ilk are latter-day velociraptors.

12. Brecht, *Mann ist Mann*, in *BFA*, 2, pp.169-227 (p.206).

13. I gratefully acknowledge the generous financial assistance provided by a British Academy Research Leave Award, which enabled me to complete the project on which this paper is based. I also wish to thank Rodney Livingstone and Elizabeth Chadwick for their very helpful comments on an earlier draft.

RODNEY LIVINGSTONE

Brecht's *Me-ti*: A Question of Attitude

The *Me-ti* has attracted sporadic critical attention, but mainly as a 'theoretischer Steinbruch', a quarry of theory,[1] a source of quotations for Brecht's opinions on a variety of mainly political subjects, rather than a work in its own right. Admittedly, it was never published and remains a fragmentary collection of aphorisms, reflections and anecdotes that was assembled from around 1934 to as late as 1955. Since the order of the contents was never fixed little can be inferred from the positioning of the individual pieces.[2] In consequence the perceived unity of the work is mainly thematic. Critics who have gone beyond this have attempted to define Brecht's ideological position.

In contrast it will be argued here that we should shift our attention from ideas to attitudes. Brecht provides a coded history of the struggles to achieve socialism and the rules of behaviour (*Verhaltenslehre*) to be derived from the contemplation of those struggles and involvement in them. This history from Marx and Engels down to Stalin, is essentially a history of basic attitudes, *Haltungen*, ways in which ideas are lived. The distinction between opinion and lived ideas emerges clearly from one of the *Stories of Mr Keuner* in which Mr Keuner tells of an encounter with a professor of philosophy, in which he refuses to listen to what the professor is saying because 'you sit uncomfortably, you talk uncomfortably, you think uncomfortably.' When the professor protests that what is important is the content of his argument, Keuner retorts,

> It has no content. I see you walking awkwardly and you reach no goal as I watch you walk. You speak obscurely and you create no light as you talk. I do not see your goal, I see your manner (*Haltung*). (13)

As formulated here, Brecht's interest might seem to be purely stylistic; he is dismissive of the professor's ideas. In the *Me-ti*, however, manner, attitude and the ideas expressed are all much more tightly intertwined; the book does give Brecht's views of specific doctrines. Nevertheless, here too his primary interest is in *Haltung*,[3] basic attitudes. The distinction being made is one between ideas as lived and ideas as a coherent body of thought. It is important because it functions at the interface between ideas and life and pays tribute to the fact that the fit between them is never perfect. The book does not contain anything like a systematic exposition of Brecht's ideas - he was not of course a (political) philosopher. Instead of attempting to create an orthodoxy, or a consistent set of ideas, the kaleidoscopic format seems designed to let conflicting voices speak. It reads like a symposium of voices: Hegel, Marx and Engels, Lenin, Plekhanov, Stalin and Trotsky, Karl Korsch and Rosa Luxemburg, among others. This is not to imply a facile eclecticism on Brecht's part. His own opinions emerge forcefully. But he allows unresolved contradictions to stand, and even emphasizes them, often through the imagery he uses.[4] We are reminded of Fritz Sternberg's comment that Brecht's train of thought did not follow a logical sequence, but 'moved like knights on a chess board, straight for a short distance, then turning radically to the right or the left'.[5]

The sense of montage is created not just by the aphoristic format but also by the Chinese setting. The title, or rather joint title *Me-ti / Buch der Wendungen*,[6] evokes two Chinese classics. Me-ti is generally referred to in English as Mo Tzu, a little-known sage who flourished around 420 BC. In the *Me-ti* Mo Tzu functions as a sage closely identified with the author's views, although sometimes distinct from Kin-jeh who stands for Brecht and whose name provides a link with Mr Keuner. Brecht learned about him from the translation by Alfred Forke that appeared in 1922 and in which Mo Tzu is presented as a social moralist (*Sozialethiker*). Mo Tzu was known in his day as an opponent of Confucius, the dominant philosopher, and for an exacting code of honour and self-sacrifice. Arthur Waley attributes his lack of fame to the fact that despite his 'on the whole sympathetic doctrines' his writing 'is... feeble, repetitive...heavy, unimaginative and unentertaining, devoid of a single passage that could be said to have wit, beauty or force.'[7]

It may come as a surprise to learn that Brecht could have been attracted to such a thinker and there are few specific echoes of Mo Tzu, but the following expression of his pacifist views may suggest his appeal to Brecht:

> If a ruler attacks a neighbouring country, slays its inhabitants, carries off its cattle and horses, its millet and rice and all its chattels and possessions, his deed is recorded on strips of bamboo or rolls of silk, carved upon metal and stone, inscribed upon bells and tripods, that in after days are handed down to his sons and grandsons. 'No one,' he boasts, 'ever took such spoils as I have done.' But suppose some private person attacked the house next door, slew the inhabitants, stole their dogs and pigs, their grain and their clothing, and then made a record of his deed on strips of bamboo or rolls of silk and wrote inscriptions about it on his dishes and bowls, that they may be handed down in his family for generations to come, boasting that no one ever stole so much as he, would that be all right?[8]

Brecht often links individual moral behaviour and political action in a similar way. For example, 'The good that Me-ti expected when two hands, a man's and a woman's, meet while performing a common task, such as carrying a bucket, Mi-en-leh [Lenin] expected for whole nations when their hands meet as they drive the wheel of history.' (173)

The second Chinese source is the *I Ching* or *Book of Changes*, one of the five Confucian classics. Its sole importance is the subtitle *Buch der Wendungen*. In the *I Ching*, a book of oracles based on 64 hexagrams, the 'changes' refer to alterations in the lines in the hexagram and these refer in turn to the different possible outcomes in real life. In Brecht, who uses *Wendungen* rather than *Wandlungen*, what is at stake is, first, dialectical reversals in history of the kind indicated in the aphorism 'On Changes', where he writes 'The introduction of democracy can lead to the introduction of dictatorship. The introduction of dictatorship can lead to democracy.' (88)   Second, because life is a process and realities cannot be definitively encapsulated in language the concepts that are applied to reality also have an ever-shifting history. Brecht analyses concepts like 'freedom' and 'morality' in order to chart their changing meanings.

The use of the Chinese background and the adoption of pseudo-Chinese names for his dramatis personae - Ka-meh (Marx), Eh-fu (Engels), Mi-en-leh (Lenin), Su (the Soviet Union) and so on - is not a piece of chinoiserie, but a distancing device, a signal that he is less concerned with an exhaustive or systematic analysis of these authorities, than with the aphoristic scrutiny of particular arguments or positions associated with them. We therefore read the text bifocally, with one eye on Ro or Ni-en, the other on Rosa Luxemburg or Stalin. Important though these identifications are, to reduce the text to Brecht's Leninism, for example, is to create an orthodoxy or a system where none exists. Instead Brecht's strategy is to test current opinions, to perform experiments on them and expose their contradictory nature. An instance is his response to Rosa Luxemburg's criticism of Leninism. According to Lenin, the people ruled, but in reality, so she thought, he ruled over the people. By way of reply Brecht tells the story of two men:

> They lived in the same house, but in different rooms. The older slept in a comfortable bed, the younger on a leather mattress. Early in the morning the older man would shake the younger one out of a sound sleep, before he was ready to wake up. At table the older man often took away from the younger one the food he liked best. If the younger man wanted a drink, the older man only gave him water or milk, and if he secretly obtained some intoxicating rice-wine the older man scolded him harshly in front of everyone. If he became angry he had to apologize publicly. One morning, I saw the older man riding a horse and driving the younger one before him. One day, I spoke to the older man and asked after his slave. He is not my slave, was the shocked reply. He is the champion and I am training him for his biggest fight. He has hired me to make sure he is fit. It is I who am the slave...(76)

Here Brecht defends Lenin's concept of the vanguard party as the servant of the proletariat, but, significantly, he does so in terms of Hegel's dialectic of master and slave. Hegel too asks who is the true master. His point is that the roles of master and slave are unstable. For example, by performing the master's work, the slave becomes the master because through his labour he transforms reality, while the master sinks into a state of hapless dependence. By using this imagery to defend the Leninist party Brecht hopes to correct an impression outsiders may glean about the relationship between people and party, but by retaining the instability of the master/slave dialectic he keeps alive the memory of the very relationship he denies: that the older man who claims to be the slave, is really in command. It follows that even if the party is the servant of the people in the Soviet Union, this is not permanent or guaranteed. It can always reverse into its opposite. Elsewhere, in the conversations with Walter Benjamin, he conceded the point with his remark that 'In Russia there is dictatorship *over* the proletariat',[9] the very situation predicted by Rosa Luxemburg and reaffirmed by Karl Korsch.

This story illustrates aspects of Brecht's understanding of dialectics, a key concept in the *Me-ti* where it occurs in the guise of the *Große Methode*, the Great Method. It takes priority over that other concept, the *Große Ordnung*, his term for socialism, and a major theme of the text, because his observations on socialism, its exponents and the degree of its realization in the Soviet Union are conducted in a dialectical spirit. The crucial features of dialectics for Brecht are, first, that reality itself is fundamentally contradictory. Dialectics thus differs from positivist logic which maintains that contradiction is a term that can be applied only to propositions about reality, not to reality itself. And second, he insists on the link between knowledge and action. In this he is following Marx's well-known Eleventh Thesis on Feuerbach, 'Philosophers have only *interpreted* the world in various ways; the point, however, is to *change* it.'[10] Brecht's formulation constantly draws attention to this link. 'Thought is something that follows difficulties and precedes action.'(62) Or again: 'The Great Method enables us to recognize and make use of processes in objects. It teaches us to pose questions that make action possible.' (104) In other words, for Brecht thought is of no interest in itself. What interests him are the tensions in it that lead us to act. We can see this in the comment on compromises taken from Lenin. Lenin distinguishes between mixing water and wine, and drinking water and wine from separate glasses. (85) The point of the distinction is the warning it contains against diluting communism by fudging the issues. By keeping the wine and water separate he keeps contradictions in the foreground and this encourages us to keep searching for solutions.

Brecht begins his history of *Haltungen* with Marx and Engels who are regarded as models of productive thought. But although he holds them in high esteem and they are described as 'the Classics', his tone is matter-of-fact rather than reverential. Despite their classical status their lives are not insulated from the travails of ordinary life: 'While one of them lived in prosperity, the other had constant money problems.' Nor did their lives consist of unbroken successes: 'A series of predictions they had made were not fulfilled. Important works were left unfinished.' For all that, they were the greatest 'teachers of behaviour' of their age. They 'lived in the darkest and bloodiest times. They were the most cheerful and sanguine of men'. (110) Elsewhere Me-ti asks 'Should Master Ka-meh drink his tea as if (*in einer Haltung, als...*) he were draining the Bay of Si? Would it not be better to drain the Bay of Si as if he were drinking a cup of tea?'(107)

One of their greatest achievements was to have abandoned hope of an immediate insurrection when they saw the situation was not propitious. They simply adjusted to the new climate. 'Neither did their anger towards the rulers abate, nor did they relax their efforts to overthrow them.' (130) This responsiveness to events is also seen as characteristic of Marx's intellectual trajectory. He is said to move from writing as a philosopher, to a non-philosophical attack on philosophers, showing in particular that it is wrong to live in order to philosophize rather than philosophizing in order to live, and ending up in 'research into practical matters'. (159) He also highlights their subversiveness, suggesting that Engels's theory that nature itself illustrates a dialectical movement will appeal to workers because it shows how the peace and order of nature arose out of unrest and disorder, and are pregnant with them. 'It may be said that when Master Eh-fu explained nature, this was no laughing matter for the oppressors and exploiters.' (183) The way things turn into their opposites, as here, is not without its comic side, and Brecht's remark that 'it is more difficult for people without humour to understand the Great Method' (113) points up the dramatic, performative aspect of dialectics.

In all of this Marx and Engels are strongly contrasted with the 'Tuis' or unproductive intellectuals. Tuis are satirized in the *Tui Novel* as 'the intellectuals of this age of markets and commodities'. (*BFA* 17, 153) They 'hire out their intellects' and relate to revolution 'not as minds, but as bellies.'(70) Brecht's targets are a broad range of the intelligentsia, but more specifically the members of the Frankfurt School, especially Adorno, Horkheimer, Pollock and Marcuse. Underlying his satire is also his need to justify his own position, both as a middle-class intellectual on the left and within a Marxism which ascribes productivity only to the working class. In the *Me-ti* the satire on intellectuals is maintained and extended. It focuses on a critique of the division of labour, which means not just the gulf between town and country and those who work with their hands or their brain, but it also includes divisions within a single identity. He discusses the case of a doctor who judges events only as a doctor, not as a human being, but comically discovers his humanity when forced to run for his life. 'How am I to continue working as a doctor, if I have been killed as a human being?' (99) Similarly with the anecdote about the painter whose father is a barge-hauler, but whose paintings reflect neither his father's hard life nor his own origins. Instead he claims to be concerned solely with the development of painting. As a human being he is a communist, but as an artist he develops the forms of painting. For Me-ti this is like saying that 'as a cook I poison the food, but as a human being I buy medicine.' (179-180) Brecht attacks intellectuals' love of things that are difficult to understand (77) and complains that notwithstanding this, they are often paralysed by the complexity of reality. Unlike Lenin they lack the 'crudeness of thought' (74) that enables you to cut through the difficulties. It is the lack of productivity and the inability to translate thought into action that really distinguishes them from the mainstream of productive exponents of the Great Method inherited from Marx and Engels. Significantly, Brecht extends the notion of Tui to intellectuals in the Soviet Union. In the controversies between the supporters of Stalin and Trotsky on the best way to build socialism, quarrelling intellectuals simply made matters worse: and 'all Tuis called each other Tuis in the worst possible sense of the word'. (169) There is obviously a risk that the word Tui will simply become a term of abuse. But it is noteworthy that Trotsky, for example, is treated fairly, something of a rarity in the 1930s. Admittedly, Brecht came down on the side of Stalin and Lenin on the question of the creation of socialism in one country - something Trotsky opposed. (96) But elsewhere he reports Trotsky's critique of Soviet Russia without comment. (172)

In many ways Lenin is the central actor in the book, the revolutionary who is able to effect the transition from theory to practice, the chief exponent of the Great Method. The moment that seizes Brecht's imagination is not the triumph of the Bolsheviks in October 1917, but the period of setbacks that followed. Brecht quotes literally from Lenin's own parable about climbing tall mountains, a story he described as 'a classical little work of realism'. (523) Here Lenin describes the plight of a climber who finds his path to the top blocked by unforeseen difficulties and who is forced to turn back to find another route. In so doing he is vilified by onlookers who accuse him of betraying his principles or are delighted by his failure. Lenin's courage in accepting the necessity of short-term expedients such as handing land over to the peasants instead of collectivizing agriculture in one fell swoop is proof for Brecht of his pragmatism, as is his willingness to make use of foreign experts whom he despises. (76) However, Brecht does not see Lenin simply as an opportunist, but as a philosopher who knows how to act, a tough-minded practical man, who is prepared to act ruthlessly, but who never loses sight of the interests of the *Verein* (the Party) and his long-term revolutionary goals. 'Mi-en-leh was practical in philosophy and philosophical in his praxis.'(90) This general stance shows him to be the true heir of Marx and Engels and in his life we can see the Great Method at its most effective.

Brecht's view of Stalin has been much debated, but although the outlines are clear, critics have reached different conclusions. Knopf, rejecting Klaus Völker's claim that the Chinese codename for Stalin, Ni-en, is an anagram of 'Nein', concludes that Brecht is 'nicht nur kritisch oder negativ', and points out that of sixteen aphorisms on Stalin only three are critical, two of them in connection with the Moscow Show Trials of 1936-38. In a wide-ranging study, John Willett, anxious to clear Brecht from Hannah Arendt's wild accusation of adulating Stalin, gives a balanced picture, but one which tends to underline Brecht's doubts: 'Critical, but *for* it [i.e. the Soviet Union].'[11]

However, there is a lot of common ground. It is agreed that Brecht praised Stalin for carrying out the industrialization of the Soviet Union (108, 168) and that he supported Stalin's policy of socialism in one country (96). To wait for revolutions to break out everywhere at once was absurdly purist, although he agrees that the revolution in Russia could only be completed if it were also begun in other countries. (120) This chimes in with Brecht's pragmatic approach. On similar pragmatic grounds he defends Stalin's alliances with 'Ausbeuterstaaten' (85), i.e. the non-aggression pact with France in 1931 and the extension of the Rapallo Treaty with Germany. A jovial picture of Stalin emerges in the story about some tree-fellers who, in their enthusiasm for a new mechanical saw, used it on harder and harder wood, finally trying it out on a huge rock, whereupon it broke. Shame-faced they ask a benign Stalin for a new one and he praises them: 'Never would we have invented saws that cut through the gnarled roots of the hardest trees if we had not, like you, always attempted the impossible.' (66-7)

The key point of Brecht's criticism is that Stalin's Russia exemplifies the decline of the Great Method (168) from its pinnacle in Lenin. 'Mi-en-leh knew everyone's weakness and could work with everyone. Ni-en could only work with very few people and did not know their weaknesses.' (108) Brecht notes the effect of Stalinism on Communist Parties outside Russia:

> The members did not elect the secretaries, the secretaries elected the members...When mistakes were made, the people who criticized them were punished; but those who had made the mistakes, remained in their posts. Soon they were no longer the best people, but only the most pliable. (168)

Because of Stalin's contributions, Brecht is willing to allow that he is 'useful' (66) (a modest enough term, but high praise in Brecht's scale of values), but he deplores the elevation of Stalin to godlike status. '[There is] so much incense that you cannot see the picture and you tell yourself: something is being concealed here.' (65) But useful though Stalin was, he 'became an emperor for the peasants, while he was still a secretary for the workers'. (171) The state apparatus became separated from the workforce and assumed a retrograde form. (171) Brecht does not condemn the Show Trials as such, but only the way they were conducted because that further undermined the Great Method: Stalin stands revealed as the high-handed autocrat who demands that people believe him, instead of delivering proofs of guilt. It is often said that Brecht defends Stalinism in public while criticizing it in private.[12] Thus Willett talks of his 'mixture of intellectual independence and outward conformity which was to characterize his attitude to the party's policy from 1929 on'.[13] This conformity was dictated by the need to support the Soviet Union in its struggle against Nazi Germany. In the *Me-ti* Brecht sees the only alternatives in Karl Korsch who on witnessing the trials 'turned away from the Great Method' and Trotsky who was led to deny that there was any good in the Soviet Union. This route was one that Brecht was unwilling to take, rather like Georg Lukács, his great antagonist. Others maintain that Brecht's position was the consequence of the erosion of the middle ground between communism and fascism.[14] Since he always saw fascism as an extension of capitalism, he could not accept liberal democracy as a viable alternative. It is easier to understand this position than to share it. But in the *Me-ti* at least Brecht was concerned to define his own contradictions to himself and we can respect this even if we regret that he felt unable to publish his criticisms. We can see his dilemma from the tensions in a passage like this one in which the disastrous conditions in the Soviet Union are faithfully described, but the communist framework is not rejected because he does not finally deny the progress made by the Soviet Union:

> The decision of the party in Su to bring about the Great Order weighs upon the people of Su like a nightmare. The progressive reforms make them stagger. Bread is hurled at people with such force that it kills many of them. The most fruitful innovations are introduced by scoundrels and more than a few virtuous people stand in the way of progress. (109)

There is an obvious overlap between 'behaviour' and 'attitudes', on the one hand, and morality, on the other. And indeed a considerable part of the text is devoted to moral issues. Here too Brecht distinguishes sharply between universal moral codes and a 'lived' morality. He emphasizes that Marx and Engels postulated no ethics (152) and condemns too active a preoccupation with morality itself. Few things do so much damage. 'People say: you must love the truth, keep your promises, fight for the good. But the trees do not say: You must be green...' (95-6) The chief ideas, familiar to readers of *Mutter Courage* and *Leben des Galilei*, are concerned to show that only societies where all is not well make great moral demands on people: 'if the [ship's] captain has to be a genius, this must mean that his instruments are unreliable.' (142) What is wanted is a society where no particular virtues are needed. Brecht's hostility towards moral absolutes and systems leads him to avoid universal commandments and instead to examine moral values in specific contexts. Thus 'useful' is generally a positive value, but he condemns it in the architecture of the Bauhaus. Mies van der Rohe believes that only the useful is beautiful, but the workers tell him that they spend their lives among machines and hence 'feel nothing but loathing for things that are only useful'. (147) Again, there is a sustained analysis of violence: the 'Classics' put forward no view of killing and were opposed to violence, but they were willing to confront violence with violence. They also point out that violence may exist where none is perceived, in the general framework of society:

> The storm that bends the birch trees
> is thought violent.
> But what about the storm
> that bends the backs of the roadmenders? (159-160)

Brecht retained one moral absolute, Thou shalt produce. (179) The advocacy of economic productivity makes sense within Marxism. Similarly, we can also see the force of his defence of intellectual productivity as a form of production that leads to action (as opposed to the production of ideas for their own sake). There is also something attractive about the idea that love is a 'production' and that it changes both lover and beloved. But the application of the logic of productivity to Ruth Berlau in the *Lai-tu* aphorisms often seems patronizing. Me-ti says to her, 'It is true that you have not produced any goods. But this does not mean that you have not produced a service. Your kindness is noted and appreciated by being made use of. In the same way an apple achieves its fame by being eaten'. (156) This reads like special pleading. Doubtless consumption is a necessary attribute of many products, but it is hardly sufficient. Brecht evidently finds it hard to extend the notion of productivity from goods to services, but the end result is that the concept becomes devoid of meaning, much like his frequent injunction to 'change the world' which it so closely resembles.[15] The ethics of productivity begin persuasively, but end up as testimony to an intellectual embarrassment comparable to the difficulties experienced by the Great Method itself.

Jan Knopf has suggested that the *Me-ti* remained a fragment because Brecht's commitment to the Soviet Union became increasingly difficult to sustain in the light of developments such as the Stalin Trials and the Stalin-Hitler Pact. While on the surface the game-playing element of the dialectic seems designed to foreground Brecht's optimism, the cheerful confidence with which he confronts growing difficulties, there is a troubling undercurrent, a sort of ground bass associated with the motif of 'coldness' and the growing awareness that he lives in 'dark times', a concept that made its appearance in the late 1930s and did not start to fade away until after the battle of Stalingrad in 1943. These dark times include not just the seemingly unstoppable advance of Hitler, but also the developments in the Soviet Union.

Faced with the harshness of modern life in the urban jungle, Brecht had carefully cultivated a hard-boiled attitude that aimed to prove itself a match for the brutality of the external world. This attitude has a number of inflections. It can be a studied ironic defiance, as in *Vom armen BB*, with its final image of the man who hopes he will never become so embittered that he will let his cigar go out. But it is a risky stance because coldness can easily degenerate into the very hardness from which it recoils. In the *Me-ti* there is an ongoing struggle between 'coldness' and 'warmth'. The coldness can be seen in the reiterated insistence on party discipline. When talking about the necessary lack of freedom under Lenin, he defends the need for 'eiserne Zucht'. (80) Freedom in the West is dismissed because it only means the freedom of the entrepreneur. In the Soviet Union, it is defended as a compulsion for all those who threaten 'the great production of goods for all'. He insists on the need for discipline for the 'plough smiths' (i.e. the workers), when they enter alliances with outsiders. In this context he sneers at intellectuals who tend to be averse to discipline. He also includes the verses from the *Svendborger Gedichte* which defend coldness:

> If I speak to you
> With cold and general words
> Without looking at you
> (I seem not to know you
> in your particular nature and difficulties)
> I am only speaking
> Like reality itself
> (Sober reality, not to be corrupted by your nature
> and fed up with your difficulties),
> A reality you appear not to perceive. (125)

This insistence on the coldness of the world goes hand in hand with a rejection of compassion (unless it is converted into anger [132]), a hankering after asceticism (157) a dislike of emotional display (as in celebrations [148]) and in general a kind of emotional poverty. Of course, we are familiar with this and may understand it as a legitimate reaction to the excesses of inwardness, one that goes naturally with a diction that privileges understatement and matter-of-factness.

On the other hand, there are also strong signs of a 'warmer' culture: as against discipline, he admits to feeling sympathy for outlaws (87). He goes even further and modifies his praise of discipline, by claiming that it need not mean 'obedience', but can be readily combined with 'a powerful disobedience' (185), political action, in short. He cites with approval an anecdote about Lenin in exile feeding birds throughout the winter - and justifying it with the assertion that they are hungry, but are unable to form a party (93). Despite his own ascetic preferences, he rejects Hitler's life-denying asceticism, since it would be easier to survive under a pleasure-seeking tyrant (162-3). There are a few moments of frank near-emotionality. When Me-ti realizes that Kin-jeh believes he has been abandoned by Lai-tu, he 'begs him, without success, not to restrain [his anguish]' 164. This may not add up to the picture of a life-enhancing warmth, but it shows that the anarchic side of Brecht has not been entirely submerged.

> 'You must close the door even when a friend takes his leave,' said Me-ti, 'otherwise it
> will get too cold.' 'It cannot get any colder,' said Kin-jeh. 'Oh yes it can,' said Me-ti.
> (121)

This grim realization, the absence of any pose of coldness, provides a compelling moment of bleakness, comparable to the tragic moments in the great plays. It is an integral aspect of the rich symphony of the *Me-ti*.

[1.]   See Klaus-Detlef Müller, 'Brecht's *Me-Ti* und die Auseinandersetzung mit dem Lehrer Karl Korsch', *Brecht-Jahrbuch* 1977, 9-29. (An English version of this essay is included in Betty Nance Weber & Hubert Heinen, *Bertolt Brecht: Political Theory and Literary Practice* (Manchester, MUP, 1980), pp.43-59. The other main commentaries are: Jan Knopf, *Brecht-Handbuch, Lyrik, Prosa, Schriften* (Stuttgart, Metzler, 1986) pp.447-4; Werner Mittenzwei, 'Der Dialektiker Brecht oder die Kunst, Me-Ti zu lesen', *Brechts Tui-Kritik*, Argument Sonderband AS11 (Berlin, 1976) pp.175-212; Roland Jost, *'Er war unser Lehrer'*, (Köln, Pahl-Rugenstein, 1981) pp.71-129.

[2.]   Quotations here refer throughout to the *Große kommentierte Berliner und Frankfurter Ausgabe* volume 18. The ordering of the contents differs sharply in the Suhrkamp *Werkausgabe* and the *BFA*, the two chief editions. The principles underlying the main editions before the *BFA* are discussed in Knopf, pp.448-50.

[3.] This is not to be confused with 'Haltung' in the sense of military self-control, composure under fire, as practised by Ernst Jünger and loathed by Walter Benjamin. Such composure is an integral part of the 'culture of coldness'. See below for Brecht's involvement in that. For a more detailed discussion see Helmut Lethen, *Verhaltenslehren der Kälte* (Frankfurt am Main, Suhrkamp, 1994).

4. This helps to explain the unusually sharp disagreements about the dominant point of view in the book, Roland Jost and Werner Mittenzwei maintaining that the book is Brecht's 'poem to Lenin', while Klaus-Detlev Müller persuasively argues for the pervasive influence of Karl Korsch. Casting his net more widely, Peter Bormans sees Brecht moving from the critique of Stalin in the *Me-ti* in the direction of Maoism: see Peter Bormans, 'Brecht und der Stalinismus' *Brecht – Jahrbuch 1974*, ed. J. Fuegi *et al.* (Frankfurt aM, Suhrkamp, 1975), pp. 53-76.

5. Fritz Sternberg, *Der Dichter und die Ratio* (Göttingen, Sachse und Pohl Verlag, 1963), p. 12.

6. The *BFA* has dropped the title *Me-ti* on the grounds that Brecht used only *Buch der Wendungen* in his typescripts and in the final note on the text, p.194.

7. Arthur Waley, *Three Ways of Thought in Ancient China* (Allen & Unwin, 1939), pp.163-4.

8. Waley, p.173.

9. Walter Benjamin, *Conversations with Brecht*, translated by Anna Bostock (London, NLB, 1973), p.121. The question of Korsch's influence on Brecht has been much debated. Knopf maintains that 'Korsch's importance for the *Me-ti* and the Great Method expounded in it is an invention of scholarship.' (Knopf, p.461) Klaus-Detlev Müller very persuasively puts the opposite case.

10. See Karl Marx and Frederick Engels, *Collected Works*, vol 5 (London, Lawrence & Wishart, 1976) p.8.

11. John Willett, *Brecht in Context* (London & New York, Methuen, 1984), p.193.

12. His defence was often provocative. He notoriously outraged Sidney Hook by saying of the arrests of Zinoviev and Kamenev in 1935: 'The more innocent they are, the more they deserve to die.' ('A Recollection of Berthold Brecht', *The New Leader*, 10 October 1960, 22-23).

13. Willett, p.184.

14. Knopf, p.472.

15. This argument is independent of claims that Ruth Berlau might have legitimately made about Brecht's failure to acknowledge his true debt to her productivity in his own work, claims recently documented in John Fuegi, *The Life and Lies of Bertolt Brecht* (Flamingo 1995), p.15.

FLORIAN VAßEN

A New Poetry for the Big City:
Brecht's Behavioural Experiments in
Aus dem Lesebuch für Städtebewohner
(Translated by Katharina Hall)

The Weimar Republic was a time of aesthetic experimentation and Bertolt Brecht one of its most important representatives.[1] For him, everything had a 'material-worth' (*BFA*, 21, 285ff). He saw world literature as a quarry to be mined, using and adapting literary genres and forms as necessary in his own literary work. In the case of his poetry, the ballad lies side by side with the song, the sonnet next to unrhymed lyric poetry of irregular rhythm, social ballads of a novel kind next to Chinese poems. In the drama, too, Brecht's work shows him to be a master of adaptation. In epic theatre and the *Lehrstück*, he created two forms of theatre which were of crucial importance to the subsequent development of twentieth-century theatre. Even in his prose he had an innovative effect through the production of calender tales of a new type, proletarian anecdotes and the specific form of the *Geschichten vom Herrn Keuner*. In addition, Brecht's practical and theoretical work with radio, his anti-culinary operas, experiments with new music, reflections on gramophone records and diverse experiments with film all testify to his interest in media.

Brecht published his works on literature and the media during a concentrated period between 1930 and 1933 in the *Versuche*.[2] 'As far as a possibly direct political effect is concerned, the *Versuche* 1-8 are the living part of his work, the theological heart in the sense of Benjamin's understanding of Marxism'.[3] One thematic focus of Brecht's works was the big city, from exoticism to Americanism, from New York to Moscow, from *Dickicht der Städte* to *Die Heilige Johanna der Schlachthöfe*. Within his poetry in particular, there is an enormous variety of themes and forms whose concern is the metropolises of the world: fascination, 'nihilistic' lawlessness, enthusiasm for and criticism of Manhattan, admiration in Moscow and irritations in Hollywood. Later on, there is horror at the destruction of German cities during the war. Above all, however, there are thirty years of fascination and disquiet, cool observation and sadness in relation to Berlin. Without doubt, Brecht is one of the twentieth century's most important German speaking poets of the city.

Already at an early point Brecht imagines the big city as a 'jungle' (*Tb*, 145). Later he thinks of it as a 'heroic landscape' (*Tb*, 208) and above all as an 'arena of struggle'. 'In the jungle of the cities', as in the play of the same name (*Im Dickicht der Städte*), people perish in this struggle, and for this reason the 'movement of mankind into the big city' demands a 'new kind of human being'.[4] When Brecht notes 'the hostility of the big city, its malicious, stony consistency, its Babylonian linguistic confusion, in short, [that] its poetry is not yet created'[5] , he sees it as his task to bridge this gap and to get to grips with the new reality of the city in his drama, poetry and prose.

The 'movement of mankind into the big city' (*Tb*, 208) produces a new contradictory social reality. Country and city, province and metropolis often collide violently with one another. What dominates is the experience of the stranger and of being strange. Thus the fear and terror of the 'jungle', the fascination and admiration of the 'heroic landscape', and finally the observation and experiment of the 'arena of struggle' constitute different forms of response to the experience of strangeness. Brecht's view of the city turns away from exoticism and Americanism to an attitude of experimentation in relation to perception, behaviour, writing technique and media communication, to a laboratory in which 'city-dwellers' are at the same time subject and object of the experimental process.

Thirteen years later, in one of the earliest and also most enlightening commentaries on Brecht's city poems, Walter Benjamin again takes up the image of the 'arena of struggle' with the characterization of cities as a 'battlefield'. He comments in relation to the *Lesebuch für Städtebewohner*:

> One cannot imagine an observer more impassive to beautiful scenery than the strategically trained observer of a battle. One cannot imagine an observer who had a more unfeeling attitude to the charms of the city than Brecht, be it the mass of houses, the breathtaking tempo of its traffic, or its pleasure industry. This lack of feeling for city decor, together with an extreme sensitivity to the city dwellers' specific types of response sets the Brechtian cycle apart from all the big-city poetry which precedes it.[6]

Is this therefore another example of a well-known genre which Brecht used, reworked, renewed, 'refunctionalized' as Brecht always advocated and practised? This essay examines Brecht's specific treatment of the big city from the perspective of Benjamin's commentary, in the context of city poetry from around the middle of the nineteenth century.

Urbanization and the Poetry of the City - Berlin

The transitory, fleeting, and provisional are not only a general characteristic of the modern aesthetic, but also specific to the thematization of the city in literature, as

Baudelaire's well known poem *A une passante* already illustrates. At the same time, there is a dominant tendency towards dissonance, distortion and dividedness, towards fragmentation, simultaneity and alternation. A particular form of perception and visualization are characteristic, along with a new experience of place in the form of crowds and masses and a sense of chaos and confusion. The individual is lonely, isolated and lost in the labyrinth of the city, as Arno Holz's *Wintergroßstadtmorgen* shows.

The artificial and constructed nature of the city corresponds to its reflection and construction in the literary text. The way impressions as well as shocking observations contrast and collide, finds a suitable form in collage, montage and the use of quotation. The ambivalence of the cityscape is dominated first and foremost by the notion of the 'nightmare city' and the 'apocalyptic landscape' (Ludwig Meidner) that was most vividly evoked by Georg Heym in poems such as *Der Gott der Stadt, Die Dämonen der Städte* or *Der Krieg*. The night-side of the big city, its intoxicating atmosphere, luxury, seduction, craving for pleasure, sex for sale and vices of every kind, is a further subject of city literature. Furthermore, from the outset writers from Alfons Petzold to Klabund focused upon exploitation, financial greed and social misery, intensified by the increasingly marked contradictions of class. There are frequent depictions of aggressiveness and destruction, of violence and brutality, heightened to the point of terror and horror by artists such as George Grosz and Otto Dix. The Biblical image of the whore of Babylon, in which all these elements are concentrated in mythological form, is developed by many writers who figure the city as a vibrant-hedonistic heroine. The fear of disaster, in which war and the city have merged since the beginning of the twentieth-century, is simultaneously a delight in disaster. The city becomes an object of fascination, as in Baudelaire's work.

At the beginning of the Weimar Republic, however, after the very real catastrophe of the First World War, the intoxication of the city is increasingly reduced to mere diversion and overstimulation. The apocalyptic landscape degenerates into a shoddy world in the style of George Grosz' *Großstadt*-triptych (1927/28), with cinema, music hall and cabaret, with pleasure palaces and department stores, characterized above all by the nocturnal artificiality of gas lanterns, lights and illuminated advertisements. *The advertisement takes over life*: this title of a poem by Walter Mehring can be seen as representative of this development. Mehring does not only focus on the artificial, all-intrusive world of advertising. With his collage of quotations he communicates its cumulative, heterogeneous form in literature, evoking the visual diversity and confusion which acts as a source of extreme stimulation of the senses. Within the general scopo-centric tendency the visual mode of perception predominates; at the same time the faculty of sight is increasingly mediated by technology and speeded up. Scopic pleasure is heightened through fleeting, quickly changing images, until the deluge produces shock effects, as Simmel had already noted in 1903 in *Die Großstädte und das Geistesleben* [7] and Benjamin after him. The flip side of this extreme stimulation is the monotony and boredom experienced in a petrified city landscape.

Through the mobilization of the masses tempo, dynamics and mobility do not only typify the street, but constitute the life-world in its entirety - from the arena of production and the workplace, the system of distribution and transport, to mass communication and everyday behaviour. The city does not mean home, let alone mother earth, or security and rootedness, but rather heterogeneity, shifting relationships and the transitory. In this context, Ernst Bloch's heading for a central chapter of *Erbschaft dieser Zeit* is given added significance: 'Transition: Berlin. Operations in a vacuum'. 'And in the vacuum created by the absence of ideology there is fresh air in the place of cynicism, instead of nihilism appearances that commit one to nothing and from which a universe is able to emerge.' [8] In 'transition' and 'vacuum', images drawn from time and space, Bloch perceives the transitory as movement and development, but also as a crossing over into a new era. Emptiness is viewed as the negation of the old and as a liberation from the burdens of tradition. The individual is reduced to his 'smallest magnitude' (*kleinste Größe*), to a 'nobody' representative of a new beginning. The individual becomes '"flat, in order to survive", "empty", in order to bear the emptiness of an alienated life, without identity in order to preserve identity'. [9] Against the cynicism and nihilism of the Weimar Republic's bourgeois intellectuals, Bloch posits 'fresh air' and 'nothingness' as a new beginning and dimension on the way to a new society.

In the Berlin of the 1920s, all these realities of the metropolis collide in a particularly violent way. At this point in time, Berlin is the largest industrial city of continental Europe. It has by far and away the worst living conditions as well as severe class conflicts. At the same time, it is the cultural heart of Europe as well as the media and newspaper capital of the world. For a short period of time, Berlin, in spite of New York and Moscow, is second only to London and Paris as the symbol of the city. Here, the 'air' is at its purest and the 'vacuum' at its emptiest.

'Decor' versus 'Types of Response'

All of this is seen by Brecht. Totally alert, he observes Berlin and gains his own city experiences as one of the many outsiders from the provinces. In the process, feelings of insecurity and fear coexist with a casual and hard-boiled attitude. He does not however, display the typical, widespread - and literary - resentment towards the city or condemn it. Brecht's literary productions, his theoretical and practical media explorations, demonstrate much more of a concern with finding an adequate aesthetic response to the city as a locus of the modern. At the same time his works thematize the 'types of response' produced by 'city-dwellers'.

Brecht is not interested in the construction of the big city or in its 'adornments' (to stay with the notion of 'decor'), but rather in the actual behaviour of the 'city-dwellers'. He is thus not drawn to expressionistic visions of doom, to 'left-wing melancholy',[10] or to new cults of technology on the part of intellectuals, for example, who worship an oiltank.[11] The threat of the 'jungle' and the enthusiasm for the 'heroic landscape', as Benjamin terms it, give way to the cool strategy of the 'battlefield'. In his negation of any inwardness and everything 'inner', and through turning towards the outward and visible, Brecht concentrates less on the city, its beauty and ugliness, the rhythm of the street and the arrangement of its buildings, and more on the behaviour of the city-dwellers. Brecht's gaze does not focus on the milieu, the ambience or the mood of the city. As Benjamin observed, it is 'insensitive to the scenic charms' of the city. The flights of streets and the 'sea of houses', the 'breathtaking tempo of its traffic' and the 'pleasure industry', social misery, luxury and vice, are for him no more than the 'decor of the city' (*GS* II.2, 556f.).

> Walt Whitman intoxicated himself on the masses; but they are not the focus of Brecht's attentions. Baudelaire perceived the frailty at the heart of Paris; but in the Parisians he perceived only what that frailty had done to them. Verhaeren attempted an apotheosis of the cities. To Georg Heym they appeared full of the omens of their impending doom. Important city-poetry generally ignored the city-dweller. (*GS* II.2, 557)

For Brecht these perspectives are, if not ideological, then at the very least unproductive. Instead of these, he becomes involved in the reality of 'city people' (*GS* II.2, 557). He describes what, in his opinion, are false responses, namely those which in all probability lead to problems, disasters or the destruction of the individual in the city. These are contrasted with other forms of behaviour which appear more suited to the reality of the big city. In opposition to all tradition and moral values, deracination, isolation, anonymity, freedom from illusion, indifference, the act of forgetting, concealment and above all, coldness[12] become the 'conditions for the circulation of the masses' or for what are termed adequate 'types of response'. They are no longer an expression of a state of life-crisis, for quite simply, 'without them communal life in these heavily populated areas would be brought to a halt'.[13]

Through his 'philosophy of the street', Brecht reworks sociological and cultural analyses in a way which attempts to develop anticipatory behavioural lessons from necessary forms of response to the new realities of the city. In order to survive in this environment - and this is not meant to be either culturally pessimistic or melancholic - radical alterations in behaviour are necessary. In the place of complaint, fear and despair there is a consent (*Ein-Verständnis*)[14] to the new reality. This signals neither obedience and discipline nor opportunism and blind conformism, but a derivation of 'dialectic from reality' instead of 'from the history of ideas'.[15] It is no coincidence that in the *Versuche* 'consent' and the 'smallest magnitude' (*die kleinste Größe*), two of the central categories in Brecht's conception of the *Lehrstück*, are used to fullest effect in the *Badener Lehrstück vom Einverständnis* which directly follows the *Lesebuch für Städtebewohner*.[16] Concepts with negative connotations in the city-literature of the past are now imbued with a new meaning as survival techniques.

Ambivalence and Abstraction - The City in Brecht's 'Lesebuch für Städtebewohner'

Today, in the face of the hypostatization of individualism and the 'tyranny of intimacy',[17] Brecht's *Lesebuch für Städtebewohner* has an irritating quality which is heightened by its ambiguous and polyvalent nature. These poems are not yet 'literature of the class struggle' like many of Brecht's texts a few years later, even if Benjamin claims to establish parallels to the 'crypto-emigration' of the 'communists' (*GS* II.2, 556). Nor, however, are they still the anarchic-hedonistic blasphemies and contrafacta found in the *Hauspostille*. Rather, the city appears both 'as the arena of existence and the arena of the class-struggle' (*GS* II.2, 556). If, thirdly, we also add the still visible markers of New Objectivity, albeit reworked and developed, the specific mixture of these three tendencies allows an understanding of the poems' idiosyncratic multiplicity of meaning and abstraction.

One might ask, however, what it is that suggests a reading of Brecht's poems as a new form of city poetry, demonstrating an 'extreme sensitivity to the city dweller's specific types of response' (*GS* II.2, 556). Without doubt, the clearest indication is the naming of the book's addressee in the title of the cycle: *...für Städtebewohner*. The substitution of the noun Großstädter with the unusual compound *Städtebewohner* ('city-dweller') indicates the separation of the city and its inhabitants and the emphasis placed by Brecht on the latter. Even within the poems themselves there are continual references to the big city and its inhabitants. It is surely not a coincidence that the cycle begins in the first line of the first poem with a situation typical of city literature: the arrival at the city railway station: 'Trenne dich von deinen Kameraden auf dem Bahnhof' ('Take leave of your comrades at the station') (*V*, 108). Already with the entry to the city all old ties are to be cut. The *Mitgebrachte* ('the ones brought with you'), in the shape of travelling companions, are discarded. In what follows, the verbs 'to go' and 'to meet' allude to the city street-life, but as a basis for an altogether different behaviour.

In the second poem reference is really only made to the new situation of the concentrated masses in the city in the closing lines, each of which is reduced to a single emphasised word; 'Und nicht schlecht ist die Welt/ Sondern/ Voll' ('And the world isn't bad/ but/ full') (*V*, 110). What is interesting here is that in place of a moral judgement ('bad') there is the laconic acknowledgement of the situation ('full'), to which the reader is supposed to respond.

Poem three, which has been particularly sharply criticised because of its apparent invitation to patricide, clearly corresponds to Bloch's image of the 'vacuum': 'Wir wissen nicht, was kommt und haben nichts Besseres/ Aber dich wollen wir nicht mehr' ('We don't know what is coming and have nothing better/ But we don't want you any more') (*V*, 110). 'Transition' and 'emptiness' are favoured over the old constrictive 'fullness'. 'The cities are allowed to change' and this is why we should 'even argue with the stones', the hardest and most unyielding things. 'House, stove and pot can stay', but the old, the traditions which keep people chained should 'not change' but 'disappear', 'vanish', 'not live', should 'not' be allowed 'to have been'. In accordance with the original title of this poem, *An Chronos*, the text is not concerned with psychologically motivated, individual patricide, nor as Benjamin asserts with the 'anti-semitism' of National Socialism or 'GPU-practice' (see *GS* II.2, 558 and VI, 540), but rather with the (mythological) liberation from the child-devouring father, the destruction of oppressive tradition and the dawning of a new age. If in the first poem name and face are discarded (in the image of the concealing hat), here it is the past. In his use of the spelling 'Chronos' (Father Time) instead of 'Kronos', which already appears erroneously in the classics, Brecht presumably makes reference to time, that is to say, an older age.

The next poem, the first in which the lyrical 'I' is a woman, contains no direct allusion to the city. The fifth, however, places the city as the locus of the new age within its final verse. Through an evolution from 'dirt' to 'hard mortar', a woman ceases her old forms of behaviour and adopts new ones (compare the last lines of five of the verses, with their repeated 'started' and 'stopped').

'Ich bin ein Dreck; aber es müssen
Alle Dinge zum besten dienen, ich
Komme herauf, ich bin
Unvermeidlich, das Geschlecht von morgen
Bald schon kein Dreck mehr, sondern
Der harte Mörtel, aus dem
Die Städte gebaut sind'
('I am dirt; but all things must
serve to the best of their ability, I

rise up, I am inevitable, the generation of tomorrow
Soon no longer dirt, but
the hard mortar, from which
cities are built') (*V,* 113).

Here too the new, the 'generation of tomorrow', is not morally legitimated, but simply an expression of reality. Just as, according to Benjamin, Brecht 'makes the revolutionary emerge from the bad, selfish type quite without any ethics' in *Der Untergang des Egoisten Johann Fatzer*, so he allows useful 'mortar' to be created from unusable 'dirt' as a productive constituent of the city.

> [These changes] do not emerge out of philanthropy, love of one's neighbour, idealism, magnanimity or the like, but out of prevailing attitudes. These attitudes can in themselves be questionable, disagreeable and selfish. If the man [or woman - F. V.] in whom they arise does not try to deceive himself [herself], if he [she] stays close to reality, then the correction will come from reality itself. Not the ethical: the man [woman] does not become better; but the social: his [her] behaviour makes him [her] useful [...] (*GS* II.2, 663)

- namely, as the 'hard mortar' of the new city-reality.

In poem six the references to the city are once more restricted to the street situation ('road', pedestrians, 'shop-windows'). In the seventh poem it is simply the street drain which evokes the city. In clear contrast to the pronounced self-confident attitude of a man in the previous poem, the drain is representative of the reduction to the 'smallest magnitude' already cited above: 'In einem Tank kommen Sie nicht durch ein Kanalgitter:/ Sie müssen schon aussteigen' ('You can't drive through a street drain in a tank:/ You'll have to get out') (*V,* 113). For 'kettle' read all belongings, for 'woman' read all, even the most intimate sexual relationships, for 'composure' read inner attitude and consistent modes of behaviour: all of these must be discarded in order to 'get through'. In concrete terms, this firstly means making yourself small enough to get through the street drain and submerge yourself in the underworld, secondly 'making do with the most essential materials' and thirdly, 'reaching your goal'. It means that you will be successful from that point onwards in 'escaping' from 'dangerous, threatening situations' and that through this you will have finally passed the 'test'.

Nor in the eighth poem is there any sign of 'city decor' although 'contract' and 'president' refer to economic and political contexts. Instead, the situation from the second poem is further intensified. The 'full' world and the 'fifth wheel' (*V,* 110) have turned into the aggressive image of the 'eaters', who are here in force and the 'mincemeat that is needed'. The radical conclusion in the one italicized line of the entire cycle of poems is 'Ihr müßt das ABC noch lernen/ Das ABC heißt/ *Man wird mit euch fertigwerden*' ('You still have to learn your ABC/ ABC means/ *They will sort you out*'). (*V*, 114f)

Lastly, in opposition to the until now dominant street scene, the images of the city in poem nine concentrate, although only in passing, on the house in the city with its variants of home, room, place to sleep, bed-chamber of the prostitute.

It is not surprising that city-decor makes no appearance of any kind in the tenth poem. In this concluding commentary to the cycle, which Brecht also uses in another teaching and learning context under the title of *Me-tis Strenge* (*BFA*, 18, 125), reality is only talked of in the most abstract terms: 'Die nüchterne, durch deine besondere Artung unbestechliche/ Deiner Schwierigkeiten überdrüssige' ('Sober, incorruptible by your particular nature/ Weary of your difficulties') (*V*, 116).

A 'Highly Suitable Model' for 'City-dwellers'

The abstract and ambivalent nature of the *Lesebuch* has time and again led to the search for a definitive meaning. This has resulted in a number of critical approaches: the 'economic mechanism of capitalism'[18] stands side by side with the psychoanalytic 'tendency to pessimism',[19] 'impersonal neutrality'[20] with 'a scornful set of instructions',[21] the 'dionysian ecstasy of self-deception'[22] with that of 'sadism',[23] the city guerilla[24] with the GPU,[25] the exponent of a Gracián-like guide to conduct[26] with the 'media-aesthetic' of the gramophone record.[27] Without wishing to lay claim to having finally found the 'right' interpretation, I would like to attempt an explanation for the particularly marked diversity of these partly reductive, partly over-emphatic or partial interpretations. 'The form' of the *Lesebuch* poems 'is strict, but only so that elements of one's own invention and contemporary style can be introduced all the more easily'[28]. The application of this characterization of the *Lehrstück* by Brecht to the *Lesebuch* seems to me to provide a possible key to its understanding. Jakobs and Rischbieter have already referred to questions of attitude in relation to forms of behaviour, and Wöhrle and Seung Jin Lee[29] have noted the close ties between the *Lesebuch* and the *Lehrstück*. However, to my knowledge, no one has focused on the aspect of the 'highly suitable models', their 'imitation' and 'the criticism which can be levelled at them through a different approach' (Steinweg, 164) as a point of departure for an exploration of the *Lesebuch* texts.

Through these texts Brecht places material at the disposal of the student, be it in the form of repeated playings of a gramophone record, or in 'the implementation of specific forms of behaviour, the adoption of specific stances, the repetition of specific speeches' (Steinweg, 164), i.e. in playing and play-acting, the imitation of models, quotations and gestures. In this context one can also understand why Brecht avoids city-decor where possible. Its evocation would create a milieu and atmosphere no longer general, translatable or applicable to the world of experience of those working in the 'laboratory' of the *Lesebuch* texts. The traditional dramatic questions, where?, when?, who?, and why? are also put to the actors, although in a completely different way. In epic theatre alienation is achieved through a distancing in time and space. In the learning situation of the *Lesebuch*, as in the pedagogical form of the *Lehrstücke*, it is their radicalization through consistent abstraction which results in gaps that stimulate the reader to provide them with a critical content. The abstraction remains, however, like that of the *Lehrstücke*, at an indeterminate level; it is not theoretical texts which are produced, but highly concentrated poetic texts in whose condensation of historical experiences a kind of distancing-experience is in force.

The *Lesebuch* texts, like the *Lehrstücke*, contain an experimental agenda in order to examine 'social reflexes' as Brecht himself calls them, and to explore behavioural forms. These 'discussions of faulty behaviour', oriented to borderline situations, lead to decisions in the test example which are applicable to reality. These texts make manifest meaningful social experiences and in the process open them up to critique. They serve as exercises in self-understanding, as 'exercises in flexibility' (Steinweg, 198) designed to destroy ideology and to develop a completely new use-value beyond moral ideas. In addition to his literary productions, Brecht wants to make use of different kinds of apparatus. In the case of the *Lesebuch* these are the gramophone record (see *V*, Heft 2, Prefatorial note) and radio, which were not only bound closely to one another in the 1920s, but in their specific orality, compression (montage and the addition of individual points of view), speed and storage capacity comprised the most advanced and at the same time - at least in Berlin - widely disseminated new communication forms of the day.

In this context the last lines of the poems, first added with their publication in the *Versuche* of 1930, can be visualized as a postscript in square brackets: 'Das wurde mir gesagt' ('That is what I've been told'), 'Das hast du schon sagen hören' ('You've heard it before'), 'So sprechen wir mit unserm Vätern' ('This is how we talk to our fathers'), 'So habe ich Leute sich anstrengen sehen' ('I've seen people struggle like this'), 'So habe ich eine Frau sagen hören' ('This is what I heard a woman say'), 'Das habe ich schon Leute sagen hören' ('I've already heard people talking like this'). There is not only a second speaker being introduced here. Within this distancing commentary, these texts partly issue an imperious invitation, partly soberly observe and are partly self-descriptive in terms of behaviour. They become question-able (*frag-würdig*) behavioural guidelines, but in the sense that they make us ask questions. Brecht's statement 'einverstanden sein heißt auch: *nicht einverstanden sein*' ('consenting also means not consenting'), which is given the heading of 'consent and contradiction' by Steinweg (62), also opens up a new dimension to the concept of *Ein-verständnis* ('consent') in relation to the *Lesebuch*. The commentary thus contains 'instructions [...] which concern the meaning and the application of the document [the text - F. V.]' (Steinweg, 73). The commentator speaks of himself, of a 'you' and a 'we', of a woman and twice of 'people': he thus addresses a range of very different people.

The Language of Gestures and Acting-Experiments

Spoken language is integral to Brecht's *Lesebuch* as one might expect given the spoken delivery which characterizes this traditional medium. In addition to this there is the 'encapsulated gesture' (*begriffene Geste*). Brecht allows Me-ti to say the following about the poet Kin-jeh (representative of Brecht himself):

> He used a language which was both stylized and natural. He achieved this by paying attention to the attitudes underlying each sentence. He merely fashioned attitudes into sentences and by means of the sentences always allowed these attitudes to shine through. This kind of language he called gestural, because it was only an expression of people's gestures. His sentences are best read accompanied by specific physical movements appropriate to them [...] (*BFA*, 18, 78f)

We have put this theory to the test and have worked with the *Lesebuch* poems using the method of the *Lehrstück*. In other words, the reading out loud of the texts was 'accompanied by specific physical movements'. We performed gestures and took up certain stances, in order to bring out the fundamental gestures of the text. In the play sequences the actors each produced very different perspectives. They filled the 'highly-suitable model' with their own physicality, with voice, mimicry and gestures, with particular forms of behaviour and not least with their own experiences. They presented their 'interpretations', making them available in the process as material to others in order to be acted out again and for critical purposes. As a rule, in accordance with the structure of the poem, a form of acting monologue was maintained, commented upon by a second player, who also took on the role of a chorus. In the case of the ninth poem, however, it seemed fitting to have the four verses, representative of the four 'invitations to a man from different sides and at different times' (*V*, 115) to be played by different people with different gestures.

We worked particularly intensively on poem number four, acting it out in six different versions. The following are summaries of each version:

1. A new day begins; a woman from a poor background, somewhat flirtatious, is not sure of her own attitude; many things are unclear and uncertain to her.

2. A self-confident woman sits with crossed legs on a chair at the analyst's. Through her stance she wants to make it clear that 'although I come to you, I don't really have

any problems'. In her self-representation she shows toughness, but only manages to do so thanks to a conscious effort.

3. A lonely, alcoholic woman sits in a dilapidated room and tells the story of her life in the spirit of 'This is what happened to me'. Her attitude is one of resignation, depression and now and then cynicism. She is disappointed in herself and the world but cannot visualize a way out, as she sees no possibility of freeing herself from her husband. Ultimately, she doesn't really care about anything.

4. A sleepy young woman sits in front of the mirror early in the morning. She puts on her make-up and combs her hair at length. She senses the mediocrity of her life and looks for change.

5. A sour, embittered woman in her mid-forties attempts to blame everything on others in an accusatory tone. She knows, or at least she thinks she knows, what's what. This inclination to apportion blame is of course not one she herself admits. Over this scene there might be the heading: 'at the moment of greatest need the middle way is fatal'.

6. A woman sits totally relaxed and at ease in a corner on the floor. She is filled with a pleasant tiredness. She is languid and stretches luxuriously. She is at peace with herself.

The model of the *Mittlere(n)* ('average behaviour') was 'filled' in different and critical ways, uncertainty next to self-confidence, resignation next to thoughts about change, the blaming of others next to a pleasurably relaxed sense of well being. 'Sleeping', 'singing', staying 'fresh', not 'exerting oneself', not giving anything away, sufficiency, eating carefully and living quietly are the activities which were each represented in different ways through the language of gesture and physical stances. The behavioural form of 'averageness', 'not-exerting-oneself', is in clear opposition to the extremes of 'dirt' and 'mortar' in the second text spoken by a woman which follows on directly from the fourth poem. This might give rise to the impression that what we see in this fifth poem is the new woman of the 1920s, equipped with 'mobility', the ability to 'adapt to different situations', 'a quick intelligence and an objective way of seeing things',[30] whilst a 'false' kind of attitude is shown in poem four. In actual fact, however, Brecht offers two possibilities to choose from, presenting them for the consideration, examination and critique of his addressees. They should experiment with these models and develop a behaviour which fits them and at the same time befits the new reality of the big city through listening to gramophone records or through an educational form of play. Through Brecht's formulation of 'learning-play' the individual is subjected to tests, observations. What is revealed is this: events are not changeable at their climax, nor through virtue and resolve, but only in their strictly ordinary process, through reason and *practice* [emphasis by F.V.] (*GS* II.2, 699)

New and Old 'City of Nets'

Brecht's *Lesebuch für Städtebewohner* 'does not formulate cognitive results, but scrutinizes thought processes'. It 'has the authenticity of the first encounter with something unknown, the shock of the first appearance of the new'.[31] This dictum of Müller's, written in connection with *Fatzer*, lends itself easily to the *Lesebuch*. It need therefore not be seen as a problematic early phase on the way to the 'mature' Brecht. There is no romanticization of reality or a harshness contemptuous of people, but rather a gaze free of illusion (see *GS* II.1, 216) directed at the 'new' aspects of the metropolis and its future radical transformation.

The *Lesebuch* 'does not condemn the city as a Babylonian whore (which of course still has a "moral" dimension), but formulates it in an emotionless way as a vast landscape'[32] in which the 'city-dwellers' live and to which they must react. Brecht's metropolis is a 'city of nets' in the traditional sense of *Mahagonny* and - in anticipation of further development - an incoherent, shapeless, dematerialized, metropolis of electronic networks, without identity, a 'non-place'. To summarize, in the words of Heiner Müller: Brecht's *Lesebuch* is `a work between the past and the future' - 'without the present'.[33] The real, always diverse present is first found in the attitudes which manifest themselves in the experiences of the reader, listener and actor: through behavioural experiments.

[1.]   See Florien Vaßen, 'Bertolt Brechts Experimente. Überlegungen zur ästhetischen Autonomie und sozialen Funktion von Brechts literarischen und theatralen Modellen und Versuchen', in *Die literarische Moderne in Europa*, vol.3, ed. Hans Joachim Piechotta *et al.*, *Aspekte der Moderne in der Literatur bis zur Gegenwart* (Opladen, Westdeutscher Verlag, 1994), pp. 146-174.

[2.]   Bertolt Brecht, *Versuche 1-12* (Frankfurt aM, Suhrkamp, 1959), cited henceforth as *V*.

[3.]   Heiner Müller, *Fatzer ± Keuner*, in Heiner Müller, *Rotwelsch* (Berlin, Merve, 1980), p. 30.

[4.]   Elisabeth Hauptmann, *Notizen zu Brechts Arbeit 1926*, in *Sinn und Form. Zweites Sonderheft Bertolt Brecht*, Berlin (o.J.), 242-3.

[5.]   Bertolt Brecht, *Tagebücher 1920-1924, Autobiographische Aufzeichnungen 1920-1954*, ed. H. Ramthun (Frankfurt aM, Surhkamp, 1978), p. 145 (cited henceforth as *Tb*).

[6.]   Walter Benjamin, *Gesammelte Schriften*, eds. R. Tiedemann and H. Schweppenhäuser (Frankfurt aM, Suhrkamp, 1977 -), II: 2, pp. 556f, cited henceforth as *GS*.

7.   Georg Simmel, *Gesamtausgabe* vol.7, ed. Otthein Rammstedt (Frankfurt aM, Suhrkamp, 1995), pp. 116-131.

8.   Ernst Bloch, *Erbschaft dieser Zeit* (Frankfurt aM, Suhrkamp, 1962), p. 220.

9.   Carl Pietzcker, *Die Lyrik des jungen Brecht. Vom anarchischen Nihilismus zum Marxismus* (Frankfurt aM, Suhrkamp, 1974), pp. 129-130.

10.   Compare Benjamin's criticism of Tucholsky and Mehring; Walter Benjamin, *Der Autor als Produzent*, pp. 683-701.

11.   See Brecht, *700 Intellektuelle beten einen Öltank an*, in *BFA* 11, pp. 174ff.

12.   Compare Helmut Lethen, *Verhaltenslehre der Kälte. Lebensversuche zwischen den Kriegen* (Frankfurt aM, Suhrkamp, 1994).

13.   See Helmut Lethen, 'Chicago und Moskau', in *Die Metropole. Industriekultur in Berlin im 20. Jahrhundert* (Munich, 1986), pp. 193-194.

14.   For an elaboration on the concept of *Einverständnis* see Brecht's *Lehrstück* theory, in particular in Reiner Steinweg, *Modell der Lehrstücke Zeugnisse, Diskussion Erfahrung* (Frankfurt aM, Suhrkamp, 1976).

15.   Brecht, *Arbeitsjournal*, 3 vols. ed Werner Hecht (Frankfurt aM, Suhrkamp, 1973), p. 86.

16.   Compare Florien Vaßen, 'Lesebuch und Schallplatte: Haltungen und Verhaltenslehren *Aus dem Lesebuch für Städtebewohner*', forthcoming in *Brecht-Jahrbuch*, 22, 1997.

17.   See Richard Sennett, *Verfall und Ende des öffentlichen Lebens. Die Tyrannei der Intimität* (Frankfurt/New York, Campus, 1994).

18.   Klaus Schuhmann, *Der Lyriker Bertolt Brecht* 1913-1933 (Munich, dtv, 1971), p. 213.

19.   Pietzcker, p. 333.

20.   Jürgen Jacobs, 'Wie die Wirklichkeit selber. Zu Brechts *Lesebuch für Städtebewohner*', in *Brecht-Jahrbuch 1974*, ed. John Fuegi *et al.* (Frankfurt aM, Suhrkamp, 1975), p.90.

21.   Henning Rischbieter, 'Zum *Lesebuch für Städtebewohner*', in *Aktualisierung Brecht*, ed. Wolfgang Fritz Haug *et al.* (Berlin, Argument, 1980), p. 196.

22.   Béla Balász, 'Sachlichkeit und Sozialismus', in *Die Weltbühne*, 18.12.28.   Cited by Lethen, *Verhaltenslehren*, p. 173.

23.   Benjamin, *GS* II.2, p. 558.

24. See afterword in Bertolt Brecht, *Gedichte für Städtebewohner*, ed. F Buono (Frankfurt aM, Suhrkamp, 1988), p. 153.

25. Benjamin, *GS* VI, p. 540.

26. Helmut Lethen, 'Brechts Hand-Orakel', in *Der andere Brecht I. Das Brecht-Jahrbuch* 17 (1992), 77-99.

27. Dieter Wöhrle, *Bertolt Brechts Medienästhetische Versuche* (Köln, Prometh, 1988) (in particular pp. 61-80); compare Hans-Christian von Herrmann, *Sang der Maschinen. Brechts Medienästhetik* (Munich, Fink, 1996).

28. Steinweg, p. 164

29. Seung Jin Lee, '*Aus dem Lesebuch für Städtebewohner.* Schallplattenlyrik zum "*Einverständnis*"', (Bern, Lang, 1993); *Aus dem Lesebuch für Städtebewohner (1)*, in *Interpretationen. Gedichte von Brecht*, ed. Jan Knopf (Stuttgart, Reclam, 1995), pp. 42-52.

30. Elke Kupschinsky, 'Die vernünftige Nephertete' in *Die Metropole*, ed. Jochen Boberg *et al.*, p. 164.

31. Müller, *Fatzer ± Keuner*, p. 35.

32. Karsten Düsdieker, 'Welcome to Wasteland: Fahren und Fernsehen in Vineland', in *Grenzgänge. Großstadterfahrungen in Literatur, Film und Musik Lateinamerikas und der USA seit 1960*, ed. Projektgruppe Neue Welt Stadt (Bielefeld, Aisthesis, 1995), p. 168.

33. Müller, *Fatzer ± Keuner*, p. 36.

JOHN J. WHITE

Brecht And Semiotics: Semiotics And Brecht

In 1968 Manfred Wekwerth published a wideranging and thought-provoking survey entitled 'Das Theater Brechts 1968',[1] a piece destined to become a milestone in the Berliner Ensemble's new-found confidence in reassessing itself, in some measure independently of Brecht's sometimes authoritarian 'Richtlinien'. Much of the thinking here, prefiguring ideas to be developed in Wekwerth's *Theater und Wissenschaft. Überlegungen für das Theater von heute und morgen*, specifically relates to the experience of staging *Die Heilige Johanna der Schlachthöfe* (premiere: 1967), a singularly post-Brechtian production hailed by Wekwerth as a watershed in the Ensemble's history: 'Bei der Arbeit an der *Johanna der Schlachthöfe* merkten wir, daß die bisherigen Linien des Spielplans [...] nicht mehr ausreichten. [...Es] stellte sich die Frage nach neuen Gesichtspunkten einer Spielplanung und Konzeption' (332).

The 1968 context is vital, for hardly more than a decade after his death Brecht is already perceived as 'in Gefahr, Gewohntes zu werden' (300). By responding to a series of all too familiar 'Gemeinplätze' and polemical questions concerning Brecht and his Ensemble's place within twentieth-century *Theatergeschichte*, Wekwerth is evidently paving the way for a major re-alignment of Epic Theatre's methods. And without doubt one of the more constructive new departures outlined takes things in a more rigorously semiotic direction.

Although Brecht had himself seldom theorized within an explicitly semiotic framework, one finds quite a number of hints that he was aware of the extent to which his theatre was indebted to the notion of theatre as a collection of signs transmitted to the audience. As Wekwerth puts it, Epic Theatre's 'Grundhaltung [ist] die des Zeigens', consequently its main instrument must be 'das Zeichen' (322). Moreover, given that '[theatrical] semiotization is clearest [...] in the case of the elements of the set',[2] it is hardly surprising that it was a series of notes on 'Bühnenbau' that gave rise to Brecht's most obviously sign-oriented remarks. In a short piece dating from the late thirties entitled 'Das Nötigste ist genug', he already declares: 'An Stätten, wo gearbeitet wird, liest man oft: "Unbeschäftigten ist der Zutritt untersagt". Das sollten die Bühnenbauer über ihr Spielfeld hängen. Was auf der Bühne steht, muß mitspielen, und was nicht mitspielt, muß nicht auf die Bühne.'[3] While the ensuing observations are above all concerned with the semiotic function of a controlled number of 'erzählende' stage-props, what Brecht has to say here, and in the related pieces 'Kennzeichen und Symbole' and 'Die Auswahl der einzelnen Elemente', offers clear evidence of an overriding pragmatic approach to theatre as an aesthetic sign-system. 'Die Auswahl der einzelnen Elemente', with its awareness of anti-capitalist theatre's need to find 'Kennzeichen für die stattfindende Produktion' and the assumption that social exploitation can only be convincingly demonstrated 'wenn wir Stücke des Ortes mit Elementen mischen, welche diesen Gebrauch [d.h. den unsere Figuren vom Ort machen] deutlich aufzeigen', comes closest to making explicit Brecht's appreciation of the sign-function of many objects on the stage. 'Wir haben den *Augenschein* aufgegeben', he notes (*BFA*, 22:1, 251f), and as a consequence of this jettisoning of devices merely serving the cause of surface mimesis, 'Dinge, die [...] nicht augenscheinlich sind' have been extensively conscripted into the cause of political theatre.

Although Brecht's sign-based observations are primarily concerned with the didactic function of stage-props and with certain commenting elements of anti-illusionistic décor, it is obvious that his concern extends well beyond just these features of staging, for one finds virtually nothing in his theatre that could not be construed as in some respect 'gestisch' and hence possessing a semiotic function. The argument which follows concerning the synecdochic nature of Brechtian sets and props has generally been assumed to relate to *Die Mutter*.

> Die Wahrheit ist: Das Ganze (das Zimmer) ist durch Teile (Fensterrahmen, Möbel, Türstock) vertreten, das realistische Ganze durch realistische Teile. Die Kleinhandelsensemble z.B. sind jedoch keine eigentlichen Symbole. Tatsächlich benötigten wir die Geschäfte selber nicht; jedoch ist im Stück die Rede von der Schwierigkeit, Kunden zu fischen. Die Embleme sind die Köder: sie stellen nicht Geschäfte dar (nicht die Idee Bäckerei oder Handschuhmacherei), sondern ihre Wahrzeichen, die den Kunden auf der Straße die Existenz eines speziellen Ladens anzeigen. (*BFA*, 22:1, 253f)

Although the formulations here build on an earlier distinction between 'die Sache selber' and theatre's '"Zeichen" dafür' (*BFA*, 22:1, 252), Brecht on the whole privileges the word 'Merkmale' (rather than 'Zeichen'). The first entry in a whole series bearing the heading 'Merkmale gesellschaftlicher Prozesse' reads: 'Unsere mobilen Elemente sind nach und nach entstanden, als Merkmale gesellschaftlicher Prozesse. [...] Proletarierwohnungen haben als Charakteristika den Platz- und Luftmangel, den geringen Erholungswert, die Krankheiten erzeugenden Umstände: Dafür sind Merkmale zu finden' (*BFA*, 22:1,252).

While Brecht's own terminology does not suggest a familiarity with the various semiotic frameworks available by this time, Wekwerth's terms rely eclectically on both Saussurean and Peircean taxonomies. In fact, since Peirce's notion of the 'iconic sign' is so central to Wekwerth's argument and has proved to be a more useful analytical tool in theatre studies, the following discussion must be seen in the context of Charles Sanders Peirce's 'Second Trichotomy of Signs'. Here Peirce distinguishes between three types of signs according to their relationship to their object:

> The icon has no dynamical connection with the object it represents; it simply happens that its qualities resemble those of that object, and excite analogous sensations in the mind for which it is a likeness. [...] The index is physically connected with its object; they make an organic pair, but the interpreting mind has nothing to do with this connection, except remarking it, after it is established. The symbol is connected with its object by virtue of the idea of the symbol-using mind, without which no such connection could exist.[4]

Thus we have three types of sign, distinguished, in Umberto Eco's more user-friendly formulation, as follows: '*icons* (similar to their object); *symbols* (arbitrarily linked with their object); and *indices* (physically connected with their object.'[5] Peirce's *symbol* is akin to Saussure's *arbitrary sign*; whereas Saussure's *motivation* overlaps with features of both the *icon* and the *index*. The problem with Peirce's trichotomy is not just that his terms diverge from normal usage and his distinctions are often opaquely expressed, it lies in the fact that he refers, invariably using nouns, to *icons* and *indices*, rather than extrapolating elements of iconicity and indexicality from any sign complex. It was Charles Morris who, in *Foundations of a Theory of Signs* (1938), eventually postulated that 'iconicity is always a matter of degree' (which is why he coined the terms 'iconicity' and 'indexicality'.[6] Wekwerth also tends to think primarily of sign-types, rather than elements of iconicity, indexicality and symbolicity within individual signs or as part of the process of semiosis. And even when he is using Peirce's terms, he seems happy to focus on the icon/symbol contrast (as if he were applying Peircean vocabulary to Saussure's two-part typology). Brecht himself, by contrast, was far more interested in indexicality than Wekwerth. Thus, the pipe in Mutter Courage's possession has indexical value, in that it not only refers to the cook of whom it is a memento, but reveals her attitude to the whole ambiguous past relationship; and Yvette's flaunted hat, when worn by Kattrin, is also an index, again of a far greater complex of things than merely its previous owner (notionally referring indexical signs to a single 'object' can be misleading). In addition, indices usually possess a marked iconic component, as is the case with Mutter Courage's waggon which Wekwerth sees as the 'Zeichen der Courage und ihrer Familie' (372). Clearly, the state of the waggon acts as a reliable barometer of Courage's fortunes (iconically representing her current economic condition); but indexically it also identifies so many other aspects of her ethos. Early images of her children harnessed to the vehicle (even Courage herself being so in the end), of the waggon as a substitute for the security of hearth and home the cook at one stage offers her, or as a screen blocking her view of things happening beyond her field of vision, show how complex aesthetic indexicality can be compared with Peirce's illustrations. Yet the common denominator of such functions is, in a Marxist context such as this, the sign's role within a political symptomatology.[7]

To say, as Brecht does of one of his more referential stage-sets, that 'die Straße ist das Resultat gesellschaftlicher Prozesse' (*BFA*, 22:1, 257) is to ascribe indexical function to an environment. One form of indexicality that was inevitably to prove attractive to Brecht relates objects to their having been bought and hence to their place within the socio-economic matrix. In Brecht's words:

> Eine Frau, die einen Stuhl unter sich zieht, um ein Kind auf den Schoß nehmen zu können, kann kaum beschrieben werden als eine Frau, die einen Artikel zum Preis von fünf Mark, wenn neu, hergestellt in einer Warenproduktion, die auf Ausbeutung beruht, unter sich zieht. Aber wie deplaziert immer ein besonderes Zeigen von Merkmalen diese Herkunft und Rolle des Stuhles sein mag, sie dürfen doch jedenfalls nicht vernachlässigt werden. Und sie können jederzeit wieder aktiv werden, z.B. wenn der Stuhl verkauft werden muß, oder zertrümmert wird. Wer je gesehen hat, mit welcher Geste eine Frau in schlechten Verhältnissen einen Stuhl zusammengelesen hat, den ihr Mann im Zorn zerbrach, eventuell ihn auf sie werfend, versteht unmittelbar, was hier gemeint ist. (*BFA*, 22:1, 256)

The above passages are almost the only places (Wekwerth calls them 'erste Schritte', 323) where Brecht – who had increasingly come to be acknowleged as having creatively explored the semiotic potential of his theatrical innovations[8] – theorizes in a way which explicitly resorts to semiotic concepts. His frequent use in the notes on 'Bühnenbau' of the words 'Zeichen', 'Kennzeichen', 'Symbol', 'Merkmal' and 'Charakteristika' – even his distinction between 'Kommerzielle Artikel und Naturprodukte'[9] – may not be rigorous or even consistent, but the chosen terms do bear witness to his interest in exploring and exploiting sign-function and the process of semiosis.

Brecht's *ad hoc* vocabulary can hardly fail to emphasize the fact that such signs are not just a part of drama's repertoire, but inform the very fabric of social interaction.[10] *Der Messingkauf*'s 'Straßenszene', the *Grundmodell einer Szene des epischen Theaters* (*BFA*, 22:1, 370-81) makes the same point. With its memorable mosaic of symbolic, indexical and iconic elements deployed to analyse public reaction to a motor accident, it reaffirms the fact that epic theatrical practice involves similar principles of semiosis to those we encounter in non-aesthetic contexts.

Although the Polish director Jan Kott enjoys a reputation as the first writer to apply Peircian semiotics to theatrical devices and conventions,[11] Wekwerth appears to have been taking the Berliner Ensemble in this direction well before him. In any case, neither was the first to be applying semiotic theories to contemporary East European drama.[12] On the other hand, although Roland Barthes' relatively early responses to Brecht's plays and theory give some indication of a semiotic framework – and some of his arguments in *Mythologies* are clearly indebted to the Brechtian principle of 'Verfremdung'[13] – he did not, despite being the leading living semiotician in Brecht's lifetime to have reacted to the dramatist's work, apply his theories systematically either to the plays he had seen or to the theoretical writings. Wekwerth was certainly opening up new avenues for Epic Theatre with 'Das Theater Brechts 1968'.

In an attempt to explain some of the basic principles of semiosis, Wekwerth begins with the axiomatic distinction between arbitrary and natural signs, also drawing attention to the importance of sign-*systems* ('das Schaffen von Zeichensystemen, die nach einer Struktur organisiert sind', 321). He also highlights the role of the audience/receiver in actively endowing something, be it linguistic element, stage-prop or didactic plot, with some form of sign-function. Wekwerth's expository stress is very much on the nature and role of *arbitrary* signs within language-systems, an approach which runs counter to the attention that has generally been paid to the imitative aspect of theatrical signs. 'It is clear', Keir Elam observes, 'that a degree of analogousness often arises between, say, representational and represented human bodies, or between the stage sword and its dramatic equivalent' that would be difficult to match in painting or sculpture, let alone the printed word. Indeed, theatre has been singled out as 'the only art form able to exploit what might be termed iconic *identity*: the sign-vehicle denoting a rich silk costume may well be a rich silk costume';[14] actors with arms, legs and voices play characters with arms, legs and voices, they tend to communicate using recognizable body language and in many productions are surrounded with relatively realistic stage-props. As Eco elsewhere puts it: 'Ein Schauspieler muß [...] Bruchstücke der realen Welt verwenden, seinen Körper, alltägliche Gegenstände und Gesten.'[15] The consensus view would thus seem to be that theatre's focus will tend to be on aspects of the imitative, rather than arbitrary, nature of the majority of signs it works with.[16]

In the light of the above emphasis, Wekwerth seems to be an exception when basing his introduction to a semiotics of theatre on non-iconic features:

> Und noch eine Entdeckung der modernen Erkenntnistheorie ist erstaunlich: Das ist das Zeichen oder Symbol selbst, der Buchstabe also oder der Laut [...]. Ein Zeichen ist immer etwas für jemanden, der seine Bedeutung weiß. Es ist nichts Natürliches, also von Natur Gegebenes. [...] Es ist eine Art Gesellschaftsvertrag – ähnlich dem Rousseaus –, der die natürliche Unordnung organisiert.
> Und es hat noch eine sympathische Eigenschaft. Es ist allein sinnlose Materie. Striche auf Papier. Oder Kehlkopflaute. Es bekommt seine Bedeutung erst durch das Dazutreten des Menschen. Es ist also ein höchst menschliches Produkt. Und es ist niemals mechanisch deckungsgleich mit dem, was es in Natur bezeichnet, und es ist kein naturgegebenes Spiegelbild, sondern bekommt seine Bedeutung erst innerhalb menschlicher Tätigkeit. Die Buchstaben B-r-e-c-h-t zum Beispiel haben mit dem Mann, der der größte Dramatiker unserer Zeit ist, zunächst nichts zu tun. Man kann sagen, sie sind sogar willkürlich. Ein Strich und ein Kreis ist ein b, ein Strich mit einem Halbbogen ein r - aber auch nur für den, der zum Beispiel nicht kyrillisch schreibt. Und trotzdem verstehen wir, was gemeint ist, wenn wir den Schlüssel haben.   Um   diese Nicht-Identität zu zeigen, möchte ich zwei Aussagen über Brecht machen: 1. Brecht hat den Ruhm, der größte Dramatiker unserer Zeit zu sein. 2. Brecht hat sechs Buchstaben. Ich will hier nicht auf den komplizierten Zusammenhang zwischen Zeichen und Objekt, Sprache und Metasprache näher eingehen. Wichtig für das Theater ist die Erkenntnis, daß zwischen dem Objekt O und dem Zeichen Z eine Nicht-Identität besteht, die erst durch menschliche Tätigkeit zu Bedeutungen führt. Und hier besteht eine verblüffende Ähnlichkeit mit der Grundstruktur des Brechtschen Theaters, das ja auch zwischen den dargestellten Vorgängen und der darstellerischen Vermittlung - also zwischen der Figur und dem Schauspieler – einen Unterschied macht, um durch die Art der Vermittlung (Verfremdung genannt) dem Zuschauer das soziale System mit auszuliefern, nach dem die einzelnen Vorgänge organisiert sind.
> Und hier muß das Theater eine große Entdeckung machen: Es muß sich seines poetischen Zeichencharakters bewußt werden. (321f.)

While the vocabulary still sounds more Saussurian than Peircean, with references to the arbitrariness of the sign being presented within a largely linguistic framework[17], the ground is gradually being prepared for bridge-building in the direction of the principle of estrangement.

> Hier werden wir erinnert an Anfänge jener Aktivität, die Brecht auf bewußter Ebene auch beim Zuschauen fordert, nicht nur als Konsumtion von Kunst, sondern als ein Selbsterzeugen. Das Schaffen von Zeichensystemen, die nach einer Struktur organisiert sind und die die Menschen, für die diese Zeichen bestimmt sind, beherrschen, um sich so der Wirklichkeit organisierend zu bemächtigen, ist der Grundvorgang jenes Verhaltens, das man Denken nennt. (321)

Although Wekwerth does go on to argue that 'der Zeichencharakter des Theaters ist besonderer Art [...] es organisiert sich seine Zeichen aus realem Verhalten und macht dies durch Auswahl, Vergrößerung und Wiederholung' (322), many of the illustrations offered do little to highlight the particularities of theatrical semiosis or to pinpoint the uniqueness of Brecht's own approach. Body language is invoked: 'ein bestimmter Gang der Weigel [...] ist Zeichen für mehr Reichtum' (323), and in the case of *Mann ist Mann*, the point is also made that 'Die kleine Geste des Händereibens, die Thate als Galy Gay ausführt, wenn er sich auf einen Fisch freut, [...] zeigt als Zeichen mehr über die Struktur des Kleinbürgers als naturalistische Genauigkeit der Kamera oder sogar als die Wirklichkeit selbst' (323), which would seem to give a new semiotic twist to the old Brechtian adage that 'Zeigen ist mehr als Sein' (*BFA*, 23, 315) – now construed as 'Zeichen ist mehr als bloßes Realitätspartikel'. A stage-set in *Die Heilige Johanna* is described as a 'Zeichen für die Schlachthöfe' (370), and much space is devoted to emphasizing the overall 'Zeichencharakter des Bühnenbildes' (371). Yet, as more detailed investigation would show, it is not mere recourse to drama's usual repertoire of semiotic processes, but the specific nature of their manipulation which makes Brecht's theatre peculiarly Brechtian.

Wekwerth's remark 'Es bliebe zu untersuchen, welch enorme Rolle auch hier die Methode der Verfremdung spielen kann, die ja eben Zeichen organisiert, die es erlauben, in einem realen Vorgang zugleich die Struktur sichtbar zu machen, die ihn hervorbringt' (324) still holds true. The following outline therefore represents an attempt to show where semiotic analysis is likely to contribute new insights into the peculiarities of Brecht's innovations.

Exhibited Semiotic Processes

The reference to a 'Sichtbarmachen' of the structures which cause an event pinpoints an important factor in relating semiotic technique to critical function. As anyone familiar with Roland Barthes' approach in *Mythologies* will be aware, this is an issue of essentially ideological importance. The 'sémiologie générale de notre monde bourgeois', as Barthes calls his *Mythologies* project, involves a process of decoding in order to reveal 'l'abus idéologique qui [...] s'y trouve caché'.[18] What I have called the 'Exhibited Semiotic Processes' in Brecht's theatre have a similar ideological purpose.

Two features of the 'wedding'-scene near the beginning of *Die Dreigroschenoper* show such politically significant processes of semiosis at work. The dominant yet simpler one relates to the transformation by Macheath's gang of a 'Leerer Pferdestall' (*BFA*, 2, 240) into a place fit for a genteel reception: *'Man hört große Lastwagen anfahren, ein halbes Dutzend Leute kommen herein, die Teppiche, Möbel, Geschirr usw. schleppen, womit sie den Stall in ein übertrieben feines Lokal verwandeln'* (*BFA*, 2, 241). One recognizable milieu, a stable, has been transformed into another one, full of deceptive emotional associations and therefore in need of estrangement. Referential décor, signifying a stable, is metamorphosed before our very eyes into its social antithesis, though of course that first simulated reality was also only to a limited extent an iconic sign for 'stable'. This classic example of Epic Theatre's exploration at *plot-level* of its own artifices is more than just an aesthetic reflection of the way the theatre's visual signs work. As Brecht says in his notes, the situation satirized in this scene is in real life itself highly artificial. We may not endorse all aspects of his cynical gloss ('Zu zeigen ist die Ausstellung der Braut, ihrer Fleischlichkeit, im Augenblick der endgültigen Reservierung. Zu dem Zeitpunkt nämlich, wo das Angebot aufzuhören hat'); but his conclusion ('Es handelt sich also um ein durchaus theatralisches Ereignis', *BFA*, 24, 63) remains incontestable. Two highly codified sign-systems, that of a euphemistic social ritual and that of its critical presentation on stage, are brought together to make a political point about marriage, exploitation and the dangers of false sentimentality.

How the semiotic principles are foregrounded comes out most clearly in another of the stage-directions: *'Das Paar stellt sich in Gratulationspositur'* (*BFA*, 2, 243). A bourgeois ritual (the giving and receiving of congratulations) is being cited – rather than faithfully imitated – by means of exaggerated iconic behaviour which highlights its underlying contractual significance (going through the required motions for reciprocal personal gain, exploitation masquerading as generosity, power-transactions disguised as bonding). But to communicate 'die Vorgänge hinter den Vorgängen' (*BFA*, 22:1, 519), the method's iconicity needs to be sufficiently non-isomorphic for both social and aesthetic signs to be recognized for what they are: deceptive sign-systems that need other sign-systems to uncover their mechanisms and real function.

The kind of effect displayed here is very close to what Wekwerth means by the 'doppelte Struktur' of a large proportion of Brecht's theatrical signs:

> *die Zeichen des Theaters* [...] *müssen nicht nur Realität abbilden.* [...] *Die Zeichen des Theaters müssen im Moment der Vorführung selbst Realität besitzen, damit der Zuschauer in doppelter Weise mit ihnen umgehen kann: als Abbild von Realität* und als Teil der Realität. Das Theater kann also nicht beliebige abstrakte Zeichen wählen (wie das die Pop-Richtung versucht oder der Symbolismus Grotowskis), sondern die Zeichen müssen selbst Ausdruck menschlichen Verhaltens sein, also realer

beobachteter Vorgänge. Sie müssen – wie Brecht sagt – gestisches Material sein, also unmittelbarer Ausdruck menschlichen Verhaltens. (370, my italics)

Obviously, one could reformulate such a statement to bring out the point that, in order to facilitate critical distance, theatrical signs have limited iconicity, offset by distancing indexical and symbolic elements. A 'Gratulationspositur' thus not only partially mimics the body-language of the real-life situation, by including non-iconic elements – and omitting other iconic features – it becomes a more critically coded version of the sign-system to which it refers. But as we can see here, changes in terminology do not necessarily bring about genuine cognitive advances. However, there are other areas where they do so.

As has been pointed out, 'while there is an iconic aspect or characteristic of things, there is nothing that is purely iconic'.[19] The idea is central to Charles Morris' approach in his *Foundations of the Theory of Signs*. Instead of locating discrete iconic signs, Morris was more interested in such qualitative concepts as 'iconicity' which allow semiotics to dissect the various *degrees* of iconicity, indexicality etc. in a given sign. And it is this idea of the impure sign or sign-system, displaying a predominant component, but possessing other sign-elements as well, which is able to cope in a more sophisticated way with some of the effects of Brechtian theatre. We can appreciate the advantages of such a methodology if we look at three familiar examples of the iconic in Brecht's work: Mutter Courage, the 'Marketenderin', as a representation of capitalism; the mask Shen Te dons to become Shui Ta in *Der gute Mensch von Sezuan*; and the circle imagery used in *Der kaukasische Kreidekreis*.

Mutter Courage is obviously an iconic representation of the capitalist type (and a recognition that characters themselves are also 'Zeichen' may help shift the focus beyond stage-props to other parts of the system). But such a sign is not isomorphic; it is possible to isolate a number of features which reveal the marked limitations to the iconicity of the Courage-sign. The word 'capitalist' denotes a modern phenomenon, whereas Courage is inserted into a parable set during the Thirty Years War. Capitalists make profit; but Courage's fortunes fluctuate, she is never affluent. Her garb, her mode of transport, even her idiom, all conspire to restrict iconicity and make the chosen sign a form of 'Verfremdung'. We may, of course, be left in no doubt about Mutter Courage's other capitalist attributes: her materialistic mode of thinking, the link between the profit-goal and warmongering, the cost she exacts from those she exploits (including herself) and her symptomatic false consciousness. Not only would it be rewarding to analyse the amalgam of iconic and other factors in the Courage-sign, one would be in a position to gauge the extent to which the sign's cognitive value depends on it not being overly iconic.

The same is true of the mask-sign in *Der gute Mensch von Sezuan*. Although necessarily iconic in some respects, masks function more complexly in Brecht's works than this implies. The Shui Ta mask is not reacted to or discussed by characters in the play; when Shen Te first appears wearing it, no one mentions it, its role is that of a direct signal to the audience, suggesting the kind of 'Härte' necessary for survival (*BFA*, 6, 220). Similarly, the link between mask and artifice reminds us of the phrase 'Etwas muß *falsch* sein an eurer Welt' (*BFA*, 6, 275, my italics). But there are other conceivable associations. Despite the fact that reference is made to Shen Te's having been torn in 'zwei Hälften', the more significant aspect of the mask-image is that the play uses only one mask, not two (there could have been one for her Shen Te persona, another for Shui Ta). The mask-sign's restricted application to Shui Ta has the rhetorical advantage of implying that the true person is Shen Te and that her ruthless cousin is a role forced upon her by social conditions, not part of her true self. As in *Leben des Galilei*, where Galilei has no mask whereas Bellarmin and Barberini self-consciously masquerade as lamb and dove, the function of the sign depends on a contrastive structure where absence is equally significant. Indeed, the interplay between the iconicity factor and the place of signs within a work's internal system is something to which Wekwerth rightly draws attention: 'Dennoch sind es nicht nur "ikonische" Zeichen, sondern auch sie bekommen ihre Bedeutung nur *über das System*, welches durch den Schauspieler, die Regie, den Stückschreiber, die Vorführung auf der Bühne organisiert wird' (370). Moreover, the mask is present both literally and figuratively: Shen Te/Shui Ta may appear both masked and maskless, but there are many characters in the play whom we are invited to read as being metaphorical mask-wearers. Clearly, despite the latitude of interpretation it permits, the mask-sign is iconic, even if only in part (it is also an index of the lengths Shen Te is prepared to go to to protect her child and of her willingness to assume the 'Verhalten' of those around herwhen the need arises). Like so many of Brecht's characterizing sign-systems, such a sign demands quite a high degree of participation on the audience's part before meaning has been created.

Much the same holds true for the circle-imagery in *Der kaukasische Kreidekreis*. In fact, we find two – possibly even three – circle-images that function as signs within the play. The most important, the one which gives the play its title, comes right at the end:

AZDAK [...] Ich werd eine Probe machen. Schauwa, nimm ein Stück Kreide. Zieh einen Kreis auf den Boden. *Schauwa zieht einen Kreis mit Kreide auf den Boden.* Stell das Kind hinein! *Schauwa stellt Michel, der Grusche zulächelt, in den Kreis.* Klägerin und Angeklagte, stellt euch neben den Kreis, beide! *Die Gouverneursfrau und Grusche treten neben den Kreis.* Faß das Kind bei der Hand. Die richtige Mutter wird die Kraft haben, das Kind aus dem Kreis zu sich zu ziehen. (*BFA*, 8, 183)

The ensuing test and its implications are too well-known to require recounting here. But for the purposes of a semiotic evaluation, we need to bear in mind that Azdak's chalk circle achieves at least some of its meaning – contrastively – by being juxtaposed with other instances of circle-imagery in the play.

The first is in some respects the opposite of Azdak's circle. It comes in the stage directions to the *Vorspiel: 'Zwischen den Trümmern eines zerschossenen kaukasischen Dorfes sitzen im Kreis, weintrinkend und rauchend, Mitglieder zweier Kolchosdörfer, meist Frauen und ältere Männer, doch auch einige Soldaten'* (*BFA*, 8, 95). This circle is the token of a community at peace with itself; subsequently it becomes the egalitarian circle of the local *soviet* where people debate harmoniously and arrive at mutually acceptable decisions. Even later, as the peasants foregather to watch the play after the 'Aufbruch [zum Essen]' (*BFA*, 8, 100) it becomes the circle of theatre-in-the-round. The initial positive circle image contrasts with the one in the chalk circle test at the end, both because of the latter's association with Natella Abaschwili's grasping response to the proposed gruesome tug-of-love and also because, as the instrument of Azdak's rough-and-ready means to justice, it compares unfavourably with the politically sanctioned circle of revolutionaries at the start of the play. There are structural differences, too. In Scene One, the circle is a containing form, with all people facing inwards, whereas the aim of the participants in the chalk circle test is to rupture the protective circle by pulling the child out with potentially disastrous consequences. Ultimately, these patterns assume even more importance because the circles are essentially emblems for different types of society. Here again, as Wekwerth noted, theatrical signs attain their meaning through the audience. Semiosis, too, is very much part of what Brecht saw as the requisite audience-response of 'Ko-Fabulieren' (*BFA*, 23, 301).

The Estranging Interplay between Icons, Indices and Symbols

A strictly taxonomic approach to Brecht's use of signs would, of course, content itself with the identification and quantification of the types deployed. Yet it is clear that much of what Brecht terms 'gegenseitige Verfremdung' was achieved, not through the privileging of just one kind of sign but by tensions between various sign-ingredients which do not normally interact in such a way. This is readily visible in the case of the technique Brecht called 'Literarisierung' (*BFA*, 22:1, 265), a major embodiment of the new kind of creative interplay between iconic, indexical and symbolic elements for fresh cognitive purposes. 'Die Literarisierung bedeutet das Durchsetzen des "Gestalteten" mit "Formuliertem"' Brecht declares in the 'Titel und Tafeln' section of 'Literarisierung des Theaters. Anmerkungen zur *Dreigroschenoper*' (*BFA*, 24, 58). Yet while 'Literarisierung' has been most frequently associated with the *Spruchbänder* and verses that tended to be used at the start of scenes, Brecht's theatre contains significantly more heterogeneous instances of the technique than the attendant theorizing would suggest. Indeed, Brecht once admitted that his early experiments with 'Titel und Tafeln' represented no more than 'ein primitiver Anlauf zur *Literarisierung des Theaters*' (*BFA*, 24, 58).

We have already encountered one instance of 'Literarisierung' in the passage concerning Azdak's chalk circle test, for what it consisted of was a strangely plodding mixture of instructions and resultant actions. A comparable image-plus-verbalization effect is employed in the following passages from *Leben des Galilei*. At the start of the play Andrea is told 'Stell die Milch auf den Tisch, aber klapp kein Buch zu' (*BFA*, 5, 189); which he duly does. But this is no more a realistic representation of an order and its execution than was the case with *Der kaukasische Kreidekreis*. On the surface, admittedly, what we are already able to observe is tautologously rendered in language: 'DER THEOLOGE *das zerbrochene ptolemäische Modell am Boden sehend*: Hier scheint etwas entzweigegangen' (*BFA*, 5, 218). Or during the scene outside the Collegium Romanum as Galilei and the clerics await Clavius's verdict: 'DER ERSTE GELEHRTE *zu Galilei*: Herr Galilei, Ihnen ist etwas hinabgefallen' (*BFA*, 5, 232), but of course the audience will have already noticed this, given that Galilei dropped his *Beweisstein* in such a demonstrative manner. Another example comes in the recantation scene: '*In diesem Augenblick beginnt die Glocke von Sankt Markus zu dröhnen* [...] VIRGINIA [...] Die Glocke von Sankt Markus!' (*BFA*, 5, 273). In 'Über die Literarisierung der Bühnen', (*BFA*, 22:1, 265f), Brecht confronts the objection that the device might be considered 'überflüssig'. His argument here, coupled with the complexity of his practice, shows quite clearly that verbal commentaries of this kind, while they may seem to do no more than duplicate information, are far from redundant because they serve a number of further functions. And one of these, due to the way in which (visual) iconic and (verbal) symbolic signs interact, is essentially an estranging one.

In the examples just cited, verbalization sometimes comes first, at other times it follows the action, in the guise of a reaction, an explanation or as a *Verfremdung* of it (cf. the verbs 'hinabgefallen'/ 'hinaufgefallen'). Brecht's recommendations concerning possible projections to some of the discovery scenes in *Leben des Galilei* are revealing. 'In der vierten Szene', he suggests, 'können auf dem Schirm [...] die Sonnenflecken wandernd gezeigt werden' (*BFA*, 24, 234); his comment 'Man kann Galilei dazu hören' suggests that he does not conceive the illustration to be a supporting dimension to the action on stage, but what is happening on stage is being thought of as standing in an illustrative relationship to the projection.

While seeming to overdetermine the message, the device in fact contributes substantially to the *Episierung* of its material. And it does so sometimes by moving not only between *iconic* and *symbolic* signs (action and commentary, images and analysis, speech and projected images), but also at other times by introducing a measure of interaction between indexical and other types of sign: the bell of San Marco, the *Beweisstein*, the broken Ptolemaic model. An analysis of the various constituents of such effects would show that 'Literarisierung' is a far more sophisticated semiotic effect than the 'Titel und Tafeln' paradigm would suggest.

Signs, Structures and Codes

In his account of Brecht's notion of Gestus, Patrice Pavis cites the canonical passage in 'Über reimlose Lyrik mit unregelmäßigen Rhythmen' where a biblical example of 'gestische Sprache' is discussed:

> Der Satz der Bibel 'Reiße das Auge aus, das dich ärgert' hat einen Gestus unterlegt, den des Befehls, aber er ist doch nicht rein gestisch ausgedrückt, da 'das dich ärgert' eigentlich noch einen anderen Gestus hat, der nicht zum Ausdruck kommt, nämlich den einer Begründung. Rein gestisch ausgedrückt, heißt der Satz (und Luther, der 'dem Volk aufs Maul sah', formt ihn auch so): 'Wenn dich dein Auge ärgert: reiß es aus!' Man sieht wohl auf den ersten Blick, daß diese Formulierung gestisch viel reicher und reiner ist. (*BFA*, 22:1, 359f)

Pavis concludes that Brecht here highlights 'one of the key problems of theatre semiology: the link between *iconic* system [...] based on the resemblance between the sign and its object, and the *symbolic* system which is based on the arbitrariness of the sign.'[20] Even though it may seem an uncontentious example by comparison with the difficulty the term 'Gestus' has generally caused commentators, the sentence represents a complex amalgam of iconic and symbolic elements, as well as thematized indexicality. Its iconic component, the

relationship between narrative order and sequence of narrated events, is the result
of an entire syntactic structure, the individual elements of which are symbols.
Just as with much shaped poetry, while the components are 'arbitrary', the
relationship between the constituent parts of the super-sign *in toto* transforms the
effect into something iconic. And sequence is iconic, not only at the micro-
structural sentence level of Brecht's plays, but in their overall epic structural
organization.

The nature of the individual signs used and the structures in which they
achieve meaning are only two of the salient features of semiosis. The third, and it
is equally important for many of Brecht's effects, is coding. The force of this can
be seen if one looks at Manfred Wekwerth's most detailed semiotic commentary:
on the Ensemble's production of the final scene of *Mutter Courage und ihre
Kinder*, where he brings out the difference between theatrically coded iconicity
and simple mimesis.

Einer der großen Eindrücke der Aufführung *Mutter Courage und ihre Kinder* war der
Schluß. Mutter Courage hat durch den Krieg alles verloren und zieht, immer noch
unbelehrbar, den zerlumpten Heerhaufen nach, um im fünfundzwanzigsten Jahr des
mörderischen Krieges doch noch ihren Schnitt zu machen. Zu dem grölenden und
müden Gesang der aufbrechenden Truppen spannt sie sich, umständlich die Traggurte
über die Schulter ordnend, vor ihren leeren Planwagen und zieht ihn mit zäher
Anstrengung den abrückenden Soldaten nach. Brecht wollte zeigen, daß sie sich in der
Unendlichkeit des überfälligen Krieges verliert. Er gab der Szene den Titel "Mutter
Courage als zuletzt gesehen". Naheliegend war es, den Wagen mit der Courage nach
hinten fahren zu lassen, um ihn auf der Hinterbühne verschwinden zu lassen, so daß
sich die Courage auf der Bühne wirklich verliert. Die Wirkung war minimal: Es war ein
normaler Abgang. Die Lösung kam durch einen Zufall: Nach einem Versuch, den
Wagen hinten verschwinden zu lassen, kam die Weigel mitsamt dem Wagen wieder
nach vorn, um zu hören, was die Regisseure sagten. Die Wirkung war enorm. Denn sie
kam nicht wirklich nach vorn, sondern es wirkte, als setzte sie ihren Weg ins
Unendliche fort, da das Rund der Drehscheibe während der ganzen Aufführung als der
"lange Weg" durch den Krieg etabliert war. Während der ganzen Aufführung fuhr der
Wagen der Courage, wenn er "kreuz und quer durch Europa" streifte, immer im Kreis
herum am Rand der Drehscheibe entlang. Dem Zuschauer war diese Verabredung
durch das ganze Stück eingegangen. Er kannte die Struktur, durch welche die Zeichen
eine Bedeutung erlangten. Selbst wenn nun der Wagen (das Zeichen der Courage und
ihrer Familie) auf ihn zurollte, nahm er dies für ein Wegfahren des Wagens, solange er
auf dem Rand der Drehscheibe fuhr.
    Wir begriffen, daß wir bei der Darstellung des "Verlierens des Wagens in die
Unendlichkeit" nicht den Wagen in Realität verlieren durften, sondern wir mußten uns
an die während des Stückes verabredeten Zeichen halten. Brecht ließ den Wagen,
gezogen von der zerlumpten Courage, nun wieder auf dem Rand der Drehscheibe
fahren. Zunächst nach hinten, dann den 12 Meter breiten Rundhorizont entlang wieder
nach vorn, direkt auf den Zuschauer zu. Schwenkte er dann wieder um nach hinten ein,
schloß sich der Vorhang. Selten ist der Unterschied zwischen der Realität des Theaters

und seiner Bedeutung als Zeichen der Realität deutlicher geworden als hier. Obwohl die Realität der Bühne dem Wegfahren widersprach (denn der Wagen kam schließlich wieder nach vorn), nahm der Zuschauer dies als *Zeichen* des Wegfahrens. (384f)

The idea that a work 'generates its own code of which [it] is the only message'[21] may, in the face of Epic Theatre's discontinuities, need to be modified to apply to the changing methods of individual scenes; but the above illustration does already give some indication of just how local the systems of codification can be. In general, however, what a semiotic approach to Brecht also needs to address is the whole interaction between the *Verfremdung* of society's own cultural codes and those used by theatre to depict and criticize them.

Supersigns, Systems and Models

In his 'Überlegungen zu einer Modelltheorie des Theaters' (297), Wekwerth has developed further his earlier ideas on the way in which individual signs – and by extension, sign-systems – operate into an account of how models function:

Es gibt die Behauptung, Theater [...] trage insofern Modellcharakter, als es Sachverhalte der Wirklichkeit isomorph (oder homomorph) in den Sachverhalten der Fabel (oder des Sujets) abbilde. Diese Behauptung ist fragwürdig, da in ihr weder das Theater noch die Kunst vorkommen. [...] Kunst ist [...] in erster Linie eine menschliche Beziehung. In ihr realisieren sich Sachverhalte [...] zu Verhalten, sowohl des einen wie des anderen. Produkt der Kunst ist nicht der Sachverhalt einer Fabel (oder eines Sujets), sondern die Produktion von Verhalten, indem sich die Sachverhalte auflösen (aufheben). So erreicht nicht etwa eine modellierte Wirklichkeit den Zuschauer, sondern ein wirkliches Modell. Diesem gegenüber tritt ein anderes Modell. Das nämlich, das der Zuschauer von seiner Umwelt, in der er produziert, im Kopf hat. Die Wirklichkeit, will sie zu Kunst werden, muß also zweimal aufgelöst (modelliert) werden: vom Künstler *und* vom Zuschauer. Nur wenn beide Systeme etabliert und genügend stabil (invariant) sind, kann im Zusammentreffen beider Kunst entstehen.

Wekwerth has here begun to integrate the 'Modell-' or 'Parabelstück' genre into his thinking about Brechtian semiosis. Again, although his theorizing is moving remarkably early in a productive new direction, Wekwerth was not to be the only person to be considering the relationship between semiotics and the theory of models at this time.

In 'Iconic Signs, Supersigns and Models', Martin Krampen indicates a number of fruitful perspectives from which the iconicity of supersigns can be investigated. In general, he argues, work on the theory of models is far more advanced than that on iconic (super-)signs. Hence, since iconic sign-systems and models in many ways function comparably, there are good grounds for attempting a 'mapping of supersigns into the domain of models'.[22] Krampen itemizes a number of two-part distinctions – between isomorphic and heteromorphic, structural and qualitative, isohylic and analogical models – and Mieczyzlaw Wallis has also differentiated between different forms of model, ranging from 'extremely simplified' ones, 'devoid of details', to which he gives the collective name 'schemata', through to those 'rich in details' which he calls 'pleromata'.[23]

The relevance of such systematizing to Brecht's use of 'Modelle' can be appreciated if one considers certain elements of *Modellhaftigkeit* in the first scene of *Leben des Galilei*, where Galilei is attempting to overcome Andrea's resistance to the heliocentric theory. His starting-point is the fact that the boy's eyes seem to be telling him that the sun *does* move across the sky each day. What follows is an object-lesson in critical thinking via the use of models. Establishing the washstand (its very cumbersomeness suggesting that it is unlikely to move) as an (iconic) sign for the sun, Galilei has the boy sit on a chair and then carries him around (i.e. boy on chair standing for man on earth). Using these simple props, he tries to demonstrate that one half-revolution of Andrea's chair puts the washstand in a different place without it having moved. But the boy is unhappy at the lack of fit between the model and what it purportedly represents:

> es stimmt nicht. Den Stuhl mit mir haben Sie nur seitwärts um sich selber gedreht und nicht so. *Macht eine Armbewegung vornüber.* Sonst wäre ich nämlich heruntergefallen, und das ist ein Fakt. Warum haben Sie den Stuhl nicht vorwärts gedreht? Weil dann bewiesen ist, daß ich von der Erde ebenfalls herunterfallen würde, wenn sie sich so drehen würde (*BFA*, 5, 193f).

With an apple and a splinter, Galilei then comes up with a more persuasive model and wins Andrea over.

By being confronted with an iconic model, Andrea is learning to think critically about an ideologically important aspect of perceptible reality. One feature of both models on offer is that they are selective and hence simplify. It is worth bearing in mind in this context a remark which Brecht made about his 'Straßenszene' paradigm: 'Die Demonstrationsmöglichkeiten unseres Straßendemonstranten sind eng begrenzt (wir haben das Modell gewählt, um zumöglichst engen Grenzen zu gelangen)' (*BFA*, 22:1, 375). Andrea is acquiring the ability to evaluate such simple models, to gauge how isomorphic and how cognitively rewarding they are, but without confusing the two properties. So too is the audience. Arguably, this incident would not be so protracted and come so early, if one of its functions were not also to introduce the audience to the methods of the 'Modellstück'. That is to say: two models of unequal didactic value are being deployed to teach both Andrea and us how iconic models work. The skill in operating with models acquired here is ultimately of importance in relating the larger model – the entire parable-play *Leben des Galilei* – to the real-life problems of which it is a representation. Adopting Wallis' taxonomy, we could say that in Scene One two 'schemata' are being used to initiate the audience into coming to terms with more complex 'pleromata'. But again, taxonomic labelling is by no means the ultimate goal. By using model-theory to relate different forms of sign-system, it would eventually be possible to quanitify and analyse not just the relationship of 'modellierte Wirklichkeit' to actual 'Wirklichkeit' (Wekwerth's terms), but to account for the structural relationship between various 'schemata' and 'pleromata' within works. Songs offering a *mise-en-abyme* of the larger model, scientific experiments which serve as miniature models of the social issues explored in *Leben des Galilei* (sinking/floating, size and the laws of gravity), even locally inserted 'schemata' such as proverbial expressions, similes, figurative descriptions or elements of the 'Bühnenbild' can, as sign-systems with varying degrees of sophistication, benefit from being analysed comparatively within the framework of a model-theory which analytically approaches the model as a system of sign-types.

Sign-Systems, Models and Ideology

One of the most striking features of Wekwerth's exploration of Brechtian sign-systems is his insistent locating of the discussion within an epistemological framework. He presents the preliminary distinction between natural and arbitrary signs, for instance, not just as a matter of linguistics or semiotics, but as 'eine Entdeckung der modernen Erkenntnistheorie' (321). Likewise he situates much of the theoretical presentation of Brechtian theatre's 'modellierte Wirklichkeit' within the framework of Georg Klaus's *Spezielle Erkenntnistheorie* (325). The reason for this stress on epistemology could, of course, simply be the fact that Wekwerth's theorizing was to some considerable extent indebted to Klaus's mediation of the thinking of others, including Peirce, Saussure and Morris. But there is another, more important factor involved – an ideological one.

One can in general distinguish between two radically different attitudes to semiosis: the one cognitively optimistic, stressing the ways in which signs, sign-systems and models assist the understanding of the world and the mediation of that understanding, the other more concerned with the way in which signs have a mystifying purpose. Earlier on I referred to the way in which Barthes used a process of semiotic decoding to reveal what he saw as the ideological manipulation of consciousness at the root of many artificial sign-systems assumed by their victims to be 'natural'. 'Ces exercices d'une grammaire aberrante auraient au moins l'avantage de porter le soupçon sur l'idéologie même de notre parole', as he puts it elsewhere.[24] Brecht's own method is to some considerable extent Barthesian, in this respect, with the signs he thematizes and de-mythologizes being presented largely as symptoms of false consciousness. The two flags hoisted in *Mutter Courage und ihre Kinder*, the one a sign of Protestant allegiance, the other Catholic, the uniforms of the two SS officers wandering drunkenly through a proletarian part of Berlin in the 'Volksgemeinschaft' scene of *Furcht und Elend des Dritten Reiches* beg to be decoded in the spirit of *Mythologies*. The uniform could have connoted officer-class material, yet this is no 'Wehrmacht' but the SS (where an anti-élite rises to the top); moreover, the Nazi uniform, although signifying one kind of political persuasion contrasts with the true class-interests and even identities of those wearing it. Signs in Brecht's theatre often have to be approached in a sceptical way for they tend to be the signs used by the enemy. However, Brecht seems on the whole reluctant to subject his own ideological semiotics to the same ruthless theoretical questioning and sceptical decoding. Marxism's signs must be assumed to be part of a cognitively dependable construct, unlike capitalism's *instrumentarium* of manipulated false consciousness. There is, however, a splendid moment of self-questioning on this subject at one point in *Leben des Galilei*, when Andrea says to Galilei, after his practical tutorial on the heliocentric system: 'Nehmen Sie nicht lauter solche Beispiele, Herr Galilei. Damit schaffen Sie's immer. [...] Mit Beispielen kann man es immer schaffen, wenn man schlau ist' (*BFA*, 5, 194).

---

1. *Sinn und Form*, 20 (1968), 542-70, re-published in Manfred Wekwerth, *Schriften. Arbeit mit Brecht* (Berlin, Henschelverlag Kunst und Gesellschaft, Berlin, 1973), pp. 298-326. My quotations from Wekwerth's writings on Brecht will be taken from this volume.

2. Keir Elam, *The Semiotics of Theatre and Drama* (London, Methuen, 1980), p.8.

3. Brecht, *BFA*, 22:1, pp.260f. Subsequent references to this edition of Brecht's works will be given in parenthesis after quotations.

4. *Collected Papers of Charles Sanders Peirce*, vol. 2: *Elements of Logic*, ed. Charles Hartshorne and Paul Weiss (Cambridge/Mass., Belknap Press, 1960), pp.168f.

5. Uberto Eco, *A Theory of Semiotics* (Bloomington/ Indiana, Indiana U.P, 1975), p. 178.

6. Quoted from Morris' *Writings on the General Theory of Semiotics* (The Hague-Paris, Mouton, 1971), p. 273.

7. In this respect, Wekwerth's approach can be seen as part of what Thomas A. Sebeok dismisses as 'a period of furious flirtation' between Marxism and semiotics in the sixties, in *Semiotics in the United States* (Bloomington and Indianapolis, Indiana U.P., 1991), p.126. On the standing of the main fruits of this interaction – L. O Rjeznikov's *Gnoseologicheskie voprosy semiotiki* (Leningrad U.P., 1964) and Georg Klaus's *Semiotik und Erkenntnistheorie* (Wilhelm Fink Verlag, Munich 1962) – see Augusto Ponzio, 'Notes on Semiotics and Marxism', *Recherches sémiotiques*, 4 (1984), 293-302 and 'Semiotics and Marxism', *The Semiotic Web*, ed. Thomas A. Sebeok and Jean Umiker-Sebeok (Berlin, Mouton-De Gruyter, 1988), pp.387-416.

8. Elam sees a key aspect of Brecht's importance for the theatre as lying in 'the gesture of putting on show the very process of semiotization involved in the performance' (*The Semiotics of Theatre and Drama*, p.9).

9. See *BFA*, 22:

10. When presenting his new '*science qui étudie la vie des signes au sein de la vie sociale*', Ferdinand de Saussure immediately saw it as a contribution to 'la psychologie sociale' (*Cours de Linguistique Générale*, ed. Charles Bally and Albert Sechehaye, Bibliothèque scientifique, 1955, p.33).

11. Elam, *The Semiotics of Theatre and Drama*, p.22. Elam's reference is to Kott's article 'The Icon and the Absurd', *The Drama Review*, 14 (1969), 17-24.

12. E.g. the symposium on 'Art as Semiotic System' (Moscow, 1962) and the two Polish International Semiological Colloquia (Kazimierz, 1966 and Warsaw, 1968), the proceedings of the latter being published as *Recherches sur les Systèmes signifiants*, ed. J. Rey-Debove (The Hague-Paris, Mouton, 1968), T. Kowzan's 'Znak w teatrze' (*Dialog 3*, 1969), as well as the influence Georg Klaus's ideas had on the 'Philosophiezirkel' connected with the Berliner Ensemble (cf. Wekwerth, p.295). Wekwerth refers to Klaus's *Spezielle Erkenntnistheorie* and to work by Karl Berka in the *Deutsche Zeitschrift für Philosophie*.

13. On the context of Barthes's Brecht-reception, see Steve Giles, 'Post/Structuralist Brecht? Representation and Subjectivity in *Der Dreigroschenprozeß*', *The Brecht Yearbook: The Other Brecht 1*, 17 (1992), 147-63.

14. 'Foundations: Signs in the Theatre', *The Semiotics of Theatre and Drama*, pp.22f.

15. 'Unser tägliches Theater', *Die Zeit*, 17 Nov. 1976, 34.

16. Cf. Elaine Aston and G. Savogna, Theatre *as Sign System. A Semiotics of Text and Performance* (London, Routledge, 1991); Marvin Carlson, *Theatre Semiotics* (Bloomington, Indiana U.P., 1990); Andre Helbo, *Sémiologie de la représentation* (Brussels, Complexe, 1975); Ernest H.B. Hess-Lüttich (ed.), *Semiotics of the Theater* (Berlin, De Gruyter-Mouton, 1981); Jarmila Hoensch, *Das Schauspiel und seine Zeichen* (Bern, Lang, 1977); and Susan Melrose, *A Semiotics of the Dramatic Text* (London, Methuen, 1994).

17. 'Das Zeichen und das Objekt haben zunächst nichts miteinander zu tun. Allein für sich genommen kann man dem Wort einer fremden Sprache nicht entnehmen, was es bedeutet,

nicht einmal der altägyptischen Bildersprache. Man muß das System kennen (das syntaktische und semantische). Und das ist die wichtigste Entdeckung, die die Linguistik für das menschliche Denken gemacht hat: Das Denken bedient sich bestimmter Zeichen, die sich im Laufe der Geschichte mit einer gewissen Willkür gebildet haben (wissenschaftlich heißen sie Symbole), die nach einem durch die Gesellschaft geschaffenen System organisiert sind, um Sachverhalte nicht direkt, sondern nur analog abzubilden (man könnte es auch metaphorisch nennen)' (Wekwerth, p.320)

[18.]   Roland Barthes, *Mythologies* (Paris, Gallimard, 1957), p.7.

[19.]   John J. Fitzgerald, *Peirce's Theory of Signs as Foundation for Pragmatism* (The Hague-Paris, Mouton), p.53.

[20.]   'On Brecht's Notion of Gestus', in Herta Schmid and Aloysius Van Kesteren (eds.), *Semiotics of Drama and Theatre* (Amsterdam and Philadelphia, John Benjamins, 1984), p.301.

[21.]   Thomas Sebeok, *Linguistic Structures in Poetry* (The Hague-Paris, Mouton, 1966), p.51.

[22.]   *Versus*, 4, iii (1973), 106.

[23.]   'The History of Art as the History of Semantic Structures', in *Sign - Language - Culture*, ed. J. A. Greimas et al. (The Hague-Paris, Mouton, 1970), p.524.

[24.]   Roland Barthes, *L'Empire des signes* (Geneva, Albert Skira, 1970), p.17

FREDDIE ROKEM

The Meanings of the Circle in Brecht's Theatre

> We're really just at the beginning.
> B. Brecht, *Life of Galileo*

Bertolt Brecht's attempts gradually to develop his theatrical language, in the broadest possible sense of this term, can be examined in a number of different ways. Brecht did not simply reject the drama and the theatrical concepts of the previous generation, but worked systematically towards creating a new integrated form of theatre which he felt would be able to serve his aesthetic as well as his ideological aims. From the point of view of the theatrical space, which is the main topic of this essay, this new form was expressed by different uses of the circle. The circular modes of representation and visuality that he experimented with are based on radically different premises from those out of which the European theatrical tradition, culminating at the end of the 19th century in the realistic theatre, had developed.

This tradition, most clearly perceived as stemming directly from the Baroque theatre, had created a visual apparatus on the basis of modes of perception primarily based on the geometrical concepts of the straight line and perspective drawing. In this article, which will examine certain aspects of *Mother Courage and her Children*, *Life of Galileo* and *The Messingkauf Dialogues*, I want to show how Brecht, in trying to create a paradigm of theatrical representation and perception which was based on the circle, revolted against this tradition. Brecht's notion of the circle also had profound implications for his comprehensive theoretical and ideological understanding of the theatre and it also influenced his theatrical practices, as a writer for the stage as well as a director.

When, in the opening scene of *Mother Courage and Her Children* the 'wagon is rolled forward against the movement of the revolving stage',[1] as Brecht prescribed in 'The Mother Courage Model', two circular movements are actually superimposed on each other. The revolving stage was turning clockwise while the wagon moved counter-clockwise from left to right, as perceived from the point of view of the audience. What the spectators saw as a result of this superimposition was a double circular movement in two opposite directions.

Such a contradictory movement is at the same time also perceived as a stasis, because the wagon in fact remains in one and the same place.

These two opposite circular movements are the basis for the complex dialectics which can be perceived and formulated simultaneously both in terms of motion and stasis. Furthermore, the theatrical machinery, and in particular the revolving stage, not only provides the support or background against which the movements and the actions of the characters gradually evolve, but can also be viewed as an active participant, a kind of resistance, or a real hindrance, against which they have to struggle. In the postscript to his short essay 'Stage Design for the Epic Theatre' from 1951, which was also included in the fragments to the *Messingkauf Dialogues*, which Brecht considered to be one of his most important projects, and to which I will return later, he notes that,

> it's more important nowadays for the set to tell the spectator he's in the theatre than to tell him he's in, say, Aulis. The theatre must acquire 'qua' theatre the same fascinating reality as a sporting arena during a boxing match. The best thing is to show the machinery, the ropes and the flies.[2]

The theatrical machinery, in this case the revolving stage, has to become an active participant in the theatrical action, delineating a central aspect of the so-called *Gestus* of Mother Courage. According to this *Gestus*, in spite of her constant movement it is not possible for her to progress from one point to another.

By incorporating the theatrical machinery as an active participant in the central dramatic action or *Gestus* of his performance of *Mother Courage and her Children*, Brecht takes advantage of the new-stage-technologies and transforms them into an integral aspect of the meaning he wishes to communicate. It was Lautenschlaeger who, on the basis of the Japanese Kabuki-stage, constructed the first revolving stage moved by electricity at the Residenztheater in Munich in 1896. And Max Reinhardt, during the first years of the 20th century, demonstrated what some of the artistic potentials of the revolving stage were. In particular Reinhardt's production of *A Midsummer Night's Dream* at the Deutsches Theater in Berlin in 1905, where the forest moved in front of the audience, contributed to the popularity of this device. According to Gosta Bergman this was an anti-realistic effect emphasizing that theatre is finally theatre and not in fact an imitation of reality[3].

Brecht developed the theatricalizing use of this stage-machinery even further. According to David Richard Jones a complex ensemble of circles was the most prevailing image which gradually developed in the production of

Mother Courage and Her Children from 1949 at the Berliner; Ensemble, which Brecht himself directed in the still war-torn city:

> On the floor was a large circle. Around the back of the circle ran the cyclorama, and at the front was the arc of the footlights. The sets were placed on this circle, scenes were acted on it, and the travelling - a central production image - took place around its great circumference. The circle was the world of Mother Courage.[4]

It is also significant that in this production, Brecht chose to disregard the opening dialogue between the Recruiter and the Sergeant, with which the printed version begins.[5] Instead the performance started by letting the half-curtain be drawn while the turntable was already moving and having the wagon gradually come into view. The first image of Brecht's production was thus, as mentioned before, that the wagon was simultaneously 'moving' and 'not moving' as it is drawn by the two sons, serving as 'horses'(!), while Mother Courage herself and her mute daughter Kattrin were seated on the wagon.

In the film-version of this production of 1960, directed by Peter Palitzsch and Manfred Wekwerth, to document the work of Brecht and to pay tribute to it, the revolving stage was not used, but it is possible to study several other details of the performance closely. In the opening scene, Mother Courage, while singing the triumphant march-song 'Christian, revive!',[6] is also simulating the marching itself, swinging her left leg back and forth in the air. But just as the wagon with its revolving wheels (and in spite of them) does not move anywhere, Mother Courage's marching leg only stirs the air. The image of the wagon drawn by different people each time is central to the performance. The first act ended with the wagon being pulled by Kattrin, after she has been wounded, who together with the Captain sang the tune of the opening march. In the last image of the performance Mother Courage is alone with her carriage, after she has covered her dead daughter Kattrin with a blanket. When Mother Courage, after some deliberations succeeds in moving the carriage, the same triumphant march is heard again, but this time from off-stage. What has in fact 'happened' during the whole performance is that while she has been marching round and round with her wagon on the 'same' spot as an expression of the paradoxical dialectics of movement and stasis, she has lost all of her three children in the war.

Obviously, the war does not lead anywhere, except to a deeper and more profound despair. Mother Courage, who unknowingly has been caught in the perpeteum mobile-impasse of a treadmill from the very beginning, moving around in a never-ending gyre, does of course neither see nor understand the tragic significance of the events. In the production at the Berliner Ensemble the call for revival under a Christian or any other banner, after the Second World War, was undoubtedly placed in an extremely ironic light. After having seen this performance George Steiner observed that, 'we cannot detach ourselves from the play and merely pass cool judgement on her faults. We too are hitched to the wagon, and it is beneath our feet that the stage turns'.[7]

This also seems to be the effect Brecht implicitly wants to achieve with his aesthetics of the circle - to force the spectator intellectually as well as emotionally to place him or herself in one of the circles, just as Brecht has placed the characters in a maze of such circles.

In order to understand the significance of these complex images created already from the opening scene of *Mother Courage and Her Children*, as well as the dramaturgical curve opened up towards the-multi-dimensional circular closure of the performance, it is necessary briefly to examine some of the strongly rooted theatrical models and conventions against which Brecht obviously revolted and therefore at the same time was also very much aware of. Brecht developed his notions of the theatre in a position of strong polemics against what he called the Aristotelean theatrical models, which he found, for example, in the realistic plays of Henrik Ibsen and August Strindberg and the theatrical practices they were based on and had engendered. It is of course impossible to exemplify the Aristotelean model as Brecht saw it with only two playwrights, but Ibsen and Strindberg, besides being modern, had gained an extremely strong footing in the German theatres with which Brecht grew up. In a 1934 interview with a Danish newspaper, while in exile there, Brecht argued that,

> I don't think the traditional form of theatre means anything any longer. Its significance is purely historic; it can illuminate the way in which earlier ages regarded human relationships, and particularily relationships between men and women. Works by such people as Ibsen and Strindberg remain important historical documents, but they no longer move anybody. A modern spectator can't learn anything from them.[8]

The narrative structures on which the realistic/naturalistic plays of Ibsen and Strindberg were based, where the conflicts between men and women are depicted as leading directly towards a gradually approaching catastrophe or crisis, are linear. These plays, as well as the theatrical practices which they reinforced, were also based on quite different visual concepts from the form of circular vision Brecht was gradually developing. In all of Ibsen's realistic plays, with their clear linear and causal narrative structure, the space is correspondingly directed towards a focal point situated in the center of the back-stage. Thus the linear structures of these plays are both narrative and visual. In the course of the action the protagonists are gradually drawn towards this focal point where they are invariably forced to a final, and as a rule, tragic confrontation with their fate and the world they live in. Sometimes this area is open to the view of the spectators, but usually it is hidden for us during this final confrontation. In this focal point there is some object or obstacle which is usually related to their distant past, to some sin or irregular action they or their parents have committed, and when they confront this place/event, what Baxtin (1978) has termed 'chronotopos', they usually meet their death. The actions of Ibsen's plays could thus be described as the protagonists' gradual approach to the area of the stage which is intimately connected with his or her fate, and usually also with their sudden death.

In the last scene in most of Ibsen's plays, for example in *Ghosts*, *The Wild Duck* and *The Master Builder*, as well as in *Hedda Gabler*, the objects and events surrounding the hero or heroine, just-like Mother Courage who clings to her wagon, are closely connected with the struggles they have faced throughout the whole action of the play. But in Ibsen's plays the protagonists are only gradually becoming more intimately connected to such an object, like the rising sun in the last scene of *Ghosts*, which signals the final madness of Oswald as well as the outbreak of the illness he has inherited from his father and which leads to his death. This is also the case with the duck which Hedvig wishes to kill in the final scene of *The Wild Duck* and the tower on which Solness is climbing and from which he falls in the last scene of *The Master Builder*. Similarly, *Hedda Gabler* is totally absorbed by her own private space, the room where she has been toying with her pistols and playing the piano under the portrait of her father. And this is where she commits suicide with one of these pistols.

The sun, the duck, the tower and the pistols are at the same time also different expressions of the inner psychological workings of the souls of the respective protagonists, who during the final moments of the respective plays are forced to confront their death through them. These objects are also in a way an integral part of the theatrical machinery and could in fact be seen as the counterpart or equivalent to the revolving stage with which Mother Courage had to struggle. But there is a fundamental difference between the visual machineries activated and the props used in the two theatrical models, of Ibsen and Brecht. In the Ibsen model the machinery has been hidden by an object in the world, or rather transformed into such an object, while Brecht directly reveals the workings of the theatrical machinery, the revolving stage as a basis for what he called *Verfremdung*.

But in addition to this Brechtian foregrounding of the theatrical machinery there is also a basic structural difference between the two models. The realistic drawing-room space is based on the principles developed by the Baroque stage, where the two side walls of the set are pointed slightly inwards, towards the focal point. In Ibsen's theatre the back wall is frequently also extended visually into an additional room, as in *The Wild Duck* and *Hedda Gabler*, or into a natural scenery[9] which can be perceived through a window or a veranda as in *Ghosts*, but which can also be concealed from the view of the spectators as in *The Master Builder*. The basic principle in Brecht, on the other hand, is that everything, even the whole universe, as in *Life of Galileo*, with the help of the telescope, should somehow, at least potentially, be visible throughout the whole performance. By placing the wagon on the front stage in *Mother Courage and her Children* Brecht made it possible for it to move around the whole of Europe, while remaining in one and the same spot. And at the same time the wagon became a focal point without being subordinated to the perspectival laws of the fictional space.

The transition for, which Brecht is largely responsible, to a conception of the theatrical space as the medium which should be exposed or foregrounded through the performance undermines the classical notion of linear perspective as a basis for realistic illusion. In the theatre as well as in painting the perspective leads to the focal point situated on the opposite side of the spectator or viewer, and from a dramaturgical perspective this focal point is clearly related to the climactic endings of Ibsen's plays. These climactic scenes all take place in the focal point of the one-point perspective, placing them in the most highly charged point of that space. In the Baroque theatre this was the area where different supernatural creatures usually entered the world of the humans with the help of what is termed the Deus ex Machina.[10] But while the Baroque conventions are deeply rooted in a metaphysical tradition, Ibsen was able to invest them with a psychological significance. At the final point in Ibsen's plays, when all the attention is drawn towards a visible or partly hidden focal point, the most hidden desires of the heroes and heroines are revealed, as an expression of their final crisis and their confrontation with death.

Brecht's Theatre, on the other hand, can be seen as an attempt to dismantle the metaphysical iconography by which Ibsen's plays are still very strongly influenced. This important development must also be considered in the context of the profound crisis with regard to the notion of visuality which occurred during the 19th century. Jonathan Crary has formulated this crisis in terms of the 'emergence of models of subjective vision', and he claims that,

> the idea of subjective vision - the notion that the quality of our sensations depends less on the nature of the stimulus and more on the makeup and function of our sensory apparatus - was one of the conditions for the historical emergence of notions of

autonomous vision, that is, for a severing (or liberation) of perceptual experience from a necessary and determinate relation to an exterior world.[11]

This development towards 'autonomous vision' has influenced not only the different forms of scientific investigation, but also the visual arts, including the theatre.

The visual apparatus of the theatre has throughout its history in different ways always been sensitive to the changes of perceptive modes and models. The development, which Crary traces to as early as the 1820's and 1830's, through which the attention is gradually shifted from the geometrical laws of optics to the physical dimensions of human sight is in many ways parallel to the developments in the theatre through which the objective modes of perception based on linear perspective are transformed into the Brechtian vision based on the circle, which places a much greater responsibility on the spectator. The responsibility of the individual for what he sees and the intellectual and ideological conclusions which have to be drawn from this field of vision is not only the central theme, but also the underlying structural principle of *Life of Galileo*. A more comprehensive examination of these issues would also have to give a fuller account of the subjective forms of visuality developed by August Strindberg. In *Miss Julie, A Dreamplay* as well as in *The Ghost Sonata* each of the individual characters constitute a focal point.

Strindberg's contribution also has to be taken into consideration when discussing Brechtian aesthetics, and I would argue that Strindberg has served as an important bridge between the realistic dramaturgy of Ibsen and Brecht's epic theatre.[12] But in opposition to the totally subjective basis for the theatre developed by Strindberg, Brecht was interested in an objective, scientific notion of the theatre. And, it is in *Life of Galileo*, by an ironic use of the telescope as the visual apparatus to perceive the whole universe, and a kind of alter ego, the scientist Galileo Galilei, that Brecht is able to bring this project to full fruition. The play about this scientist-hero is at the same time both a dramatic-theatrical and a theoretical formulation of Brecht's aesthetics of the circle. And furthermore the aesthetic principles of this play are a dialectical reflexion of the structure of the universe as it has been revealed by scientific laws and the principles of scientific experimentation.

The fundamental principle of this scientific aesthetics, based on the Copernican understanding of the universe, could be described as a dynamic network of circular movements around an infinite number of different centers. In fact each individual subject in the world is such a center, around which all other bodies move. The important thing is that the position of the subject has to be constantly redefined. It can never be regarded as constant, because then according to the position of Galileo/Brecht there is an immediate regression to the Ptolemaic world-picture, which is authoritarian and inflexible. *Life of Galileo* thus presents a dynamic view of the center as a subject-position which has to be constantly redefined and re-evaluated in a larger perceptual and ideological framework.

This concern with circles and the possibility of transforming any particular point in the universe into a center starts already in the opening lines of the play. Andrea says that the milkman must be paid, 'Or he'll start making a circle round our house', which Galileo, while he is busy washing himself, immediately corrects by saying 'Describing a circle'[13], a more abstract and more scientific formulation. The description of the bailiff who will come for the money in a straight line, the shortest distance between two points, draws the attention to the fact that Galileo and Andrea are living in a world based on the laws of geometry. The question this attitude immediately raises is which geometrical model will fully explain this world, not only the house in which they live and study, but also the order of the social world surrounding them, with its unique and quite fixed hierarchies of power.

Life of Galileo presents two basic theoretical models. In the very beginning of the first scene Galileo makes a demonstration of the Ptolemaic system, exemplified by a wooden model which shows 'how the planets move around the earth, according to our forefathers'(5) with the earth in the center and eight rings situated 'one inside another'.(6) After throwing the towel, with which he has been drying himself, as if to demonstrate the laws of gravity to Andrea, Galileo explains what the limitations of the old system are. At the same time Andrea is rubbing his back, with this action physically making Galileo his center. According to Galileo the old Ptolemaic system, on which the hierarchical social norms have also been based, is

> walls and spheres and immobility! For two thousand years people have believed that the sun and all the stars rotate around mankind. Pope, cardinals, princes, professors, captains, merchants, fishwives and schoolkids thought they were sitting motionless inside this crystal sphere.(6)

But, continues Galileo 'we are breaking out of it [the crystal sphere], Andrea, at full speed [...] Because everything is in motion, my friend.' (6)

In the long and enthusiastic speech which follows Galileo explains to his pupil that a new time has begun, explaining when and how the changes began. But Galileo is also concerned with how these changes will affect the future:

> It is my prophecy that our own lifetime will see astronomy discussed in the marketplaces. Even the fishwives' sons will hasten off to school. For these novelty-seeking people in our cities will be delighted with a new astronomy that sets the earth moving too. The old idea was always that the stars were fixed to a crystal vault to stop them falling down. Today we have found the courage to let them soar through space without support; and they are travelling at full speed just like our ships, at full speed and without support. And the earth is rolling cheerfully around the sun, and the fishwives, merchants, princes, cardinals and even the Pope are rolling with it.
>
> The universe has lost its centre overnight, and woken up to find it has countless centres. So that each one can now be seen as the centre, or none at all. Suddenly there is a lot of room. (8)

The new understanding of astronomy, heralded by Copernicus and carried further by Galileo, is clearly not limited to the spheres of science, and as we know, the reason why Galileo has to recant his ideas was not 'geometric', but because these ideas directly threatened the existing social order.

I will, however, not develop this specific issue further in detail here, but rather examine some examples where the two competing conceptions of the universe, as well as of the circle, are presented in the play. They are not only revealed through dialogue, but have become fully integrated into the theatrical machinery itself. In order to make it possible for Andrea to understand the new picture of the world, Galileo stages a small demonstration placing Andrea on a chair, which within the framework of the short demonstration represents the earth. Galileo asks Andrea how it is possible for the wash stand, which represents the sun, to rise on one side of the earth and to sink on the other side. Andrea, quite logically, argues that by moving the washstand from one side to the other, 'I can see with my own eyes that the sun goes down in a different place from where it rises'. (9) It is however quite simple for Galileo to show Andrea, that by turning the chair around instead of moving the washstand, there is an alternative way for the 'sun' to move from Andrea's left side to his right. This small scene is constructed exactly like two alternative scientific experiments, showing that the answers can be given according to two alternative, and plausible, hypotheses.

Andrea, and Brecht, too, are clearly aware of the fact that 'examples always work if you are clever' (11) and that Galileo's demonstrations do not prove anything unless you already have a hypothesis which has already been tested on reality. But Galileo, and Brecht, are interested in showing Andrea, as well as the spectators, that these demonstrations, like theatrical performances, are only models which have to be critically and empirically examined on the basis of the physical and social realities of the world itself. This is finally the dialectics of the theatre, or as Galileo says to Andrea at the end of the first scene,

Look at Felicia down there outside the basket-maker's shop breast-feeding her child: it remains a hypothesis that she's giving it milk and not getting milk from it, till one actually goes and sees and proves it. Faced with the stars we are like dull-eyed worms that can hardly see at all. (18)

But Andrea is gradually learning to see the world through these demonstrations, not just by 'gawping' (9) as Galileo complains when his student does not understand the alternative solutions to the chair and wash stand demonstration, but to see it dialectically, as Brecht's theatre demands. The ending of *Life of Galileo*, with Andrea saving for the world the *Discorsi*, which Galileo has kept hidden inside the globe, is the optimistic aspect of this complex dialectic.

But how is this constantly ongoing dialectic, not only between the different theatrical models, but also between these hypothetical models and the world, constructed? The *Messingkauf Dialogues* project, which remained uncompleted, is probably Brecht's most developed answer to this question. Here I will only deal with the notion of circular vision as it has been briefly outlined in this project.[14] According to Brecht it is possible to describe the two basic modes of the theatre as the merry-go-round-type and the planetarium-type. The merry-go-round, or the so-called *K-Typus*, is based on the Ptolemaic conception of the universe. It is a theatre which has a fixed centre with everything moving around it, causing dizziness to everyone situated in the theatre. This for Brecht is represented by the Aristotelean theatre, aiming at catharsis, where the spectators identify with the events and characters on the stage. According to Brecht this model was practised by Stanislavski, and it is the theatrical model found in Ibsen, as analysed above, where the whole attention is directed towards one focal point.

The second type, or the so-called *P-Typus*, is based on the visual model of the Copernican conception of the universe, where the centre constantly has to be redefined. It is supposed to enable the spectators, through a demonstration, first of all to observe and to understand, and only after that to judge. This is for Brecht also the model of the theatre which he wished to realize through his own scientific conception of the epic theatre. It is a form of theatre where the point from which the theatrical space is observed can always be changed, depending on which aspect of the fictional universe is going to be exposed. The planetarium also enables every spectator to observe the circular movements of the heavenly bodies objectively, while at the same time it reveals the truths about the universe from the exclusively subjective point of view of each individual spectator, as the central point in the universe.

Ideally, the planetarium concept of the epic theatre liberates the perception of the fictional universe from the constrictions that buildings and cities, social strata and ideologies, impose on the spectators when they move around in the real world. It is the aim of Brecht's epic planetarium to free the spectator from these limitations, in order to sharpen his or her abilities to perceive the real world and to critique it. *Life of Galileo* is a dialectical play confronting this issue on two levels. First, the play itself is acutely aware that it is only a model in the same sense that the Ptolemaic and the Copernican conceptions of the universe are models which have to be constantly re-examined in relationship to the universe. Such a re-examination is also a form of demonstration, like for example what Galileo and Andrea do with the washstand and the chair. And such a demonstration is in itself a theatrical performance, a *Lehrstück* in the true Brechtian sense.

Second, *Life of Galileo* is in itself a dialectical play, because it contains both the *K-Typus* and the *P-Typus* as the two major forms of perception which are not only confronted on the level of astronomy, but are also placed in opposition to each other in social and ideological respects as well. *Life of Galileo* can be seen as a linear play, showing a middle aged scientist who has just finished his breakfast in the first scene, and the same man who in his old age is having his supper in the last scene of the play. But at the same time it is also a play about the ideas that constantly reappear at different times in history, ideas and the repression of these ideas which are constantly re-cycled, to use an expression from our own contemporary world of circles.

As the conclusion of this analysis of the meanings of the circle in Brecht, one could argue that in spite of its constant dialectical embeddedness in complementary forms of perception, the ultimate aim of the theatrical planetarium is to establish a utopian vision, where only the radically subjective can make claims of being truly objective. On the one hand such a utopian vision totally frees the theatre from the limitations of its own architectural space. This is because from any point around which a circle is drawn, enclosing its space, creating a center, it is possible to make new circles, placing the individual spectator in any point s/he wishes to watch the events from, including his or her own ideological commitments. The stage is only one such circle and the spectator may even choose, either to include, or to exclude him - or herself from this planetarium space. But at the same time, such an open strategy also places a very heavy responsibility on the individual spectators, which it is still doubtful if they/we have really been able to manage or even been willing to accept. This Brecht must also have been aware of this, giving Andrea the last words of his play about Galileo, quoted as the motto at the beginning of this essay, which are circular in more than one way - 'We're really just at the beginning'. (113)

1. Bertolt Brecht, *Mother Courage and Her Children*, translated by Ralph Manheim, in *Collected Plays*, vol. 5 (New York, Vintage Books, 1972), p.340.

2. Bertolt Brecht, *Brecht on Theatre*, translated by John Willett (London, Methuen, 1978), p.233.

3. Gosta Bergman, *Den Moderna Teaterns Genombrott 1890-1925* (Stockholm, Albert Bonnier, 1966), p.125.

4. David Richard Jones, *Great Directors at Work: Stanislavsky, Brecht, Kazan, Brook* (Berkeley, University of California Press, 1986), p.96.

5. John Fuegi, *Bertolt Brecht: Chaos, According to Plan* (Cambridge University Press, 1987), p.116.

6. Brecht, *Mother Courage*, p.136.

7. Georg Steiner, *The Death of Tragedy* (New York, Alfred A. Knopf, 1958), p.358.

8. *Brecht on Theatre*, p.66.

9. M. Baxtin, 'The Forms of Time and Chronotopos in the Novel', *Poetics and Theory of Literature*, 3 (1978), 493-528.

10. For a detailed discussion on the Deus ex Machina in the modern theatre, including Brecht's *Threepenny Opera*, see Freddie Rokem, 'Der Deus ex Machina im Theater der historischen Avantgarde', *Theater Avantgarde: Wahrnehmung - Körper - Sprache*, ed. Erika E. Fischer-Lichte (Tübingen & Basel, Francke Verlag, 1995), pp.324-368.

11. Jonathan Crary, 'Unbinding Vision', *October*, 68 (Spring 1994), 21-44 (21). See also Michael Lynch & Steve Woolgar, *Representation in Scientific Practice* (Cambridge, The MIT Press, 1990).

12. For discussions on the visual modes developed by Strindberg see Freddie Rokem, 'The Camera and the Aesthetics of Repetition: Strindberg's use of Space and Scenography in *Miss Julie, A Dream Play* and *The Ghost Sonata*' in *Strindberg's Dramaturgy*, ed. Goran Stockenstrom (Minneapolis, University of Minnesota Press,1988), pp.107-128; and 'Strindberg's Optical Unconscious', in *Strindberg's Post-Inferno Plays*, ed. Kela Kvam (Copenhagen, Munksgaard and Rosinante, 1994), pp.71-84. It is also possible to find support for this view concerning Strindberg's importance for Brecht in Peter Szondi, *Theory of Modern Drama*, tr. Michael Hays (Cambridge, Polity Press, 1987).

13. Bertolt Brecht, *Life of Galileo*, translated by John Willett (London, Methuen, 1980), p.5. Subsequent page references to *Galileo* will be included in parentheses in the main text of this essay. See also Patricia Ann Simpson, 'Revolutionary Reading: The Circulation of Truth in Brecht's *Leben des Galilei'*, *Versuche über Brecht - The Brecht Yearbook*, 15 (1990); Freddie Rokem, 'The Erotic, The Scientific and the Aesthetic Gazes in the Theatre' *Assaph*, 7 (1991), 61-73; and Rudolf Arnheim, *The Power of the Center: A Study of Composition in the Visual Arts* (Berkeley, University of California Press, 1982).

14. Brecht, *The Messingkauf Dialogues*, trans. John Willett (London, Methuen, 1965).

MARK W. ROCHE

Comic Reduction and Comic Negation in Brecht

Many comedies end happily – either because of artifice, as when the comic protagonist suddenly inherits a fortune from a distant relative, or because of genuine development, as when the comic character overcomes an (often self-imposed) obstacle and joins in an overarching harmony. Brecht's comedies are not of this kind. Instead, Brecht works with those subgenres of comedy that stress unresolved contradictions and ask viewers to resolve the tensions portrayed on stage outside the dramaturgical arena – in consciousness and in life. I would like to sketch the two forms of comedy Brecht employs, what I call comic reduction and comic negation. Much of the discussion of Brecht and comedy has focused on the extent to which epic theater draws on the comic tradition.[1] Certainly the concepts of contrast and contradiction and the breaking of the illusion of verisimilitude are common to both forms of drama, but this tells us little about the general and specific ways in which works by Brecht can be related to the comic tradition. This essay, therefore, attempts to view Brecht's comedies more fully in the light of different comic types. After defining what I call the comedy of reduction and illustrating it with what is arguably Brecht's greatest comedy, *Herr Puntila und sein Knecht Matti*, I turn to what I call the comedy of negation and illustrate it with aspects of several of Brecht's other comic dramas.[2] The essay seeks to render transparent Brecht's development of certain basic comic structures and to shed light on individual comic works.

Comic Reduction

In a subgenre of comedy I call the comedy of reduction, the comic protagonist longs for truth and goodness but reduces these values to the lowest, most primitive level. Though the comic subject has valid goals, he cannot attain them owing to a lack of insight or will. Failing in this way, the protagonist reduces his goals, ending in effect with invalid goals. Consider, for example, Lessing's *Die Juden*, where intersubjectivity is reduced to a limited move toward recognition of the rights of the other, or Schnitzler's *Anatol*, where love is reduced to ephemeral and instrumental relationships. Like much of comedy, reduction thematizes the base inclinations, passions, and drives of the self: sexuality, desire for power, insatiable hunger or thirst. The protagonist of reduction is far from free, for his actions are determined not by reason but by his lower desires and the external world that feeds these desires. Our laughter and enjoyment are especially pronounced when the protagonist views this apparent spontaneity – whereas he is in fact determined by circumstance and arbitrary, finite desires – as the highest expression of freedom.

In the comedy of reduction the hero does not hold his goal high and simply fail to attain it; on the contrary, he reduces his goal and generally sees himself as realizing it. He is like the drunk who decides to pass by the pub without entering and after passing it decides to go in to reward himself for having passed it. Where the tragic hero remains consistent and accepts consequences, including guilt, the comic hero gives in, indulges himself, and shifts perspectives. Again, the hero of reduction is not consciously or intentionally evil or corrupt. He is simply led to violations of proper behavior by way of his weak reasoning or lack of will, yet spares no imagination in creating deceptions that serve to justify his reduced existence. At times the comic deed arises from appropriate reasoning but a false premise. So, for example, the actions of Shakespeare's Malvalio, who has – like many a comic hero of reduction – so high an opinion of himself that he is easily fooled by his vanity.

Brecht's most successful comedy, *Herr Puntila und sein Knecht Matti*, is an example of the comedy of reduction. In Brecht's play we see the two major forms of asymmetry in comedy: the Don Quixote motif of the subordination of the servant, and the Don Juan motif of the subordination of women. The inversion of truth (and intersubjectivity) we see in the comedy of reduction is mirrored in the frequency with which asymmetrical master-servant and male-female relations arise. Puntila desires friendship, yet his friendship remains asymmetrical. Puntila *commands* Matti to be his friend and so cancels the attempt at friendship. We also see Puntila's intuitive desire for love in his collecting brides, but again his actions undermine this higher form of intersubjectivity. Puntila cannot take each one as his wife; his attempts at love quickly pass over into possession.

The attaché illustrates another limited form of intersubjectivity. Admittedly, the attaché is a fool, but because of his lack of knowledge and resulting lack of subjectivity he is unable to think or act with prejudice. The attaché doesn't even recognize that the joke he hears is not a bad joke missing a punchline, but an anti-Semitic joke understandable only to those aware of prejudice (*BFA*, 6, 344).[3] The positive moment here is the attaché's lack of prejudice, but the negative side is his inability to recognize enmity in others. His intersubjectivity is, if for different reasons, as deficient as that of Puntila.

A symmetrical conversation takes place only on the fringe of this society. Laina and the Pröbstin discuss mushrooms. Though cooking mushrooms is a hobby for one and a necessity for the other, the stress here is on equality, on energetic discourse that bridges two spheres of society. Again it is intersubjectivity at the lowest level: the conversation is restricted to the trivial (it is not about love or friendship but about food), and the exchange takes place only among one segment of society, women.

A hidden irony in the piece is that even when drunk Puntila remains a master: he orders his servants, he talks about himself, and he fails to listen to others.[4] His vision of the world becomes increasingly simplistic: Puntila fancies himself a near Communist, he thinks that everyone should be his friend, and he is convinced that work contracts are no longer needed. Puntila's lack of perception is brought to the fore in a comic passage where he holds up one fork and states that when he's sober he sees only one (*BFA*, 6, 289). (Not only is his vision incorrect, but when he's drunk, he sees more.) Puntila's getting drunk satisfies his *individual* desires. It is a very particular structure; there is nothing universal or tragic about it. I disagree, therefore, with Walter Sokel's reading of the play as in many respects tragic.[5]

Indeed, critics often misinterpret comic reduction as tragic. This misreading derives from two factors. First, theoreticians of tragedy often stress not the greatness that leads to tragic suffering but rather the so-called tragic flaw, which in some respects resembles comic reduction. Second, critics overlook the extent to which comedy includes the parody of tragedy. Parody of tragedy may reduce tragedy to the contradictions of society and evoke a comic world in which fate is not pre-determined; if contradictory social structures or the categories with which the comic figure sees the world were altered, a seemingly inevitable fate could be overcome. Parody of tragedy can also involve a critique of a particular tragic author's presuppositions and style. It can mock a particular tragic moment, for example, tragic pathos. At times comedy mocks the tragic hero's obsession with greatness and inability to compromise, which leads to a suffering that more balanced individuals might know how to avoid.

Above all, however, the parody of tragedy targets not the tragic hero but the comic protagonist who claims for himself tragic stature. The comic protagonist, unstable, inadequate, and without character, deems his situation noble or tragic. Comedy includes not only a negation of the substance of tragedy but also an ironization of this negation of substance. We laugh not only at comedy's justified mockery of tragic pathos and pessimism but at comic insufficiency, the unjust erasure of tragic substance. The parody of tragedy frequent in comic reduction normally revolves around the instability, inadequacies, and characterlessness of the protagonist who nonetheless deems his situation noble or tragic. Lamenting that happiness is illusory, that nothing is secure, that the forces of the world make chaos of our lives, the hero attempts to justify, from a broader perspective, his self-indulgent despair, his inconsistency, his weakness. The comic hero is not great, and his suffering is not deep. To suffer deeply and not to speak of it is great; the comic hero, in contrast, suffers mildly and speaks obsessively of his suffering. Preoccupied with his suffering, the comic protagonist is unwilling to be hard on himself. We see a comic inability on the protagonist's part to transform himself, to learn and to change; there is no evidence of the recognition we see in the tragic hero.

The comic contrast between Puntila's weakness and his inflated view of himself comes to the fore in many ways: through comparisons with God, assertions of his own strength, and his unabashed confidence that everyone wants to be his friend. Puntila is presented as an imitation of the divine: in his position as the father of Eva; his constant adoption, and twisting, of the words of Christ; his apparent *deus ex machina* at the end of scene 3; and his creation of a mountain in scene 11. But where the primary mark of divine existence has traditionally been *manere*, or immutability, Puntila is ever fluctuating, a comic reduction of the divine. Similarly, Puntila is a reduction of the tragic ruler who seeks omnipotence and, beyond his isolation, intersubjectivity: in Schiller's *Don Carlos* King Phillip announces, 'Jetzt bin ich wach und Tag soll sein,' and longs for the friendship of the great Marquis Posa;[6] Puntila cries out, 'Es soll Freitag sein' and longs for the friendship of his driver Matti (*BFA*, 6, 286).

Puntila desires friendship, but he does not receive it from an equal, and so it is not friendship. Puntila is ignorant of the other: he unintentionally marks his ignorance by declaring work a form of fun, glibly announcing his wish to be poor, and calling herring a delicacy (for he rarely eats what is for the servants a staple). Not knowing the other, Puntila cannot recognize the other as other. The other is forced to recognize him and so does not exist as other; in short, there is no genuine recognition. Puntila treats humans as inanimate objects and, accordingly, speaks to objects, such as telephone poles, as if they were human (*BFA*, 6, 298). The object-status of other persons is already manifest – aesthetically – in the title of scene one, 'Puntila findet einen Menschen.' The comic hero's reduction of humans to objects is especially present in the following reply to Matti: 'Was heißt: einen Menschen? Bist du ein Mensch? Vorhin hast du gesagt, du bist ein Chauffeur. Gelt, jetzt hab ich dich auf einem Widerspruch ertappt! Gib's zu!' (*BFA*, 6, 287). The line is not only superficially comic:

because Puntila does not treat his servants as humans, Matti cannot be both a chauffeur and a *Mensch*. In rendering the other an object, Puntila undermines his own sense of self, for true subjectivity depends on recognition from another subject, rather than someone who has been reduced to an object and forced to recognize the other. Puntila's self is split (the idea is cleverly dramatized in the image of his calling himself on the phone), but his crisis cannot be taken seriously. Brecht was right to place him in a comedy.

Puntila views himself as tragic because he has an inflated view of his own importance, but the play undermines this notion. Puntila's parody of tragedy arises on several occasions: he'd rather be dead than break Finnish law (a tragedy of self-sacrifice to which he does not adhere (*BFA*, 6, 299ff), and he states that he will never again touch alcohol just as he begins to do so (*BFA*, 6, 361ff). Fate rules Puntila. He suffers a collision, but it is of his basest desires, and it stems, as the prologue and epilogue state, not from his inner greatness but from the circumstances in which he lives.

Other characters and spheres of society contribute to this theme. Matti says to Eva: 'Wenns einen Chauffeur heiraten wollen, ist das eine Tragödie, denn da müssen Sie sich nach der Decke strecken, und die ist kurz, Sie werden sich wundern' (*BFA*, 6, 353). A tragedy requires that the hero or heroine reach his or her limits. Whether we read *sich nach der Decke strecken* as an allusion to the chauffeur's limited means, as the idiom suggests, or, more boldly, as a pun on stretching to the low ceiling of the chauffeur's car, the thrust is the same: reaching one's limits is in this context easy. The farmers are not free of this parody either. The advocate discusses the fact that they easily renounce their steadfast opinions for financial reasons (*BFA*, 6, 342). Even Matti fits the theme. The names 'Matti/Athi' invite comparison: clearly the latter hero holds to principles and is not determined by external circumstances; Matti meanwhile becomes cynical, avoids ever taking Puntila seriously, never speaks against him, and is himself guilty of asymmetrical relations toward Eva. He, too, is a comic figure.

Matti finally leaves not on the basis of an empirical event (Puntila's recurrence of drunkenness and the dismissal of Surkkala have occurred before) but rather on the basis of his general insight into master-servant relations ('Wer wen?' [*BFA*, 6, 370]). Matti will accept no master until he is recognized in his subjectivity; but then no master will be recognizable, for the master will be an equal. Brecht's play demonstrates that ephemeral goodness on the part of rulers (Puntila) and momentary heroism on the part of the opposition (Athi) fail to change society.[7] A substantial and overarching symmetry is necessary.

Brecht was appropriately attracted to the comedy of reduction, for this form creates great distance toward the characters and stops short of any solutions. It stresses the contradictions of society. The blocking character, Puntila, is not converted at the end; he still fluctuates, continuing along his mistaken path. Puntila's allusions to a *deus ex machina* in scene 3 do not lead to resolution; they are eventually unveiled as forms of his arrogant subjectivity. Despite Puntila's charm and vitality, the audience as – Brecht insists – remains sufficiently distant to preserve the freedom of criticism (*BFA*, 24, 301-302). Comedy and morality work in harmony.

Reduction is among the most successful and popular of comic subgenres. It raises significant issues by way of the characters' unsuccessful attempts to recognize and realize truth. Unlike harmonic comedy, reduction will never risk the danger of an unearned happy end. The primary danger of reduction is that the audience, depending on the performance, may identify with the protagonist rather than recognize his inadequacies. Reduction may or may not be received as comic in the sense of a negation of the negation. The observer of comic reduction plays a central role, for the hero is comic only if the observer can distance himself from the hero and recognize the absurdity of his actions. Thus, if the first negation, the negation of substance, takes place on stage, the second negation, the recognition of the comic as comic or absurd, takes place in the consciousness of the audience. The extent to which the object is viewed as comic varies, because the values of different spectators vary as well, though the play can in its argument, its *reductio ad absurdum*, encourage the viewer to *change* his values. Nonetheless, the viewer may well be content with the appearance of the hero as he is and fail to recognize his absurdities. Because we do not take the hero seriously, we are lulled into a relaxed, indulgent view and are tempted to identify with the first negation. This was not the view of the comic dialectician Brecht, whose critique of comic inadequacy would plant the seeds for its own transcendence.

Comic Negation

In the comedy of reduction, the hero has valid goals but insufficient means; in the comedy of negation, we see the reverse. The subject has insubstantial goals and fails, but in failing demonstrates substantial means. The audience, aware of the untenability of the hero's aspirations, is not disappointed to see him fall. Consider as examples Johnson's *Volpone*, Molière's *Tartuffe*, Goldoni's *Il bugiardo*, or Kleist's *Der zerbrochene Krug*. In this subgenre, the subject knows himself to be independent of norms of justice and duty. He decides for himself what is right. The hero of negation sees the world as something made by humanity and thus alterable by it. Because the comic hero's subjectivity is all-important, the hero is unwilling either to enter into relations with others or to treat others as equals. Instead, the hero unscrupulously seeks his own advantage. To the extent that the hero of negation himself unveils the absurdity of his position – as when Falstaff's lies, for example, become clearly recognizable as lies – we are not disturbed by the presence of negation; we know that it will undermine itself. In this contradiction lies the comic moment. Despite the comic hero's charm and dazzling intellect, he isn't as strong as he thinks he is. His lawlessness is as self-destructive as it is fascinating.

The idea of negative subjectivity generally engenders a plurality of negative subjects. Here Brecht's comedies enter, for Brecht was concerned less with individual than with social evil. For Brecht the negation of the good is not restricted to a single individual but rather permeates an entire society or at least most of that society; accordingly, one can speak of the comedy of social negation. Just as there are finite parallels to the comedy of reduction – for example, stuttering, deafness, and so forth – so, too, are there parallel forms for the comedy of negation. Especially important here is the concept of doubling, which represents a transition to social negation. It is mildly comic when a protagonist peeps through a keyhole to spy on another; it is more comic when whoever is spying is also being spied upon, when two heads move to the keyhole simultaneously. The expansion of negation and the subsequent structure of doubling are not only comic, but in a self-reflexive sense predictable; the deceiver is himself deceived. This multiplicity creates a new dramatic constellation. Not only the hero is corrupt; the egotistical concerns of the subject are spread over society. The good hero, if there is one, is isolated in his stance against this society. All relationships are now instrumentalized. By virtue of its self-contradictions, such a society is seen to be on the verge of destroying itself. The expansion of negative subjectivity brings with it, ironically, an undermining of subjectivity. No single hero has a privileged status. While each individual claims a position of strength, the spread of power undermines these claims.

Instead of highlighting individual deviance, the comedy of social negation offers a critical portrait of the age. In many works of social negation, as, for example, Brecht's *Aufstieg und Fall der Stadt Mahagonny*, not a single character is morally admirable. The good intentions of reduction are absent. When the comedy of social negation does introduce a counter-hero, the character is usually cunning and clever but faces an uphill battle; power lies with the forces of society, and society is not converted. The comedy of social negation is, like the comedy of reduction, a comic form with a muffled happy end. The counter-hero may succeed against society, but society is not cured of its ills. He is at first the victim of a society that treats not only the outsider but even its own members asymmetrically. The counter-hero, however, resists this asymmetry through trickery. Such works proffer a spiritual countermodel to the antiquated concept that the comic hero is of lower rank; here the butt of the comedy is the higher echelon of society, those in power; the hero is the resourceful and tenacious underling. The structure of the outsider donning the disguise or imitating the actions of the forces to be ruined does more than serve the plot. Works such as Nestroy's *Der Talisman*, Zuckmayer's *Der Hauptmann von Köpenick*, or Brecht's *Schweyk im Zweiten Weltkrieg* seem to suggest, on either the symbolic or literal level, that these societies are ultimately self-destructive. The outsider who adopts the tricks and techniques of the targeted society merely accelerates its internal decline.

The instrumentalization of others characteristic of social negation is especially strong in Brecht's *Mann ist Mann*, which argues that a person has no fixed identity and is determined by his environment; thus, it is possible to make him over into something else. The play suggests not only that we can externally manipulate this raw material ('Daß man mit einem Menschen beliebig viel machen kann' [*BFA*, 2, 123]), but also that one can transform it internally. It doesn't pay to preserve any identity that holds one back; thus, the self is willing to relinquish its entire past. Galy Gay is transformed from a weak individual – by way of lack of resistance (he can't say 'no'), bribery, intimidation, and ultimately a shift in desire – into a fierce and successful soldier, a 'menschliche Kampfmaschine' (*BFA*, 2, 157). What began as Galy Gay's decision to call an old elephant head a pole, and some maps an elephant, a decision that reflects the transformation of essence into function (if he can sell it as an elephant, it is an elephant), ends as a transformation of himself, the erasure of any private essence; he denies his identity so that he can survive (and flourish) as a soldier. In an inversion of Narcissus, he decides it is best not to be attracted to himself. In a further inversion, those who transform Galy Gay are later subject to his whims. In the comedy of social negation individuals act out roles; they do not develop their subjectivity as much as assume the stances society offers them. If our function in the collective is more important than our individuality, we can be made into whatever the forces of society deem fit. The malleable self easily becomes the instrument (or victim) of an evil collective. Whereas identity-crises normally originate from a character's preoccupation with his own subjectivity, Galy Gay's crisis in *Mann ist Mann* stems from his lack of subjectivity and his being nothing but a victim of social manipulation. The tragic motif of heroic consistency, 'Mann ist Mann' with the implication 'one remains oneself,' gives way to the comic motif of ephemerality and manipulation, 'Mann ist Mann' with the implication that we are all interchangeable – and without individual dignity.

Die Dreigroschenoper also underscores the lack of any core ethical substance. The police officer is a friend of the criminal, and the criminal appears to be a respectable, sociable member of society. The play highlights such incongruities throughout: the gangsters dress in dinner jackets, but their deportment is at odds with their dress — this mocks not only the gangsters' pretensions but the hidden ruthlessness of the business world. Polly thanks the bandits for their (stolen) gifts and notes their extraordinary kindness. The contradiction is especially clear in the play's music: when, for example, in the first finale Peachum speaks of justice, the music is gloomy, and when he describes a brutal and pessimistic world, the music is uplifting. The audience is encouraged to see through these incongruities and recognize the self-deception and self-destruction of a society whose only measure is enhancement of the individual self at the expense of others. The play's parodistic happy end mocks our continuing blindness to these structures.

Brecht's *Furcht und Elend des Dritten Reiches* has been viewed as his most realistic, least epic, play,[8] yet by its use of comic incongruities, the play creates the kind of distance intrinsic to epic theater. Its critique of National Socialism is achieved by way of a portrayal of contradictions in the ideology, institutions, and everyday life of the Third Reich. Like Kleist's *Der zerbrochene Krug*, but on a larger scale and with more at stake, Brecht's play illustrates a form of subjectivity obsessed with itself and with no regard for universal values; such a subjectivity exhibits only secondary virtues, such as discipline or obedience, which, when abstracted from the primary virtue of justice, can lead only to internal destruction. The fall of this regime is, however, not tragic, but comic; the play's parody of tragedy makes this amply clear. Brecht does not challenge National Socialism from an external measure of the good; he shows that National Socialism, by violating the law of non-contradiction, is immanently untenable. National Socialism will cancel and destroy itself.

The task of the play is to demonstrate this immanent critique and hasten the destruction of the regime before it destroys all those caught in its internal web. The situation confronting Judge A in the scene 'Rechtsfindung' illustrates this structure: the conflicting demands of different parts of society render the situation so complex that the reader is as perplexed as the judge. The presentation is intentionally confusing: there is no way out. Judge A is willing to do anything, but one cannot please a regime that is unjust toward itself. The factions of this society will cave in on each other and destroy one another.

Inconsistencies also surface in 'Die jüdische Frau'; the circumstances under which the Jewish wife lives force her to lie – even to her husband. Whereas this borders on the pathetic, the scene 'Der Spitzel' highlights the comic and absurd implications of this contradictory society. Not only does the couple lie, the family unit breaks down through the devaluation of trust. The parents even fear criticizing the weather, and they wonder whether the ten cents they gave their child to buy candy could be interpreted as a bribe. The father fears the son's revenge for his having taken away his frog, calls him a Judas, and puts on his Iron Cross. The situation drives the characters into grotesque behavior.

In Brecht's *Schweyk im Zweiten Weltkrieg*, which also mocks the Third Reich, the forces in power treat each other and minorities as objects. A hero stands up against this society and fights it – not heroically, but comically – by becoming, in an ironic fashion, part of that very society. In the comedy of social negation society appears on the verge of destroying itself; in some such comedies this destruction is aided by a hero who stands up to resist the society and does so by imitating the society to the extreme, thus exhibiting its absurdity. Schweyk is the witty underdog who knows how to keep afloat. His survival illustrates the incompetence of the regime. The state, in turn, battles with itself; in scenes 2, 6, and 7, for example, the Gestapo fights the SS. These contradictions will inevitably lead to self-destruction: the play ends with 'Das Lied von der Moldau,' an assertion of the passage of time, the destruction of the powerful, and the renewal of society.

Earlier comedies of negation, in many cases even comedies of social negation, have explicit happy ends; a fine example is Sheridan's *The School for Scandal*. More modern works tend toward muffled happy ends. First, we may see an isolated happy end where the hero prevails but society remains the same. Titus, in Nestroy's *Der Talisman*, adopts asymmetrical tactics in order to ascend in society. Such ascension can hardly generate a justified happy end. The happy end must be tacked on, through chance, to demonstrate that until society changes (and not that the individual accustom himself to the ways of the unjust society) an earned happy end is mere fiction. Second, we may see an ironic happy end where the hero gets his goal only after giving in to the conditions imposed on him by society. We have analyzed such a structure above in Brecht's *Mann ist Mann.* Zuckmayer's *Der Hauptmann von Köpenick* is an equally good example: the comic protagonist Voigt will receive his pass, but only after serving a prison term. Third, the work may suggest, at times quite subtly, that society is destroying itself. Schnitzler's *Der grüne Kakadu* moves in this direction, as does Brecht's *Furcht und Elend des Dritten Reiches*. In every case the moment of harmony is either ironized or postponed.

The comedy of social negation is generally filled with tendentious themes and a critical-satirical spirit, with the forms of negativity portrayed ranging from frivolousness to brutality.   To the extent that it becomes polemical, it is privileged by those who equate literature with social criticism and disparaged by those who view art as autonomous.   Social negation is endangered whenever it becomes all message.   An interesting dialectic surfaces in this genre: the more extreme the characters' inadequacies are, the clearer the message; to the same degree, however, the less likely the audience is to recognize its own weaknesses in the action.   Plays of this subgenre are most successful when they stress not the victimization of a character but the comic contradictions in a society that victimizes itself.

Conclusion

Brecht's comedies do not portray the traditional happy end, but they can still be seen in the light of two comic traditions or types.   Either they reveal the inadequacies of a protagonist with good intentions, who is too weak or too embedded in his age, to reach his goals, or they portray a society of opportunists who instrumentalize one another and who are ironized through their internal contradictions or absurdities and their self-destructive tendencies.   Despite the numerous studies of comedy in Brecht and the many commentaries on individual plays, no other work has attempted to see basic structures of comic action in Brecht's plays.   This lens offers us a heuristic device to see more clearly how Brecht uses comic contradictions to undermine weak heroes who are given to self-pity or inaction and brutal heroes who pursue evil ends at all costs.   By linking comedy and contradiction in this way, Brecht shows that such characters eventually self-destruct, but not without creating victims in their wake, such that the audience's conscious attention to their actions and motivations may indeed limit the often less than comic destruction of others in life.

[1.]   The connection between epic theater and comedy is supported, for example, by Reinhold Grimm, 'Komik und Verfremdung', in *Strukturen: Essays zur deutschen Literatur* (Göttingen, Sachse, 1963), pp. 226-247 and Helmut Arntzen, 'Komödie und episches Theater,' *Der Deutschunterricht* 21/3 (1969), 67-77. It is questioned, for example, by Jan Knopf, *Bertolt Brecht: Ein kritischer Forschungsbericht* (Frankfurt, Athenäum, 1974), pp. 32-37 and Rainer Warning, 'Elemente einer Pragmasemiotik der Komödie' in *Das Komische*, ed. Wolfgang Preisendanz and Rainer Warning (Munich, Fink, 1976), pp. 279-333. The thesis is also weighed by Peter Christian Giese in his lengthy study of Brecht and comedy, *Das Gesellschaftlich-Komische: Zur Komik und Komödie am Beispiel der Stücke und Bearbeitungen Brechts* (Stuttgart, Metzler, 1974).

2.·   These two subgenres of comedy are analyzed more fully in my forthcoming book, *Tragedy and Comedy: A Systematic Study and a Critique of Hegel* (Albany, SUNY, 1998).

3.·   Brecht is cited according to the *Große kommentierte Berliner und Frankfurter Ausgabe*,

4.   See E. Speidel, 'Brecht's "Puntila": A Marxist Comedy,' *Modern Language Review* 65 (1970), 319-32 (esp. 325-331).

5.   See Walter Sokel, 'Brecht's Split Characters and His Sense of the Tragic', in *Brecht: A Collection of Critical Essays,* ed. Peter Demetz (Englewood Cliffs, NJ, Prentice Hall, 1962), pp. 127-37.

6.   Schiller, *Dramen II*, ed. Gerhard Kluge (Frankfurt, Deutscher Klassiker Verlag, 1989), p. 865.

7.   Athi's heroism is momentary, owing not to the hero's fickleness but to the inevitable demise of the consistent resistance fighter.

8.   See, for example, Georg Lukács, 'Es geht um den Realismus,' in *Die Expressionismusdebatte: Materialien zu einer marxistischen Realismuskonzeption*, ed. Hans-Jürgen Schmitt (Frankfurt, Suhrkamp, 1973), pp. 229-230.

ANNE MOSS

Limits of Reason: An Exploration of Brecht's Concept of *Vernunft* and the Discourse of Science in *Leben des Galilei*

May you now guard science's light
Kindle it and use it right
Lest it be a flame to fall
Downward to consume us all.
Galileo - final scene[1]

Since antiquity, man has trusted increasingly the laws of causality and logic as axioms for the rational comprehension and explanation of physical phenomena. Conceived and employed during the Renaissance by Galileo and Bacon, and mathematically codified by Newton, science provided a seemingly reliable instrument which would hopefully unlock the mysteries of nature and eventually even master it. With these new secular insights, metaphysics and Christian teaching were no longer seen as the only valid keys for deciphering the world. Jürgen Habermas notes that '*Reason* was validated as equivalent for the unifying power of *religion* (emphasis added, AM).'[2] In his epic play *Galileo*, Brecht depicts the Italian mathematician, astronomer, and physicist at the very point in history at which entrenched metaphysical beliefs were being brought into question. Galileo's faith in the 'gentle power of *reason*,' (210) which manifested itself in his dedication to empirical science as a means for deciphering the world, signaled a shift in paradigm. Although this process did not reach its philosophical peak until the dawning of the Age of Enlightenment, its scientific beginnings date from an earlier period: that of Copernicus. In search of rational answers, all supposedly within reach of human intellect, enthusiastic confidence in science was a volatile force. Verifiable theories were formulated, and their implementation provided an explanation to overcome humankind's fear of nature. Francis Bacon prefaced his celebrated aphorism 'knowledge itself is power' with the pointed assertion: 'I am come in very truth, leading to you Nature with all her children, to bind her to your service and make her your slave.'[3] The earth was no longer flat, the stars could be charted, machines could be invented as tools to control and suppress nature. In their 1944 essay *Dialektik der Aufklärung*, Max Horkheimer and Theodor Adorno summarize this optimism: 'The goal of Enlightenment was the de-mystification of the world. With the help of science, myths and illusions could be dissolved.'[4]

Science in the Age of Enlightenment assumed that the universe was rational and that nature could be controlled by the systematic development of scientific knowledge and rational thought. Science as method was responsible for such great success in its discovery and manipulation of the physical world that it engendered faith in its ability to resolve social problems as well. It was the belief of advocates of Enlightenment, such as Hobbes, Spinoza, Descartes, Locke, Leibnitz, Lichtenberg, Mendelssohn, and Kant, that society unfolded by causal process. If one could emancipate oneself from the oppression of Church and State and acquire a complete system of scientific and philosophical truth, one would behave 'by nature' socially, responsibly, virtuously, and *reasonably*. Emancipation was to be the first step. In his 1784 definition of Enlightenment, Kant describes this emancipation as 'man's emergence from a self-imposed tutelage,' offering as its motto: 'Sapere aude! Dare to know, take the risk of discovery, exercise the right of unfettered criticism.'[5]

Society evolved from obedience to Church fathers to obedience to the Scientist. Science as method - an end in itself - was redefined as scientific method - a means for not only explaining but actually restructuring the world. Central to the revolutionary application of scientific method was the concept of progress. As scientist Thomas S. Kuhn has noted, 'The result of solving problems or puzzles that science's paradigms define must inevitably be progress.[...]The outcome of a revolution must be progress.'[6] Fantasies of attainable omnipotence would eventually drive and empower society toward an entwining of science and industry and, subsequently, capitalism.[7]   Contained in the Enlightenment, however, was the seed for its own destruction, as Horkheimer and Adorno reflect in their essay:

> Since its earliest beginnings, the Enlightenment strove - in the broadest sense of progressive thought - to relieve man of fear and place him in a position of power. But our fully enlightened earth now hovers under the brand of triumphant disaster.[8]

Following in the footsteps of Horkheimer and Adorno, German sociologist Ulrich Beck provides a late twentieth century perspective on this dialectic, portraying what he sees as today's 'risk society.' Just as science and other forces of modernity dissolved the feudal hierarchy to set the stage for the Industrial Revolution, that framework is now crumbling to reveal the next historical phase. 'Whereas danger was once seen as external to man (gods, nature), today the real dangers come from within science through their own scientific and social construction.'[9] Beck draws attention to a shift he perceives from the focus on progress and belief in science as truth - to the present obsession with science itself as definer and producer of risks. Like Brecht, Beck considers the capitalist mode of production to be a primary agent in the creation of the risk society, and he echoes Adorno and Horkheimer's critique of technological over-development, of instrumentalized *reason*. The concept of science addressed in *Galileo* has, of course, attained a higher level of complexity and complicity in today's risk society. Beck maintains, however, that, despite 'Verwissenschaftlichung,' the project of Enlightenment could, with a dose of modernized *reason*, actually be resuscitated:

> The project of Enlightenment is not completed. Its calcification - as witnessed in predominant scientific and technological thought - could be dissolved by renewing our faith in *reason* and by introducing a dynamic theory of *scientific rationality* in order to digest the bulk of history and to ensure continued learning. (emphasis added, *Risikogesellschaft*, 258)

It is this call for the revival of Enlightenment *reason* which I would like to examine more closely, through the discourse of science - as put forth in Beck's *Risikogesellschaft*, and as seen, in Brecht's *Leben des Galilei*, where the playwright appears to be wrestling with *reason* as his favored stated means of human progress. Focus in this discussion will be on the following questions:
(i) What forms of *reason* are being celebrated by the dramatist, the natural scientist, and the sociologist, and are distinctions being made between them? (ii) Does the scientist assume responsibility for the products of his *reason*? (iii) Are there limits to *reason*? (iv) How might a new discourse of science begin to evolve?

'Leben des Galilei' as a Celebration of Reason

Leben des Galilei serves as an example of Brecht's later parable works designed didactically to produce a critque of the capitalist status quo. It is one of the dramatist's most popular works, and his involvement with it spanned nearly twenty years. Three versions of the play are most easily accessible: (1) the 'Danish version' (conceived in Svendbørg in 1938/39, entitled *Die Erde bewegt sich/Leben des Galilei*, and premiered in Zurich in 1943 after Brecht had left Scandinavia for California); (2) the 'American version' (an English adaptation entitled *Galileo*, presented in Los Angeles and New York in 1947); and (3) the 'Berlin version' (translated back into German to be presented in Cologne in 1955, and further revised during rehearsals with the Berliner Ensemble until the playwright's death in 1956). Set against a canvas of severe clashes between the Church and the main character of the Scientist, it chronicles the life of Galileo during the Inquisition in seventeenth-century Rome. The historical Galileo, pioneer of the empirical method and advocate of the Copernican hypothesis, which refuted the Aristotelian view by purporting that the earth circled the sun, shunned prevailing metaphysical explanations for phenomena, thus championing the verifiable science of the new era. In reflections from 'Das ungeschmickte Bild einer neuen Zeit,' Brecht chronicles his own interest in the genesis of the play:

> Das 'Leben des Physikers Galilei' wurde in jenen finsteren letzten Monaten des Jahres 1938 geschrieben, als viele den Vormarsch des Faschimus für unaufhaltsam und den endgültigen Zusammenbruch der westlichen Zivilisation für gekommen hielten. In der Tat stand die große Epoche vor dem Abschluß, die der Welt den Aufschwung der Naturwissenschaften[...]gebracht hatte. [...]Nur wenige sahen die neuen Kräfte sich bilden und spürten die Vitalität der neuen Ideen. (*BFA*, 24, 239)

While writing *Leben des Galilei* during his exile in Denmark, the dramatist was privy to news of the latest scientific discoveries through assistants to the physicist Niels Bohr, who were researching the smashing of the atom in their laboratory. In support of his inquiry into the life of Galileo, the physicists contrasted for Brecht the old ptolemaic view of the solar system with the Copernican. Inspired by the idea of a shift in paradigm, Brecht noted: 'The play follows the onset of the new age and attempts to revise some of the misconceptions associated with such new ages.' (*BFA*, 24, 237) For the playwright, the Scientific Age began with Galileo.[10] In his study of the character, Brecht applies Marxist principles of dialectical materialism to a dramatic examination of the astronomer's revolutionary insights seen before the historical backdrop of Inquisition, poverty, disease, and economic exploitation.

Brecht's political aims challenged the existing order, shedding light on anachronistic thinking and attacking bourgeois values. In the first version of the play, the character of Galileo appears as a positive figure in opposition to the medieval Catholic Church, which is represented as holding not only spiritual but also worldly hierarchical power.[11] This version portrays the scientist as optimist on an exuberant quest for empirically verifiable truth, believing unquestioningly in science and trusting in *reason* through sensual experience. For the entire physical universe, scientific explanations seem attainable. Galileo rejoices at the desire expressed by young scientists to light up the Dark Ages. And why shouldn't all share in the knowledge and power, which will enhance human life? (193) The scientist's confidence is placed firmly in *reason* as source of motivation and even as ultimate goal: 'I believe in the brain,' (144) says Galileo, 'I believe in man, and that means I believe in his *reason*.[...] Thinking is amongst the greatest pleasures of the human race.' (emphasis added, 210-11)

The scientist appears to be echoing Kant's perception of the new human being endowed with *reason*, who not only arrives at fresh scientific insights but comes to new interpretive conclusions as well. Galileo's subsequent questions and discoveries raise doubts in the minds of believers, thereby potentially destabilizing the prevailing concept of the world. When *reason* and *doubt* continue to fuel one another, the old order becomes apprehensive. The astronomer has aimed his telescope at their heavens, threatening their *Weltbild* and their power. The Cardinal protests that, in doing so, Galileo has 'removed man from the center of the universe and placed him somewhere on the periphery.' (232) To a wary Church authority this is heresy, since the fathers of the Catholic Church cannot tolerate in their system change or doubt. Galileo's disclosures could undermine the ecclesiastical hierarchy which has so effectively manipulated the masses for centuries: in keeping the Earth at the center of the universe, 'the Pope may then retain his seat at the center of the Earth.' (245) Galileo confirms their worst fears that, by peeking behind the heavenly curtain and recording what he sees not in scholarly Latin but in the vernacular, the scientist has challenged received wisdom and seriously overstepped the limits.

An actual interpretive consequence of Galileo's new perspective would allow those once yoked to the old, inflexible metaphysical system and impelled to accept the Pope as the final authority to throw off their shackles. Intent on avoiding at all costs critical investigation of its authority by protagonists of a 'subversive' scientific method, the Grand Inquisitor expresses his displeasure at the disturbing unrest which has come into the world. (267) Since Galileo has become too dangerous, the Church forces him in 1633, under threat of torture, to publicly recant his conviction that the earth rotates around the sun. On October 30, 1947, during the postwar American witch hunts, exactly three months after *Galileo* had opened in Beverly Hills, California, Brecht was summoned to testify before the House Committee on Un-American Activities in Washington, where, sounding surprisingly like the historical Galileo, he denied being a member of the Communist party, ostensibly 'recanting' his own political position.

Aspirations of the Scientist

Brecht was committed to *reason* as springboard for social change, as personified by the figure of Galileo, who asserts that the goal of science is to alleviate the hardships of human existence. 'For the love of God the work we do is exacting. Who would go through the strain for less than the population at large?' (159) In this spirit of science for human welfare it seems then ironic that Galileo is not loath to sacrifice his own eyesight, the health and safety of his faithful housekeeper and the happiness of his daughter. A single-mindedness binds him to his telescope, diverting his focus from his own household and blinding him to impending harassment by the authorities. His friend Sagredo cautions: 'Galileo, you are traveling the road to disaster. You are suspicious and skeptical in science, but in politics you are as naive as your daughter!' (134) Passionately in the service of the science of inquiry, the astronomer has neglected to inquire after the allegiance of his patrons until the ecclesiastical tribunal for the suppression of heresy, the Grand Inquisitor, is at his door. The impact of his submission to the Inquisition is felt in all corners of Europe. Despite loss of eyesight, colleagues and friends, reputation and freedom, Galileo risks further persecution by making an illegal copy of his *Discorsi* treatise. In an analysis of the first version of the play, Brecht himself summarizes the meaning of Scene Thirteen by observing that through foresight and cunning Galileo had completed his writings in great secrecy, later assuring that his visiting student Andrea would smuggle the book out of Italy. His strategically calculated recantation had actually allowed him the opportunity to prepare a radical and far-reaching contribution to the scientific community. He was a wise old scientist, after all. (*BFA*, 24, 247-48)

Alterations in the versions of the play reflect actual revisions in the perspective of the scientist and in the world of science as seen by the playwright. While Brecht holds that the scientist's responsibility is to illuminate truth and spread knowledge, there is no guarantee that science may not suddenly turn back on humankind. With the bombings of Hiroshima and Nagasaki in 1945, science in the service of capitalism has assumed a frightening new dimension. Brecht sees the atomic bomb, both technically and socially, as classic end product of Galileo's scientific achievements and as his 'betrayal of society.' (*BFA*, 24, 240) The playwright is confronted with the shortcomings of an overly optimistic view of science as 'progress' and is shocked into preparing a major revision of his play in collaboration with actor/translator Charles Laughton.[12] In the preface to the resulting American translation Brecht elaborates on this shift:

> The 'atomic age' made its debut in Hiroshima in the midst of our work on the play. From one day to the next, a radical shift was felt in the significance of the biography of the founder of modern physics. The infernal effect of the great bomb put Galileo's conflict with the power elite of his time in a new, sharper light. (*BFA*, 24, 241)

Reflecting Brecht's 1945 perspective, his revised protagonist makes the shattering discovery that the same truth which was supposed to enlighten the masses can just as easily be perverted to wipe out humanity. The playwright explores this challenge: by turns he blames the 'Obrigkeit' - the Church in Galileo's day and the power structures and industry in his own - and the scientist.

In Scene Thirteen of the post-Hiroshima American version of the play, the Church suffers less harsh an indictment than the scientist, who is no longer portrayed as wise and heroic but as grim and apprehensive. The astronomer has transformed his prison into an ivory tower, where he has defiantly continued his 'analytical thought experimentation' in isolation from the scientific community.[13] Jan Knopf interprets Galileo to have not been oblivious to possible social-political consequences of his research, although the astronomer emphasizes that they are not his affair, repeatedly demanding time and money to pursue that research.[14] In defence of what he has accepted as his larger commitment to that study, Galileo argues: 'Are we as scientists concerned with where the truth might lead us?' (137) 'I have written a book about the mechanics of the firmament, that is all. What they do or don't do with it is not my concern.' (166) In Brecht's own view, 'Galileo's crime can be seen as the 'original sin' of modern science (*BFA*, 24, 240), to which Knopf adds that the scientist's fall from grace is contingent on his choice of an 'Elfenbeinturm' existence over service to society.[15]

In Berlin several years later, Brecht reinstates some of the material he had deleted for the American audience and attempts to refocus much of the content. Important revisions are undertaken in Scenes Nine, Ten, Eleven, and particularly in Scene Fourteen, the aforementioned *Discorsi* transaction. Galileo warns Andrea that, if he should pocket the manuscript and transport it over the border, he alone would bear the responsibility for repercussions. Admonishing his former student, Galileo asserts that science can be crippled if the scientist persists in stockpiling knowledge for its own sake alone:

> Your new machines may simply suggest new drudgeries. You may in time discover all there is to be discovered, but if you yield to coercion your progress must be a progress away from the bulk of mankind. The gulf between you and humanity may even grow so wide that the sound of your cheering at some new achievement could be echoed by a universal howl of horror. (180)

The moral vacuum surrounding scientific progress has left this disillusioned Galileo character in severe conflict with his responsibility as scientist. No longer the hero who had his *Discorsi* spirited out of the country at the end of the optimistic Danish version of the play, Galileo bemoans his fate: 'I have betrayed my profession. Any man who does what I have done must not be tolerated in the ranks of science.' (180)

Vernunft remains Vernunft

Following the bombing of Hiroshima, concurrent with the Hollywood production of *Galileo*, physicists employed in Pentagon laboratories across the United States

became suddenly aware of the weighty responsibility for the consequences of
their discoveries. Many fled their jobs, including Albert Einstein. 'Es war
schimpflich geworden, etwas zu entdecken.'[16]   But as Galileo confesses to
colleagues and as Cardinal Barberini confesses to Galileo in a moment of
camaraderie in Scene Six, a flirt with astronomy can be 'harder to get rid of than
the itch.' (144) Who can resist the call of the laboratory? Possessed by an
apparent Faustian thirst for knowledge, scientists and intellectuals were to
succumb to that 'itch', which holds sway over other considerations. Thanks to
such relapses, defense research positions were manned anew and the Cold War
could commence. While on his modern scientific trajectory, Brecht recognizes
the predicament facing the experimental scientist: unable to abolish his desire to
know, he is enticed by discernments, calculations, computations, logical
conclusions, and, of course, fame and money. What became of the ideological
solidarity? The playwright sees Kant as ultimately responsible for initiating the
fatal separation of scientific knowledge from ideology. (*BFA*, 21, 415)
Attempting to clarify the relationship between different applications of science,
Brecht found himself grappling with catagories of the intellectual *reasoning*
power of the theoretical scientist, the instrumentalized use of *reason* by those
holding political power, and social *reason* which he attributed to intellectuals and
to the oppressed classes. In his essay entitled 'Rede über die Widerstandskraft
der Vernunft' (1937), indicting the German prewar propaganda machine, Brecht
describes the political atmosphere of the time as one in which intellectuals were
persecuted for their exercise of intellect. Challenging Nazi perversion of the
concept of *Vernunft* which was politicized and denounced as 'intellectual
dissidence,' he contends that, while the fascists publicly attacked *reason* and
denounced the intellect as bestial, they felt compelled to train the populace to
reason. Ironically, in order to broadcast such propaganda, they needed radios,
which are products of *reason*. Brecht concludes that fascist oppression is actually
threatened by its own appetite for the *Vernunft* produced in the act of oppressing.
(*BFA*, 22:1, 336)

We find Brecht defending a term: *Vernunft* - exposing the double-edged sword of
reason as both tool for domination and means for resisting domination; the
playwright saw the fascists as requiring as much *reason* to support their regime
as the masses would need to topple those in power. (*BFA*, 22:1, 336) Brecht
appears, however, to be conflating the important interplay between *reason* and
ideology with engineering, the mechanistic thinking which allowed for radios to
be brought into existence. Evidence of this sort of conflation can be found in
other sections of the same essay. Such a lapse may well stem from the

dramatist's predilection for a utopian vision of *reason* as man's unique capacity for practical intelligence, cognitive acuity and ideological thinking - none of which may necessarily be informed by sound judgment.

In versions of *Galileo* written after 1947, Brecht plays with distinctions between shrewdness (*Schlauheit*) and critical reason (*Vernunft*), again evoking the dialectic of ideology and *reason*. Scene Three finds Sagredo still criticizing what he perceives as Galileo's naiveté: he discloses that his own forty years amongst humans have taught him that the vast majority does not display appreciable quantities of *Vernunft*. 'How can you confuse their wretched shrewdness with reason?' (210) In vain he urges Galileo to use common sense, step away from his telescope, and open his eyes long enough to observe that the world is not gravitating towards critical *reason*, which, if consciously applied, would lead by way of insight to action, which in Marxist terms would mean revolution. Instead of revolutionary transformation, Brecht is faced with the inevitable march from Industry and 'Progress' in Science to Enlightenment and the 'Verwissenschaftlichung' of Modernity.

The Responsibility of the Scientist

Within this context, the theoretical work of Ulrich Beck again enters the discussion with a hypothetical sociological solution. He has crystallized Brecht's dilemma by reconceptualizing science (and, implicitly, *reason*) as 'accountable' in terms of its capacity to predetermine its own supposedly unpredeterminable side effects:

> Whether or not science finds ways to facilitate the process of controlling its own practical risks is dependent not on scientists being given a say in the application of their own findings, but on *what type of science* is practised in view of its consequences and side-effects. (emphasis added, *Risikogesellschaft*, 258)

Beck appears to have manoeuvered himself into circular reasoning - seeking scientific solutions to scientific dilemmas as posed by scientists.

Believing scientists can practise safe science by avoiding the overkill effect of 'Verwissenschaftlichung' and unforeseen side-effects, Beck conjures up a super-scientist who has a comprehensive prognosis and solution for the consequences of all he discovers. By drafting a proposition by which *reason* is contingent on a superhuman cognitive perspective, and *responsibility* for scientific consequences is 'assured,' Beck is in danger of trapping himself in the pretensions of omni*science*, while avoiding confrontation with the inevitable. Although mathematical probability of degrees of danger may be calculated with the aid of *reason*, neither our most scrupulous context-thinking nor confidence in the predictability of scientific outcomes can prevent the risk of irresponsible technological application, no matter what type of science is practised, no matter how responsibly such technology may be calculated, pondered or plotted.[17]

Both Brecht and Beck strive to assure accountability for social consequences in hopes of resolving the dilemmas of science. Brecht holds to the Marxist view in which *reason* is tied to the struggle of the oppressed and responsibility must begin with the redistribution of wealth;[18] Beck maintains that society and the scientist can act in a morally responsible manner by exercising sufficient quantities of *reason* to select the best science and thus ward off possible catastrophies. It must be noted, however, that much of the optimism which once surrounded the idea of technological progress has been shattered. Adorno/Horkheimer's prior diagnosis of the collision course of Enlightenment anticipates the predicament: in order to advance its societal objectives, the scientific method proceeds in a way which, paradoxically, subverts some of those social goals. The *reasoning* of Enlightenment 'reifies' itself to an automatic process that imitates the machine it created, so that the machine may someday replace it, converting it into *machine reason*.[19] Put it in a nutshell: 'On the way to the new science, we sacrifice reason.'[20] It is Brecht who provides us with a strikingly relevant example of this sacrifice:

> Das Ziel des Forschers ist die 'reine' Forschung, das Produkt der Forschung ist weniger rein. Die Formel E = mc2 ist ewig gedacht, an nichts gebunden. So können andere die Bindungen vornehmen: die Stadt Hiroshima ist plötzlich sehr kurzlebig geworden. Die Wissenschaftler nehmen für sich in Anspruch die Unverantwortlichkeit der Maschinen. (*BFA*, 24, 252)

The scientist is left holding the baby - the irresponsible machine for which his indulgence in 'Verwissenschaftlichung' is responsible. Both Brecht and Beck fall victim to this paradox not only in their failure to question the limitations of the scientific method, but also in their reluctance to recognize their inclination to subsume *reason* under their respective scientific concepts and to elevate it to a status from which it supplies all the answers, including the moral one. By means of logic, depending on the axiom in place at the time, one can rationally argue anything. Given what Beck sees, however, as the almost uninterrupted cognitive dissonance between reality and 'expert' interpretations of reality, the individual is now compelled to live in a state of denial, virtually blind to impending nuclear holocaust (*Risikogesellschaft*, 7) Truly employing all of one's intellectual faculties to ascertain and acknowledge the degree of danger could be unbearable.

In his farewell to Andrea in the final Berlin version of the play, Brecht concludes that *reason*, which led us into disaster in the first place, will lead us out again. Regretting that he had perpetuated the misuse of science by not resisting the machinations of the Inquisition, completing instead the *Discorsi* and obediently handing over to his captors the pages of the manuscript, Galileo laments:

> If only I could have resisted, if only scientists could have developed an Hippocratic Oath like physicians have, a promise to use their *knowledge* only for the good of mankind! As it now stands, however, the best that scientists can ever hope for is to become a species of resourcefully researching dwarfs who can be rented out and used for everything. (emphasis added, 5, 248)

If only, by swearing an oath to diffuse his *knowledge* of potentially lethal discoveries, the scientist could ward off power-brokers who pervert scientific insights! In his attempt to make the disreputable scientist reputable, Brecht appears to be reaching for a pre-rational, mythological image: his dwarf-analogy evokes a giant-dwarf dichotomy. Hard pressed to prescribe how the explosive force of science is to operate innocuously, Brecht offers one desperate hope: an Hippocratic oath which might encase gigantic discoveries in an all-encompassing morality - a pledge, in actuality, to *more reason*. His Galileo character, who yearned to become a *reason* Riesen, has neatly internalised the giant-dwarf syndrome: 'For some years I was as strong as the authorities, and I surrendered my knowledge to the powers that be, to use it, abuse it, just as it suits their needs.' (180) As slave to his research passions, he allowed himself to be exploited, thus unwittingly fueling the fires of disaster. The scientist who was envisioned at the vanguard of the Enlightenment is now portrayed in dark isolation, a mere wage labourer who can be baited and bought with money, power, status, ideology, and, in Galileo's case, wine and a plucked goose: a despicable species of 'dwarf.'

The Limits of Reason

This discourse of the absolutization of science and the instrumentalisation of *reason* can best be described today as a cul-de-sac. Whether man is viewed as under- or over-dimensional, whether he operates through alchemy or ideology, mathematical abstraction or its translation into mega-weaponry, the old Cartesian partition between the observer and the observed is breaking down. Although a pledge cannot be substituted for wisdom, cooperation, and a human conscience, it may be seen as an important first step in rejoining the superscientist with society. The next requisite steps would involve changing the structure of science to integrate connection, consensus, compassion, and conscience back into the equation. The limits of *reason* must be recognised and acknowledged. One danger experienced by the scientist Galileo - the politics of telling the truth and trusting that the other person is *reasonable* - was a pitfall which apparently did not entrap the playwright Brecht before the House Committee on Un-American Activities. As shrewd 'Bearer of Truth,' whose main duty must be to survive, Brecht was practised in detecting the *unreasonableness* of oaths sworn before representatives of state. It is not enough, however, to be on the 'right' side. Given the limits of *reason*, no oath would suffice, as the kernel of destruction already dwells within science. Neverthless, the Federation of American Scientists has created a voluntary Hippocratic Oath for scientists: it holds that scientists will not participate in any project involved in destruction of the earth. Without compliance by the individual scientist, scientific data cannot be applied, as was stressed by Dr. Joseph Rotblat upon receipt of the Nobel Peace Prize in 1995. It is his contention that 'the momentum of the nuclear arms race was maintained not by the military-industrial complex but individual scientists in weapon laboratories and positions of governmental power and influence.'[21]

As the curtain closes, the responsibility has fallen upon the super-scientist who has assumed the power to comprehend, predict and oversee all eventualities. Faced with such dilemmas, Brecht stands 'ratlos,' as I feel Rudolf Heukenkamp demonstrates.[22]   Unable to arrive at a decision on the trustworthiness of scientists, Brecht offers instead two explanations: a social-historical interpretation of relations between Galileo and the physicists of the 20th century (that Galileo's betrayal brought forth the modern bomb-building specialists) and an ethical interpretation (that without an Hippocratic Oath scientists serve as mere 'inventive dwarfs'). For Brecht, I extrapolate, contradictions in the role of the scientist – who on the one hand, looms gigantic 'as strong as the authorities' and yet cowers dwarf-like, having 'surrendered his knowledge' to them - are exacerbated by the fear that no plan can be drafted nor agreed upon by which an oath could be enforced. Through the attempted balancing act and through his final indecision, it is Heukenkamp's contention, Brecht had hoped to overcome his helplessness ('Ratlosigkeit').

In the end, the dramatist could not resolve the issue of how knowledge should be used, though his persistence brought him to a point of recognisable impasse. Brecht's plea for an oath to confine the uses and proliferation of science may be an impractical and utopian vision, but it dramatises the now universal quandary which scientists had previously felt called upon to face alone. What is at stake goes beyond a theoretical discussion of *Vernunft* as it has heretofore been understood. Recalling Galileo's optimistic first glorification of the '*gentle* power of reason' as it contrasts with Bacon's pretentious 'knowledge itself is power,' it is the discourse of power and the quality of human relations with each other and with nature which require humanity to reexamine the meaning of *Vernunft* and the scientific tradition. Such a reconceptualization might best begin with the scientist's confessed helplessness and defencelessness in the face of the overkill effect of 'science-gone-wild.' Seen in this light, Brecht's humbling indecisiveness, which clearly stands contrary to an idealized application of the scientific method, might well represent a first honest reaction to 'Verwissenschaftlichung.' In fact, the ability to exist within the dynamic contradictions of reality could be one of the initial requirements of a new era.[23]

---

[1]   Bertolt Brecht, *Leben des Galilei: Schauspiel*, in *BFA, Stücke 5* (Frankfurt aM, Suhrkamp, 1988), pp. 8-289. Bracketed references to the play are henceforth cited by page number. All English quotations are taken from the Laughton translation.

[2]   Jürgen Habermas, *The Philosophical Discourse of Modernity: Twelve Lectures*, trans. Frederick G. Lawrence (Cambridge, MIT Press, 1987), p.84.

[3]   Benjamin Farrington, *Temporis Partus Masculus: An Untranslated Writing of Francis Bacon*, (Centaurus, 1, 1951), p.197, cited in Evelyn Fox Keller, *Reflections on Gender and Science* (New Haven, Yale Univerity Press, 1985), p.17.

[4]   Max Horkheimer and Theodor Adorno, *Dialektik der Aufklärung: Philosophische Fragmente*, (Frankfurt aM Main, Fischer Taschenbuch Verlag, 1988), p.9.

[5]   Immanuel Kant, 'Beantwortung der Frage: Was ist Aufklärung?' in *Die Deutsche Literatur in Text und Darstellung: Aufklärung und Rokoko* (Stuttgart, Reclam, 1980), pp.42-45.

[6]   Thomas S. Kuhn, *The Structure of Scientific Revolutions* (Chicago, University of Chicago Press, 1962), p.165. In his discussion of *progress*, the author details 'inextricable connections between our notions of science and technology and of *progress*.' 'We tend to see as science any field in which *progress* is marked.' (pp.160-65; emphasis added)

[7]   The Industrial Revolution was, in a sense, a stepchild of the Newtonian revolution. Concomitant with industrialization, the capitalist mode of production furthered the modernisation process. For Adorno and Horkheimer, the Enlightenment begins with capitalism and its instrumentalized exchange of people and things.

[8]   Horkheimer and Adorno, *Dialektik der Aufklärung*, p.9. The authors appear to be referring to Auschwitz. Among the disasters one might also include are the products and manipulations of the bourgeoning postwar military-industrial complex: the atomic, hydrogen and neutron bombs. See also Horkheimer's discussion of questionable outgrowths of

Enlightenment *reason* in Zur *Kritik der instrumentellen Vernunft. Aus den Vorträgen und Aufzeichnungen seit Kriegsende*, ed. Alfred Schmidt (Frankfurt aM, Fischer, 1967).

9. Ulrich Beck, in *Risikogesellschaft: Auf dem Weg in eine andere Moderne* (Frankfurt aM, Suhrkamp, 1986), p.254. Bracketed references to Beck's book are henceforth cited by page number.

10. See also Peter Gay, who provides background on the astronomer in his book, *The Enlightenment: An Interpretation. The Rise of Modern Paganism* (New York: W.W. Norton and Company, 1977), p.228.

11. In journal notes made in 1939, Brecht cautions against branding Galileo's struggle for freedom to conduct research as one purely against the Church, for it would deflect attention from the reactionary and utterly secular authorities of the day - the criminal engineers and commanders of the Third Reich (*BFA*, 24, 238).

12. During his three-and-a-half-year collaboration with Laughton, Brecht made extensive journal notations detailing the process, some of which are included in 'Das ungeschminkte Bild einer neuen Zeit' (*BFA*, 24, 241).

13. 'Analytical thought experimentation,' according to Thomas S. Kuhn, 'bulks large in the writings of Galileo and is perfectly calculated to expose the old paradigm to existing knowledge in ways that isolate the roots of crisis with a clarity unattainable in the laboratory.' (*Structure of Scientific Revolutions*, p. 88).

14. Jan Knopf, *Brecht-Handbuch: Theater: eine Ästhetik der Widersprüche*, (Stuttgart, J.B.Metzlersche Verlangsbuchhandlung, 1980), p.164.

15. Knopf, *Brecht-Handbuch*, p.169.

16. Knopf, *Brecht-Handbuch*, p.169.

17. In this connection see Kant's discourse on *Vernunft* [reason] and *Erkenntnis* [knowledge, realization, cognition] in his discussion of the transcendental dialectic in *Kritik der reinen Vernunft* (1781) (Hamburg, 1956). There he defines his terms by stating that *reason* actually leads dialectically away from empirical use of the Kantian categories and that this restricts cognition. In the last analysis, he implies, *Vernunft* operates with ideas under which all phenomena and terms are subsumed.

18. The limits of *reason* may have led, ironically, to Brecht's gradual loss of faith in the paradigmatic shift started by the Russian Revolution.

19. Horkheimer and Adorno, *Dialektik der Aufklärung*, p.31.

20. Horkheimer and Adorno, *Dialektik der Aufklärung*, p.11.

21. The Einstein-Russell Manifesto, which called upon scientists to abandon their 'ivory towers' and assemble to discuss the social, moral, and ethical implications of the advent of thermonuclear weapons, was issued in London in July 1955. Albert Einstein, Bertrand Russell,

Linus Pauling, and Joseph Rotblat were among the 22 founders of the annual Pugwash Conferences on Science and World Affairs. Rotblat's quote is cited in the science section of *The New York Times*, 21 May 1995, pp.C1 and C7.

22. Brecht conceived the Hippocratic oath passage for the American translation but inserted it only in his final version. Rudolf Heukenkamp interprets the passage to mean that he did not trust scientists with a solution to the atom bomb problem. As proof, he cites Brecht's proposal of an oath as a corrective to society's dilemma - the lack of responsibility - in his 'Vorschlag anläßlich der außerordentlichen Tagung des Weltfriedensrates in Berlin 1954.' Rudolf Heukenkamp, 'Dichter im Dienste der Nuklearrüstung? Literarische Beiträge zum Atomdiskurs der DDR zwischen 1945 und 1957,' in *Militärische und zivile Mentalität. Ein literaturkritischer Report,* ed. Ursula Heukenkamp (Berlin, Aufbau-Verlag, 1991), pp. 282-302. My sincere thanks to Helmut Peitsch for this specific reference from pp.298-99.

23. I gratefully acknowledge the German Graduate Students Association at New York University for their 1994 publication of an earlier version of this paper in the *Proceedings and Commentary of the GGSA Conference.* I also wish to express gratitude to Margret Herzfeld, Imke Lode, David Palmer, and Robert Cohen for their helpful comments on earlier drafts.

TERRY HOLMES

The Suppressed Science of Society in *Leben des Galilei*

Galileo's self-denunciation towards the end of *Leben des Galilei* seems to encapsulate Brecht's case against his unheroic hero. Galileo condemns himself for having publicly recanted his scientific discoveries under pressure from the Church. He insists that if he had stood firm at that critical moment his example could have inspired a far-reaching social upheaval ensuring that scientific knowledge would be used only for the good of humanity. His failure to resist the threat of torture has resulted in the complete subjugation of science to the powers that be.[1]

Gert Sautermeister sharply criticizes Brecht for representing Galileo's recantation in this light. The scientist's self-arraignment is judged by Sautermeister to be unconvincing because it is not consistent with the handling of social issues in the rest of the play. If the drama as a whole reflects the Marxist view of history as a process determined by class struggle, the ending completely overturns this approach by attributing such momentous historical responsibility to a failed martyr:

> Am Ende lenkt das Drama den Blick [...] auf den todbereiten Individualheroismus als eine die Gesellschaft erlösende Kraft. [...] Da ist nicht mehr materialistische Dialektik, sondern säkularisierte Religion und barockes Welttheater im Spiel. Mit der 14. Szene bricht sich Brechts kritisch aufklärende Dramaturgie an einer anachronistischen Helden- und Märtyrerkonzeption.[2]

Sautermeister's argument presupposes that the dramatist himself is addressing us through the medium of Galileo's final speech, that this entire statement is articulated by a composite of figure and author, by 'Brecht-Galilei' (Sautermeister, 144-5). On the face of it this may appear to be a perfectly obvious view. When Brecht collaborated with Charles Laughton on the fundamental revision of the play in America, the main point of the exercise was to underline the social consequences of Galileo's capitulation, and Brecht certainly spoke of this intention in terms that are echoed by Galileo in the drama.[3] The great scientist was to be depicted as the 'technischer Schöpfer' of the Industrial Revolution, but also as its 'sozialer Verräter'.[4] The dramatist rejected the idea that Galileo's recantation could be excused as a deliberate ploy enabling him to continue with his scientific research - just as Galileo dismisses the same suggestion when it is put to him by Andrea (*BFA*, 5, 282). Brecht insisted: 'In Wirklichkeit hat Galilei die Astronomie und die Physik bereichert, indem er diese Wissenschaften zugleich eines Großteils ihrer gesellschaftlichen Bedeutung beraubte' (Hecht, 56), which is in effect exactly what Galileo affirms. To this extent we may agree with Sautermeister that 'Brecht hat diese Selbstverklagung Galileis energisch bekräftigt' (137). But that is not sufficient reason to posit a complete equation of Galileo's words with Brecht's own treatment of the problem. I will argue that Galileo's self-accusation reveals significant misunderstandings about what he has done wrong, and that this failure of analysis may be seen as an integral part of Brecht's more subtle and complex arraignment of him. Brecht wants to show that by the end Galileo has actually rendered himself incapable of giving a proper account of his guilt, because that guilt is incurred when he ceases to apply his critical intelligence to social and political processes as well as to such things as the structure of the universe and the properties of solid bodies. It is a cruel but fitting irony that Galileo, though clearly aware in general terms of the damage he has caused, cannot in retrospect correctly identify the precise social issues that he declined to think about at the time when they directly confronted him.

The reason given by Galileo for thinking that his resistance would have triggered off 'große Erschütterungen' is that his scientific theories had reached the market-places and inspired a critical and rebellious attitude amongst the common people (*BFA*, 5, 284). The implication is that the people were capable of challenging the ruling class if only he, Galileo, had given the lead by defying the Church. We can test this theory by reference to the carnival scene, which depicts the popularization of Galileo's scientific ideas and their translation into questions about the validity of the social order (*BFA*, 5, 259-62). Brecht said that this scene depicts 'die italienische Bevölkerung, Galileis revolutionäre Lehre mit ihren eigenen revolutionären Forderungen verknüpfend' (Hecht, 100), and indeed the crowd is entertained with a subversive street performance linking the overthrow of the Ptolemaic system with the inversion of social hierarchies and the expropriation of the expropriators. The people are encouraged to learn from Galileo 'des Erdenglückes großes Abc' and to adopt a more fractious and critical attitude, since 'Gehorsam war des Menschen Kreuz von je!' (*BFA*, 5, 262).

We find nevertheless that Brecht has been careful to point up the limitations and hesitancies of this popular radicalism. The prospect of social change comes across as a wistful fantasy rather than a political programme. The refrain 'Macht man den Strick uns ums Genick nicht dick, dann reißt er!' suggests that the rope of social control is indeed a good thick one and that the faint prospect of escaping from it would depend on the carelessness of the oppressors, not on the determination of the underdogs. The purely hypothetical status of the social revolt is also established by the subjunctive mood and the distancing 'auch mal' in that other snatch of the refrain, 'Wer wär nicht auch mal gern sein eigner Herr und Meister?'. It is not really plausible to view this scene as prefiguring imminent proletarian revolution, as Alfred White seems to do when he comments that the stirrings of discontent 'here lead straight to Utopia'. If that were so, then White would be right to say that Brecht 'short-circuits the history of the proletarian idea'.[5] But Brecht himself is not responsible for any such impression of an abbreviated class struggle; he stresses the tentative and imaginary character of the 'revolutionäre Forderungen' voiced in the carnival scene and thus indicates that we are dealing with an urban crowd in early modern times, not with the proletarian mass under developed capitalism. The very form in which the demand for economic justice is made serves to underscore this point. The labourers' appropriation of the fruits of their labour figures here as the personal retention of a personally produced commodity at that moment when it is about to pass into the possession of another:

> Der Maurer hebt den Baugrund aus
> Und holt des Bauherrn Stein
> Und wenn er's dann gebaut, das Haus
> Dann zieht er selber ein! (*BFA*, 5, 261)

This bears only a distant relation to the Marxist theory of proletarian revolution, in which the working class takes *collective* possession of the *means of production*. The highest ambition articulated in this scene is an individualistic wish that also has little to do with the aspirations of the Marxian proletariat: it is the dream of becoming 'sein eigner Herr und Meister', that is, to be free from the tyranny of guild master and feudal overlord, to be an autonomous individual rather than a servant in the traditional chain of hierarchy. This is not what Helmut Jendreiek calls it, 'ein Aufruf [...] zur revolutionären Solidarität' marking 'die Chance der historischen Stunde des Volkes'.[6] The lack of a collective purpose amongst the crowd reflects their lack of collective strength and collective identity, the absence, in short, of a revolutionary class consciousness in the Marxist sense. However, this does not mean that the people's desire for individual freedom is unrealizable; in the historical perspective disclosed by the play that wish is destined to be fulfilled, but it will turn out to be something very different from genuine emancipation. Ironically, the people's yearning for the freedom to dispose of their own powers anticipates the free labour market that capitalism will establish in order to develop its massive productive potential at the expense of the common people.

Brecht undoubtedly depicts the popularization of science as a significant factor in the social ferment of Galileo's day and age. The Inquisitor and the landowner Ludovico voice the establishment's unease about the effect of the new doctrines on the people (*BFA*, 5, 256, 269), and the clamp-down on Galileo comes immediately after the carnival scene. But whereas Galileo at the end of the drama seems to view the people's disaffection as having a revolutionary potential of its own, Brecht follows an orthodox Marxist line in treating the popular unrest as a contributory moment in the incipient bourgeois revolution, the only revolution possible at that stage in the history of the forces of production. In the American version of the play, Brecht introduced a representative figure of the rising bourgeoisie, the iron-founder Matti (renamed Vanni in the version of 1955/56). In Scene 11 (*BFA*, 5, 263-7) he seeks out Galileo at the Florentine court and offers him help in his conflict with the Church, an offer that is brusquely dismissed by the scientist, who prefers the more comfortable option of trusting in the friends that he thinks he has in high places. The central importance of this episode is clearly indicated by Brecht's own commentary:

> Der Stückeschreiber zieht es vor, den *Widerruf* des Galilei hier zu plazieren, anstatt denselben vor der Inquisition stattfinden zu lassen. Galilei vollzieht ihn, wenn er das Angebot der fortschrittlichen bürgerlichen Klasse, gemacht durch den Eisengießer Vanni, ihn in seinem Kampf gegen die Kirche zu unterstützen, ablehnt und sich darauf beruft, er habe ein unpolitisches wissenschaftliches Werk geschrieben. (Hecht, 101)

This is an extremely important argument, for it shifts the crisis of the play from the formal recantation scene to this brief private encounter. The scene with Vanni represents the true moment of recantation, since this is where Galileo denies the social relevance of his scientific research: 'Ich habe ein Buch geschrieben über die Mechanik des Universums, das ist alles. Was daraus gemacht oder nicht gemacht wird, geht mich nichts an' (*BFA*, 5, 265). This statement is a direct contradiction of Galileo's own previous insistence that scientific questions cannot be considered in isolation from their social repercussions. In his argument with the little monk he even asserts that the problem of social justice is the real point at issue behind the cosmological disputes: 'es handelt sich nicht um die Planeten, sondern um die Campagnabauern' (*BFA*, 5, 245). Galileo's retraction of this insight, a retraction in effect of his own commitment to the cause of humanity, is a much more serious and fundamental betrayal than his later repudiation of the scientific facts.

At this turning point Galileo commits not only a grave moral offence, but also a fatal tactical blunder. He refuses to escape in Vanni's coach, declaring that he cannot see himself as a fugitive; but a few moments later the trap closes and he is on his way to Rome, where he will be forced to recant and then condemned to life-long house arrest. When Galileo later condemns himself for failing to defy the authorities when he was hauled up before them in Rome, he is interpreting his own case quite differently from the way Brecht presents it. The drama demonstrates that Galileo's crucial failure was to put himself in a position where the Church could isolate him from his supporters and subject him to irresistible pressure. The central issue is not one of heroism or martyrdom, rather Galileo's guilt lies in his refusal to think clearly about the politics of his situation while he still has time to evade the long arm of the Inquisition. That is why I think Sautermeister is mistaken in arguing that Brecht burdens his anti-hero with 'eine heroische, uneinlösbare Verantwortung' (127); it is Galileo who places himself in this dilemma by rejecting out of hand Vanni's offer of an alliance.

Whilst recognizing the importance of the Vanni episode for the moral and political argument of the play, Ernst Schumacher is sceptical about the historical assumptions that led Brecht to invest it with such weighty significance. Brecht maintains that the rise of the bourgeoisie gave Galileo the opportunity to link his fight for scientific truth with the interests of a dynamic and ambitious social class:

> es handelte sich nicht nur mehr um wissenschaftliche Leistungen, sondern um Kämpfe, sie groß und allgemein zu verwerten. Die Verwertung erfolgte in vielen Hinsichten, mußte doch die neue Klasse, um ihre Geschäfte betreiben zu können, zur Macht kommen und eine herrschende Ideologie zertrümmern, die sie daran hinderte. [...] Galilei wurde zum Schädling, als er seine Wissenschaft in diesen Kampf führte und den Kampf dann verließ. (Hecht, 98)

Schumacher objects, however, that the image of a rampant bourgeoisie, although valid for countries like England and Holland at that time, is not applicable to Galileo's Italy:

> Das italienische Bürgertum [...] befand sich ökonomisch auf der absteigenden Linie und war politisch entmachtet. [...] [Brecht] gliederte Galilei schematisch in die europäische Gesamtentwicklung ein, ohne die besonderen Umstände zu berücksichtigen, die in Italien herrschten. (161, 164)

But in fact Brecht has not ignored the unevenness of capitalist development, which is very distinctly reflected in the play in Vanni's litany of complaints about the backwardness of Italy in comparison with other parts of Europe:

> Im letzten Jahr allein eschienen fünf Bände über Agrikultur in London. Wir wären hier schon dankbar für ein Buch über die holländischen Kanäle. Dieselben Kreise, die Ihnen Schwierigkeiten machen, erlauben den Ärzten von Bologna nicht, Leichen aufzuschneiden für Forschungszwecke. [...] Wissen Sie, daß sie in Amsterdam und London Geldmärkte haben? Gewerbeschulen ebenfalls. [...] Hier haben wir nicht einmal die Freiheit, Geld zu machen. Man ist gegen Eisengießereien, weil man der Ansicht ist, zu viele Arbeiter an einem Ort fördere die Unmoral! (*BFA*, 5, 264)

It is simply not true that Brecht places Galileo in an unhistorical context of bourgeois triumph; for all his generalizations about the energy and enterprise of the new social class, Brecht does make it quite obvious in the drama that the Italian bourgeoisie is on the defensive and has a very long way to go to achieve its aims. But in any case that consideration hardly justifies Galileo's refusal to join forces with Vanni. Admittedly the industrialist does not promise Galileo the certainty of success, he promises him only an opportunity to continue the struggle; but that is the best offer Galileo can expect, since the bourgeoisie is the only class with definite ambitions for the future that coincide with his pursuit of scientific truth. And although Vanni's opponents may have the upper hand, the way Galileo talks about that relation of power is undifferentiated to the point of obtuseness: 'Ich kenne Macht von Ohnmacht auseinander' (*BFA*, 5, 265). It emerges from the discussion about the star charts in the very next scene that Italy's commercial class does possess some measure of influence; despite the fact that the charts are based on Galileo's heretical teachings, the Inquisitor himself concedes that the maritime city-states must be allowed to use them: 'Man wird ihnen nachgeben müssen, es sind materielle Interessen' (*BFA*, 5, 269). Galileo seems unwilling to recognize that the dynamics of social conflict may be every bit as complex as the physical laws of the universe and just as needful of scrupulous analysis. But it is Vanni who makes the essential point: 'Sie scheinen Ihre Freunde nicht von Ihren Feinden auseinanderzukennen, Herr Galilei' (*BFA*, 5, 265). The objective class interests of those in whom Galileo puts his trust clearly require the suppression of his novel views. It makes no sense for Galileo to choose the side of the powerful to defend his science when he has already understood that the prevailing power structure rests on the very dogmas that are challenged by his science, when he has already deduced that the earth has to be placed in the centre of the universe 'damit der Stuhl Petri im Mittelpunkt der Erde stehen kann!' (*BFA*, 5, 245).

Ronald Speirs has argued that Galileo refuses Vanni's support 'for what seem to him to be good reasons', one of which is 'the fact that the Pope is a trained scientist'.[7] Brecht himself acknowledged that this scene offers 'hinreichend Gründe für Galileis Zögern, aus Florenz zu fliehen und sich in den Schutz der oberitalienischen Städte zu stellen', but he added: 'Trotzdem mag das Publikum sich ausmalen, daß er sich dem Eisengießer Matti anvertraute und auch hierfür so manche Tendenzen im Charakter und in der Situation Galileis ausfinden' (Hecht, 68). In other words, we may question, from Galileo's own standpoint, the reasons that lead him to make the wrong choice. And Galileo's trust in the new pontiff is an eminently questionable reason for acting as he does, for he has already met Barberini at a masked ball before he became Pope, and in that encounter the scientifically minded cardinal reveals very clearly the limits of his tolerance. Barberini explains that he is able to speak frankly to Galileo only because he is wearing a mask and hence relieved for the moment of his duty as a dignitary of the Church; but what he says *incognito* actually confirms his commitment to uphold the vested interests of the Church: 'In einem solchen Aufzug können Sie mich murmeln hören: Wenn es keinen

Gott gäbe, müßte man ihn erfinden' (*BFA*, 5, 240). This may be a cynical and impious remark, but on the other hand it plainly indicates that Barberini is prepared to defend the tenets of belief even if he can no longer believe in them himself - because religious belief serves the purpose of social control, as his 'gelehrte[r] Freund' Cardinal Bellarmin (*BFA*, 5, 237) explains in an equally cynical tone with reference to the landowners' brutal treatment of the Campagna peasants:

> Wir haben die Verantwortung für den Sinn solcher Vorgänge (das Leben besteht daraus), die wir nicht begreifen können, einem höheren Wesen zugeschoben, davon gesprochen, daß mit derlei gewisse Absichten verfolgt werden, daß dies alles einem großen Plan zufolge geschieht. (*BFA*, 5, 238)

In effect these two enlightened prelates issue Galileo with an unmistakable warning that they will not be on his side in an open contest between faith and science, because faith underpins the social order that guarantees *inter alia* the privileged access they evidently have to 'alle Arten von Genüssen, himmlische und irdische' (*BFA*, 5, 237). If he still thinks that the new Pope's scientific training is a good reason to rely on him - and he does, as witness his euphoric outburst: 'Barberini im Aufstieg! Das Wissen wird eine Leidenschaft sein und die Forschung eine Wollust' (*BFA*, 5, 254) - then that simply illustrates the point I am trying to make: that Galileo's principal fault is his failure to think about politics with the same consistent clarity, attentiveness, and rigour that he brings to his scientific research.

It seems to me that Brecht does succeed in making Galileo's encounter with Vanni into the focal point of the drama, a moment when the scientist not only abjures his conviction that science must be used to improve human life, but also disdains to think seriously about the political strategy by which the freedom of science might be preserved. In the dramatic context we are persuaded that Galileo makes the wrong decision, that it is a fateful decision, and that he is culpable, since it lay within his moral and intellectual capacity to decide on the right course of action. But there is a larger, historical context within which this construction of the problem may appear to be questionable. If Galileo had made what Brecht presents as the correct choice and thrown in his lot with the bourgeoisie, would that not have meant in effect that he was switching allegiance from one oppressive system to another one? After all, where Galileo does achieve genuine moral insight in the play, his ethical standard is the well-being of ordinary people. Are the ordinary people going to be any better off under capitalist exploitation than they were under the feudal yoke? Are the horrors of the proletarian experience in the Industrial Revolution any less shocking than what Galileo sees of peasant life in the Campagna? In the Marxist perspective, of course, the rise of capitalism is a necessary prelude to the eventual triumph of communism. But to invoke that theory in bare outline seems a rather remote and schematic justification. I believe that Brecht had a more definite conception of the role that Galileo might have played in shaping and hastening the historical movement towards communism. If we follow Brecht's invitation to suppose that Galileo did take sides with Vanni, then it is possible to extrapolate a pattern of development showing how the critical thinking with which Galileo supports the bourgeoisie in its bid for hegemony is transformed, at the next stage of the class struggle, into a revolutionary critique of bourgeois hegemony.

I shall begin this phase of the argument by asking how much we can infer about the kind of society that Vanni wants to create. What makes him the predestined ally of Galileo is his pursuit of freedom. He admires in Galileo 'de[n] Mann, der für die Freiheit kämpft, neue Dinge lehren zu dürfen', but above and beyond freedom of research and information he also desires 'die Freiheit, Geld zu machen', which implies the right to run his business along the lines he reckons will maximize his profit. But the Church tries to interfere with his managerial freedom, just as it tries to curb Galileo's intellectual freedom: 'Man ist gegen Eisengießereien, weil man der Ansicht ist, zu viele Arbeiter an einem Ort fördere die Unmoral! Ich stehe und falle mit Männern wie Sie, Herr Galilei'. Evidently the concentration of labour is a technical exigency of the production methods that Vanni wants to adopt. That is also implied in the term he uses to refer to his own interest group when he assures Galileo 'daß wir von der Manufaktur auf Ihrer Seite sind' (*BFA*, 5, 264). For a Marxist like Brecht that term has a quite definite historical meaning. In *Das Kapital* Marx closely examines manufacture as a particular phase in the early development of capitalism, where profit is increased by the systematic division of labour. The task of making a given article is subdivided into a series of distinct manual operations, each of which is carried out by a different worker or group of workers. As Marx pointed out, the economics of this new procedure entail the concentration of many workers in the place of work: 'die manufakturmäßige Teilung der Arbeit [entwickelt] das Wachstum der angewandten Arbeiterzahl zur technischen Notwendigkeit'.[8] Brecht puts it a bit more vividly in 'Das Manifest', his versification of part of the *Communist Manifesto*, which he wrote during a break in the American revision of *Leben des Galilei* whilst Laughton was acting in a pirate film:[9]

> Manufaktur überflügelt das Handwerk. [...]
> Viele sitzen sie nunmehr
> Eng aneinander gereiht in der einen, größeren Werkstatt.
> (*BFA*, 15, 150, 397)

Crowded together and narrowly specialized, the workers are, in Marx's view, reduced to abnormalities, mechanical mutations of humanity imprisoned in the soul-destroying discipline devised and imposed by the capitalist: 'Die manufakturmäßige

Teilung der Arbeit unterstellt die unbedingte Autorität des Kapitalisten über Menschen, die bloße Glieder eines ihm gehörigen Gesamtmechanismus bilden' (*Das Kapital*, 377). This image of the manufacturing workforce belies Vanni's clarion call for freedom. Vanni is fighting against the authority of the Church in order to impose his own 'unconditional authority' on those who work for him. In the name of freedom, he will deny others not only *their* freedom but also their very humanity as they become mere cogs in his productive machine. Marx comments scathingly on the bourgeois double standard whereby the complete subjugation of the worker is celebrated for its productive results, whilst any restriction of the capitalist's activity is denounced as an attack on property rights and individual freedom:

> Dasselbe bürgerliche Bewußtsein, das die manufakturmäßige Teilung der Arbeit, die lebenslängliche Annexation des Arbeiters an eine Detailverrichtung und die unbedingte Unterordnung der Teilarbeiter unter das Kapital als eine Organisation der Arbeit feiert, welche ihre Produktivkraft steigre, denunziert [...] ebenso laut jede bewußte gesellschaftliche Kontrolle und Reglung des gesellschaftlichen Produktionsprozesses als einen Eingriff in die unverletzlichen Eigentumsrechte, Freiheit und sich selbst bestimmende 'Genialität' des individuellen Kapitalisten. (*Das Kapital*, 377)

In the drama Vanni's particular line of manufacture and the direction of Galileo's scientific research both point forward beyond the period of manufacture to the Industrial Revolution, the era of machinery. Attached to the end of Scene 13 is an excerpt from the historical Galileo's *Discourses on Mechanics and Motion* that deals with the problem of the resilience of a structure relative to its size (*BFA*, 5, 274-5). This passage reflects on the observation that bigger organisms are proportionately less robust than smaller ones; nature could produce a horse twenty times as big as normal only by 'Veränderungen der Proportionen aller Glieder, besonders der Knochen, die weit über das Maß einer proportionellen Größe verstärkt werden müssen'. The quotation concludes by applying this insight to mechanical engineering: 'Die gemeine Annahme, daß große und kleine Maschinen gleich ausdauernd seien, ist offenbar irrig'. A later section of the *Discorsi* provides an answer to the question of how to make bigger structures work efficiently without having to use disproportionately bigger components:

> if one wished to maintain in an enormous giant those proportions of members that exist in an ordinary man, it would be necessary either to find much harder and more resistant material to form his bones, or else to allow his robustness to be proportionately weaker than in men of average stature [...].[10]

In the drama Galileo's practical involvement with industry points in the same direction. The disproportionate strengthening needed for bigger machines will be achieved not through a geometric increase in the size of their parts, but through the development of a much stronger construction material. By designing a 'Schmelzanlage' for Vanni (*BFA*, 5, 263) Galileo has already contributed to the technical solution of the problem. In *Das Kapital* Marx points out the role of iron-making technology in the evolution of fully automatic machinery; the 'Anwendung von schwer zu bewältigendem Material, z.B. Eisen statt Holz' was an essential precondition for replacing the 'Zwerginstrument', the hand-tool of the craft and manufacture periods, with the 'Riesenglieder' of modern industrial machinery (402-4). Brecht's Galileo is fully involved, by virtue of both his theoretical and his technical efforts, in preparing the way for this future revolution in the forces of production.

But far from redressing the evils of the manufacture system, the capitalist machine age will, according to Marx, intensify the process of exploitation. As the main requirement of industry shifts from muscle-power to machine supervision, women and children can be drafted *en masse* into the workforce, which has the effect of eroding family life as well as driving down wages. And because profit accrues to the capitalist only from his variable capital and not from his fixed capital, the increased proportion of fixed to variable capital resulting from investment in costly machinery means that the variable capital embodied in the workforce must be more fully exploited, which is achieved by the lengthening or intensification of the working day to the very limits of human endurance (*Das Kapital*, 223-5, 425-32). Under capitalism, a great technological advance that might have been expected to relieve the burden of human labour actually imposes a far greater demand on the time and effort of the working class. Marx speaks of 'das ökonomische Paradoxon, daß das gewaltigste Mittel zur Verkürzung der Arbeitszeit in das unfehlbarste Mittel umschlägt, alle Lebenszeit des Arbeiters und seiner Familie in disponible Arbeitszeit für die Verwertung des Kapitals zu verwandeln'. Who could have foreseen such a perversion of progress? Marx quotes Aristotle at this point, to show that even the greatest thinker of antiquity associated the dream of automation with the prospect of universal leisure and freedom:

> 'wenn jedes Werkzeug auf Geheiß, oder auch vorausahnend, das ihm zukommende Werk verrichten könnte, wie des Dädalus Kunstwerke sich von selbst bewegten oder die Dreifüße des Hephästos aus eignem Antrieb an die heilige Arbeit gingen, wenn so die Weberschiffe von selbst webten, so bedürfte es weder für den Werkmeister der Gehilfen noch für die Herrn der Sklaven.' (*Das Kapital*, 430)

Brecht also makes use of the same passage from Aristotle in *Leben des Galilei* to indicate the hopes that Galileo and his followers attach to the coming of the machine. The dramatic context is the Inquisitor's diatribe against the exponents of scientific progress:

> Dieser Galilei hat schon als junger Mensch über die Maschinen geschrieben. Mit den
> Maschinen wollen sie Wunder tun. Was für welche? Gott brauchen sie jedenfalls nicht
> mehr, aber was sollen es für Wunder sein? [...] Der Aristoteles, der für sie sonst ein toter
> Hund ist, hat gesagt - und das zitieren sie - : Wenn das Weberschifflein von selber webte
> und der Zitherschlägel von selber spielte, dann brauchten allerdings die Meister keine
> Gesellen und die Herren keine Knechte. Und so weit sind sie jetzt, denken sie. (*BFA*, 5,
> 268-9)

This is no mere invective, but a very accurate insight into the social motives of
Galileo's science prior to his meeting with Vanni. In his argument with the little
monk in Scene 8 Galileo rejects the idea that the peasants' submission to grinding
toil is a virtue, and adds: 'meine neuen Wasserpumpen können da mehr Wunder tun
als ihre lächerliche übermenschliche Plackerei' (*BFA*, 5, 245). And in Scene 14
Andrea's definition of 'das eigentliche Geschäft der Wissenschaft' is clearly an echo
of Galileo's own convictions: 'd[as] Studium der Eigenschaften der Bewegung,
Mutter der Maschinen, die allein die Erde so bewohnbar machen werden, daß der
Himmel abgetragen werden kann' (*BFA*, 5, 282).

It is obvious that we are meant to admire the sentiment behind these
expectations, but they may appear rather utopian when we contrast them with the
grim realities of the machine age. Our perspective on the very different future that
actually ensued would seem to undercut the whole debate over Galileo's betrayal of
his ideals, for it suggests that what Brecht saw as the right choice for him to make -
to fight alongside Vanni in the name of those ideals - would merely have helped to
establish and justify a new system of oppression. At this point, however, we need to
examine more closely the character, or perhaps we should say the *technique*, of that
social criticism which is the complement to Galileo's idealism. In his *Kleines
Organon für das Theater*, written in 1948/49 soon after the American version of
Leben des Galilei, Brecht refers to the historical Galileo in connection with the
concept of the 'Verfremdungseffekt'. Brecht is explaining what it is like for
someone to overcome their sense of familiarity with the world and see things in that
questioning and critical light:

> Damit all dies viele Gegebene ihm als ebensoviel Zweifelhaftes erscheinen könnte, müßte er
> jenen fremden Blick entwickeln, mit dem der große Galilei einen ins Pendeln gekommenen
> Kronleuchter betrachtete. Den verwunderten diese Schwingungen, als hätte er sie so nicht
> erwartet und verstünde es nicht von ihnen, wodurch er dann auf die Gesetzmäßigkeiten
> kam. (*BFA*, 23, 82)

We may call this a dialectical method insofar as the train of thought is set off by a
contradiction, in this particular example the contradiction between the movements of

the chandelier and some contrary expectation on the part of the observer: '[...] als hätte er sie so nicht erwartet und verstünde es nicht von ihnen'. We find the same dialectical pattern, the same stimulus through contradiction, in the way that Brecht's Galileo thinks critically about social problems. This is particularly evident when Galileo argues with the little monk, who treats poverty as an ineluctable given and wants religion to be preserved as a consolation to the poor. Galileo questions the premise of this plea, looking at poverty as a surprising phenomenon that needs a special explanation - because it stands in such stark contradiction to the fruitfulness of the countryside: 'Warum ist denn nichts da? Warum ist die Ordnung in diesem Land nur die Ordnung einer leeren Lade und die Notwendigkeit nur die, sich zu Tode zu arbeiten? Zwischen strotzenden Weinbergen, am Rand der Weizenfelder!' By way of this 'Verfremdungseffekt' Galileo arrives at the 'Gesetzmäßigkeiten' of the matter: 'Ihre Campagnabauern bezahlen die Kriege, die der Stellvertreter des milden Jesus in Spanien und Deutschland führt' (*BFA*, 5, 244-5). The income from the produce is needed to finance the wars of the Counter-Reformation and safeguard the position of the Catholic Church, that is why there is nothing left for those who work the land. The same alertness to contradiction is again shown a little later in the scene when Galileo mentions the attempts of the authorities to buy his silence with gifts of wine. Their intention is to keep the people in ignorance by means of a bribe that the people themselves have produced 'im Schweiße ihres Antlitzes, das bekanntlich nach Gottes Ebenbild geschaffen ist' (*BFA*, 5, 245). This last remark brings out with bitter emphasis the contrast between the veneration of humanity in the abstract and the cruel and contemptuous treatment of real human beings, though it is also clear from the little monk's argument that the theological glorification of humanity plays an important part in reconciling the people to a life they would otherwise find unendurable; it is both a contradiction and a function of their enslavement, it is at once grotesquely incongruous and, as the ironic 'bekanntlich' implies, generally believed in.

These glimpses into Galileo's social criticism are important not only for what they tell us about the prevailing structures of power, but even more so for what they reveal about the transferable structure of the critical approach itself. It is a technique that seizes on patterns of contradiction and would therefore be equally responsive to the emerging contradictions of capitalism. Just as the conception of man's divine image facilitates his social degradation under feudalism, so too the freedom Vanni demands is a function of the very system that will destroy the freedom of those who work under it. And just as the burgeoning fields of the Campagna represent for the peasants a milieu of deprivation, so too the labour-saving marvels of the mechanized factory will turn out to be an instrument for the exaction of still more labour from the working class. These analogies indicate that if Galileo's mode of social criticism had played a major part in the bourgeois upheaval and thus continued as a living tradition into the period of bourgeois ascendancy, it would have registered the contradictions of capitalism as they made their appearance. There is the fleeting intimation of such a critique in Galileo's remark that if the superstitions imposed by the 'Machthaber' go unchallenged, then it is possible that 'eure neuen Maschinen mögen nur neue Drangsale bedeuten' (*BFA*, 5, 284). We see, then, that what was referred to above as Galileo's 'utopian' attitude to the future does not make his technique of social criticism invalid for the pattern of things to come. Indeed it is precisely the utopian expectations built into his social critique of the present which render that critique transferable into the dystopian future; for it is on the basis of those expectations that the practitioner of the Galilean method would begin to question and analyze the developments of capitalist society, 'als hätte er sie so nicht erwartet und verstünde es nicht von ihnen'. This refocusing of the social 'Verfremdungseffekt' would of course mean the end of its alignment with bourgeois class interests, but also the beginning of its role as an ideological weapon of the emerging proletariat. As we have seen, Galileo's subversive ideas cannot precipitate a unified revolutionary consciousness amongst the people in the carnival scene, because they are divided by their separate occupations and correspondingly limited in their conception of social change, each dreaming of having for themselves the things they individually produce or sell. But the proletariat is a quite different social formation, increasingly concentrated and homogenized by the progress of capitalism. As Brecht puts it in *Das Manifest*:

> es wachsen die Großindustrieen
> Ballend das Proletariat zu immer gewaltigern Massen.
> Mehr und mehr gleicht ein Prolet auch dem andern [...]
> (*BFA*, 15, 131)

As the contradiction between the demands of capital and the interests of labour becomes ever more acute, so too the labourers become ever more numerous and their interests ever more uniform. In this way the dynamic of capitalist exploitation constantly tends to increase the strength and solidarity of the exploited. Applied to capitalism, then, the analysis of social contradictions has a universal relevance for the great mass of the working class, because it is the analysis of their collective plight and of their collective power to change it.

The social critique that Galileo begins to develop and bring to bear on feudal conditions can thus be seen as the prototype of Marxist theory, and his abandonment of it implies a delay in the evolution of scientific socialism. In Brecht's view that delay had enormous repercussions reaching right up to the present. In his *Kleines Organon für das Theater* he characterizes the modern age as the age of science, but he acknowledges that scientific enquiry has not spread evenly to cover all areas of life. Whereas modern natural science began 'vor einigen hundert Jahren' with the rise of the bourgeoisie, the scientific understanding of social relations came into its own 'vor etwa hundert Jahren', with the publication of the *Communist Manifesto*. The consequence of that time lapse is 'daß die neue Denk- und Fühlweise die großen Menschenmassen noch nicht wirklich durchdringt', and one reason for the delay is that the bourgeoisie has, in its own interests as a ruling class, resisted the scientific examination of social phenomena:

> Die bürgerliche Klasse, die der Wissenschaft den Aufschwung verdankt, den sie in Herrschaft verwandelte, indem sie sich zur alleinigen Nutznießerin machte, weiß gut, daß es das Ende ihrer Herrschaft bedeuten würde, richtete sich der wissenschaftliche Blick auf ihre Unternehmungen. (*BFA*, 23, 70-72)

We see now the point of Brecht's emphasis on the straitened position of the Italian bourgeoisie in Galileo's time. Once the capitalist class is firmly established in power, it will be interested only in the kind of knowledge that will bring technological progress and increasing profits. But Vanni and his friends are hard pressed and badly in need of ideological ammunition as well as scientific know-how. It is in their interests at this particular moment to encourage and disseminate Galileo's critique of the feudal system - with its unsuspected convertibility into a critique of their own exploitative designs.

At this stage in history, the bourgeoisie is the only class that can translate the discoveries of science into a great productive enterprise. Galileo is still contributing to that enterprise at the end of the play, when his discourses on *due nuove scienze* are smuggled out of Italy. But what he fails to do is to use the impetus of the bourgeois revolution to inaugurate one more new science complementary to the others, a science of society capable of grasping and exposing the contradiction between the new productive forces and the capitalist relations of production that will prevent them from operating to the benefit of all humanity. The 'früher Morgen des Beginnens' invoked at the outset of the play (*BFA*, 5, 192) has not yet dawned by the end, because an essential part of its promise was the birth of dialectical materialism out of the spirit and methodology of Renaissance science.

[1.] Page numbers for the play refer to: Bertolt Brecht, *Leben des Galilei*, BFA, 5 (1988).

[2.] Gert Sautermeister, 'Zweifelskunst, abgebrochene Dialektik, blinde Stellen: *Leben des Galilei* (3. Fassung, 1955)', in Walter Hinderer (ed.), *Brechts Dramen. Neue Interpretationen* (Stuttgart, 1984), pp.125-61 (pp.138, 140).

[3.] For a detailed examination of this rewrite, and of the new, more critical attitude to Galileo that prompted it, see Ernst Schumacher, *Drama und Geschichte. Bertolt Brechts 'Leben des Galilei' und andere Stücke* (Berlin, 1965), pp.136-55.

4.   Werner Hecht (ed.), *Brechts 'Leben des Galilei'*, suhrkamp taschenbuch materialien (Frankfurt a. M., 1981), p.72.

5.   Alfred D. White, *Bertolt Brecht's Great Plays* (London and Basingstoke, 1978), p.74.

6.   Helmut Jendreiek, *Bertolt Brecht. Drama der Veränderung* (Düsseldorf, 1969), pp.278-9.

7.   Ronald Speirs, *Bertolt Brecht* (London and Basingstoke, 1987), p.128.

8.   *Das Kapital. Kritik der politischen Ökonomie*. Erster Band (Berlin, 1972), p.380.

9.   'Das Manifest' was intended, in Brecht's words, as the 'Kernstück' of a 'Lehrgedicht in der respektablen Versart des Lukrezschen *De rerum natura* über so etwas wie die Unnatur der bürgerlichen Verhältnisse' (*BFA*, 15, p.387). For a detailed account of Brecht's work on this project, see ibid., pp.386-96.

10.   Galileo Galilei, *Two New Sciences*, translated with introduction and notes by Stillman Drake (Wis. and London, Madison, 1974), p.128.

JÜRGEN THOMANECK

B. Brecht and A. Seghers: Utopian additions to the Critique of the Gotha Programme

In a recent statement on the role of ideology in the former German Democratic Republic, Richard Schröder makes a fundamental assertion about the relationship between real existing socialism and Marxism.   He also alleges fundamental negligence by Marx himself. Schröder says:

> In der Tat: ohne Macht kann niemand handeln.   Macht wird aber erst durch Machtbegrenzung human. Machtbegrenzung wird politisch durch Machtkontrolle und Gewaltenteilung organisiert. Ursprünglicher noch aber findet Machtbegrenzung statt durch Recht und Moral, d.h. durch intersubjektive Anerkennung.   Es war ein Geburtsfehler des Marxismus, der bis zu Marx selbst zurückreicht, daß Recht und Gerechtigkeit für ihn keine leitenden Kategorien waren. Statt dessen hieß es: 'Das Recht ist immer ein Machtmittel der herrschenden Klasse.' Dieser Satz mag ja als heuristische These einer Ideologiekritik, die Mißbrauch diagnostiziieren will, brauchbar sein. Als Definition des Rechts beweist er bloß, daß nicht begriffen worden ist, was Recht ist, oder: daß der Mißbrauch zum Gebrauch umdefiniert wird.[1]

Schröder's assertion in respect of Marx and the reduction of Marx's thinking on law to the one sentence is a gross misrepresentation of Marx's position. Schröder's *reductio ad absurdum* is untenable in view of section 3 of Marx's 'Randglossen zum Programm der deutschen Arbeiterpartei', (*Kritik des Gothaer Programms*) or Engels' introduction to his *Herrn Eugen Dührings Umwälzung der Wissenschaft*. Nevertheless it is also true that Engels himself near the end of his life commented critically on the fact that both he and Marx had emphasized the politico-economic aspect too much in their consideration of the law. This had already resulted in a situation where Marxists neglect

> die formelle Seite über der inhaltlichen [...] : die Art und Weise, wie die aus den ökonomischen Grundtatsachen abgeleiten politischen, rechtlichen (!) und sonstigen ideologischen Vorstellungen und durch diese Vorstellungen vermittelte Handlungen zustande kommen.

Engels' assessment proved to be less than adequate critically and his historical optimism unjustified ('die Geschichte wird das alles schließlich in Ordnung bringen'). The subsequent concentration of real existing socialist practitioners

was on the *Machtfrage*: 'Die entscheidende Frage ist die Machtfrage, denn nur
wenn wir die Macht haben, können wir unser humanistisches Projekt, den
Aufbau des Sozialismus, verwirklichen.'[2] In this context Schröder's conclusion
is correct:

> Die Verführung zum Allmachtswahn, der sich in den zitierten Sätzen eine
> ausdrückliche theoretische Begründung gab, war ermöglicht durch das hochmoralische
> Ziel: eine Gesellschaft ohne antagonistische Widersprüche, eine Gesellschaft der
> Befriedigung aller Bedürfnisse schaffen zu wollen. Das hochmoralische Ziel war eine
> Gesellschaft, in der Menschen überhaupt nicht mehr für andere Menschen Mittel,
> sondern nur noch Selbstzwecke sind, eine Gesellschaft der universellen menschlichen,
> menschheitlichen Selbstverwirklichung.[3]

In this context Schröder also correctly draws attention to the great German
philosopher of the 18th century enlightenment: 'Kant hat behauptet, daß selbst
die vollständige Bedürfnisbefriedigung ... das Defizit verweigerter Anerkennung
nicht ausgleichen kann.' He then provides a lengthy passage from Kant's 'Der
Streit der Fakultkäten' to substantiate this view:

> Warum hat es noch nie ein Herrscher gewagt, frei herauszusagen, daß er gar kein
> *Recht* des Volks gegen ihn anerkenne; daß dieses seine Glückseligkeit bloß der
> *Wohltätigkeit* einer Regierung, die diese ihm angedeihen läßt, verdanke, und alle
> Anmaßung des Unterthans zu einem Recht gegen dieselbe ... ungereimt, ja strafbar sei?
> Die Ursache ist: weil eine solche öffentliche Erklärung alle Unterthanen gegen ihn
> empören würde; ob sie gleich, wie folgsame Schafe, von einem gütigen und
> verständigen Herren geleitet, wohlgefüttert und kräftig beschützt, über nichts, was
> ihrer Wohlfahrt abginge, zu klagen hätten. - Denn mit Freiheit begabten Wesen
> genügt nicht der Genuß der Lebensannehmlichkeiten ... ; sondern auf das *Princip*
> kommt es an, nach welchem es sich solche verschafft. Wohlfahrt aber hat kein Prinzip,
> weder für den, der sie empfängt, noch der sie austheilt.[4]

The purpose of this essay is to demonstrate how the two most acknowledged
German communist writers of the twentieth century addressed the question of
law, justice, and interpersonal recognition, and how they redressed Engels'
dictum as formulated in his July 1893 letter to Mehring:

> Sonst fehlt nur noch ein Punkt, der aber auch in den Sachen von Marx und mir
> regelmäßig nicht genug hervorgehoben ist und in Beziehung auf den uns alle gleiche
> Schuld trift. Nämlich wir alle haben zunächst das Hauptgewicht auf die *Ableitung* der
> politischen, rechtlichen und sonstigen ideologischen Vorstellungen und durch diese
> Vorstellungen vermittelten Handlungen aus den ökonomischen Grundtatsachen gelegt
> und *legen müssen*.[5]

This essay will seek to demonstrate how Seghers and Brecht took recourse to enlightenment concepts and utopian devices. It will proceed to discuss the relevance of these two writers for the post-modernist age. Anna Seghers and Bertolt Brecht manifestly had much in common: they were born within two years of each other in southern Germany; they became communists early on in their lives; they were both blacklisted by the Nazis; they both spent the years of the Third Reich in exile, predominantly in North America; they both returned to what was to become the German Democratic Republic; they both became 'official' writers of the GDR, they were both vilified in the West. Occasionally their paths crossed, for example with their common interest in Joan of Arc. So far no comparative study of these two writers has been undertaken. The focus of this chapter will be on *Der gerechte Richter* by Anna Seghers and Bertolt Brecht's *Der kaukasische Kreidekreis*, and in particular the first scene or *Vorspiel*. Both *Der gerechte Richter* and *Der kaukasische Kreidekreis* are placed in countries of real existing socialism: in the case of Seghers an unspecified country, and in Brecht's case in the former Soviet Union. Both works are placed at the end of hostilities in World War II. *Der gerechte Richter* starts with the following opening paragraph:

> Nach dem Krieg lebte Jan eine Zeitlang allein mit seiner Mutter. Der Vater war früh gestorben. Der älteste Bruder kehrte aus der deutschen Gefangenschaft nicht zurück, er war im Lager verhungert. Der mittlere war im Widerstandskampf in den Bergen gefallen.[6]

Der kaukasische Kreidekreis starts as follows:

> Der Streit um das Tal
>
> *Zwischen den Trümmern eines zerschossenen kaukasischen Dorfes sitzen im Kreis, weintrinkend und rauchend, Mitglieder zweier Kolchosdörfer, meist Frauen und ältere Männer; doch auch einige Soldaten. Bei ihnen ist ein Sachverständiger der staatlichen Wiederaufbaukommission aus der Hauptstadt.*
> Eine Bäuerin links *zeigt:* Dort in den Hügeln haben wir drei Nazitanks aufgehalten, aber die Apfelpflanzung war schon zerstört.[7]

Both works are permeated by a spirit of a new beginning, an *Aufbruch*. It is said of Jan in *Der gerechte Richter*: 'Jetzt stürzte er sich aufs Lernen, Rechtswissenschaft erschien ihm ein großes Ziel: durch seinen Beruf Recht und Gerechtigkeit durchzusetzen, nach einer Zeit voll Gewalt und Gemeinheit'. (5f) Scene I of Brecht's play refers to *Wiederaufbau,* but not merely rebuilding the old: 'Der benachbarte Obstbaukolchos "Rosa Luxemburg" - *nach links* - stellt den Antrag, daß das frühere Weideland des Kolchos "Galinsk", ein Tal mit spärlichem Graswuchs, beim Wiederaufbau für Obst- und Weinbau verwertet wird.' Or: 'Die Gesetze müssen auf jeden Fall überprüft werden, ob sie noch stimmen.' Or: 'Genossen, im letzten Winter, als wir als Partisanen hier in den Hügeln kämpften, haben wir davon gesprochen, wie wir nach der Vertreibung der Deutschen unsere Obstkultur zehnmal so groß wiederaufbauen könnten.' Or: 'Unser Gedanke war dabei, daß unsere Soldaten, unsere und eure Männer, in eine noch fruchtbarere Heimat zurückkommen sollten.' And: 'Verschiedene Weine zu mischen mag falsch sein, aber alte und neue Weisheit mischen sich ausgezeichnet.' (*BFA*, 8, 9-14; 95-100)

This spirit of a new beginning, of *Aufbruch*, is motivated by a feeling that all the human and material sacrifices of the past must be given some meaning: a new future must justify the past; as Anna Seghers formulated it in the story 'Der Führer', which was written at about the same time as *Der gerechte Richter*: 'Wenn es keine Zukunft mehr gibt, ist das Vergangene umsonst gewesen.'[8] In their treatment of a future new society, a society emphasizing interpersonal recognition, both Seghers and Brecht home in on the subject of law and justice.

Anna Seghers' literary device is simple. Jan, a young man, had studied law before the war. His studies were interrupted by the war when he became a soldier. After the war he resumes his law studies with renewed vigour and a new motivation. Jan soon becomes a public prosecutor who is respected inside and outside his profession. 'So jung er noch war, es hieß, wenn sein Name in einem Prozeß vorkam: "Der kennt sich aus, dem macht man kein X für ein U vor. Der ist gerecht." ' (7f.) Jan is not only directly involved professionally with law and the dispensation of justice, he himself is seen as the embodiment of justice. As a lawyer he is highly sensitive to the deformation of socialist ideas. He realizes that interpersonal relations are suffering from a lack of openness (*Offenheit*) and trust (*Vertrauen*).[9] Interpersonal recognition is not practised. After he loses regular contact with his friends Stefan and Andreas he thinks to himself: 'Doch kam es ihm vor, er könne mit diesen nicht so unumwunden, so offen sprechen wie mit Andreas und Stefan.' (7) Trust (*Vertrauen*) becomes a cause for a major psychological trauma. The following episode with his wife illustrates this at a time when he reaches new professional heights under the protection of an influential public prosecutor and law professor: 'Sie sah ihn aufmerksam an, und sie sagte: "Man hat dir ein großes Vertrauen geschenkt." Worauf er sagte: "Das ist es eben." ' (11) His involvement in the case of Viktor Gasko makes him realize that people live in fear: 'Vielleicht war dieser und jener auch bange, er könne als Gaskos Freund in die undurchsichtige Sache hineingezogen werden.'(11)[10] Later on, while Jan is still investigating the Gasko case, Stefan terminates their friendship out of fear. (29)

Jan eventually, like Viktor Gasko, becomes a victim of Stalinist show trial procedures, and like Viktor Gasko Jan is not prepared to make confessions which are not true, nor does he give in to the temptation 'Unrecht als Recht zu erklären, wenn auch zwangsläufig, wenn auch nur als Notbehelf.' (40) It is during his imprisonment that Jan firms up his most fundamental belief. During his remand in custody he asks himself about the investigating judge: 'Ist er überzeugt, wie ich es bin, daß zu unserem Leben Gerechtigkeit gehört wie Luft?' (36) And later on while in a labour camp the following conversation takes place between him and a doctor (47):

> Jan sagte: 'Ja, und ich liebte meinen Beruf.'
> 'Warum?'
> 'Weil dieser Beruf, wenn man ihn ernst nimmt, besonders stark mit etwas verbunden ist, was das Leben zum Menschenleben macht.'
> 'Und zwar womit?'
> 'Mit Gerechtigkeit.'

Through Jan, Anna Seghers produces an axiomatic statement where justice is the most fundamental and most desirable aspect of human existence. It is important to realize that this axiom 'Gerechtigkeit macht das Leben zum Menschenleben' is not only the most central statement in *Der gerechte Richter*, but it also stands in direct contrast to the most fundamental tenet of Marxist anthropological philosophy known generally as 'Menschwerdung durch Arbeit'. The simplest and most succinct statement of this tenet is to be found in Friedrich Engels' 1876 essay 'Anteil der Arbeit an der Menschwerdung des Affen', where the first paragraph reads:

> Die Arbeit ist die Quelle alles Reichtums, sagen die politischen Ökonomen. Sie ist dies - neben der Natur, die ihr den Stoff liefert, den sie in Reichtum verwandelt. Aber sie ist noch unendlich mehr als dies. Sie ist die erste Grundbedingung alles menschlichen Lebens, und zwar in einem solchen Grade, daß wir in gewissem Sinn sagen müssen: Sie hat den Menschen selbst geschaffen.

Much has been made of the unfinished state of *Der gerechte Richter*, and in particular the lack of cohesiveness or at least the hiatus between the first part of the story and the ending. Yet two questions have not been properly addressed in this context. Firstly, when Jan quite axiomatically postulates that justice is the most fundamental aspect of human existence, does that mean that the *Novelle* abrogates the most basic tenet of Marxist socialism, or did Anna Seghers introduce the justice axiom as a simple but essential corrective to real existing socialism? Secondly, how does the reader reconcile the following statements in the *Novelle*? In the first part of the story when Jan meets up with Viktor Gasko in the Gulag, Gasko accuses the political class of the new society as having ruined its ideational base for ever: 'Es ist euch also gelungen, unsere Idee ganz zu verhunzen, endgültig - .' (57) At the very end of the story, however, Viktor says: 'Das dachte ich jeden Abend, ... , wir müssen kommen, wir sind im Recht.' Jan's reply to this *Leitmotif* 'wir sind im Recht' is as follows '"Das zu denken, immerfort, war gar nicht leicht", sagte Jan, und er dachte an den Abend, an dem Viktor völlig verzweifelt war - ihm schien es, der Freund hätte diesen Abend bereits vergessen'.(56) The reader knows in respect of the last statement that Viktor and Jan have been released, that they are now 'in Freiheit'. The reader has no information whether 'in Freiheit' means no more than the two having been released, or whether society has changed, which would explain Viktor's new historical optimism. The reader does, however, know that all along Jan individualizes the state of injustice and societal deformation in the person of the omnipotent Kalam who seems to control the rather Kafkaesque trial procedures. For instance, during the last recounted conversation between Jan and Viktor in the Gulag hospital, Jan answers Viktor's question; 'Dann sag mir, bist du nicht verzweifelt, du? Warum nicht?' with the following jejune analysis:

'Vielleicht', sagte Jan, 'weil ich ihm [i.e. Kalam] nicht gehorchte. Ich kann es dir nicht genau erklären. So schnell nicht. Du sprichst von unserer Idee. Wovon sprichst du? Von einem einzelnen Mann? In einem einzelnen Mann hab ich mich bös geirrt. Ich tät ihm einen Gefallen, wenn ich deshalb verzweifeln würde.'(54)

This analysis of the state of injustice explains Jan's earlier assertion when asked whether he would choose this state again: 'Dann würde ich ihn wieder wählen, ... und diesen Staat, nur diesen, gerade diesen so gut wie möglich machen!' (38) Jan clearly believes that injustice is brought about by deformed individuals, and not by a deformed society allowing deformed individuals in power to exert their corrupt practices. He does not question the system of subalternity and believes in the reformability of the system as a whole. It is in this sense that within the context of the story the postulation of the axiomatic 'Gerechtigkeit macht das Leben zum Menschenleben' is to be seen as no more than a corrective to existing socialist society. As the story stands and ends, Viktor was clearly wrong when he argued that the 'idea' itself had been deformed beyond repair. Viktor and Jan both believe in a future in justice when their time will come and there will be *gerechte Richter* only.   This does, however, mean that Jan's axiom of justice stands side by side with materialist socialist tenets.

This axiomatic postulate does not appear for the first or last time in Anna Seghers' writings.   She has laid herself open to being criticized as fideistic in her approach to socialism.   This was first mooted by Marcel Reich-Ranicki during the sixties and more recently discussed by Frank Quilitzsch in his article 'Werden die "Letzten" die "Ersten" sein?   Fragen, nicht nur an Anna Seghers.'[11]   *Der gerechte Richter*, however, presents the clearest statement of this axiomatic approach and could be viewed as pure fideism.   It is doubtful whether a completed version would have remedied this basic inherent fideism.   While attempting to redress the balance between power on the one side and law, justice, and interpersonal recognition on the other, Anna Seghers does not derive justice on a materialist basis in the Marxist post-Hegelian sense but rather along utopian lines.   Anna Seghers, and in particular her character Jan in *Der gerechte Richter*, would come under Friedrich Engels' critique of the utopian socialists as outlined *inter alia* in his introduction to his *Herr Eugen Dührings Umwälzung der Wissenschaft ('Anti-Dühring')*:

> Die Anschauungsweise der Utopisten hat die sozialistischen Vorstellungen des 19. Jahrhunderts lange beherrscht, und beherrscht sie zum Teil noch.[...]Der Sozialismus ist [ihnen allen] der Ausdruck der absoluten Wahrheit, Vernunft und Gerechtigkeit, und braucht nur entdeckt zu werden, um durch eigene Kraft die Welt zu erobern; da die absolute Wahrheit unabhängig von Zeit, Raum und menschlicher, geschichtlicher Entwicklung ist, so ist es bloßer Zufall, wann und wo sie entdeckt wird. [...]   Um aus dem Sozialismus eine Wissenschaft zu machen, mußte er erst auf einen realen Boden gestellt werden.[12]

As with Seghers' *Novelle,* Brecht's *Der kaukasische Kreidekreis* is also clearly located in place and time.   Within the context of an *Aufbruch* to a better future certain key concepts are acclaimed by the participants in the discussion in Scene 1.   These are *Gesetze, Nützlichkeit, Vernunft, Ökonomie,* and *Weisheit.* These key concepts are clearly and positively enunciated in turn:

1.   'Die Gesetze müssen auf jeden Fall überprüft werden, ob sie noch stimmen.'
2.   'Es ist richtig, wir müssen ein Stück Land eher wie ein Werkzeug ansehen, mit dem man Nützliches herstellt, aber es ist auch richtig, daß wir die Liebe zu einem besonderen Stück Land anerkennen müssen.'
3.   'Wie der Dichter Majakowski gesagt hat, >die Heimat des Sowjetvolkes soll auch die Heimat der Vernunft sein< !'

4.   'Wir befassen uns eigentlich mehr mit Ökonomie.' ' - Ihr bringt Ordnung
      in die Neuverteilung von Weinreben und Traktoren, warum nicht von
      Gesängen?'
5.   'Verschiedene Weine zu mischen mag falsch sein, aber alte und
      neueWeisheit mischen sich ausgezeichnet.'(*BFA*, 8, 9-14; 95-100)

The first scene also tells us that the play *Der Kreidekreis* is an old legend. It will
be performed at the end of the deliberations and after the refreshments. It
reflects upon the question under discussion, i.e., the future of the valley. Much
has been written about the relationship between the original *Vorspiel* and the
later Scene I. Much controversy has also been generated on the question of the
relationship between the *Vorspiel*/Scene I and the chalk circle story itself, and on
its relevance, topicality, and purpose.[13] This chapter will argue that the opening
scene conjures up a new society, a socialist society, a new future where Brecht
takes recourse to pre-Marx 18th century enlightenment concepts. The central
concept of 18th century enlightenment thinking is *Vernunft, reason, raison.*

Whereas all key concepts of the *Vorspiel*/Scene I can easily be related to
the story and statements of the chalk circle, the concept of *Vernunft* is an
exception. As such it does not appear in the story of the chalk circle.
Furthermore, it did not occur in the 1944 version of the *Vorspiel*. There its place
was taken by 'vom wissenschaftlichen Standpunkt aus' and 'auf
wissenschaftlicher Basis'. In this context it is also to be noted that the following
are also later additions: 'Die Gesetze müssen auf jeden Fall überprüft werden,
ob sie noch stimmen' and 'Es ist richtig, wir müssen ein Stück Land eher wie ein
Werkzeug ansehen, mit dem man Nützliches herstellt, aber es ist auch richtig,
daß wir die Liebe zu einem besonderen Stück Land anerkennen müssen.' These
two statements clearly function as anticipations of what is to follow in the story
itself and are necessary insertions because of the changed relationship between
the *Vorspiel*/Scene I and the story itself. For in the later version the two parties
have determined the fate of the valley before the story is enacted.

Scene I informs the audience that the chalk circle legend consists of two
stories. The first story is that of Grusche and the child, the second that of Azdak
and the chalk circle. It is generally agreed that the first story is about love, both
caritas ('Schrecklich ist die Verführung zur Güte') and eros; it is about
motherhood ('Es ist meins: ich hab's aufgezogen') and humanity. The second
story is about Azdak whose appointment to judicial office is made by the
Panzerreiter: 'Immer war der Richter ein Lump, so soll jetzt ein Lump der
Richter sein.' (*BFA*, 8, 83; 182) Azdak remains the judge for two chaotic
years, and is remembered at the end (*BFA*, 8, 91; 185):

> Aber das Volk Grusiniens vergaß ihn nicht und gedachte noch
> Lange seiner Richterzeit als einer kurzen
> Goldenen Zeit beinah der Gerechtigkeit.

There is no disagreement between critics that Azdak dispenses justice most of the time because he recognizes both law and laws as class law and class laws. More importantly he recognizes justice (*Gerechtigkeit*) as being class justice, and thus arbitrary in nature and application. Azdak says to Grusche during the trial: 'Ganz richtig.   Von euch Hungerleidern krieg ich nichts, da könnt ich verhungern. Ihr wollt eine Gerechtigkeit, aber wollt ihr zahlen?' (*BFA*, 8, 86; 179) Azdak recognizes justice as a commodity. This contradicts the traditional differentiation where a code of law is perceived as a universal medium, whereas justice presupposes the singularity of the individual case. He is, however, fully aware of social justice,   which is only possible in a class society in times of chaos and through serendipity.

Brecht's treatment of justice is fundamentally different from Seghers'. Brecht depicts not only law as class law, but also justice as class justice. Justice is not an axiom for Brecht but a material condition. Passages from *Me-ti / Buch der Wendungen* illustrate this, e.g.:

> Über Gerechtigkeit
> Die Gerechtigkeit jedoch, deren Verkörperung das Recht zu sein vorgibt, während sie nur seine Vergeistigung ist, wischt alle Widersprüche aus und kann das, weil sie sich niemals in menschlichen Vorfällen bestätigen muß. So scheint sie vollkommener als das Recht. (*BFA*, 18, 100)

In *Der kaukasische Kreidekreis* Brecht is still evidently continuing his dispute with Kant, the philosopher of the enlightenment. This dispute started with *Die heilige Johanna der Schlachthöfe* on the issue of *Güte* and, as Hans Mayer pointed out, continued on the same topic to the Grusche story of *Der kaukasische Kreidekreis*.[14] But it extends also to the issue of *Gerechtigkeit* which is in conflict with Kant's more general *Princip* as in the above passage from Kant's 'Der Streit der Fakultäten'. This is illustrated by Brecht's stated views on *Gerechtigkeit*. It should also be noted that Brecht's *Me-ti* statements were written during the gestation period of *Der kaukasische Kreidekreis*.

The same *Me-ti* statements contain a passage 'Die Große Ordnung verwirklichen' (*BFA*, 18, 106)

> Viele halten die *Große Ordnung*, von der Ka-meh, En-fu und Mi-en-leh gesprochen haben, für eine aller vorhandenen Ordnung oder Unordnung ganz entgegengesetzte

Ordnung, einen fertigen Plan, den es zu verwirklichen gilt. Nun ist sicher, was wir haben, Unordnung, und was wir planen, Ordnung, aber das Neue ergibt sich aus dem Alten und ist seine nächste Stufe. [...] Das Neue entsteht, indem das Alte umgewälzt, fortgeführt, entwickelt wird. [...] Deshalb kann man nicht erwarten, daß die *Große Ordnung* auf einen Schlag, an einem Tag, durch einen Entschluß eingeführt werden kann. Die Einführung der Großen *Ordnung* ist, weil ihre Gegner gegen sie Gewalt anwenden, ein Akt der Gewalt, ausgeübt durch die große Mehrheit des Volkes, aber ihr Aufbau ist ein langer Prozeß und eine Produktion.

The latter part of this passage underlines what Jost Hermand described as follows:

Die Vorstellung > fertiger Bilder < lehnt er [Brecht] stets entschieden ab. Er nähert sich damit - wenn auch wohl unbewußt - in manchen Punkten recht auffällig den prozeßhaft-konkreten Utopievorstellungen von Ernst Bloch . . . Statt jedoch wie Bloch auch die theologische Tradition in diese Zukunfterwartungen einzubeziehen, legt Brecht den Hauptakzent immer wieder auf den nüchternen Wechselbezug von Theorie und Praxis, der rein auf die Gegenwart bezogen ist.[15]

Jost Hermand's interpretation requires a correction, however, especially in the context of an analysis of *Der kaukasische Kreidekreis*. It would seem that in his *Me-ti* and *Der kaukasische Kreidekreis* Brecht enunciates views which are described as *Luxemburgismus* by orthodox Marxist-Leninist ideologues. One of the points of contention in the Lenin-Luxemburg controversy was a statement by Rosa Luxemburg at the Stuttgarter Parteitag in October 1898 where she said:

Drittens hat er [Vollmar] mir die Unterschiebung gemacht, daß ich für Gewaltmittel schwärme. Ich habe weder in meinen Ausführungen, noch in meinen Artikeln gegen Bernstein in der 'Leipziger Volkszeitung' den geringsten Anlaß dazu gegeben. Ich stehe gerade auf dem entgegengesetzen Standpunkte, und ich sage, das einzige Gewaltmittel, daß uns ᴢum Siege führen wird, ist die sozialistische Aufklärung der Arbeiterklasse im alltäglichen Kampfe.[16]

The interesting point in respect of *Der kaukasische Kreidekreis* is the fact that one of the farming cooperatives is called 'Rosa Luxemburg'. Brecht clearly flags up his own ideological stance in the context of a real existing Stalinist Soviet Union. It is also noteworthy that the original *Vorspiel* figured the kolkhoz Rosa Luxemburg as the 'loser' in the argument whereas the re-written final Scene I had 'Rosa Luxemburg' as the 'winner'.

The statement 'Verschiedene Weine zu mischen mag falsch sein, aber alte und neue Weisheit mischen sich ausgezeichnet' is a dramatic manifestation of the first part of the above statement 'Die Große Ordnung *verwirklichen*': 'aber das

Neue ergibt sich aus dem Alten und ist seine nächste Stufe.' The dramatic aspect
is clearly stated by Brecht in May 1954 in a letter to P.S:

> Daß das Vorspiel Ihnen nicht gefällt, verstehe ich nicht ganz. Es war das erste, was ich
> von dem Stück schrieb, in den Staaten. Die Fragestellung des parabelhaften Stücks
> muß ja aus Notwendigkeiten der Wirklichkeit hergeleitet werden, und ich denke, es
> geschah in heiterer und leichter Weise.(*BFA*, 24, 27)

'Die alte Weisheit' is clearly defined at the end of the play in terms of
Nützlichkeit: (*BFA*, 8, 301)

> Ihr aber, ihr Zuhörer der Geschichte vom Kreidekreis
> Nehmt zur Kenntnis die Meinung der Alten:
> Daß da gehören soll, was da ist, denen, die für es gut sind, also
> Die Kinder den Mütterlichen, damit sie gedeihen
> Die Wagen den guten Fahrern, damit gut gefahren wird
> Und das Tal den Bewässerern, damit es Frucht bringt.

The conclusion of the play makes clear the question of the ownership of
the means of production, which is based on the Grusche story and Azdak's
judgment. The criteria for the ownership of the means of production are that
those who work with them should own them. That would ensure their maximum
development and productivity (*Nützlichkeit*) i.e., the disappearance of the
contradiction between the methods of production (the 'material productive
forces') and the existing property relationships ('the relations of production'). In
the process of the discontinuance of this contradiction a new quality of social
relationships will develop. Marx in his preface to his *Kritik der Politischen
Ökonomie* points out that the sum total of the relations of production constitutes
the economic structure of society on which rises a legal and political
superstructure to which correspond definite forms of social consciousness. With
the change of the economic foundation the entire superstructure will also be
transformed.

But in respect of *Weisheit* Brecht also makes the following statement about
Stalin and the Soviet Union in *Me-ti:*

> Aufbau und Verfall unter Ni-en
> Unter der Führung Ni-ens wurde in Su die Industrie ohne Ausbeuter
> aufgebaut und der Ackerbau kollektiv betrieben und mit Maschinen versehen ...
> In Su wurde alle Weisheit auf den Aufbau verwiesen und aus der Politik
> verjagt. (*BFA*, 18, 147)

In this statement Brecht points to the continuation of contradictions in the Soviet Union, whereas in the Scene I of *Der kaukasische Kreidekreis* these have been overcome. Property issues are resolved peacefully by means of wisdom. It is also characteristic that in the new society a judge is no longer required. Brecht himself pointed this out:

> Die Geschichte des Vorspiels findet statt in einem Lande, in dem schon eine sozialistische Gesellschaftsordnung besteht. Der Streit um den Besitz eines Tals, in dem ein ganzer Kolchos beheimatet war, wird innerhalb kurzer Zeit, in gemeinsamer Diskussion und ohne Zuhilfenahme formalen Rechts oder eines Richters, auf gütlichem Wege und für alle befriedigend gelöst. (*BFA*, 24, 31)

The question arises at this point whether Brecht did indeed depict an idealized propaganda picture of the contemporary Soviet Union. This conflicts with his realistic assessment of the Soviet Union as recorded in *Me-ti* or his letters to Karl Korsch. On the other hand it has been argued that Brecht depicted a future society, most cogently by Hans Bunge, whose essay concludes: 'Unter diesem Gesichtspunkt wird der >Streit um das Tal< zum >Vorspiel< einer erstrebenswerten >goldenen Zeit beinah der Gerechtigkeit<.'[17]

However, not only wisdom and new legal practice determine the discussion of the opening scene. The young tractor driver exclaims: 'Wie der Dichter Majakowski gesagt hat, >die Heimat des Sowjetvolkes soll auch die Heimat der Vernunft sein<!' It has already been pointed out that this demand for reason to find a home in the Soviet Union does not correspond to anything thematically in the story of the chalk circle. It has also been pointed out that in the 1954 Scene I *reason* has taken the place of the science of the 1944 *Vorspiel*. Brecht seems to have deliberately taken recourse to a pre-Marxist central concept of 18th century enlightenment, promulgated amongst others very forcefully by Kant and yet condemned by Marx and especially Engels. In his introduction to his *Anti-Dühring* Engels wrote:

> Jetzt erst brach das Tageslicht, das Reich der Vernunft an; von nun sollte der Aberglaube, das Unrecht, das Privilegium und die Unterdrückung verdrängt werden durch die ewige Wahrheit, die ewige Gerechtigkeit, die in der Natur begründete Gleichheit und die unveräußerlichen Menschenrechte.
> Wir wissen jetzt, daß dies Reich der Vernunft weiter nichts war, als das idealisierte Reich der Bourgeoisie; daß die ewige Gerechtigkeit ihre Verwirklichung fand in der Bourgeoisjustiz; daß die Gleichheit hinauslief auf die Bürgerliche Gleichheit vor dem Gesetz; daß als eins der wesentlichsten Menschenrechte proklamiert wurde - das bürgerliche Eigentum.[18]

And later on Engels declares the redundancy of idealist philosophy in the face of historical materialism:

> Was von der ganzen bisherigen Philosophie dann noch selbständig bestehn bleibt, ist die Lehre vom Denken und seinen Gesetzen - die formelle Logik und die Dialektik. Alles andre geht auf in die positive Wissenschaft von Natur und Geschichte.[19]

The immediate context for the tractor driver's Majakowski quotation is a farmer's explanation for their plans: 'Unser Gedanke war dabei, daß unsere Soldaten, unsere und eure Männer, in eine noch fruchtbarere Heimat zurückkommen sollten.' (BFA, 8, 12; 98) This context would indicate that reason is defined in terms of material productive forces, i.e., in the context of the play in terms of *Nützlichkeit* and *Weisheit*. Brecht himself was most emphatic on this issue; he states in his notes on the *Vorspiel*:

> In einem Gleichnis soll erzählt werden, wie das Recht auf eine Sache abhängig ist von der Arbeit, die man dafür leistet. Und durch die Darbietung sollen alle erkennen, was sie soeben erlebt haben: daß es in der bestehenden Gesellschafts-ordnung möglich geworden ist, auf vernünftige Weise vernünftiges Recht zu finden und vernünftig durchzusetzen. (BFA, 24, 33)

It could therefore be argued that with *Der kaukasische Kreidekreis*, and in particular through the relationship between the first scene and the chalk circle story, Brecht attempted to demonstrate dialectically a material basis for love, humanity, justice, and reason. It could be argued that in dramatic guise Brecht attempted to further develop Marx and Engels 'zu einer auch theoretisch höheren Form des Gedankens.'[20] Much of the theoretical background to this dramatic attempt can be found in *Me-ti* and the *Arbeitsjournal*. The dialectical structure of *Der kaukasische Kreidekreis* focuses on an issue highlighted by Korsch in his Marx book:

> Die materialistische Kritik der Politischen Ökonomie im >Kapital< ... geht methodisch davon aus, daß mit der Erforschung der bürgerlichen Produktionsweise und ihrer geschichtlichen Veränderungen bereits alles erforscht ist, was Gegenstand einer streng empirischen, >naturwissenschaftlich treu< verfahrenden gesellschaftlichen Wissenschaft bilden kann ... Für andere Zweige der materialistischen Gesellschaftslehre bleibt dann nur noch ein der streng wissenschaftlichen Erforschung mit der Entfernung von der ökonomischen Grundlage immer weniger zugängliches, immer weniger >materielles<, immer >ideologischeres< Gebiet übrig, welches schließlich überhaupt nicht mehr positiv und theoretisch, sondern nur noch kritisch im engsten Zusammenhang mit den praktischen Aufgaben des revolutionären Klassenkampfes zu behandeln ist.[21]

The latter part of this statement places *Der kaukasische Kreidekreis* and in particular the first scene squarely into the context of developments in the Soviet Union during the Stalin era. In that sense the first scene is either a glorifying propagandistic lie, or a counter-statement to real existing Stalinism, or an attempt to add to Marx's economically restricted vision of the future in the *Kritik des Gothaer Programms*. Such an attempt would have been motivated by an *Aufbruchstimmung* at the end of World War II which focused on a new future. Such an addition to Marx's vision of a future society is conjured up by the criticism of the *Sachverständiger* in the *Vorspiel*/Scene I who had stated: 'Wir befassen uns eigentlich mehr mit Ökonomie.' The answer he receives is: 'Ihr bringt Ordnung in die Neuverteilung von Weinreben und Traktoren, warum nicht von Gesängen?' An overemphasis on the economic is too one-sided, unacceptable, and must be rectified, but not only in the context of Engels' confession of guilt in his letter to Mehring. The criticism of the *Sachverständiger* as representative of the state is a criticism of the state's emphasis on the economic (*Me-ti*: 'In Su wurde alle Weisheit auf den Aufbau verwiesen und aus der Politik verjagt'). It also demonstrates a rejection of the Soviet Union's propagation of the new man. In December 1940 Brecht writes in his *Arbeitsjournal*:

> In Wirklichkeit ist der neue Mensch der alte Mensch in den neuen Situationen, d.h. derjenige alte Mensch, der den neuen Situationen am besten gerecht wird, den die neuen Situationen nach vorn treiben, das neue Subjekt der Politik. Alle Postulate an den Menschen, welche über die Postulate hinausgehen, welche die Situationen stellt, sind zu verwerfen. (*BFA*, 26, 161)

The relationship between the first scene and the chalk circle story could be further explained on the basis of this statement together with Brecht's statement on the *Vorspiel*: 'Die Fragestellung des parabelhaften Stücks muß ja aus Notwendigkeiten der Wirklichkeit hergeleitet werden.' It is, after all, individual characters who have to deal with the necessities of reality.

The comparison between Seghers' *Der gerechte Richter* and Brecht's *Der kaukasische Kreidekreis* has shown that World War II marks an important hiatus in their thinking. In the context of an *Aufbruchstimmung*, the feeling of a new era, both Seghers and Brecht re-assess the development of real existing socialism, and emphatically re-introduce concepts such as justice and reason. Both writers clearly realize that socialism is impossible without justice, although both take different philosophical approaches. Their realization foreshadows what was to happen after 1985:

The political and economic collapse of Eastern Europe is the clearest current example of a failed strategy of justice. Whatever the precise external reasons may have been, it remains a fact that a domestic policy which proclaimed social justice while infringing the just claims of human rights ultimately allowed these states to fall apart internally. The residents of these states terminated their contract with their respective governments.[22]

In their attempts to redress imbalances in real existing orthodox socialist ideology, it is no coincidence that Seghers and Brecht take recourse to enlightenment concepts which Marx had cavalierly banished to the superstructure and subsequently neglected. At the end of World War II and for some years to come, Brecht and Seghers like many others still believed in the reformability of real existing socialism. History has proven them wrong. What is the legacy of these writers fifty years hence on the doorstep of the new millenium? Where do they fit into the dispute where one side claims that when the Berlin Wall fell the viability of Marxist discourse collapsed along with it, and the other side is of the view: The DDR is dead, let the history of true socialism begin.[23] In terms of Heiner Müller's statement it is undoubtedly an advantage that real existing socialism has collapsed. The performance of *Der kaukasische Kreidekreis* and its first scene can now be finally detached from Stalin's Soviet Union. The direct historical references can be changed, as has already been done from time to time.[24] At worst the play would turn into a Utopian vision of the future, at best it would be experienced as an analytical dialectical Marxist play. A recent performance in Edinburgh in October 1995 resulted in a review in *The Scotsman* which posed as its first sentence the question 'How is Brecht faring in the post-Communist world?' The reviewer makes the point that the conventions of Brechtian performance are ripe for revision and that it is wrong to faithfully reproduce 'yesterday's modernism without finding any contemporary idiom in which to present it.'[25] If, however, post-modern audiences find difficulties with Brecht's *Modelle*, and he is presented in a post-modern idiom (if that is at all possible) then Brecht would finally become a classic of timeless art.[26] In the post-modern context it might be difficult to stage *Der kaukasische Kreidekreis* with its modernist systemic view. After all it is probably the most complete of all of Brecht's plays. On the other hand there is only one truly prophetic Brecht play which forecasts the post-modern age: *Aufstieg und Fall der Stadt Mahagonny*. It vehemently enacts Neil Postman's analysis of postmodnity *Amusing Our-selves to Death. Public Discourse in the Age of Show Business*. The ultimate danger here, however, would be the reduction of *Mahagonny* to a variety show. *Mahagonny*, like *Der kaukasische Kreidekreis*, finishes with a

trial. Whereas Grusche is sentenced to life because she is motherly and poor,
Paul Ackermann is sentenced to death because of lack of money:

Wegen Mangel an Geld
Was das größte Verbrechen ist
Das auf dem Erdenrund vorkommt.

Paul Ackermann's final conclusion about his life reads:

Jetzt erkenne ich: als ich diese Stadt betrat, um mir mit Geld Freude zu kaufen, war
mein Untergang besiegelt. Jetzt sitze ich hier und habe doch nichts gehabt. Ich war es,
der sagte: Jeder muß sich ein Stück Fleisch herausschneiden, mit jedem Messer. Da
war das Fleisch faul! Die Freude, die ich kaufte, war keine Freude, und die Freiheit für
Geld war keine Freiheit. Ich aß und wurde nicht satt, ich trank und wurde durstig.
Gebt mir doch ein Glas Wasser.(*BFA*, 2, 386)

Post-modern producers have the choice between the depiction of the *Große
Unordnung* or the *Große Ordnung*.   It should, however, be remembered that
Der kaukasische Kreidekreis embodies the great motif of human dreams and
literature, which is found in pre-modernist human yearning and will no doubt
continue into the new post-modernist millenium: the return to the Garden of
Eden. In the final analysis *Der kaukasische Kreidekreis* is held together by
Azdak's dream and hope for future generations: 'Die Güter fallen an die Stadt,
damit ein Garten für die Kinder draus gemacht wird, sie brauchen ihn, und ich
bestimm, daß er nach mir >Der Garten des Azdak< heißt'. (*BFA*, 8, 90f.; 184).
The other part is Scene I where human beings are in the process of constructing
the new Garden of Eden which of course in terms of *Nützlichkeit* is an orchard:
'Das benachbarte Obstbaukolchos >Rosa Luxemburg< . . . stellt den Antrag,
daß das frühere Weideland des Kolchos >Galinsk<[. .] beim Wiederaufbau für
Obst- und Weinbau verwertet wird'. (*BFA*, 8, 9; 95)

     When Anna Seghers takes recourse to *Vernunft* and *Gerechtigkeit* as basic
components of socialist society, she does so in an *a priori* fideistic utopian
fashion. Those works by Anna Seghers which embrace such a fideistic attitude
are incongruous in a post-modernist age and are likely to survive only as
historical documents. When Brecht introduces *Vernunft* and *Gerechtigkeit* in the
later and final version of *Der kaukasische Kreidekreis* it is done in terms of a
further development of Marxian philosophy and in contradiction to Stalin's real
existing socialism. The reference to Majakowski states: '*soll auch* [my
emphasis] die Heimat der Vernunft sein.' Reason is defined in terms of material
productive forces (*Nützlichkeit*) in *Der kaukasische Kreidekreis* and not

introduced as an *a priori* concept.   Dialectical thinking is not restricted to modernism or post-modernism, and nor are Brecht's dialectical plays.

[1]   Richard Schröder, 'Verführtes Denken? Zur Rolle der Ideologie in der DDR', in: Wolfgang Hardtwig and Heinrich A. Winkler, eds., *Deutsche Entfremdung: Zum Befinden in Ost und West* (Munich, Verlag C.H. Beck, 1994), pp. 144-161, (p.149)

[2]   Friedrich Engels letter to Mehring, London 14 July 1893; see also Korsch's 1930 review of two law books in Karl Korsch, *Die materialistische Geschichtsauffassung und andere Schriften* (Frankfurt aM, Europäische Verlangsanstalt, 1971), pp. 157-166.

[3]   Schröder, p.149.

[4]   Schröder, p.149.

[5]   Engels to Mehring.

[6]   Anna Seghers, *Der gerechte Richter* (Berlin and Weimar, Aufbau-Verlag, 1990), p.5. The Novelle was written in 1957 and 1958.   It was never finished, nor was it published or submitted for publication during Seghers' lifetime.

[7]   *BFA*, 8, p.9 (1949), p.95 (1954).

[8]   Seghers, 'Der Führer', in *Die Kraft der Schwachen* (Berlin, Aufbau, 1965), pp. 29-45   On the relationship between sacrifice and new beginning, past and present, see the first part of Sonja Hitzinger's essay 'Opfer, Täter und Richter: Versuch einer Annäherung an die Novelle "Der gerechte Richter",' in *Argonautenschiff: Jahrbuch der Anna-Seghers-Gesellschaft* 1 (1992), 50-64.

[9]   For a treatment of Offenheit and Vertrauen in Seghers' works see. J.K.A. Thomaneck, 'The Iceberg in Anna Seghers's Novel *Überfahrt*', *German Life and Letters*, 28 (1974), 36-45. It should also be noted in this context that the official arrival of glasnost in the Soviet Union after 1985 contributed to its downfall, and the demand for openness in the former GDR in 1989 ('Wir sind das Volk') propelled its disappearance.

[10]   For the probable actual background to the Novelle, i.e. the Janka trial, see J.K.A. Thomaneck, 'Anna Seghers and the Janka Trial: A Case Study in Intellectual Obfuscation', *German Life and Letters*, 46 (1993), 156-161.   Viktor Gasko, a communist with a heroic pedigree, is the victim of Stalinist persecution.

[11]   In: *Argonautenschiff* 1 (1992), 65-71

[12]   Friedrich Engels, *Herrn Eugen Dührings Umwälzung der Wissenschaft* (Berlin, Dietz Verlag, 1956), p.21.

[13] For still by far the best 'Forschungsbericht' on *Der kaukasische Kreidekreis* see Jan Knopf, *Brecht-Handbuch Theater* (Stuttgart, J.B. Metzlersche Verlagsbuchhandlung, 1980), pp.254-271.

[14] Hans Mayer, *Anmerkungen zu Brecht* (Frankfurt aM, Suhrkamp, 1970), p.102f.

[15] Jost Hermand, 'Utopisches bei Brecht', in: *Brecht-Jahrbuch* 1974, ed. Fuegi *et al.* (Frankfurt, Suhrkamp, 1975), pp. 9-33 (p.20).

[16] Rosa Luxemburg, 'Reden auf dem Stuttgarter Parteitag der Sozialdemokratischen Partei Deutschlands', in: Rosa Luxemburg, *Ausgewählte Reden und Schriften* (Berlin, Dietz Verlag, 1951), vol.2, pp. 28-34 (p.31). For a full treatment of the Lenin-Luxemburg controversy see Annette Jost, 'Rosa Luxemburgs Lenin-Kritik', in: *Jahrbuch Arbeiterbewegung*, vol.5: *Kritik des Leninismus*, ed. Claudio Pozzoli (Frankfurt aM, Fischer, 1977), pp. 77-103.

[17] Hans Bunge, 'Der Streit um das Tal,' in: *Materialien zu Brechts >Der kaukasische Kreidekreis<*, ed. Werner Hecht (Frankfurt aM, Suhrkamp, 1966), pp.144-153, (p.153). For a different view see. Peter Bormans, 'Brecht und der Stalinismus', in *Brecht-Jahrbuch* 1974, pp. 53-76.

[18] Engels, *Anti-Dühring*, p.18.

[19] Engels, *Anti-Dühring*, p.29.

[20] Korsch, p.17, footnote 16

[21] Quoted in Karl Korsch, p.vii, footnote 7.

[22] Helga Geyer-Ryan, 'Justice, Literature, Deconstruction: Homer to Kafka,' in *New Comparison* 18 (1994), 152-164 (152).

[23] Statement by Heiner Müller in: Tom McGrath, 'An echt Brechtian', *The Scotsman* 9/1/96, p.16.

[24] See Ernst Schumacher, *Brecht-Kritiken* (Berlin, Henschelverlag, 1977), p.140-142 and Jan Knopf, p.271, which refer to Indian and Cypriot performances.

[25] Colin Donald, 'The Caucasian Chalk Circle', *The Scotsman* 16/10/95, p.15.

[26] G. Bartram and A. Waine, eds., *Brecht in Perspective* (London and New York, Longman, 1982), p.viii.

PETER DAVIES and STEPHEN PARKER

Brecht, SED Cultural Policy and the Issue of Authority in the Arts: the Struggle for Control of the German Academy of Arts

A relatively uncharted area in Brecht studies concerns Brecht's membership of the German Academy of Arts.[1] This gap is due largely to the limited access before 1989 to documents recording the Academy's turbulent early history. Brecht's own texts on Academy matters in the Academy's Brecht Archive were included in editions earlier than the *Grosse kommentierte Berliner und Frankfurter Ausgabe*.[2] Yet the new edition continues to make only limited use of documents from other Academy archives, principally the Central Academy Archive, which houses material concerning the institution's administration, committees and events. As a result, Brecht's statements on Academy matters are sometimes inadequately contextualised, while his activities in this élite institution continue to be underestimated.

Through reference to the period leading up to the 17 June 1953, we intend to show that Brecht's great authority amongst his fellow artists in East Berlin was intimately bound up with his defence of certain artistic principles in the face of ferocious attacks on him and fellow academicians by SED cultural politicians and their supporters in the Academy. Yet Brecht's own dependence on the SED prevented him from exploiting the leadership's acute insecurity as well as its immediate disarray, and the opportunity was lost to capitalise in the medium to long term on the advantageous position that, most improbably, had been achieved.

In 1950 Brecht was one of the Academy's founding members, and when he died he was one of its Vice-Presidents. The all-German orientation of the Academy's foundation was in keeping with Soviet Union's German policy. A variety of political and artistic views was represented amongst a broadly 'progressive' membership. Whilst the SED's presence was strong, it did not command clear working majorities in committees. Under Arnold Zweig's presidency, an atmosphere of open debate and exchange was fostered amongst the artistic élite. This was reflected in Peter Huchel's editorship of the Academy's journal *Sinn und Form*, in the development of which Brecht took a keen interest.[3] For Brecht, the Academy represented the opportunity for the open, socialist discussion which was a central tenet of his dramatic theories, developed since the 1920s within the Marxist avant-garde. These theories were, however, bitterly opposed by many SED figures. Like Zweig and other non-SED academicians, he was inclined to attribute such opposition to the meddling of petty bureaucrats rather than to genuine political pressures from the SED leadership, to whose higher authority he and Zweig repeatedly appealed. Evidence of success only fostered the illusion.[4]

From the outset, leading SED figures were dismissive of the 'misconceived' Academy. Despite the demand of Marxist-Leninist theory that the SED should be the sole source of authority in the arts as in all matters, in the immediate post-war years it was hamstrung by Soviet German policy. The SED's hold on power depended on the GDR's integration into the Eastern Bloc, yet Stalin's German policy was inconsistent and ambivalent, focusing on his unrealistic ambition to seek a unified, neutral Germany as a safeguard against renewed German militarism and as a source of reparations payments. Even though Stalin's policy was constantly frustrated by the demands of European *Realpolitik* and by the conflicting agendas of his subordinates, the SED leadership could not feel secure in power without the unequivocal backing of the Soviet leader. Only after the arrest of Beria in July 1953, following his reckless attempt to jettison the GDR, could the SED leadership begin to expect such backing. The tensions between Moscow and East Berlin manifested themselves at all levels, including culture, in the battle between the 'integrationists' around Ulbricht and the supporters of the all-German approach, whose linguistic space was relentlessly attacked in Ulbricht's aggressive appropriation for the SED of 'patriotic' values located in the 'progressive' elements of the German tradition. [5] In order not to be decried as traitors, SED members had to toe the Ulbricht line. The assault was sanctioned by the policy, agreed at the Third SED Congress in 1950 and re-affirmed with the launch of the Formalism Campaign in March 1951, of creating an image of the GDR as a viable state in its own right and as the legitimate successor to all progressive political and intellectual movements.[6] This, in turn, sanctioned the imposition of demands on the artistic community, not least the prestigious Academy, whose legitimising presence was required to promote the image. Socialist Realism, with its demand for positive images of revolutionary development with which citizens could identify, presented itself as the appropriate vehicle for the urgent task of national legitimation. Yet the Academy under Zweig was not the body to deliver such a ringing endorsement of the SED's historic mission, and the SED repeatedly charged it with failing to provide the clear lead in artistic matters that was expected of a generously-funded institution of the state.

Nor could Brecht's theatre remotely begin to provide such legitimation. Two related areas of disagreement that had emerged in Brecht's exchanges with Lukács and other proponents of Socialist Realism in Moscow in the mid-1930s were the treatment of the cultural heritage and dramatic theory. The disagreements were carried over to East Berlin, where figures such as Friedrich Wolf and Wolfgang Langhoff were powerful voices in the theatre and the Academy. The criticism of the 'negativity' of Brecht's own productions, beginning in 1949 with Fritz Erpenbeck's attack on *Mutter Courage*, centred on the absence of uplifting examples with which the audience could identify. Despite great popular and critical acclaim, the charge of 'negativity' was levelled against Brecht's adaptation that same year of Lenz's *Der Hofmeister*. With that production, Brecht initiated his exploration of the German classics and German 'bourgeois' intellectuals in terms of the theme of the 'deutsche Misere', an approach quite consistent with Brecht's development but wholly at odds with the SED's self-legitimising needs.

Ulbricht's 'integrationist' line required the creation overnight of a legitimising German identity for the GDR, which would allow it to take its place among the People's Democracies and which would therefore put an end to the dangerous uncertainty about the future of the GDR and the regime. The 'deutsche Misere' theory, as expounded by Alexander Abusch in 1945 in his book *Der Irrweg einer Nation*, but from which he distanced himself in the early 1950s, held that the development of the German nation and state had, for various reasons, not been able to follow the course laid down in orthodox historical materialism, and that, therefore, the reactionary forces in German history had been stronger than the progressive forces. One symptom of this had been the failure of the 'intelligentsia' to cooperate with the 'revolutionary peasantry or proletariat', producing a disastrous separation of 'Geist' and 'Macht' which led intellectuals either to collaborate with repressive regimes or to retreat into aestheticism. Nazism is seen as the most extreme expression of this tendency in German history, and of the collective failure (with notable exceptions) of the intellectual class. Brecht's explorations of the 'Misere' aimed to generate a new sense of responsibility in his audiences, which would gradually restore broken links and continuities within the German nation, eventually allowing Germany to take its place within the mainstream of historical development. For the 'integrationists', however, any admission that the course of German history had been an exception to historical materialist norms would call into question the right of the GDR to exist as a fully-fledged People's Democracy, and thus to enjoy the comforting security of the Soviet Bloc; paradoxically, the achievement of legitimacy as a state entailed the abandonment of national autonomy.

Thus, interpretations of history were not merely of theoretical interest for the SED leadership, but were a matter of political survival: the SED's legitimacy as a governing party was guaranteed only if they could be sure of Soviet military support. The 'integrationist' line required a legitimising continuity of progressive forces in German history in order that there could be no question of a German 'Sonderweg', and that the division of Germany could be characterised as the final, geographical expression of the conflict between progressive and reactionary social and historical forces. Brecht's belief system meant that he accepted this dialectical model and that he constantly glossed over the intimate connection between the ideological position, of which he approved, and the attacks on freedom of expression, which triggered his protests.

It followed from Brecht's approach to Marxism-Leninism that he not only expected, but positively welcomed tough ideological exchanges on artistic issues. At last an insider in a new, socialist Germany, he saw himself as influencing the direction that the arts would take in the GDR from within the emerging socialist discourse of its artistic institutions. Brecht's expectations were by no means always disappointed: unlike his collaborator Paul Dessau, in 1951 he derived obvious pleasure from debate with figures such as Wilhelm Pieck, in the light of which he made alterations to *Das Verhör des Lukullus*. He contrasted Pieck's intervention with the meddling of narrow-minded bureaucrats and took it as proof positive of the SED leadership's appreciation of the contribution that the arts had to make. Yet the attacks continued on him in the SED's Formalism Campaign. In June 1951, the SED's Cultural Department undertook an analysis of the Academy's achievements. Its many criticisms included the following comment on the Performing Arts Section, 'Die Brechtsche Art, Theater zu spielen, herrscht vor ... Genossin Rodenberg, Mitarbeiterin dieser Sektion, sagte hierzu: "Brecht ist gut, doch darf er keine Schule machen. Dieser Sektion muß neues marxistisches Blut zugeführt werden"'.[7]

With the Berlin Ensemble, Brecht maintained the terms of enquiry that he had established for his successful, early productions. He followed up the 'deutsche Misere' theme with another examination of the fateful historical role of the German 'bourgeois' intellectual in his treatment of Goethe's *Urfaust*. For all the fact that the reviewer for *Neue Zeit* by now referred to Brecht's 'Igelstellung' towards the press, that paper and others responded positively to the Potsdam premiere on 23 April 1952.[8] However, in a letter to the *Märkische Volksstimme*, the SED Party Organisation for Brandenburg Theatres launched a violent attack on Egon Monk's 'formalist' production with its 'decadent' Faust and its 'falsification' of the classics. Vehement altercations followed in the theatre and the production was discontinued on 22 June.

The Construction of the Foundations of Socialism was intended to signal the end of the 'compromises' in the arts, in which such a key SED figure as Johannes R. Becher had engaged. Becher's return to the fold, apparently after a severe personal crisis in mid- to late 1952, strengthened the hand of the Party group considerably.[9] After the still inconclusive attacks, SED members in the Academy had to improve their tactics in order to present a more united front in the face of hesitant, or downright awkward, artists within their own ranks, let alone outside the Party itself. The SED resolved to install its people in key Academy positions and to bring its work into line with the party leadership's requirements. Becher colluded with the Academy's Director, Rudolf Engel, the main conduit for SED instructions, in order to pressurize Zweig into resignation from his post. In the autumn of 1952, Brecht acquiesced in that action and, despite Zweig's protests, in the unconstitutional elevation of Alexander Abusch simultaneously to membership of the Academy and to the post of Secretary of the Literature Section, which Becher had vacated. All the other key positions of Section Secretaries, who were *ex officio* members of the Presidium with Becher and Engel, were occupied by tried and tested figures.

Abusch, seeking to ingratiate himself with the SED leadership,[10] was instrumental in the organisation in the Academy of a series of events designed to force the adoption of official cultural policy upon recalcitrant members. Through its choice of topics for discussion, the SED brought into a single focus the closely related problems of Brecht and the Academy. Abusch ensured that he was confronted in a concerted manner on those very issues where the SED's need for self-legitimation clashed with Brecht's artistic practice. In January 1953, in an act which undermined the Academy's authority, the State Commission for Artistic Affairs announced that the Academy would be the venue for the First German Stanislavsky Conference on 17-19 April. Stanislavsky's theories of drama had been used in the mid-1930s in the Soviet Union as a model for Socialist Realism in the attack on the avant-garde and were now promoted as a model for GDR drama in opposition to Brecht's theories.

Brecht was subjected to pressure on a second front when a new forum for discussion in the Academy was announced, the *Mittwoch-Gesellschaften*. The first item chosen for debate was the libretto *Johann Faustus*, written by Brecht's friend Hanns Eisler, and Ernst Fischer's laudatory *Faustus* essay. Both had appeared in *Sinn und Form* in late 1952 and, together with the journal's editor, were subjected to severe criticism in the Academy's committees, principally on account of the quite unacceptable depiction of the 'deutsche Misere'. Brecht could be in little doubt that these attacks were ultimately directed at him and that however 'small' he might make himself in the manner of his Herr Keuner, the prospect was that he would be subjected to unrelenting pressure until such time as he recanted.

In early 1953, an extremely cautious Brecht took great pains to put his defences in place for the Stanislavsky Conference. His attendance at Academy meetings became infrequent. From early February, entries in his journals almost ceased, as he and his collaborators at the Berlin Ensemble devoted themselves to the intensive study of all available Stanislavsky material. Aiming to enter into a constructive dialogue if at all possible, Brecht produced a series of texts, which followed the spirit of his notes made in 1951, 'Was unter anderem vom Theater Stanislawskis gelernt werden kann'. (*BFA*, 23, 167) Meanwhile, the Berlin Ensemble's productions were now all but ignored, as the SED-controlled press took its cue from earlier official attacks and treated his work as of peripheral interest. An entry in his journal on 4 March 1953 stands out in its resigned, weary tone,

> Unsere Aufführungen in Berlin haben fast kein Echo mehr. In der Presse erscheinen Kritiken Monate nach der Erstaufführung, und es steht nichts drin, außer ein paar kümmerlichen soziologischen Analysen. Das Publikum ist das Kleinbürgerpublikum der Volksbühne, Arbeiter machen da kaum sieben Prozent aus. Die Bemühungen sind nur dann nicht ganz sinnlos, wenn die Spielweise späterhin aufgenommen werden kann, d.h. wenn ihr Lehrwert einmal realisiert wird. (*BFA*, 27, 346)[11]

Brecht, however, signalled his intention to continue his exploration of the 'deutsche Misere', whilst sounding out the views of his supporters. He wrote to Hans Mayer on 22 February 1953, seeking Mayer's views on the supposed 'negativity' of Eisler's *Faustus*.[12] Mayer informed Brecht that he had declined a request from *Aufbau* to provide a detailed discussion of Brecht and Stanislavsky and from *Neues Deutschland* to write about Eisler's *Faustus*.[13] Brecht proceeded with Monk's *Urfaust* at the Kammerspiele of the Deutsches Theater on 13 March 1953. He overstated things somewhat in claiming that it was a 'völlige Neuinszenierung', though changes had been made. He wrote in the programme notes that the aim was,

> der so großartigen Widersprüchlichkeit der Goetheschen Faustfigur gerecht zu werden und ihr das Positive zu verleihen, die Humanität, Radikalität in Denken und Fühlen, die innere Weite, durch die sie tief in das Bewußtsein der Deutschen eingedrungen ist. (*BFA*, 24, 433)

However, during rehearsals the SED Party Organisation at the Deutsches Theater, following the Potsdam example, lodged protests at the 'negativity' of the production, and in doing so demonstrated that as long as the Berlin Ensemble did not have its own theatre but had to rely on figures such as Langhoff at the Deutsches Theater, Brecht would not be able to exercise the control that he desired. After only three public performances in March, all during the day rather than in the evening, the production was permitted three closed performances, before it was dropped on 5 May. The view of *Neues Deutschland* was yet to be heard.

As the head of the Berlin Ensemble, Helene Weigel received the invitation to attend the Stanislavsky Conference. Weigel, not Brecht, attended the opening sessions. It was an open secret that the conference was to be an 'Auseinandersetzung mit dem Brecht-Theater',[14] promoted by the organs of the state, the aim of which was, 'Brecht zu isolieren und zur Zurücknahme einiger seiner "theoretischen Marotten" zu bewegen'.[15]   The anti-Brecht tone was maintained throughout. On the second day, Weigel delivered the conciliatory text that Brecht had written. Brecht took his place in the audience on the final day, when he extemporised on 'Gemeinsamkeiten und Unterschiede bei Stanislawski und Brecht'.[16]   Knopf summarises the outcome, 'Brecht reagiert ... weise und zurückhaltend, im Wissen, eine Schlacht verloren und doch recht zu haben'.[17] And yet, the motives for Brecht's 'Zurückhaltung' are complex, and it would be too simple to explain his behaviour simply in terms of a tactical retreat; a closer analysis of his statements and actions, particularly in the 'Faustus-Debatte' of 1953, when set in the context of Beria's panicky German policy after Stalin's death, shows that Brecht's *Realpolitik* is shot through with a self-deception born of his ideological and institutional dependence.

Brecht's journals record that he had a hand in the composition of Eisler's libretto.[18] The avant-gardist sensibility at work in Eisler's text, which reflects Brecht's own attitude to the classics, aims for a radical juxtaposition of present conditions with a past moment of defeat (in this case, the aftermath of the Peasants' War), in order to expose the underlying connections and the development of the historical dialectic. The exploration of the failure of the German 'intellectual class' to lend its weight to the peasant uprisings puts *Faustus* firmly in the tradition of Brecht's explorations of the 'deutsche Misere', and is clearly intended as a commentary on German intellectuals who opposed the GDR or remained neutral. Eisler's support for SED rule is clear, and the violence of the attacks on his text can only be explained in the light of the regime's insecurity.

The first *Mittwoch-Gesellschaft* of three took place on 13 May 1953.[19] Brecht's defence of Eisler began badly. Party discipline was a clear constraint on Eisler. Abusch had ensured majorities for the anti-Eisler camp, while Becher maintained the posture of neutrality as chairman. Abusch set the agenda by reading out his essay, 'Faust - Held oder Renegat in der deutschen Nationalliteratur?',[20] in which he took issue with the 'Misere' theory and the idea that the intellectual class had betrayed the progressive forces in German history. Goethe's Faust is seen as 'ein großer positiver Held des klassischen Nationaldramas'[21] and thus as an antecedent of Socialist Realism. He represents the spirit of progressive striving in the German bourgeois intellectual, which reached its highest expression in the figure of Goethe himself. Eisler's Faustus, by contrast, is driven in his quest for knowledge by the bad conscience brought about by his betrayal of his peasant roots. For Abusch, this is an attempt to 'take back' Goethe's achievements. Parallels with Thomas Mann's *Doktor Faustus* are drawn. It is certainly the case that, as in Brecht's explorations of the 'Misere', bourgeois intellectual and revolutionary forces are shown to be irrevocably at odds. Yet, at stake here is a vision of GDR society in 1953, where the 'integrationists' within the SED needed to place the fledgling GDR within a progressive German tradition in order to buttress their precarious hold on power. If intellectuals departed from that line, Ulbricht's hold on power was threatened, particularly at a time when Beria and Malenkov were beginning to demand liberalisation. Thus, loyal artists like Eisler were attacked: the independent thinking which their methods required was construed as a direct threat.

In the first *Mittwoch-Gesellschaft*, Brecht puts his faith in open discussion, claiming that the negative figure of Faustus can have a positive effect on the audience, and that the essential conflict of the opera takes place within this character.[22] This attempt to relocate Eisler within the mainstream of Marxist, if not Socialist Realist, artistic theory makes good tactical sense, but the two sides talk past each other, as the SED grouping is concerned with national legitimacy. Thus, Girnus contends that a negative conception of the German intellectual and of a German 'Sonderweg' actually amounts to an attack on the GDR,

> Es ist absolut unerfindlich, warum das deutsche Volk als einziges eine Ausnahme von den geschichtlichen Gesetzen machen soll, die in anderen Nationen Geltung haben. Ich meine, hier kommt bei Hanns Eisler eine Fremdheit gegenüber dem deutschen Volk, gegenüber den nationalen Traditionen des deutschen Volkes, gegenüber seiner Geschichte zum Ausdruck.[23]

If German history is an exception, then the GDR forfeits its right to be an independent state and to retain its place in the community of progressive nations, as a People's Democracy. The circle is squared in favour of Ulbricht's line, so that the GDR's national consciousness as a state separate from the FRG is reconciled with its integration into the Soviet Bloc. Eisler's defenders were caught up in a game far bigger than any of them realised, and any attempt to reconcile support for the existence of the GDR with a desire for greater freedom of expression must stumble on these questions of national legitimacy. What was not wholly clear to Brecht and his colleagues was that the basis of this legitimacy was so fragile, that popular support for the regime was negligible, and that the debate in the Academy was paralleled by conflicts within the leadership which were to come into the open in June 1953.

Brecht and his supporters came under even greater pressure at the second *Mittwoch-Gesellschaft*. The atmosphere was openly hostile following the scathing review of *Urfaust* in *Neues Deutschland* and an attack by Ulbricht.[24] By the end of the meeting, the dominance of Abusch's faction, achieved with Becher's connivance through manipulation of cadres rather than force of argument, has become clear, and the exchanges become more ritualised, threatening to become a standard 'Kritik und Selbstkritik' session. Brecht's response had been cautious, testing the water with his 'Thesen zur Faustus-Diskussion', but he clearly still viewed the debate as a discussion of artistic principle. (This became the official GDR version of the debate.) Eisler and his defenders were forced onto the defensive, and their attempts to stress the ambiguity and complexity of the German intellectual tradition - 'Können wir 1945 von einem *Sieg* des deutschen humanistischen Geistes sprechen?'[25] - are dismissed as little more than treason. The avant-gardist Eisler's approach to history, which treats the past as a discontinuous textual resource rather than as a continually unfolding narrative, threatens those who rely on a legitimising continuity in history, according to which the division of Germany is simply the physical and geographical expression of the opposing currents in German history. The problem faced by artists and intellectuals like Brecht and Eisler was that their attachment to Marxism made it hard for them not to share this view of the GDR - as the potential synthesis of 'Geist' and 'Macht' - and they were thus unable to follow through the consequences of their artistic techniques to their logical conclusion, namely that the legitimising narrative spun out by the SED was simply one possible narrative amongst many.

In a number of ways, Brecht differs radically from Abusch's line in his defence of Eisler's approach to the 'kulturelles Erbe'; he espouses a strictly dialectical approach to the development of artistic forms, and thus considers that Eisler's Faustus is an antithesis, 'eine kritische Weiterentwicklung' of Goethe's figure.[26] This attitude towards revered cultural icons clashes with the narrative which sees the GDR as the logical development of Goethe's humanism; according to Abusch, a truly socialist development of the Faust legend would show, 'daß eben diese Persönlichkeit in einem sozialistischen Sinne vollendet wird, d.h., daß das Dilemma Gesellschaft und Persönlichkeit gelöst wird'.[27]

Brecht had sharply criticised tenets of Socialist Realism in preparatory discussions with members of the Berlin Ensemble, 'Aber der neue Mensch kann nicht durch die Dichtung produziert werden, das ist ein Aberglaube. Er muß sich selbst produzieren. Die Dichtung kann ihn anregen, nicht schaffen'.[28] Yet the idea of the perfectibility of humanity under a socialist system has authoritarian implications which lead Brecht to support the rule of the SED. His beliefs are bound up with his image of the Soviet Union. Whatever doubts he had about Stalin, he mentions the Slánský trial with approval, comparing Slánský's final 'confession' with Faustus' belated recognition of his own treachery.[29] His support for the principle of purges of 'renegades' weakens his ability to defend his friends, despite the leeway which such compromises grant him. The aims expressed here by Brecht and Abusch are the same; the difference lies in the method. The former's artistic practice claimed to return to the spectator/reader the responsibility for decision-making which had been appropriated by the author in 'bourgeois' drama, and a regime struggling with its own illegitimacy could not afford to give licence to such independent approaches to history. Yet the conclusions towards which Brecht leads his audiences are clear, as he considered them to be the outcome of inevitable dialectical processes which made support for the GDR a matter of historical necessity. His application of the dialectic is more consistent than that of the SED leadership, but the self-deceptive sleight-of-hand involved in this kind of reasoning restricted his ability to think independently.

The limits which Brecht set on his discourse of opposition and compromise result to a great extent from his ideologised view of circumstances in the GDR, and his self-image as *Machtpolitiker* begins to look distinctly threadbare.The transcripts of the debate demonstrate that Brecht convinced himself that the discussions were generally constructive and show how his self-conscious application of the dialectic to problems of culture and of intellectual history led him to endorse Ulbricht's regime, which, however wretched the immediate situation, he took to embody the next stage in the progress of this dialectic. Up to a certain point in the second meeting, he sought the point of principle in his opponents' words, whereas the 'Faustus-Debatte' was intended as a showpiece, stage-managed through the SED's deployment of a coercive dialectic against intellectuals whose own legitimacy depended on the GDR. This forced him into positions of compromise with the line which he opposed.

The declaration of the 'New Course' on 9 June increased the pressure on all parties, although the extent of the changes which Beria's policy could have brought were clear to few at the time. Nevertheless, the signs that the SED leadership was having to retreat from its hard-line positions brought a significant fightback in the Academy, at the third *Mittwoch-Gesellschaft* on 10 June.This shows that increasing resistance in the artistic community began before 17 June, as hints of the precariousness of Ulbricht's position begin to appear. There are courageous contributions to Eisler's defence from Hermann Duncker, Helene Weigel and particularly Arnold Zweig, whose scholarly humanism is alien to the majority of the participants. Zweig is the only contributor to consider Goethe's use of irony in his portrayal of Faust, an idea which has been notably absent from the discussions, as it tends to undermine any attempts to claim a work of art for political purposes, whether from the perspective of Brecht or Abusch. Brecht brings the discussion onto ground where he and his colleagues can put up a more spirited defence of Eisler; by emphasising his revised 'Thesen', he ensures that the debate revolves to a certain extent around his own personal standing, which is still high, despite the press campaign against the Berlin Ensemble. That the administrative structure of the Academy obliges such views to be heard is an expression of the tenacity of its all-German foundation and the emphasis which it put on individual personalities rather than on the functions of a 'mass organisation' like the Kulturbund. Brecht's increasing confidence is reflected in the aggressiveness of his attacks on Eisler's critics - for example, he turns on Walter Besenbruch when the latter describes Eisler's *Faustus* as 'Wühlen im Dreck'[30] - and a certain defensiveness on the part of functionaries like Besenbruch enables him to exploit his room for manoeuvre. The difficulty of the situation for the SED grouping comes out very clearly when Becher appears to switch sides in an attempt to relieve some of the pressure on Eisler. He criticises Besenbruch and Girnus for the ferocity of their attacks, hypocritically turning the tables on the faction whose success he had tried to guarantee, in a foretaste of the abrupt turnaround in the Academy's affairs in the wake of 17 June.

The strikes and demonstrations on 16/17 June shattered the fragile authority that the SED exercised following the announcement of the New Course and transformed the situation in the Academy, behind whose closed doors Brecht moved quickly and courageously in a series of emergency meetings.[31] He was instrumentally involved in the formulation of the Academy's recommendations for the restructuring of cultural life that were first debated at a Plenary Session on 26 June.[32] At that meeting, Brecht, supported by Eisler and others, took revenge on Abusch and Friedrich Wolf for their assault on Peter Huchel and *Sinn und Form*. Brecht and his supporters pressed home their advantage on 2 July, when Huchel joined Brecht in a furious condemnation of Abusch and Wolf. Yet there were clear limits to Brecht's criticisms of the SED, whose fundamental illegitimacy he would not entertain, especially at a time when the prospect of securing his own theatre was finally very real.[33] His actions remain within the bounds of the critical loyalty of his infamous letter to Ulbricht concerning the manner in which the SED had tackled the Construction of Socialism.[34] Although Brecht's criticisms of Abusch over *Faustus* and *Sinn und Form* are stinging - he condemns Abusch's 'sehr eigentümliche Art und Weise, hier Einfluß zu gewinnen' - he still maintains that the debate has been 'eine sehr anständige Diskussion', despite his own awareness, demonstrated in the changing dynamics of the debate after the declaration of the New Course, that the outcome rested on political developments in the GDR.[35] In his juxtaposition of an idea of open debate with Abusch's machinations, Brecht demonstrates a sleight-of-hand. Firstly, he downplays his own role as tactician in the defence of Eisler, and his ability to select arguments according to the needs of the situation. Secondly, and more seriously, his attachment to the idea of open discussion among socialist artists suppresses the fact that the 17 June uprising has called into question the very basis of that discussion. It is not a case of artist versus bureaucrat, but of the radical exposure of Brecht's *Weltanschauung* and his dependence on the institutional privileges afforded to him.

He went on to argue, in similar vein, of *Sinn und Form*, 'Wir brauchen Beiträge, die die großen historischen Errungenschaften der DDR beschreiben, so daß die Leute in Westdeutschland und in der DDR sie wirklich als sachlich aufnehmen und verstehen können. Die Fakten sind überwältigend'.[36] The limits to the new discourse of intellectual freedom are set by the suppression of the implications of 17 June. An open-minded appraisal of the uprising's significance for the legitimacy of SED rule would have disrupted the ideological self-justification of Marxist intellectuals on which their work in the GDR was based. Brecht cannot acknowledge the significance of the Soviet intervention in Berlin. He employs an ideologised view of conditions in the GDR, which regards that state as absolutely opposed to the Federal Republic and Nazi Germany, in order to shift onto them much responsibility for the disaster of the Construction of Socialism. In doing so, he defines the limits of the crisis that the 17 June triggers in him. Brecht's famous journal entry of 20 August captures that crisis, 'Buckow. *Turandot*. Daneben die *Buckower Elegien*. Der 17. Juni hat die ganze Existenz verfremdet'.(*BFA*, 27, 346) *Turandot* remained a fragment: the resurgence of fascism in the GDR was a subject that defied his dramatic gift. However, he wrote a foreword in which he sought to exculpate SED politicians with drastic claims concerning the forces truly acting as the government,

> Unter neuen Befehlshabern setzte sich also der Naziapparat wieder in Bewegung. Ein solcher Apparat kann durch Kontrolle von oben nicht mit neuem Geist erfüllt werden; er benötigte Kontrolle von unten. Unüberzeugt, aber feige, feindlich, aber sich duckend

begannen verknöcherte Beamte wieder gegen die Bevölkerung zu regieren. (*BFA*, 24, 410)

The GDR bureaucracy became the butt of his scathing satire after 17 June. One thinks of publications such as 'Das Amt für Literatur' and 'Nicht feststellbare Fehler der Kunstkommission'. *Buckower Elegien* such as 'Der Einarmige im Gehölz' and 'Vor acht Jahren' show that he was plagued throughout the summer by the traumatic vision of a resurgent Nazism.

In this way, Brecht protected himself from a deeper crisis, rescuing his belief in Marxism beyond the 17 June. His early death spared him the severe trials that followed the Soviet suppression of the Hungarian government, after which Becher, terminally ill and humiliated by Ulbricht and Abusch, renounced socialism.[37] Zweig had no doubt how Brecht would have responded. On 3 December 1956 he wrote to Lion Feuchtwanger, 'Immer wieder sagt einer aus unserem Kreise: "Das müßte man dem Brecht sagen! Der würde sich einen Fall des Wolfgang Harich nicht haben gefallen lassen!"'[38] In the light of the above analysis, it is difficult to share Zweig's view. There was nothing in the political situation in 1956-7 that Brecht could have exploited as he did in 1953; and a direct challenge to the SED leadership was simply not on Brecht's agenda. Brecht emerges, instead, as the paradigm for that particular intertwining of criticism and loyalty that characterised the artistic élite's relationship to the SED leadership during the forty years of the GDR's history.

[1.] Research for the present essay was undertaken with the support of a Research Fellowship from the Alexander von Humboldt Foundation and a British Academy Research Studentship.

[2.] The texts are collected in Bertolt Brecht, *Grosse kommentierte Berliner und Frankfurter Ausgabe*, 23, *Schriften 3*, ed. by Barbara Wallburg (1993). Subsequent references to the edition (*BFA*) will be given in the main body of the essay, with volume and page numbers within parentheses.

[3.] In his *Das Leben des Bertolt Brecht oder der Umgang mit den Welträtseln*, 2 vols (Berlin and Weimar, Aufbau, 1988), Werner Mittenzwei points out that *Sinn und Form* was Brecht's 'wichtigste literarische Plattform, von der aus er die Öffentlichkeit in sorgfältiger Auswahl mit neuen oder bereits im Exil entstandenen Arbeiten bekannt machte'.(ii, p.379)

[4.] In May 1950, for example, Brecht was instrumental in securing confirmation of the Academy's status as the GDR's highest authority in the arts, over which the Cultural Commission had no say. (*BFA*, 23, p.478).

[5.] We have used the term 'integrationist' to refer to the tendency within the SED leadership, represented principally by Walter Ulbricht, which aimed for the absolute and unconditional integration of the GDR into Soviet-dominated security structures as a means of guaranteeing the viability of the new state. Although this line became increasingly dominant in the years after 1945, capitalising on and contributing to the increasing tensions in Europe, it by no means represented a unified policy within the SED, nor even within the Soviet leadership. For an analysis of this process see Peter Davies, *Ideology, Resistance and Complicity in the*

'*Deutsche Akademie der Künste*' *in the Context of Stalin's German Policy 1945-1953*, doctoral dissertation, University of Manchester, 1997, especially chapter 3.

6.   See Davies, pp.267-73, for a fuller discussion of these issues, including the connection between the 'deutsche Misere' theory and the abandonment of the 'German Road to Socialism'. See also Sigrid Meuschel, *Legitimation und Parteiherrschaft in der DDR* (Frankfurt am Main, Suhrkamp, 1992), pp.59-70.

7.   See the documentation '*Die Regierung ruft die Künstler*': *Dokumente zur Gründung der* '*Deutschen Akademie der Künste*' (*DDR*) *1945-1953*, ed. by Petra Uhlmann and Sabine Wolf (Berlin, Henschel, 1993), p.171.

8.   See Deborah Vietor-Engländer, *Faust in der DDR* (Frankfurt a. M.: Lang, 1987), pp. 139-54 for details of the Potsdam and Berlin productions. Unless otherwise indicated, subsequent details of those productions are taken for this source.

9.   See Davies, pp.216-7.

10. See '*Die Regierung ruft die Künstler*', p. 29 for discussion of Abusch's removal from all SED positions of responsibility in 1950 due to his alleged involvement with Noel Field. For details of Abusch's recruitment by Erich Mielke for the Stasi in 1951 see Joachim Walther, *Sicherungsbereich Literatur* (Berlin, Ch. Links, 1996), p. 563.

11. The adaptation of Anna Seghers' radio play *Der Prozess der Jeanne d'Arc zu Rouen 1431* illustrates press neglect: the premiere was on 23 November 1952 and the decidedly cool reviews were still appearing in influential newspapers like *Neues Deutschland* the following March.

12. Bertolt Brecht, *Briefe*, ed. by Günter Glaeser, 2 vols (Frankfurt, Suhrkamp, 1981), i, pp. 689-90.

13. Details of Mayer's reply on 24 February are in Brecht, *Briefe*, ii, pp. 1129-30.

14. Mittenzwei, ii, p. 447.

15. Manfred Jäger, *Kultur und Politik in der DDR 1945-1990* (Cologne, Edition Deutschland Archiv, 1994) p. 62.

16. It is suggested in *BFA* (23, p. 538) that Brecht's piece 'Einige Gedanken zur Stanislawski-Konferenz' (23, p. 236) may be 'eine zur Publikation bestimmte Fassung seines Diskussionsbeitrages'. However, 'Einige Gedanken zur Stanislawski-Konferenz' takes issue with Langhoff's interpretation of Stanislavsky in his production of *Egmont* rather than comparing Brecht and Stanislavsky.

17. Jan Knopf, *Brecht Handbuch*, 2 vols (Stuttgart, Metzler, 1986), ii, p. 465.

18. See Brecht's journal entries for 25-30 August 1952. (*BFA*, 27, p. 333)

19. Transcriptions of the *Mitwoch-Gesellschaften* are collected in Hans Bunge, *Die Debatte um Eislers 'Johann Faustus': Eine Dokumentation* (Berlin, BasisDruck Verlag, 1991).

20. Abusch's essay was published in *Sinn und Form*, 4 (1953), 3/4, 179-94, where it was juxtaposed with Brecht's 'Thesen zur Faustus-Diskussion', 194-7. Abusch's essay is an attempt to redeem himself for his earlier ideological errors by repositioning his text of 1945, *Irrweg einer Nation* - the classic statement of the 'Misere' theory - as a contribution to the SED line of 1953.

21. Abusch, p.185.

22. Bunge, p.62.

23. Bunge, p.71.

24. See Johanna Rudolph, 'Weitere Bemerkungen zum "Faust"-Problem', *Neues Deutschland*, 27.5.1953 in Bunge, pp.117-126. For details of Ulbricht's speech on the same day, see Vietor-Engländer, p. 154.

25. Bunge, p.141.

26. Bunge, p.168.

27. Bunge, p.172.

28. Bunge, p.115.

29. Bunge, p.115.

30. Bunge, p.208.

31. See Stephen Parker, '*Sinn und Form*, Peter Huchel und der 17. Juni 1953: Bertolt Brechts Rettungsaktion', *Sinn und Form*, 46 (1994), 738-51.

32. Parker, '*Sinn und Form*, Peter Huchel und der 17. Juni 1953', 745. Quite misleadingly, the editorial commentary on Brecht's draft in *BFA* (23, pp.549-50) gives the date of that meeting as 16 June and places the affair in the context of the New Course without any reference whatsoever to the 17 June!

33. See Brecht's letter to Grotewohl of 15 June 1953 in Brecht, *Briefe*, i, pp. 692-3.

34. The letter to Ulbricht of 17 June is in Brecht *Briefe*, i, pp. 693-4.

35. Brecht's statements are taken from the protocol of the Academy Plenary Session on 26 June 1953, which is deposited in Stiftung Archiv, Akademie der Künste Berlin-Brandenburg, 118.

36. Parker, '*Sinn und Form*, Peter Huchel und der 17. Juni 1953', 749.

37. Becher's reflections following 1956 were first published in *Sinn und Form* in 1988. For a discussion of the SED leadership's response to their publication see Stephen Parker, 'Re-establishing an all-German identity. *Sinn und Form* and German unification', in *The New Germany: Literature and Society after Unification*, ed. Osman Durrani *et al.* (Sheffield, Sheffield Academic Press, 1995), pp. 14-27 (18-19).

38. See *Lion Feuchtwanger - Arnold Zweig. Briefwechsel 1933-1958*, ed. Harold von Hofé, 2

RENATE RECHTIEN

Relations of Production?
Christa Wolf's Extended Engagement with
the Legacy of Bertolt Brecht

Two years before the demise of the GDR and the eventual break up of the entire Eastern block, Christoph Hein stressed the important role which the cultural life and history of Eastern Europe would come to play in ensuring the survival of the richness and complexity of all European culture, including that of important strands of Western European culture. In the face of dominant trends in Western European capitalist societies towards market concentration and internationalisation, Hein envisaged a situation where a few multinational publishing houses would gain control over the majority of all literary distribution, leading to the exclusion not only of a growing number of authors but also of entire literary traditions. Eventually, Hein predicted, we would witness the death of an important part of our culture, 'ein[es] so wichtig[en] Teil[s], daß die Kultur Westeuropas insgesamt gefährdet sein wird.'[1] Given recent events in European history in general and Germany's unification process in particular, Hein's warnings have certainly not lost their relevance today. On the contrary, in view of the tendency in the West German cultural media to write off the GDR as a short-lived Stalinist monstrosity and reduce its memory, as Stefan Heym put it, to a footnote in history, it seems more important than ever before for academic investigation and analysis to form and communicate a more differentiated view of the GDR's life and culture. Within the context of European literature and tradition, we now face the task and also have the opportunity to reread East German literary texts with a view to reassessing their contribution to *our* life and culture as well as accepting the challenges offered therein. As part of this process we should also renew our understanding of the role which literary tradition and its handling by individual East German authors has played in the development of GDR literature as a literature which forms an important part of, but is also distinct from, modern and contemporary writing in the West.

For no other generation of GDR authors did the engagement with the ideas of their forebears assume as important a role as for Christa Wolf's generation. The complex interrelationship between their desire to develop a distinctive literary identity and tradition on the one hand, and the demands made on them by the state at crucial stages of the GDR's socio-political history on the other, frequently forced these writers to define and redefine their roles. In this process, a critical examination and re-examination of literary heritage played an important part. Wolf herself has consistently linked her work to the experiences and ideas of other writers in an endeavour to establish lines of literary tradition in the GDR. These were intended to constitute an alternative to dominant cultural trends in the West and, at least as importantly, to the narrow dogmatic proscriptions of SED cultural functionaries. In Wolf's critical engagement with tradition and literary heritage as well as in her discussion of poetics from ancient and modern traditions, Bertolt Brecht has played a seminal role.

In the opinion of Sara Lennox, Christa Wolf's entire work may be said to exist in a tension between the two poles Brecht and Bachmann, with the influence of Bachmann growing progressively stronger from the seventies. Lennox suggested that pursuing Brecht's influence on Wolf and her growing disenchantment with him would be a fascinating enterprise.[2] In raising this issue Lennox is echoing Wolf herself, who stated in her 1966 essay on Brecht: 'Es könnte eine interessante Studie werden, wenn jemand es unternähme, das Verhältnis meiner Generation zu Brecht zu untersuchen', before reminding herself that Brecht would have preferred to have this relationship expressed in terms of 'Spannungen' and 'Entwicklung'.[3]

This essay seeks to illuminate the nature of this tension along with some of its possible causes. It will re-examine also the extent to which Wolf's work develops and refines some of Brecht's ideas on the basis of her own experiences with prose rather than dramatic writing and as a member of a generation younger than that of Brecht and his contemporaries. It will focus on two key stages in Wolf's development as a writer, when the question she had first posed in 1964: 'Wie aber soll man heute schreiben?'[4] assumed a new and urgent relevance: in the later 1960s, as part of Wolf's search for new prose forms, and in the 1980s, when the crisis within her own society as well as within the Eastern block and Western civilisation at large prompted her to challenge the received truths of Marxism as well as some of the fundamental assumptions on which European culture rests. For Wolf, this has involved a complete rethink of her role as a woman writer in European society. But it also led her to renew her interest in Brecht, as the intertextual references to Brecht in Wolf's *Störfall* indicate.

Appropriation and Development

In his 1974 analysis of Brecht in the GDR, David Bathrick stressed the controversial role and the contradictory function which the dramatist played throughout the cultural and political history of that society, which Bathrick discusses in terms of 'the dialectics of legitimation'.[5] This he takes to describe the two diametrically opposed, yet intricately linked functions of Brecht's revolutionary theatre within GDR culture. On the one hand, beginning with his return to the GDR in 1948 and his production of *Mutter Courage* in 1949, his theatre was supported as a distinctive feature of 'socialist national culture', and thus served the cultural aims of the SED. On the other hand, however, Brecht was always at odds with the prevailing official affirmative notion of culture, and continuously sought to challenge, undermine and transform it. Forged as a means of transforming society, art, Bathrick pointed out, was understood by Brecht to be more than simply a superstructural affirmation of reality. Brecht defined its role as active and critical appropriation of reality, with the artist confronting, exposing and acting upon real societal contradictions with a view to bringing about social change.

Going back to his debate about realism in art with Georg Lukács in the 1930s, Brecht was particularly at odds with the prominence given in the official 'Kulturerbe' of the GDR to the literature of Weimar classicism as well as with the dogmatic and unidimensional manner in which the works of Goethe and Schiller were being proposed as models for contemporary authors. In the early 1950s Bertolt Brecht and Hanns Eisler fought passionate battles against the SED's cultural apparatchiks, insisting that a socialist literature could not be based on the classical bourgeois tradition but had to develop alternatives which were rooted in a proletarian, socialist culture. With his experimentation with alternative art forms (montage, techniques of *Verfremdung*, epic theatre), Brecht drew on the artistic and political tradition of the Formalists and Futurists of post-revolutionary Russia (Tretjakov, Arvatov) and introduced production aesthetics into the GDR as an alternative and challenge to socialist realist art. In fact, Brecht's ideas on heritage and aesthetics were much closer to the essence of Marx's thought on history than the favoured interpretations of SED cultural functionaries at the time. Brecht aimed in his aesthetics as well as in his dramatic technique to create genuinely democratic and emancipatory art forms, rejecting hierarchical concepts of social, political or artistic production. In so doing he captured the spirit of Marx's conception of *revolutionary practice*.[6] It is precisely this challenging and potentially more subversive dimension of Brecht's work which official GDR criticism tended to ignore or play down, as it was considered too threatening to the ideological programme and hegemony of the SED.[7] At the same time, it is precisely this emancipatory and democratic potential of Brecht's notion of unfettered production and particularly the notion of the writer as co-producer, not merely recorder, of the social process which has acted as an inspiration to both playwrights and writers alike in the GDR.

There can be little doubt that Christa Wolf's work also stands within the dialectical critical tradition of Brecht. As a fellow Marxist and committed socialist of a subsequent generation of artists in the GDR she has, whether consciously or unconsciously, addressed a number of the issues and concerns which had also been of importance to him. Wolf first became acquainted with Brecht's work as a student at Leipzig University in the early 1950s. Her first reaction to Brecht's theatre is perhaps best described as a mixture of admiration, curiosity and - according to her own analysis [8]- a considerable degree of misunderstanding. Her account of visiting the Berlin Ensemble expresses with unconcealed admiration the deep and lasting impression which above all the innovative, fresh and provocative nature of Brecht's theatre made on her. Brecht seemed to have captured in his dramatic technique as well as in his plays the essence of Marx's thought and of socialism. In contrast to classical drama with its tendency to idealise and seek unity, coherence, harmony and certainty, Brecht confronted his audience with contradiction, disharmony and uncertainty - without sacrificing either his love of life or his belief in and respect for the integrity of the individual human being. The contradictions expressed in his drama, Wolf felt, were those of a modern, scientific age, and Brecht's dramatic technique of involving the audience emotionally, while at the same time appealing to its desire for a rational understanding of why the characters act in a particular manner, clearly aroused her curiosity. However, due partly to the manner in which GDR Germanists at the time taught Brecht, and partly to the over-confidence and gullibility of her generation, whose members were only too keen to consider themselves the 'Menschen des wissenschaftlichen Zeitalters'[9] whom Brecht had addressed, many of the fundamentally critical and challenging aspects of Brecht's aesthetics and theatrical practice were overlooked. As a consequence, most of Wolf's generation also failed to understand Brecht's message regarding their own role in the historical process and in shaping the future of their society. Looking back in the later 1960s, Christa Wolf deplores the fact that people in the GDR of the 1950s had not been ready for Brecht's revolutionary theatre; as a result, it tended to be imitated rather than properly understood.[10] Wolf's theoretical and prose writing of later years bears testimony to the fact that her engagement with Brecht did not end with the views she had first absorbed in the GDR of the 1950s. While her interest in Brecht in the early stages focused almost exclusively on his dramatic technique, the ethical issues of works such as *Leben des Galilei* or *Urfaust* later assumed great importance for Christa Wolf.

Both in her dialectical understanding of history as an open and contradictory process of change rather than a linear progression towards a pre-given finite goal, and in the prominence which she gives to the role of the individual in the process of change, Christa Wolf's work echoes the ideas of Brecht and other socialist intellectuals of his time. For Wolf, who has been as committed to social change as Brecht was before her, prose writing in the GDR also had to be firmly anchored in the contradictions arising out of the everyday experiences of people in society, since 'der Vorstoß zu den Fragen unserer Zeit ist - jedenfalls in der Prosa, wenn sie sich nicht im Gleichnishaften bewegen will - an das Alltägliche gebunden.'[11] For her, as for Brecht, art has little to do with spreading comfortable truths or ideas of harmony and certainty in the manner in which socialist realist dogma would have it, but springs from the 'anstrengenden[n], schmerzhafte[n] Versuch, nicht zu Vereinbarendes miteinander zu vereinbaren', which has always been 'eine Wurzel für den Zwang zum Schreiben.'[12] In her essay 'Tagebuch - Arbeitsmittel und Gedächtnis' (1964) Wolf quotes from Brecht's poem Lektüre ohne Unschuld (1944) and from his diary of 1955 in order to stress the fact that one such fundamental contradiction in modern society, which Brecht had already indentified in the 1940s and 1950s, had lost none of its topicality and urgency in the GDR of the mid-1960s, namely the gap between the 'Entwicklungsstand der Wissenschaft und den vielerorts zurückgebliebenen Gesellschaftszuständen' (DdA I, 22). Picking up Brecht's warnings against the dangerous destructive potential of technological and scientific advance as it had been revealed in twentieth century warfare, Christa Wolf reminds her readers that this dangerous contradiction has remained very much unresolved. Furthermore, she holds it responsible also for the many manifestations of politically apathetic attitudes and behaviour patterns in modern socialist society. Like Brecht, Wolf believes that artistic and literary production have an important, if not essential role to play in helping to bridge this gap and in seeking to help people overcome a deep-seated resistance to and disbelief in the possibility for change. Wolf clearly identifies with Brecht's method of confronting his audience with complex issues rather than offering easy answers as a means of promoting independent, mature and critical thought. And when she writes, referring to the works of Gorki, Seghers, Thomas Mann, and others, that what they all share with Brecht is 'daß die Struktur ihrer Arbeiten auf eine sehr komplizierte, öfter durchaus indirekte Weise mit der Struktur ihrer Wirklichkeit übereinstimmt, mit der sie andererseits, Veränderung wünschend und verändernd, dauernd im Streit liegen',[13] she comes close to Brecht's concept of realism itself. For Werner Mittenzwei, Brecht's essential partisanship and commitment to the political struggles of his time manifests itself through the 'Lust am Erkennen' and the 'Spaß an der Veränderung' which his theatre inspires.[14] While she does not seek to emulate Brecht, Christa Wolf, too, clearly considers the particular merit of Brecht's work for her as an author to be the 'Ermunterung zu eigenen Entdeckungen.'[15]

Wolf's essay 'Lesen und Schreiben' (1968), in which she first formulated her own prose theory, as well as her narrative *Nachdenken über Christa T.* (1968), where she put these ideas into literary practice, demonstrate that by the late 1960s Wolf had clearly made productive the encouragement which Brecht's work had provided. In contrast to Brecht's revolutionary theatre which had already addressed an audience of the scientific age in the 1950s, prose writing in the GDR of the 1960s in the form prescribed by the doctrine of socialist realism seemed, for Wolf, to be more and more dangerously out of step with actual social developments. But modern prose, Wolf demonstrated, could go further than drama in addressing big political questions as well as the seemingly banal, everyday experience of the individual in society and it could help to gain greater understanding of the dilemmas and contradictions of the individual as a moral agent in a complex social reality. In his drama Brecht sought to dispel false consciousness by applying Marx's theory of historical materialism. In this theory, Marx argued that we must understand individuals '[...] not as they may appear in their own or other people's imagination but rather as they really are, that is, as they work, produce materially, and act under definite material limitations, presuppositions, and conditions independent of their will.'[16] Brecht considered that, to gain a rational understanding of individuals' actions, it was necessary to portray these in the way that Marx's theory of historical materialism had proposed.

Wolf's prose theory and her literary practice take the interpretation of Marx's theory of historical materialism an important step further than Brecht had done. While her exploration of 'individuals as they really are' continues to include the dimension of outer material, socio-political and historical reality as it impinges on the individual's ability to act, her prime focus of attention shifts towards those aspects of human experience that are less easily penetrable by rational or scientific observation and thought, namely to the domain of the inner emotional and psychological reality of subjective individual experience. Wolf's writing has explored with increasing intensity the complexity of levels on which tensions and crises in outer reality interact with the inner, emotional and psychological circumstances of the individual, insisting that the 'Spuren, die die Ereignisse in unserem Innern hinterlassen' (*Chr.T.*, 170) deserve as much attention and critical reflection as those phenomena more readily accepted as significant social facts within the institutional discourses of modern society.

Modern prose must seek to support 'das Subjektwerden des Menschen'[17]through the honest and open reflection of the totality of human experience, which Christa Wolf takes to involve:

> everything that happens to a person [...] not only what he actually experiences, but what he has thought about and what has affected him, as well as any ideas he may have assimilated from ideology or literature or knowledge from any other field, in fact all those things that come together to mould his mind, the way he feels and thinks as an individual.[18]

Moreover, where Brecht's emphasis had been on encouraging a rational understanding of human action by his audience, Wolf's prose has aimed also at an equally strong emotional response from her reader, at an understanding which is based on empathy, compassion and love. This approach, she stated in a conversation with Hans Kaufmann in 1973, could, like Brecht's theatre, still be explained within the framework of historical materialism:

> Wenn Brecht den Akzent für seine Untersuchungen zeitweise stärker auf die Herausarbeitung der sozialen Determinanten, heutige marxistische Autoren ihn stärker auf die Erforschung der Rolle des Individuums [...] legen, - sollte man nicht auch dies mit Hilfe historisch-materialistischen Denkens erklären können?[19]

In contrast to drama which, according to Christa Wolf, tends to objectify characters by placing them outside the dramatist's self and his or her direct personal experience into a constructed reality,[20] prose writing, as Wolf envisaged it, should also express the authentic, subjectively mediated experience of the writer, the dimension of authorship. According to her own statement, as a result of the revelations made about the crimes of the Stalin era at the XX. Party Conference of the CPSU in 1956, a fundamental learning experience for her, Christa Wolf resolved: 'künftig wollte ich zu meinen Erfahrungen stehen und sie mir durch nichts und niemanden ausreden, verleugnen oder verbieten lassen. - Sonst hätte ich ja übrigens niemals eine Zeile schreiben können.'[21] Wolf's approach to prose writing presupposes that the writer can no longer be the conduit for unalienated reality or agitational didacticism. Instead, the writer's mediation would entail a refraction of that 'external' reality: 'Lassen wir Spiegel das Ihre tun: Spiegeln. Sie können nichts anderes. Literatur und Wirklichkeit stehen sich nicht gegenüber wie Spiegel und das, was gespiegelt wird. Sie sind ineinander verschmolzen im Bewußtsein des Autors.'[22] While Brecht had already rejected the crude socialist realist notion of the artist as passive recorder of reality in his essay 'Wir müssen nicht nur Spiegel sein' of the 1950s,[23] Wolf's poetological statement develops his ideas further and stresses in particular the role of the author as conscious subject in history who both acts upon and perceives reality in a manner which is inseparably linked with his or her entire way of being. Wolf's poetics therefore attach particular importance to the role and integrity of the individual, whether as writer or reader. In *Nachdenken über Christa T.*, where Wolf put her ideas into literary practice, the act of writing itself has become the subject of narration in such a manner as to allow reality to become manifest only to the extent in which the possibility of depicting it is being problematised. And it is precisely this new function which Wolf ascribes to literature which Karl Robert Mandelkow considers to be the genuinely new and revolutionary element of her work: 'Damit hat Christa Wolf den dogmatischen Vorlauf wissenschaftlicher Welterkenntnis in die poetische Reflexion zurückgenommen und die nur attributive Wahrhaftigkeit ihres Erzählerstandorts in die konstitutive der Wahrheitsstiftung verwandelt.'[24] On the basis of my exposition so far, Christa Wolf's aesthetic positions of the 1960s may be said both to draw on and to develop aspects of the critical dialectical tradition emanating from Brecht. As a fellow Marxist who had been as concerned, as Wolf was later, to distinguish between Marxism as it was being propagated by Party functionaries and his own interpretations of Marx's thought, Brecht without doubt played an important role in Wolf's aesthetic emancipation from the discourse of the state during the later 1960s. But the ideas of Brecht and his colleagues continued to be of importance also in Christa Wolf's handling of literary heritage during the years that followed.[25]

Re-emphasizing Past Warnings Unheeded

Wolf's prose writing of the 1980s has been informed by an acute awareness of the destructive path towards annihilation and self-annihilation on which European culture and politics have been headed. The intensification of the very real possibility of a nuclear confrontation between the superpowers, followed by the first acknowledged nuclear accident on Russian soil in 1986, left little doubt about the fact that the leadership in any modern society, whether East or West, would go to any length in order to protect the supposed progress and achievements of modern civilisation. In such a climate, any claim to moral superiority traditionally upheld by socialist ideologues had clearly become unmasked as false consciousness by the events themselves. For Wolf as a writer, the full conscious acknowledgement of these complex and dangerous realities forced a final abandonment of the notion of art as a didactic instrument which Brecht had upheld. In *Kassandra* (1983) she makes this point through an intertextual allusion to Brecht's Galilei, who had rejected the classical notion of the value and merit of individual heroism by emphasising instead the hope which lay in a socialist conception of the collective assuming this role. For Wolf in the 1980s, this conception had become equally invalid, as: 'Gegen eine Zeit, die Helden braucht, richten wir nichts aus.' (*K*, 156). For her, any notion of heroism, whether individual or collective, remains trapped in conventional patterns of antithetical thinking in terms of victor and victim, subject and object, which Wolf's aesthetics seek to overcome. In contrast to this, Wolf's protagonist develops a contradictory understanding of herself as both subject and object of history, as both resisting and at the same time collaborating and colluding in present circumstances. While Kassandra apportions blame where it is due and distances herself from the warmongering tactics, attitudes and actions of the palace world, she also critically reflects the deeply internalised awareness of herself and others as victims as a first step towards genuine emancipation. This juxtaposition of a self which is resisting and in opposition as well as collaborating reflects not only current feminist thought, but also a postmodern recognition that the old dualistic modes of thinking can no longer be of validity in today's world.

Christa Wolf's narrative *Störfall* (1986) reflects similar ideas on a much more autobiographical level. By letting the reader witness the thought-processes of her narrator over the course of one day in the aftermath of the Chernobyl accident, Wolf depicts the process of seeking emancipation and inner independence from deeply internalised values, attitudes and patterns of thought and behaviour. In this narrative, Wolf continues to put into literary practice an intention she expressed in her Frankfurt lectures (1983): 'Ich will zusammentragen, was mich, uns, zu Komplizen der Selbstzerstörung macht; was mich, uns befähigt, ihr zu widerstehn.' (*FPV*, 109). As a highly intertextual work, *Störfall* also contains overt as well as indirect allusions to Brecht's work. After the news of the nuclear accident has reached her, the narrator of *Störfall* can no longer continue to look upon the world in her accustomed way: 'Wieder einmal, so ist es mir vorgekommen, hatte das Zeitalter sich ein Vorher und Nachher geschaffen' (*Stf.*, 43). Just as Brecht's Galilei had turned the belief system of a millenium on its head with his discovery: 'Die alten Lehren, die tausend Jahre geglaubt wurden, sind ganz baufällig'[26], the narrator of Wolf's narrative has to learn a 'neues Sehen' in order to transcend the false appearances of outer reality. But for Wolf, this new way of seeing involves also attacking the deeply internalised values and beliefs transmitted through Western culture and society over the millenia, and it also has final implications for her socialist commitment. In the course of the narrative, Wolf critically re-examines how our thought has been shaped by theories of evolution, history, biology and even religion.

Attacking preconceived ideas about outer and inner reality seems to involve first of all overcoming the fear of doing so, for, as *Kindheitsmuster* had already established, 'Lust und Angst' are 'innig miteinander verbunden' (*KM*, 13). The narrator's reflections begin, therefore, with an attack on the obvious, outer enemy: the nuclear accident is the result of scientific progress. In contrast to the promises made by GDR scientists of the earlier years that scientific progress in socialist societies would be guided by ethical and humanitarian principles[27], the scientists depicted in *Störfall* have cast aside all ethical and humanitarian considerations. Wolf's narrative depicts them in terms reminiscent of the Faust characters of Brecht and Eisler's suppressed works[28], with the emphasis on the dangerous and ruthless side of their nature, as 'Wissenschaftler[n], die, von keiner Ehrfurcht gehemmt, was die Natur im Innersten zusammenhält, nicht nur erkennen, auch verwerten wollen' (*Stf.*, 34) and as 'Faust, der nicht Wissen, sondern Ruhm gewinnen will.' (*Stf.*, 73). A further indirect allusion to Brecht's warnings against the dangers of scientific and technological advance contained in *Störfall* is the narrator's scream of horror towards the end of the narration which reminds the reader of Galilei's words:

> Ihr mögt mit der Zeit alles entdecken, was es zu entdecken gibt, und euer Fortschritt wird doch nur ein Fortschreiten von der Menschheit weg sein. Die Kluft zwischen euch und ihr kann eines Tages so groß werden, daß euer Jubelschrei über irgendeine neue Errungenschaft von einem universalen Entsetzensschrei beantwortet werden könnte.[29]

While Brecht's apocalyptic vision of a universal scream of horror has not yet become a reality, Wolf reminds us that Brecht's warnings, which had been issued with a view to the abuse made of scientific progress in Western capitalism and German fascism, have lost none of their relevance and poignancy in modern European societies, whether socialist or capitalist. The reference to Brecht's poem *1940*, which is about the early days of the Second World War, 'daß die Mütter entgeistert den Himmel durchforschen nach den Erfindungen der Gelehrten', serves a similar function of underlining the narrator's sense that the horrors of Chernobyl were not new but familiar, predictable and perhaps avoidable.

In the face of a massive nuclear accident, ordinary people are shown to have no meaningful course of action open to them. Even full contemplation and comprehension of the extent of the accident has been rendered impossible, for events are dominated completely by the language of science in a conspiratorial pact with political power. For the narrator of *Störfall*, who is a writer, this has serious implications. While Brecht, in his essay 'Fünf Schwierigkeiten beim Schreiben der Wahrheit' (1934) had still been able to conceive of literature as a process of communication: 'Die Wahrheit aber kann man nicht eben schreiben: man muß sie durchaus jemandem schreiben, der damit etwas anfangen kann',[30] the narrator here seems to have lost any belief that she could communicate the truth as she sees it to anyone:

> Mir ist ein Brieftext durch den Kopf gegangen, in dem ich - beschwörend, wie denn sonst - irgend jemandem mitteilen sollte, daß das Risiko der Atomtechnik mit fast keinem anderen Risiko vergleichbar sei und daß man bei einem auch nur minimalen Unsicherheitsfaktor auf diese Technik unbedingt verzichten müsse. Mir ist für meinen Brief keine reale Adresse eingefallen. (*Stf.*, 113)

But Wolf by no means depicts people as mere victims of outer circumstances. The narrator of *Störfall* also identifies the political apathy, disinterest and passivity of ordinary people in society as important contributory factors. The dangerous contradiction Brecht had pointed to in the 1950s, which Wolf had reiterated in her essay 'Tagebuch' in 1964, is shown to have remained very much unresolved in the GDR of the late 1980s as well. And the 'Übereinstimmungssucht und Widerspruchsangst' (*Stf.*, 23) of people in the village also highlight the fact that behaviour patterns and attitudes which Brecht and Eisler had traced back to the impact of Lutheranism on the German psyche[31], have also survived well into the late 20th century.

However, Wolf's critical excursion into the blind spots of modern civilisation does not end with her reminders of past warnings unheeded and an examination of the manner in which present circumstances and the persistence of false consciousness collaborate in and contribute to the present crisis. The narrator of *Störfall*, albeit reluctantly, takes her questioning much further than Brecht had done by also probing the depths of her own psyche in order to gain greater understanding of the extent to which she, as a member of an intellectual elite, has collaborated in these conditions. As in *Kassandra*, collaboration and resistance are juxtaposed in the recognition that she has to cast aside her own preconceived ideas and acquired modes of 'seeing' in order to gain greater understanding of her own need to think in terms of 'Feindbilder[n]', which she unmasks as a means of self-protection, as it allows the projection of unwanted aspects of herself onto an apparent enemy. What she learns is the 'Verzicht auf den Feind' (*Stf.*, 114) which forces her to take a closer and more critical look at herself. As in *Kassandra*, Wolf's questions and reflections in *Störfall* move far beyond the ethical issues addressed in Brecht's *Galilei*.

In conclusion, I have demonstrated that Christa Wolf has, in her prose and essay work, repeatedly engaged with Brecht's work and aesthetics. During the 1960s, this centred to a large extent around her search for new prose forms and the development of an aesthetics which would challenge and oppose the officially propagated dogma of socialist realism. In this quest, Brecht's theatre was able to act as inspiration as well as offer important theoretical insights on which Wolf could build. Wolf's attitude to tradition and her reception of other writers has been informed throughout by the essentially Marxist understanding that such relationships should be productive and lead to personal as well as professional growth. But it has also been underpinned by the need for close identification and affinity with other authors - whether contemporary or of earlier generations - in an endeavour to counteract the kind of objectification of their work to which literary criticism has frequently given rise. With her growing disillusionment with really existing socialism' and her heightened awareness especially of the objectification of women in society in European culture and history, Wolf became increasingly influenced by women's literature and feminist aesthetics. But Brecht continued to play a role in terms of the ethical guidance his work could offer Wolf during a time of crisis in the 1980s. In a manner not dissimilar to Brecht's own approach to literary heritage and conventions, Wolf's intention has never been to invalidate the important insights and developments of other writers before her, but rather to arrive at necessary new positions on the basis of a fresh examination of tradition. Brecht (above all through *Galilei* and *Urfaust*) continued to play an important role for Wolf in terms of his deep commitment to the development of a humanitarian and ethical socialism, and Wolf picks up his warnings against ruthless scientific and technological progress. In her essay on Hans Mayer which was written after the demise of the GDR,[32] Wolf describes her pain and horror at the sight of Bertolt Brecht's grave which had been vandalized by a generation that was obviously no longer able to differentiate between their experience of the GDR version of socialism, and the ideas and hopes which Brecht and his generation had stood for. Above all in view of the very real dangers which the survival of GDR literature as an important part of our European cultural traditions faces today, this essay has intended to make a contribution to keeping alive these ideas and the challenges they can continue to offer both in aesthetic and ethical terms.

[1.] Christoph Hein, speaking as a member of the 'Arbeitsgruppe IV, Literatur und Wirkung' on November 25th 1987, in *X. Schriftstellerkongreß der DDR. Arbeitsgruppen* (Cologne, Pahl-Rugenstein 1988), pp. 224-305, (p. 231).

[2.] Sara Lennox, 'Christa Wolf and Ingeborg Bachmann: Difficulties of Writing the Truth', in Marilyn Sibley Fries (ed.), *Responses to Christa Wolf: Critical Essays* (Detroit, 1989), pp.128-148, (p. 128).

[3] Christa Wolf, 'Brecht und andere', in *Lesen und Schreiben*, Neue Sammlung (Frankfurt aM, Luchterhand, 6th edition, 1985), pp. 161-163, (pp. 161-162) (abbreviated in the text hereafter as *LS*). Other references to Wolf's work in the text are: *DdA = Die Dimension des Autors. Aufsätze, Essays, Gespräche, Reden*, vol. I and II (Berlin, Aufbau, 1986); *CT = Nachdenken über Christa T.* (Frankfurt/aM, Luchterhand, 1971); *KM = Kindheitsmuster* (Frankfurt/aM, Luchterhand 1976); *Stf. = Störfall. Nachrichten eines Tages* (Frankfurt/aM, Luchterhand, 1987); *FPV = Voraussetzungen einer Erzählung: Kassandra,* (Darmstadt und Neuwied, 1983); *K = Kassandra. Erzählung* (Frankfurt/aM, Luchterhand, 1984).

4. Christa Wolf, 'Tagebuch - Arbeitsmittel und Gedächtnis', in *DdA* I, pp. 13-27, (p.22).

5. David Bathrick, 'The Dialectics of Legitimation: Brecht in the GDR', in *New German Critique* (Spring 1974), 90-103, (91).

6. In *The German Ideology* (1845-6) Karl Marx opposed Feuerbach's materialist doctrine, arguing that this 'forgets that circumstances are changed by men and that it is essential to educate the educator himself' and declaring that this 'doctrine must, therefore, divide society into two parts, one of which is superior to society'. See David McLellan, *Karl Marx. Selected Writings* (Oxford, 1977), p. 156.

7. Werner Mittenzwei was one of the first critics in the GDR who, on the occasion of the 70th anniversary of Brecht's birth, recognised him as 'the great model for the theatre of the GDR'. Mittenzwei was also the first critic in the GDR to analyse in detail Brecht's debate with Georg Lukács, which had remained entirely unpublished in the GDR until 1967. See Werner Mittenzwei, 'Die Brecht-Lukács-Debatte', in *Sinn und Form* 19 (1967), 235-269. Only five years after Mittenzwei's positive evaluation of Brecht's work, the official verdict on Brecht was reversed and both Brecht and Mittenzwei came under severe attack for their sacrilegious attitudes toward the German classical literary tradition. See Werner Hecht (ed.), *Brecht-Dialog 1968* (Berlin, 1969), p.31. See also Bathrick, 'The Dialectics of Legitimation'.

8. Christa Wolf, 'Brecht und andere'.

9. Christa Wolf, 'Brecht und andere'.

10. Wolf comments on this in her essay of 1966 on Brecht as well as in 'Lesen und Schreiben', written two years later.

11. Christa Wolf, 'Tagebuch - Arbeitsmittel und Gedächtnis', in Wolf, *DdA* I, pp.13-27 (p.18).

12. Christa Wolf, 'Auskunft', in *DdA* I, pp.64-66 (p.65).

13. Christa Wolf, 'Brecht und andere', p.85.

14. Werner Mittenzwei, 'Die Brecht-Lukács-Debatte', 257

15. Christa Wolf, 'Brecht und andere', p.85.

16. Karl Marx, quoted here from McLellan, *The Thought of Karl Marx*, p.37.

17. Christa Wolf, 'Lesen und Schreiben', in *LS*, p.48.

18. 'Christa Wolf in Edinburgh. An interview', edited by Karen McPherson, *GDR Monitor*, 1 (1979), 1-12, (4).

19. 'Die Dimension des Autors. Gespräch mit Hans Kaufmann', in *LS*, pp.68-99 (p.78).

20. Christa Wolf made this point in a discussion at Ohio State University when she replied to the question why women rarely write drama: 'Man hat das Problem, die Figuren aus sich herauszustellen, ganz zu objektivieren und in eine Konstruktion zu bringen.' See 'Aus einer Diskussion. Gespräch mit Christa und Gerhard Wolf', in *DdA* II, pp.440-455, (p.451). As a woman writer, Wolf stressed in a conversation with Therese Hörnigk in the late 1980s, she felt alienated by: 'die Art von Selbstaufgabe, die Brecht Frauen abverlangte.' See Therese Hörnigk, *Christa Wolf* (Göttingen, 1989), p.24.

21. Christa Wolf in conversation with Hörnigk, *Christa Wolf*, p.21.

22. Christa Wolf, 'Lesen und Schreiben', p.41.

23. Bertolt Brecht, 'Nicht nur Spiegel der Wahrheit', *BFA*, 23, p.132. Here Brecht had stated: 'Wir müssen nicht nur Spiegel sein, welche die Wahrheit außer uns reflektieren. Wenn wir den Gegenstand in uns aufgenommen haben, muß etwas von uns dazukommen, bevor er wieder aus uns herausgeht.'

24. Karl Robert Mandelkow, 'Neuer und sozialistischer Realismus. Zu Fragen der Rezeption von DDR- Literatur in der Bundesrepublik', in *Kontext*, 1 (1976), 175-198, (193).

25. As I have argued elsewhere, Christa Wolf's work from the mid-1960s consistently links with literary traditions which may be considered the antithesis of the dominant culture and ideology in the GDR. In contrast to the unidimensional image of man propagated through the heritage reception of SED cultural functionaries, with its idealisation of qualities such as action, thirst for knowledge and industriousness, Wolf's protagonists have in common characteristics such as love, compassion, imagination, and reflection. Wolf's reception of the works of the Early Romantic poets in the mid-1970s marks the culmination of her endeavours to establish alternative lines of literary traditions to those imposed by the Party in the GDR. See Renate Rechtien, 'The Faust Theme in Christa Wolf's Work', in Ian Wallace (ed.), *Christa Wolf in Perspective* (Amsterdam, Rodopi, 1994), pp.107-125.

26. Brecht, *Leben des Galilei*, BFA, 5, p.10.

27. In Wolf's conversation with the GDR biologist Hans Stubbe in the later 1960s, the latter had affirmed his belief that scientific progress in the GDR will and must occur along such fundamentally humanitarian and ethical principles: 'Die Frage: Sollen wir weiterforschen? ist müßig. Wir *werden* weiterforschen. Was erfindbar ist, wird erfunden werden. Aber wir werden unsere eigenen Erfahrungen nur *als Menschen* überleben, als vernunftbegabte Wesen in vernünftig organisierten Gesellschaften - oder gar nicht.' Christa Wolf, 'Ein Besuch', in *DdA* II, pp.239-270 (p.268).

28. Hans Bunge's recent account has re-emphasized that Brecht and Eisler debated passionately against Party functionaries in the early 1950s to defend their separate adaptations of Goethe's *Faust*. Brecht and Eisler each approached the Faust myth from a different angle to that favoured by the SED. In their adaptations, Faust is no precursor of the positive hero of scientific socialism, but rather a complex figure riddled with self-doubt and incapable of piercing through the complexity of

the wider political circumstances and power struggles of his time. While Brecht's Urfaust character might be described as a mixture of a scientist and criminal, Eisler's Johann Faustus is characterised by negativity and political apathy, and his thirst for knowledge does not spring from a desire for true 'Erkenntnis', but rather for social recognition and status. As they were considered too uncomfortable for the political programme of the SED, both Brecht's *Urfaust* and Eisler's opera libretto *Johann Faustus* were ruthlessly suppressed. See Hans Bunge (ed.), *Die Debatte um Hanns Eisler's 'Johann Faustus'. Eine Dokumentation* (Berlin, 1991).

[29.] Brecht, *Leben des Galilei, BFA*, 5, p.284.

[30.] Brecht, 'Fünf Schwierigkeiten beim Schreiben der Wahrheit', *BFA*, 22:1, p.80.

[31.] Karl Otto Maue comes to the conclusion that official interpretations of German cultural history in the GDR, rather than being interested in overcoming this particular legacy, had contributed significantly to ensuring the survival of these very characteristics. GDR efforts to re-establish links to German humanism and Goethe's classicism had been far less significant than had been generally claimed: 'Statt zuwenig Sozialismus und zuviel Humanismus, wie der DDR-Führung jener Jahre in der Sekundärliteratur häufig vorgeworfen wird [...], scheint die festgestellte Ideologisierung auch der Faust-Dichtung ein Beispiel dafür zu sein, daß von der DDR-Führung gar nicht so sehr an die Ideale des Humanismus angeknüpft wurde, sondern vielmehr an solche, die vor der Zeit des Humanismus entstanden und mehr mit dem Namen Martin Luthers in Verbindung zu bringen sind als mit dem Goethes: Gemeint sind Strebsamkeit, Unterordnung, Obrigkeitsgläubigkeit, Duckmäusertum und Anpassungswille', in Karl Otto Maue, *Hanns Eisler's 'Johann Faustus' und das Problem des Erbes: Interpretation des Libretto und seine zeitgenössische Diskussion in der DDR 1952/53* (Göppingen, 1981), p.89.

[32..] Christa Wolf, 'Ein Deutscher auf Widerruf', in *Neue Deutsche Literatur* 2 (1991).

ASTRID HERHOFFER

Brecht: an Aesthetics of Conviction?
(Translated by Martyn Saville)

> Ich will zum Beispiel leben mit wenig Politik. Das heißt, ich will kein politisches Subjekt sein. Aber das soll nicht heißen, daß ich ein Objekt von Politik sein will. Da also die Wahl nur lautet: Objekt von Politik zu sein oder Subjekt, muß ich wohl Politik machen.[1]

Any author who makes this idea the fundamental principle of their public appearances and writings must naturally assume that their life history will be questioned by later generations according to the consequences of this premiss. Acting in the public eye, they are responsible for the consequences of their behaviour. The question of the political responsibility of the author is therefore a quite legitimate one, so long as possible answers are not sought in his or her literary works alone. And yet that is precisely what has happened since the discussion about political responsibility was rekindled at the beginning of the Nineties by the debate over Christa Wolf's text *Was bleibt*. The accusation was made against the author that her works contained propaganda rather than 'pure' art and had therefore served to support the preservation of the East German state. In the course of this discussion the term *Gesinnungsästhetik* (aesthetics of conviction) was coined, stemming from Max Weber's term *Gesinnungsethik*,[2] and has now entered the language of literary criticism. *Gesinnungsästhetik* denotes artistic production which feels itself obliged to a moral authority and therefore does not rely solely on the artistic value - tied exclusively to aesthetic criteria - of the work of art itself.[3] Art which leaves no doubt as to the moral and political intentions of its creator has since then been subsumed under this pejorative label by a particular train of thought in German literary criticism.[4]

And this intellectual approach itself has a tradition. H.D.Zimmermann, in his book *Der Wahnsinn des Jahrhunderts. Die Verantwortung der Schriftsteller in der Politik*, cites György Konrad: 'Jeglicher Wahnsinn des Jahrhunderts kam aus Büchern. Die Akteure des Geistes sind tatsächlich verantwortlich für das, was ihre Zeitgenossen anstellen'.[5] Following this premiss, Zimmermann's essay on the politicisation of Bert Brecht's aesthetics comes rather quickly to the conclusion that Brecht in his didactic plays had voiced the principle of Stalinism, a principle which became fully noticeable in the bloody 'purges', and had thereby to a certain extent made it socially acceptable (Z, 73). Leaving aside the characteristic causality which Zimmermann here ascribes to art, it is be rather difficult, if not quite impossible, to substantiate this thesis with historical facts or even with the help of Brecht's own texts, as we shall see below. Zimmermann here illustrates a variant of literary criticism based on *Gesinnungsästhetik*, in which the literary text is placed in immediate relation to a given reality as if it were a question not of art, but rather solely of mirrored reality. Even the objection that the author intended this direct relationship between text and (political) reality is entirely irrelevant to what actually happens in the act of reception, for relationship between the author's intentions and the actual effect on the reader/audience is ultimately fractured in various ways; factors such as the personal experiences of the reader and the concrete economic situation of the time of reception play a decisive role here.

The second variant of this type of criticism measures the conduct of authors against the moral claims of their literary characters. Zimmermann also makes use of this method in his Brecht essay, thereby building a bridge to the discussion of the Nineties when he presents the following argument:

> Brechts persönliches Verhalten gegenüber der stalinistischen Sowjetunion und gegenüber der stalinistischen DDR unter dem unsäglichen Ulbricht war auf verhängnisvolle Weise vorbildlich für die Schriftsteller der DDR: nämlich sein Opportunismus, den er so drastisch in der Figur seines Galilei darstellte. Um des lieben Friedens willen, damit man gutes Essen hat und guten Wein, eine Datscha und eine Westreise, hält man das Maul. Aber insgeheim oder zwischen den Zeilen riskiert man eine große Lippe und hält sich für einen großen Mann oder eine große Frau. Mutig zu sein braucht man nicht, denn traurig ist doch das Land, das Helden nötig hat, wie es im >Galilei< heißt. (Z, 80)

With this peculiar mixture of moral consideration and literary criticism, Zimmermann joins the attacks of Nineties' West German literary criticism as expressed by its leading representatives, Ulrich Greiner (*Die Zeit*) and Frank Schirrmacher (*Frankfurter Allgemeine Zeitung*) in connection with the dispute over Christa Wolf. The idea that the morality of a text must be vouched for by the morality of its author leads to the assumption that literary heroes may embody no higher moral worth than their author has attained in his own life, and that literature be provided with a 'Sauberkeits- und Ehrlichkeitspostulat'[6]. In Zimmermann's case, this reads as: 'Brechts Charakter war seinem Talent nicht gewachsen.' (Z, 78)

Yet only a mixture of the two variants detailed above permits us to accuse Brecht's works of justifying repressive state systems, and claim that his personal behaviour vis-à-vis the Soviet Union and the GDR served as an appalling example to East German authors, that he politicised his aesthetics and made art the slave of ideology, thereby cancelling out the achievements of bourgeois aesthetics (Z, 79-80). Zimmermann insinuates, knowing quite well that art can indeed be committed, that Brecht had subjugated his art to a party or regime; he believes to have found proof of this in his interpretation of Brecht's *Lehrstücke*. The following discussion attempts to liberate Brecht's didactic plays from the suspicion of *Gesinnungsästhetik*, essentially using *Die Maßnahme* as an example. For if one further analyses this concept, Brecht appears as its founding father in modern writing, and his work must be liberated from ideology if it is to be saved for future generations (Z, 80). In connection with the apparently incompatible entities of ideology and art, the question of the responsibility of the artist will always be posed, but in the following discussion this question will be extended to cover the responsibility of the recipient when appropriating Brecht's works.

Brecht's plays did not come under suspicion of embodying *Gesinnungsästhetik* when the two German states, at different points in time and with different intentions, tried in vain to monopolise Brecht for themselves, but rather in 1947, when he was forced to give a full explanation of the political content of his plays to the investigating committee of the United States. The intention here was to use *Die Maßnahme* to condemn Brecht for his political convictions, both as *zoon politikon* and as author. The starting point was an approach to interpretation, again to be found in Zimmermann's analysis, which saw the play as praising the Communist Party and blind obedience, as well as the subjugation and extermination of the individual.[7] Were this the case, we would indeed be dealing with an extreme form of sycophancy and tendentious writing, with a literature reduced to the level of propaganda, 'deren willfährige Gestalt alles Engagement des Subjekts verhöhnt'.[8] According to Adorno, commitment only moves into the dangerous vicinity of tendentiousness when it loses its ambiguity, the very element which makes that same work of art open to a variety of interpretations:

> Engagierte Kunst im prägnanten Sinn will nicht Maßnahmen, gesetzgeberische Akte, praktische Veranstaltungen herbeiführen, wie ältere Tendenzstücke gegen die Syphilis, das Duell, den Abtreibungsparagraphen oder die Zwangserziehungsheime, sondern auf eine Haltung hinarbeiten [...]. Was aber das Engagement künstlerisch vorm tendenziösen Spruchband voraushat, macht den Inhalt mehrdeutig, für den der Dichter sich engagiert.(A, 113)

This reflection of Adorno's, in which tendentiousness and commitment are clearly differentiated from one another, will be applied below to a selection of

Brecht's *Lehrstücke*, for it presents a terminology which does not condemn from the outset literature which has political aims.

Bert Brecht commits himself in his work to the cause of the humiliated and the offended, and it is in this political commitment that lies the strength of his literary work. Attempts to 'liberate' his works from their political intention - or from ideology as Zimmermann calls it - are doomed to failure, as Brecht's texts would then be distorted out of all recognition. The fact that even his fiercest critics feel obliged to speak of the salvation of Brecht's work, cannot simply be traced back to the linguistic sensitivity and dramaturgical skill of the author; it is ultimately his pugnacious portrayal of social relations and those acting within them, which makes Brecht and his works so attractive and at the same time so repulsive. It was his conception of political agency - and according to Brecht remaining passive and apathetic is also a form of political action - which attracted more criticism than praise from both sides. It was clear to Brecht that with his political theatre he was contravening a cliché which still today - or even once again - dominates German cultural life: the demand for art's autonomy.[9] Traditional theatre, he explains in the *Kleines Organon*, is emptied of social content. With this didactic impetus of his theatre, Brecht disregards the principle of *l'art-pour-l'art*, and the *Lehrstück* takes up a special position. Adorno sees in it the substance of Brecht's authorial artistry, which he criticises in three fundamental aspects: the technique of reduction unique to Brecht's *Lehrstücke* is said to misrepresent that very objective, the distillation of which is the ultimate aim of the *Lehrstück* (121); political untruth defiles the aesthetic shape (122); and that which is politically bad of necessity also becomes artistically bad (123).[10] It is the last two critical points which place the *Lehrstück* close to *Tendenzliteratur* and must therefore be analysed more closely.

For the *Lehrstück*, described by Brecht himself shortly before his death as the theatre of the future, Brecht developed a theory which stemmed from the premiss that man learns in daily life by conscious or unconscious imitation and by testing modes of behaviour. In the *Lehrstück* it is thus not the audience, but primarily the actor who takes part in the learning process:

> Das Lehrstück lehrt dadurch, daß es gespielt, nicht dadurch, daß es gesehen wird. Prinzipiell ist für das Lehrstück kein Zuschauer nötig, jedoch kann er natürlich verwendet werden. Es liegt dem Lehrstück die Erwartung zugrunde, daß der Spielende durch die Durchführung bestimmter Handlungsweisen, Einnahme bestimmter Haltungen, Wiedergabe bestimmter Reden gesellschaftlich beeinflußt werden kann. Die Nachahmung hochqualifizierter Muster spielt dabei eine große Rolle, ebenso die Kritik, die an solchen Mustern durch ein überlegtes Andersspielen ausgeübt wird. [...]
> Die Form der Lehrstücke ist streng, jedoch nur, damit Teile eigener Erfindung und aktueller Art desto leichter eingefügt werden können.[11]

The experiences of the actors are to embody fixed modes of action, whereby predetermined patterns of behaviour are subjected to the individual criticism of the actors, and the traditional roles of the audience and the actor melt into one another. It is therefore not a case of establishing absolute maxims of behaviour or formulae for political action, but of enabling the individual, on the basis of his experiences and the awareness acquired through them, to make decisions. In Brecht's case these decisions concern revolutionary practice. The closeness to revolutionary practice and Brecht's own view of this attracted criticism from almost all political camps. Thus it is argued by some, as mentioned earlier, that Brecht, through *Die Maßnahme*, had made the Stalinist Terror with its show-trials socially acceptable[12]. If we take seriously Adorno's contention that that which is politically bad also becomes *nolens volens* artistically bad, then the play will be dismissed *a priori* as artistically worthless *Tendenzliteratur*. Marxist criticism at the time of the work's appearance, on the other hand, essentially accused Brecht of being totally ignorant of revolutionary practice and of lacking revolutionary experience.[13] And the post-war period made it no easier for the play: Brecht research devoted itself primarily to the great dramas of the time of exile; Brecht's theorems on the *Lehrstück* continued to be ignored, and against the backdrop of the Cold War numerous misinterpretations of *Die Maßnahme* presented themselves, which led to Brecht himself distancing himself from the play so as to prevent 'die bürgerliche Annektion des Stücks für den Kanon der Tragödien'.[14] Only in the Seventies, starting with Reiner Steinweg's *Lehrstück* theory, were serious attempts made by literary critics to devise an adequate theoretical framework and thereby open up new possibilities for the *Lehrstück*.[15] And yet this discourse too is characterised by the difficulties of definition which have accompanied the *Lehrstück* genre since its emergence, though the recent *Lehrstück* theory did quite clearly attempt to lay the foundations of a new practice of performance. What is interesting in this attempt is 'weniger die Verwirklichung des Brechtschen Lehrstückkonzepts in seiner >reinen< Form als seine produktive Anwendung und Modifizierung gemäß den heute vorfindlichen, veränderten Voraussetzungen und Einsichten'[16]. This radical way of dealing with the *Lehrstücke*, which is prepared to develop their semantic potential on the basis of current historical conditions and possibly even against the intentions of its author, is often felt to be problematic in the most recent Brecht research.[17]

The key point in the controversy surrounding the interpretation of *Die Maßnahme* could well be the pedagogical aim of the play. Where some see it as being to educate unquestioning fighters obedient to the party for the communist cause, more well-meaning voices explain that the aim here is to highlight the problematic nature of this unquestioning obedience to the party. The Marxist Left was for a long time not able to admit that those events in its history described in *Die Maßnahme* could happen, nor that they had indeed done so:

> In der >Maßnahme< spitzte Brecht einen solchen Fall bis zur äußersten Konsequenz zu: Wie verhalte ich mich zu einem Genossen, der aus Ungeduld gegen die Anordnung der Partei verstößt, weil er im Augenblick glaubt, einen besseren Weg zu wissen? Ist es gerechtfertigt, ihn zu töten, wenn es die Notwendigkeit verlangt?
> Die ganze Fragestellung, die Brecht hier vorbringt, ist natürlich äußerst abstrakt, äußerst konstruiert, äußerst unreal.[18]

The German term *Lehrziel* (pedagogical aim), which stems from the term *Lehrstück*, chosen by Brecht himself, is undoubtedly an unfortunately chosen and misleading one. Learning should not actually, as is often falsely assumed, come about via the ideas and opinions of the author as conveyed by the play, but rather through the actors and the experiences they bring to the play. Emphasis is therefore not laid upon a pre-fabricated and intended message, but upon the process of learning, which, in changing historical situations, necessarily produces different messages. The *Lehrstück* follows its own rules, which Brecht himself had developed and presented in his *Lehrstück* theory, in which, as explained above, the framework for such plays' conditions of impact is defined. Critics who are prepared to make these framework conditions the starting point of interpretation must necessarily come to a similar conclusion to Douglas Kellner, who, with regard to *Die Maßnahme*, sees the audience (should one even exist) simply *confronted* with fundamental questions of revolution, such as violence, discipline, party structure, justice etc., without any generally valid doctrine being developed.[19] Brecht, in his remarks on the *Lehrstück*, leaves no doubt that it is for him a matter of the discussion of and the positioning towards basic questions of revolutionary practice, and not a matter of applauding or justifying it.

This idea is completely ignored by Zimmermann, whose criticism is based on the premiss that the *Lehrstück* had been 'eher als Provokation der satten Bürger gedacht', and at the same time 'als Unterwerfungsangebot an die Kommunistische Partei, als Entreebillet eines entlaufenen Bourgeois, der das Mißtrauen der Partei doch nie ganz beseitigen konnte' (Z, 73). The unreadiness to be drawn into the premisses laid out by the author would actually make any discussion unnecessary, if this point of view were not so widespread and did not stubbornly rear its head again and again over the years. And Zimmermann himself points out in his observations on the school opera, *Der Jasager*, that Brecht rewrote the end of the play in 1930 at the request of the pupils of a Neukölln school who were to put on the play: *Der Jasager* became *Der Neinsager*. Brecht stayed true to his theory, he respected the right of the actors to share in decisions and viewed the draft of the text as a variable model, which conformed to his intention and yet which was to be filled out with the experiences of the actors. And so what actual differences come to light in the two versions, the end of the first of which was deemed nonsensical by Zimmermann, compared to the end of the second which he deemed acceptable? Both plays tell a similar story. In *Der Jasager*, a teacher sets off into the mountains with a group of students to fetch medicine which is to cure the village of an epidemic. One of the teacher's pupils joins up with them in order to bring his ailing mother the curative medicine. On the way he falls ill and endangers the whole expedition. In order to reach their goal the group must leave the pupil behind, and yet custom decrees that he must give his consent. This he does and asks the others to help him to die. Together they push him into the chasm.

In *Der Neinsager* a pupil once again joins an expedition in order to bring his mother the urgently needed medicine. He is not up to the strains of the journey and falls ill. Custom demands that he be thrown from the cliff, but also demands the ritual consent of the victim. The pupil refuses and a new custom is established. The expedition makes its way home without having achieved anything and takes the boy with it. Whereas the individual in *Der Jasager* bows to custom and the collective will and dies, his counterpart in *Der Neinsager* refuses to comply and it thus able to alter established customs: he is portrayed as being wiser than the collective and the collective is depicted as being teachable. Whichever way the conflict is solved: the pattern and questions lying at the heart of both plays (the relationship between individual and community) are the same.

In their discussion of *Der Jasager*, the children of the Neukölln school came to exactly that conclusion which finds its way into the altered version, in *Der Neinsager*, namely rejecting the boy's death as senseless. If such an effect on actors and even on the author himself is possible, then the argument that the play teaches blind obedience, as used by Zimmermann, is taken *ad absurdum*. And what is more, it is in no way clear whether the boy in *Der Jasager* accepts his fate quite so voluntarily; his request to be thrown from the rockface also allows another interpretation. It can be interpreted as a demand to reconsider the custom:

Knabe:	Ich will etwas sagen: Ich bitte euch, mich nicht hier liegenzulassen, sondern mich ins Tal hinabzuwerfen, denn ich fürchte mich, allein zu sterben.
Studenten:	Das können wir nicht.
Knabe:	Halt! Ich verlange es.
Lehrer:	Ihr habt beschlossen, weiterzugehen und ihn dazulassen. Es ist leicht, sein Schicksal zu bestimmen

Aber schwer, es zu vollstrecken.
Seid ihr bereit, ihn ins Tal hinabzuwerfen?[20]

The *Lehrstück* thus paradoxically remains without a rigid message for actor and audience alike. The conflict and possible reactions to it are structured in such a way that they can be repeatedly scrutinised. It is Brecht's stated aim to enable the actors to read his texts critically and to change them. To make such a course of action possible, the text itself must consist of apparently formal and exchangeable clichés which can be copied and criticised by the actors. According to this, it is not the problematic nature of the contents which primarily distinguish the *Lehrstück*, but its structural peculiarities which promote the act of learning.

In this light, Lehmann and Lethen's thesis, which states that the whole point of the *Lehrstück* consists precisely in the fact that its message is put at risk by confronting theory and message with the incorrigibly spontaneous refusal of life, appears to be the only one to support the attempt to read and perform the *Lehrstück* in a new way.[21] They come to this conclusion by means of their structural analysis of the *Lehrstück*, with the help of which they are able convincingly to give reasons for its impact. They take as their starting point two related levels of the *Lehrstück*, whereby the first level confronts two opposing positions: a 'right' one and a 'wrong' one. Whereas the conflict on level 1 proves to be thoroughly solvable, the conflict which is developed on level 2 remains insolvable. On level 2 are to be found spontaneous action, immediacy and sensory-moral impulses, and rationality, discipline and inexorable logic on level 1 (L, 307). The interaction between the two levels makes it possible - even independently of Brecht's intentions - to view the *Lehrstück* as a variable onto which different political usages can be projected. Yet because level 2 exists and influences level 1 (or colours level 1, as Lehmann and Lethen put it), neither pre-fabricated solutions nor singular truths are offered in Brecht's *Lehrstücke*. This is also the basic principle of its general functioning and literary worth, which goes beyond cheap *Tendenzliteratur* and does not forcedly present disaster as salvation (A, 124). The rational first level, moreover, ensures that the interpretation of *Die Maßnahme* is not simply reduced to 'die große Tragödie des moralischen Dilemmas des sowjetischen Kommunismus'.[22] Using the example of *Die Maßnahme*, it is possible to clearly follow how the concrete question, bound to the historical subject matter and the historical situation, expands into universally applicable, topical problems, which are to be answered anew time and again:

Die Frage, >Aufstand jetzt oder nicht?< ist ganz vergänglich, in jeder historischen Situation neu zu entscheiden; die Ebene >Warten, bis man stark genug ist?< schon allgemeiner, öfter verwertbar; die Ebene >Unterordnung oder Beharren auf dem eigenen Standpunkt?< schon sehr allgemein, die Ebene >Einsicht der Vielen geht über die Einsicht des Einzelnen< eine immer neu zu bewahrheitende Frage. Die Ebene >Mein Leben - Prozeß der Geschichte< ist in überschaubaren Zeiträumen permanent aktuell. (L, 312)

In *Die Maßnahme* Brecht takes up the themes developed in *Der Jasager*.[23] If it was his intention to propagate party discipline and loyalty with this play, he was not successful; his play is too ambivalent, too complex to merely be propaganda material. And besides, modern literary scholarship reformulated long ago the question of what the writer wanted to say in his work into the question of what the work itself says to the reader in its hermeneutic complexity. The answer to this question can thus differ from recipient to recipient. Should one want to develop Brecht's works productively, it is absolutely necessary to go beyond the political intentions of the author, if indeed these can be clearly identified at all.

Viewed superficially, his plays can be summarised as a critique of capitalism and praise of communism, and yet, upon closer inspection, it becomes clear - and this is the really interesting aspect for the actor (reader/spectator) - that the conflicts in his plays are based on general human and eschatological questions, which, in the context of a different historical situation and the various prior experiences of the actors, can be answered in a variety of different ways. As regards the *Lehrstück*, three such thematic areas stand out, the complexity of their treatment transcending any hint of an aesthetics of conviction: the tension between rebellion and consent (discipline), the tension between ends and means, and the humanitarian question of sacrifice and its justification. The latter will be dealt with in more detail because it is precisely this problematic which clarifies Brecht's approach to *Die Maßnahme*.

Marxism uses a paradigm which Brecht would repeatedly deal with on both an artistic and personal-private level: the paradigm of the historically justified sacrifice, which arises from a theory which sublates the rights of the individual in favour of the common good: you can't make an omelette without breaking eggs. In this context Storch argues that Brecht was concerned to rethink Christ's sacrificial death and to redefine it for our age.[24] He states that Brecht, in order to reach the era of 'Liebe und Erleuchtung', had to recast Christ's sacrificial death, writing *Die Maßnahme* when Majakowski committed suicide. (S, 648). Storch develops a line of argument in his analysis of Brecht's relationship to the Christ-figure which appears fruitful in the context of our theme: 'Ich denke, diese Linie >Die Bibel<, >Die Maßnahme<, >Die Antigone des Sophokles< eröffnet Brechts Werk.' (S, 646) This lineage is not only convincing because the question of the necessity of sacrifice or sacrificial death is raised, but it also credibly illustrates the fact that Brecht dealt intensively with this problem: *Die Bibel*[25] is probably Brecht's first completed play. He wrote it at the age of 15 as a pupil of the *Realgymnasium* in Augsburg, and published it in 1914. Brecht wrote *Die Maßnahme*[26] in 1930 at the age of 32, and *Die Antigone des Sophokles*[27] is one of Brecht's later works, written in 1948.

Die Bibel is a one-act play: a besieged protestant town in the Netherlands is about to be captured and the enemy commander informs the mayor that he will spare the town on the condition that the inhabitants convert to catholicism and that a virgin spends the night with him. The mayor's daughter must make the decision. Here are to be found the first signs of the conflicts which are to repeatedly play a role in Brecht's later works: the question 'To sacrifice or not to sacrifice', and on the other hand the question of advice and help in making this decision. In this play, the advice of the Bible is brought in to help. The chain of events is portrayed from a distance and without bias, in a way which is later to be found in the *Lehrstücke*, though in the later works the place of the Bible is taken by custom (*Jasager*) or party discipline (*Maßnahme*). The grandfather praises the Bible: 'Dieses Buch ist so schön. Weil es stark ist. Die Menschen sollten es mehr lesen.'(*BFA*, 1, 10), and yet the girl recognises the danger which comes from it: 'Deine Bibel ist kalt. Sie redet von Menschen, die stärker waren als wir.' (*BFA*, 1, 10) It is cold, like the party discipline of the agitator in *Die Maßnahme* which forbids him from acting humanely; cold like the tyrant Kreon's command (*Die Antigone des Sophokles*) that forbids Antigone from burying her slaughtered brother.

The girl does not sacrifice herself in the way the enemy commander had wished, and yet, with her grandfather, who refuses to leave the house, she will perish in the flames. She consciously decides against the sacrifice expected of her, through which she could have saved the town, and for the biblical text with which she eventually declares herself in agreement. The idea - maybe also the desire - of being permitted to sacrifice oneself for the people is placed by the adolescent Brecht in the mouth of the brother: 'Ist es nicht schön, für Tausende zu leiden?'(*BFA*, 1, 12). As the brother bombards the girl more and more and wants to force her to give her consent, the father intervenes: 'Junge! Laß ab von ihr! Ich befehle es! Es ist genug.'(*BFA*, 1, 13). What happens, happens here too on the basis of the agreement of the individual, a dimension which is later to play a significant role in the *Lehrstück*. In this context, this movingly naive and adolescent play of Brecht's appears to be very important, as it already contains the seeds of some of Brecht's major themes and thus to a certain extent assumes a key role in the analysis of his further literary development.

At the end of the play the reader/spectator is left alone to ponder the question which decision would have been the right one. He is also left with doubts as to the usefulness of the consulted teachings - in this case the teachings of the Bible - in the decisions which the individual must get right when faced with his own possible demise and that of his fellow humans. The question as to whether there is a sacrifice which can be called historically justified was to remain one of the central questions of Brecht's works throughout his life.

Whereas in this one act play the problem of sacrifice is portrayed in a single-layered and linear manner, in *Die Antigone des Sophokles* it gains multiple dimensions. This play, an adaptation based on the Hölderlin translation, is preceded in Brecht's version by a prologue: Berlin, April 1945. Two sisters find at their door the body of their deserter brother, hanged by the SS. As cries for help had reached them in their room, one of the two had wanted to go and look, but the other had held her back, so they would not endanger themselves: 'Bleib sitzen, du; wer sehn will, wird gesehn.' (*BFA*, 8, 196)   Good intentions, however, played no part in their decision, the dark premonition of something terrible is paired with the knowledge of their own inappropriate behaviour. As the first sister leaves the house with the words: 'Laß mich, bin schon nicht gegangen / wie sie ihn uns aufgehangen' (*BFA*, 8, 198), an SS-officer associates her with the hanged deserter, and she picks out the conflict as a central theme: 'Da sah ich meine Schwester an. / Sollt sie in eigner Todespein / Jetzt gehn, den Bruder zu befrein?' (*BFA*, 8, 199)   Thus the question of sacrifice remains unanswered in the prologue.

From the very beginning, Antigone, on the other hand, never wavers from her intention, in direct contravention of Kreon's decree, of wanting to bury her brother Polyneikes, who had deserted during the war and had therefore been murdered at the hand of the tyrant. Polyneikes had learnt how his elder brother, Eteokles, had been trampled to death by the hooves of the horses in battle and had ridden out of the battle early in tears, on the one hand not ready to offer himself as a sacrifice to Kreon's war of conquest, on the other hand knowing, however, that this flight from the enemy would be punishable by death. A hero's death, or lost honour and an ignominious end are the possibilities open to Polyneikes, but these are naturally not real alternatives as life (and survival) is not an option in either case. He decides - like the soldier in the prologue - against sacrifice in the service of the tyrant.

Antigone, who has decided to bury her brother, seeks support from her sister Ismene who, however, refuses, since: 'Vergebliches nämlich / Zu tun ist unweis.' (*BFA*, 8, 202) Antigone shows no understanding for the opinions of her sister, who is not ready to make the sacrifice demanded of her and sacrifices herself alone. Kreon gives her one last chance to escape sacrificial death: 'So frag ich dich: da du's gemacht hast heimlich / Und es ist jetzt offen worden, würdst du sagen / Und schwere Straf so meiden, daß dir's leid tut?'. (*BFA*, 8, 11-12) Antigone does not take up the offer. She also rejects Ismene's offer to die with her; her sister is no longer worthy of such a sacrificial death. Self-sacrifice means self-surrender, but also guarantees a certain gratification, intensifying into a feeling of happiness which depends upon being *allowed* to sacrifice oneself. Just as the brother in *Die Bibel* feels sacrifice for others to be beautiful ('Ist es nicht schön, für Tausende zu leiden?'), the greatness of the deed plays a role for Antigone as well: 'Folge dem Brauch und begrabe den Bruder. / Sterb ich daran, was ist's? Gestillt werd ich liegen / Mit den Stillen. Hinter mich hab ich / Heiligs gebracht [...].' (*BFA*, 8, 202) As with the *Lehrstücke*, here too the basic premiss is consent to the sacrificial deed, which itself stems from the need to serve that which is good and human, indeed to serve humanity per se through the extinguishing of one's own being. The heroic dimension of sacrifice never lost its significance for Brecht, and yet from the Thirties onwards he seems to have been clear that the beautiful idea and the humanist ideal are called into question as soon as one's view switches from abstract human redemption to concrete individual fate.[28]

Against this background of evolved self-knowledge, *Die Maßnahme*, in which sacrifice for the redemption of humanity is likewise picked out as a central theme, can be interpreted as questioning the meaning of this sacrifice. If this approach is not taken, then given the conditions of reception created by the Thirties this *Lehrstück* can in fact only be seen as 'Opfer von Entwicklungen, die es weder meinte, noch zu verantworten hat' (K, 197). But does this mean, that because the chorus declares its consent to the sacrifice of the fourth comrade - who gives his consent to the extinguishing of his own existence - that the reader/spectator must also consent to it? All of the reactions to the play known to us indicate that the consent of the chorus in no way gives rise to the consent of the actors or the spectators. On the contrary: precisely because this consent does not present itself, *Die Maßnahme* counts, from our point of view, as one of those plays by Brecht which even today have lost none of their topicality, and can be categorized neither as *Tendenzliteratur* nor as a product of an aesthetics of conviction: it lacks the unequivocal and moralising tone. Brecht performs a stroke of genius with the question of consent in *Die Maßnahme*: a cruel awakening awaits any actor or spectator tries to empathise with the young comrade or even to identify with him, as Eric Bentley indicates in his Brecht commentaries:

> [...] it was quite cunning of Brecht to permit us an identification with the Young Comrade, then, suddenly, to shock us out of that identification. At this point, indeed, we withdraw angrily from our entanglement in history with the word No! On our lips. Well, such is dialectic drama.[29]

The consent of the young comrade is the result of a political argument, which convinces him that all trace of him must be erased forever; and yet the destruction of his individual experiences and lifetime shows, despite all historical necessity, a certain contradictoriness which remains unresolved: 'Hinter der klaren >dialektischen< Lösung des Problems wird im Lehrstück der Schrecken nicht wegdisputiert. Es bleibt ein *Rest*. Hüllt man ihn in Schweigen, versteht man die Lehrstücke nicht.' (L, 302) And with this residue we can defend Brecht against Adorno's attack, which views Brecht's tone as being poisoned by the untruth of his politics:

> Weil, wofür er wirbt, nicht, wie er lange wohl glaubte, bloß ein unvollkommener Sozialismus ist, sondern eine Gewaltherrschaft, in der die blinde Irrationalität der gesellschaftlichen Kräfte wiederkehrt, der Brecht als Lobredner von Einverständnis an sich beisprang, muß die lyrische Stimme Kreide schlucken, damit sie dich besser fressen kann, und sie knirscht. (A, 124)

Yet this residue of terror constitutes the play's unacceptable ambivalence. The sacrifice and murder motifs in *Die Maßnahme* are unacceptable in the context of Enlightenment:

> Weil sich niemand mit der Erschießung des jungen Genossen abfinden kann, werden Sänger/Spieler und Zuhörer zu Widerspruch und Auseinandersetzung gezwungen, sie setzt den Reflexionsprozeß in Gang, der Zweck der Lehrstückübung war. Die bis heute andauernden Debatten um *Die Maßnahme* belegen, daß das provokante Motiv diese Funktion auch tatsächlich erfüllt hat. (K, 197)

And yet, in the same breath, Krabiel points to the fact that it was primarily the complicated conditions of reception in the Thirties that led to the misunderstanding that the play was concerned to legitimize the physical removal of opposition within the party. This reading, however, places the play in immediate relation to actual historical events and no longer allows the metaphorical character of the murder-motif; moreover, this method of dealing with art and literature is simply unacceptable, particularly since the example of

Die Maßnahme shows that the play can work in a way that resists the unequivocal and the tendentious.

Such a reading presupposes a willingness not to encounter Brecht's texts in the narrow framework of those ideologically bound aims which Brecht had imposed on his art from the outside. This does not mean freeing the texts from ideology, as demanded by Zimmermann, but rather differentiating clearly between ideological intention and artistic statements. Under these conditions the reader does not encounter the text via the framework of the prefabricated ideological categories of modern literary criticism, but rather takes up the challenge of an approach to literature which takes seriously the subjective experiences and the objective knowledge of the recipient. This, in turn, thereby makes possible the development of new semantic potential and opens the way towards a modern approach to Brecht's works.

When R. Mueller comes to the conclusion that the challenge of the *Lehrstück* is as topical today as it was at the time of its writing,[30] she refers essentially to the theatrical *form* developed by Brecht, which allows a rethink and a new positioning of the *Lehrstück*'s contents, which were never completely fixed. And such a rethink of contents must never be forgotten in any approach to the *Lehrstücke*, because, as Krabiel points out, they have often been subordinated to a concrete purpose and are thereby more subject to an ageing process than other texts (K, 318). Clearly it remains open to question whether the *Lehrstück*, which presupposes the existence of consensual solutions to basic social problems (K, 319), is still appropriate in our modern world without certainties. This question generally underlies dichotomy of autonomous and politically intended art. Politically intended art will always search for suggestions for solutions. However, when the recipient is partly responsible for the development of these solutions - as suggested in the *Lehrstück* model - the author's convictions become irrelevant to the act of reception and are of merely literary-historical interest.

---

1. Bertolt Brecht, 'Über den Staat', *BFA*, 22:1, p.304.

2. In his essay '"Es geht nicht um Literatur": Some Observations on the 1990 "Literaturstreit" and its Recent Anti-intellectual Implications', Hans Hahn convincingly analyses the relationship between *Gesinnungsästhetik* and *Gesinnungsethik* with reference to the Enlightenment and German idealism. (*German Life and Letters*, 50:1 (January 1997), 64-81).

3. Ulrich Greiner, 'Die deutsche Gesinnungsästhetik. Noch einmal: Christa Wolf und der deutsche Literaturstreit. Eine Zwischenbilanz', in *Die Zeit*, 2. November 1990.

4.   Here it was not the literary text *Was bleibt?* that was evaluated on aesthetic criteria, but instead its author was judged as a person and moral instance. See: *Der Literaturstreit im vereinten Deutschland. 'Es geht nicht um Christa Wolf'*, Hg. Thomas Anz (Munich, Spangenberg, 1991); *Der deutsch-deutsche Literaturstreit oder 'Freunde es spricht sich schlecht mit gebundener Zunge'*, Hg. Karl Deitritz und Hannes Krauss (Hamburg/Zürich, Luchterhand, 1991).

5.   Epigraph to Hans Dieter Zimmermann, *Der Wahnsinn des Jahrhunderts. Die Verantwortung der Schriftsteller in der Politik*   (Stuttgart/Berlin/Cologne, Kohlhammer, 1992).

6.   Jörg Magenau, 'Strukturelle Befangenheiten.   Die Intellektuellen-Debatte', in *Verrat an der Kunst? Rückblicke auf die DDR-Literatur*, Hg. Karl Deiritz and Hannes Krauss (Berlin, Aufbau, 1993), p.59.

7.   Brecht's appearance before the investigating committee for un-American activities is documented in *Brecht. A Collection of Critical Essays*, ed. Peter Demetz (Prentice Hall, 1962), pp.30-42. In comparison to this, see Zimmermann, pp.76-79.

8.   Theodor W. Adorno, *Noten zur Literatur III* (Frankfurt, Suhrkamp, 1973), p.110. (Cited as A)

9.   See 'Bertolt Brecht and Politics', in *Bertolt Brecht. Political Theory and Literary Practice*, ed. Betty Nancy Weber and Hubert Heinen (Athens, University of Georgia Press, 1980), p.15.

10.   Furthermore, Adorno assumes that art, by making past injustice a central theme - as is generally the case with committed art - also to a certain extent legitimises it: 'Indem noch der Völkermord in engagierter Literatur zum Kulturbesitz wird, fällt es leichter, weiter mitzuspielen in der Kultur, die den Mord gebar.' (p.127).   This therefore means that an alternative political practice can only be awakened, 'um sie sogleich wieder sinnberuhigend einzuschläfern' (Christian Enzensberger, *Literatur und Interesse* (Frankfurt, Suhrkamp, 1981), p.140).   This position ultimately leads any commitment (not just artistic commitment) *ad absurdum* and is not shared by the author of this article.

11.   Brecht, 'Zur Theorie des Lehrstücks', *BFA*, 22:1, p.351.

12.   If literature really had such an effect, 'müßte demnach der fleißigste Leser im Laufe der Zeit auch zum rollengeschicktesten, hierarchieempfindlichsten, sprachgewandtesten, sensibilitätsgeübtesten, nebenbei noch klassenkämpferischen Wundertier geworden sein - und wer will mir (oder sich) weismachen, daß damit der Normaltypus des Literaturprofessors treffend beschrieben wäre?' (Enzensberger, *Literatur und Interesse*, p.19)

13.   See *Die Linkskurve*, January 1931, and Alfred Kurella, 'Ein Versuch mit nicht ganz tauglichen Mitteln', in: *Literatur der Weltrevolution*, Moscow, No.4, 1931.   Both sources quoted in Martin Esslin, *Brecht. A Choice of Evils* (London, Heinemann, 1973), p.139.

14.   Reiner Steinweg, 'Das Lehrstück - ein Modell des sozialistischen Theaters', in *alternative* 78/79 (1971), 103.

15.   Probably most important forerunner of this development was Reiner Steinweg; see *Das Lehrstück. Brechts Theorie einer ästhetischen Erziehung* (Stuttgart, Metzler, 1971); *Brechts Modell der Lehrstücke, Zeugnisse, Diskussionen, Erfahrungen* (Frankfurt, Suhrkamp, 1976); *Auf Anregung Bertolt Brechts: Lehrstücke mit Schülern, Arbeitern, Theaterleute* (Frankfurt, Suhrkamp, 1978).

16.   Steinweg, *Auf Anregung Brechts*, p.7.

17. One of the most topical and comprehensive analyses of Brecht's *Lehrstücke* was produced by K.-D. Krabiel, whose basic proposal is to classify the *Lehrstücke* as a musical genre, and who subjects Steinweg's *Lehrstück*-theory to a comprehensive critique: 'Seine Lehrstücktheorie war nicht das Ergebnis einer geschichtlichen Rekonstruktion, sondern ein abstraktes Konstrukt jenseits geschichtlicher Prozesse und Wirkungszusammenhänge.' See Klaus-Dieter Krabiel, *Brechts Lehrstücke. Entstehung und Entwicklung eines Spieltyps* (Stuttgart, Metzler, 1993), p.3 (cited as K).

18. Werner Mittenzwei, *Brecht. Von der <Maßnahme< zu >Leben des Galilei<* (Berlin, Aufbau, 1965), pp.57-58.

19. Douglas Kellner, 'Brecht's Marxist Aesthetics: The Korsch Connection', in: *Bertolt Brecht. Political Theory and Literary Practice*, p.35.

20. Brecht, *Der Jasager*, BFA, 3, p.64.

21. Hans-Thies Lehmann and Helmut Lethen, 'Ein Vorschlag zur Güte. Zur doppelten Polarität des Lehrstücks', in: *Auf Anregung Bertolt Brechts*, p.310.

22. Enzensberger, *Literatur und Interesse*, p.140

23. Krabiel (p.163) points to the fact that the theme of the consent of the individual to the demands of the community to the point of self-sacrifice ought to be transported into a contemporary and politically concrete context and that the first hand-written draft of the play, known to us today as *Die Maßnahme*, was entitled: *der jasager (konkretisierung)*.

24. Wolfgang Storch, 'Brief über Brecht', *Sinn und Form* (1994), 645.

25. Brecht, *Die Bibel*, BFA, 1, pp.9-15.

26. Brecht, *Die Maßnahme* [Fassung 1931], BFA, 3, pp.100-125.

27. Brecht, *Die Antigone des Sophokles*, BFA, 8, pp.192-242.

28. Numerous examples of this are to be found in the life of the author, as well as in his literary works. On being asked why he had emigrated to the West rather than to the Soviet Union, which must have been closer to him both ideologically and politically, Brecht replied that he preferred his tea with sugar, rather than unsweetened. His Galilei seems to be speaking from his own heart when he says: '[...] ich verachte Leute, deren Gehirn nicht fähig ist, ihren Magen zu füllen'.

29. Eric Bentley, *The Brecht Commentaries 1943-1983* (London, Methuen, 1981), p.279.

30. Roswitha Mueller, 'Learning for a New Society: the *Lehrstück*', in *The Cambridge Companion to Brecht*, ed. P.Thomson and G.Sacks (Cambridge, CUP, 1994), p.94.

CARL WEBER

Is there a Use-value? Brecht on the American Stage
at the Turn of the Century.

Brecht lived in the United States for less than half of his fourteen year long exile from Germany, but American culture had an impact on his writing and thinking that exceeded that of any other country, aside of Germany. He left the U.S. the day after his appearance before HUAC, the Congressional Committee investigating 'Un-american Activities'. Having been summoned as a resident alien under suspicion of subversive Communist activities in the American film industry, he convinced the committee that he was neither a dangerous Bolshevik agitator nor a Soviet spy. His testimony has been recorded, today it sounds like an exquisitely devised comic performance from one of his plays. Brecht, the performer, was indeed recommended for his cooperative attitude by the committee's chairman. The next day, 31 October 1947, Brecht took a plane for Paris. It was not because of the hearing, as has been speculated by some scholars. He had been planning his return to Germany since the collapse of Hitler's Reich, in May of 1945. After four years in the U.S., the playwright appears to have realized that he would not achieve the success he had hoped for (and had become used to before his emigration from Germany) in the America that had engaged his imagination more consistently than any other foreign land. His efforts to establish himself as a screenwriter in Hollywood, where many of his fellow immigrants prospered, had come to naught. The three of his plays that were professionally produced, *The Private Life of the Master Race*, *The Duchess of Malfi*, and *Galileo*, received mixed reviews and were commercial flops.

Despite his profound contempt for Capitalism's mode of cultural production, it seems that Brecht still harboured some illusions about the American theatre when he arrived in California in 1941. In an essay written in 1935/36 [1] he had stated that during the twenties and early thirties only Berlin, Moscow, and New York were the 'theatre capitals' that were 'modern, i.e. introduced artistic and technical innovations.' By the time Brecht decided to return to Central Europe, however, he had lost his trust in the American theatre's potential to explore an innovative, politically progressive aesthetics that might be responsive to his work.

This disappointment must have been particularly hard for a European playwright who devoted so much of his writing to America's culture and mythology: eight completed works for the stage (among them four plays about — 'the cold Chicago'), numerous poems, and several unfinished projects for plays or novels. American culture had fascinated Brecht from his late teenage years when he discovered its literature and watched its silent films. Yet, while he was living in the country, American culture ignored this foreigner whose concept of theatre seemed incompatible with the values cherished by the indigenous entertainment industry.

After his return to Europe, Brecht never had occasion to visit America again. The times were not propitious for an American recognition of Brecht's work. The Anti-Communism that prompted Brecht's hearing before the HUAC of Washington had become increasingly virulent during the following years. By the time Brecht established his Berliner Ensemble, in 1949, the Cold War was acutely heating up, Germany had been divided in two states hostile to each other, and the writings of a professed Marxist had no chance in an American theatre whose actors, directors, and designers were smarting from the purges enforced by McCarthyism, while its commercial producers wouldn't touch anything that smacked even remotely of Communism. It may have been a traditional, proudly defended independent attitude versus political pressure that made some American universities more hospitable to Brecht's work. In 1948, *The Caucasian Chalk Circle* and *The Good Person of Szechwan* were performed at College theaters in Minnesota, in Eric Bentley's translations which were published the same year; there also had been an earlier university production of *The Private Life of the Master Race* at U.C. at Berkeley when Brecht was still living in the U.S. While Brecht had been recognized as an important writer by a number of Left-leaning intellectuals as well as German emigrants who were familiar with his work from the twenties and early thirties, the majority of American theatre artists barely had heard of him at the time he returned to Europe.

There were two events that suddenly and quite surprisingly changed the situation. In 1954, the year when Senator McCarthy's power was beginning to crumble, an Off-Broadway production of *The Threepenny Opera* opened in the American composer Marc Blitzstein's version that had somewhat tempered the text's social attack. The production became a huge success. With 2,611 performances in six years, it broke all records for the run of a musical theatre piece at the time.[2] The other event was the Berliner Ensemble's invitation to the original 'Festival Mondial du Théâtre' at Paris, in the summer of 1954. Brecht's company was competing with the Peking Opera, Laurence Olivier's and Peter Brook's *Titus Andronicus*, a widely praised American production of *Medea* with Judith Anderson, the Dublin Gate Theatre's *The Playboy of the Western World*, with Cyril Cusack and Siobhan McKenna, and many more performances by artists who were regarded as the world theatre's cream of the crop in the fifties. Brecht's own staging of *Mother Courage*, with Helene Weigel playing the lead, won the prize of the festival, and thus the Berliner Ensemble was established as one of the leading theatre companies in Western civilization. Quite a number of American artists and critics had seen the company perform at Paris; others came to see it the following year when it returned with Brecht's staging of *The Caucasian Chalk Circle*, during the Ensemble's first London season, in 1956, or at the Paris festival of 1960 when it won the first prize of the 'Théâtre des Nations' with *Galileo* and *The Mother*. During subsequent years, many Western theatre people ventured into what was then East Berlin to observe Brecht's work and later that of the young directors he had groomed at the Berliner Ensemble. Among the visitors were Herbert Blau (who was to direct the American premiere of *Mother Courage* in 1957 at the San Francisco Actors Workshop), Alan Schneider (soon one of Brecht's advocates and a pioneering director in the American resident theatre movement), Lee Strasberg (of The Group Theatre and The Actors Studio), Peter Brook, Lawrence Olivier, John Gielgud and Kenneth Tynan who became the champion of Brecht's theatre in the English-speaking world. By the time Brecht died, in 1956, he was acknowledged as the playwright/director who had no peer in his time.

The American theatre took notice – of the commercial success of *The Threepenny Opera* as well as the award-winning appearances of Brecht's company in Paris – and by the mid-sixties, Brecht was firmly established as a leading contemporary playwright and theatre theoretician, be it in academe, the resident nonprofit theatre movement, Off-Broadway, or even on Broadway. Broadway's flirt with Brecht didn't last long, how ever. After both *Mother Courage* (1963) and *Arturo Ui* (1964) were commercial flops – though *Arturo Ui* with Christopher Plummer had won critical acclaim – the commercial Broadway theatre abstained from Brecht with the exception of John Dexter's staging of *The Threepenny Opera* with the rock star Sting as Macheath, in 1989, which also failed to succeed. Brecht and a Broadway audience which abhors to be aesthetically challenged didn't mix. On the other hand, the regional nonprofit theatre movement and its rapidly growing audience embraced Brecht like no other playwright-in-translation with the exception of Molière, Chekhov and Ibsen. These four authors alone have achieved a permanent position in the American repertoire of foreign drama; only Shakespeare, maybe Shaw, and a few other English-writing playwrights, exceed them in the number of productions at nonprofit resident theaters.[3]

In the academic theatre Brecht is also one of the most frequently performed playwrights in translation, and his texts have attained an assured place in the syllabi of Drama, German, and Comparative Literature departments.[4] American scholars founded in 1970 the International Brecht Society, emulating the model of Brecht's never realized plan for a Diderot Society; it has matured into an international organization dedicated to Brecht criticism and the promotion of Brecht's theory and practice. The I.B.S. convenes periodic symposia and publishes *The Brecht Yearbook* and a bi-yearly journal *Communications*.

All is well then, it may seem, with Brecht in America. The once ignored and then for political reasons rejected playwright/poet has a firm place in the repertoire of the American theatre and the curriculum of the academy. In recent years, however, a growing number of voices have criticized Brecht's work for being outdated, 'politically incorrect,' morally corrupt, or even counterfeit. His intellectual and political positions are again being attacked, from both sides of the political spectrum, and often with a vengeance that matches the fervor of an earlier Cold War Anti-Communism.[5] At the same time his writings are attracting renewed curiosity since they have been freed of their bonding to a stalemated state Socialism . After a period of declining interest during the eighties, theatre artists are again exploring and adopting Brecht's dramatic paradigm and discovering its 'use-value' – to employ a term Brecht once adopted from Marx.[6]

On the other hand, there are respected scholars who joined his detractors. An early example was Allan Bloom and his 1987 best-seller *The Closing of the American Mind*. The remarkably long-lived popularity of the song 'Mack the Knife' (whose first widely acclaimed version had been recorded by Louis Armstrong in the mid-Fifties, following the New York success of *Threepenny Opera)* offers, as Bloom argues, conspicuous proof of American culture's embrace of 'that ambiguous Weimar atmosphere...[where] anything was possible for people who sang of the joy of the knife in cabarets.' Blithely ignorant of the song's dramaturgical function in Brecht's fable, Bloom assigns responsibility for such dubious morals to, among others, the 'two heroes of the artistic Left, Bertolt Brecht and Kurt Weill' and their American interpreters.[7] The most notorious recent effort to debunk the icon Brecht is a hefty volume whose British edition trumpeted its intention with the title *The Life and Lies of Bertolt Brecht,*[8] whereas the American publishers decided on a less sensational one, *Brecht and Company: Sex, Politics, and the Making of the Modern Drama.,*[9] (Does this reveal something about the publishing strategies that are deemed to be effective in the two markets?) John Fuegi's book was touted as the result of more than twenty years of painstaking research. He claims his labors led him to the discovery that many of Brecht's works were actually written by his female friends/lovers, and that Brecht traded sex for text while cheating his collaborators of their royalties. Given Fuegi's strongly biased agenda it is not all too surprising that the published text contains a staggering number of factual and scholarly errors, as an exhaustive analysis by leading British, American, and Danish Brecht scholars has revealed.[10] Yet, Fuegi did not lack supporters. Many of the reviews in the American press honored his book with more or less positive assessments. Some of the critics appeared just to have waited for a chance to see this Marxist writer clobbered; his enduring success in the U.S. must have been sticking in their craw for a long time.[11] Fuegi even received the 'Bernard Hewitt Award' for the outstanding scholarly book of 1995, awarded by a panel of three judges who were not exactly known for their familiarity with Brecht's work and criticism. Quite a number of Brecht scholars protested the panel's decision. Nevertheless, Fuegi's book will have its inevitable impact on the way many American intellectuals and theatre artists perceive Brecht and his work.

Fuegi tried hard to align himself with feminist scholarship in his argumentation. Since the seventies feminist scholars have submitted Brecht's portrayal of women in his plays to a thorough analysis and pointed out many instances where Brecht, conditioned as he was by his Bavarian middle class background, appears to have fashioned his female protagonists according to the conventional models of Mother/Whore. Scholars also scrutinized Brecht's relation to his women friends/lovers/collaborators, long before Fuegi published his own interpretation. If indeed Brecht's plays were written to a significant extent by his women friends – as Fuegi maintains – then it raises the question why these women became accomplices in creating female characters that were tainted, as some feminists have claimed, by Brecht's male chauvinist attitude. This is not the place, however, to discuss American feminist criticism of Brecht's work in detail – let it suffice to mention some of the issues raised and also point out recent studies that represent a quite different view of the ways 'Brecht and Company' were 'writing women.'[12]

For better or for worse, during some time to come the American discourse on Brecht may be focussed again on his morals and politics while blithely disregarding that they belong to past history and need to be evaluated in the context of their historical moment. Such an approach articulates only too well with a contemporary American trend that is fond of negating a historic trajectory. However, at a time when conservative thinking appears to be on the rise in the U.S., Brecht's work might become as timely again as it seems to be unsettling the conservative mind. Its provocative potential of content and form has been opened to new modes of interpretation after the collapse of a petrified Communism. In view of the various displacements that are shaking up the social stratification of the U.S., new readings of Brecht's texts will become viable and maybe some rather old ones, too. There has not yet been a noticeable increase in the number of Brecht productions,[13] and it remains to be seen if and when such a phenomenon is going to happen. But many theatre artists appear to sense new possibilities in Brecht's paradigm.

Some selected statements by directors who occupy prominent positions in the contemporary American theatre may illustrate the attention Brecht is attracting again. Though nearly each of them is careful to point out his reservations about some aspects of Brecht's legacy, they all concur that his plays are still significant – disagreeing only as to which aspect of his work may be of special relevance in the nineties. The experimental director Anne Bogart, for instance, argues: 'The earlier plays have more to do with the present-day New York. The chaos and the poeticism reflect the contemporary city. The later plays are too pat. People like me are more drawn to the earlier plays.' (Weber, 185) Others are attracted to the didactic plays, which may be surprising given their original political agenda, but not so if the texts will be approached in new ways that won't read them merely as Communist pedagogics. Internationally known director Peter Sellars states: 'I'm interested in the extremely didactic Brecht, the only texts that are not corrupted and maybe incorruptible.' (Weber, 186) Oscar Eustis, artistic director of Trinity Theatre at Providence, Rhode Island, explains: 'I'm most excited about the *Lehrstuecke*, and they were formerly the least interesting to me. Now we see under the text's surface something much darker: the collision of the collective and the self.' (Weber, 186) Tony Kushner, the noted playwright who is also a talented director concurs: 'I'd like to do the *Baden Play of Learning* and *Jasager/Neinsager* ... The *Lehrstuecke* are so much of this moment [...] less so *Caucasian Chalk Circle, Galileo*, or *Puntila*.' (Weber, 186) Aside from their advocacy of the *Lehrstueck*, Kushner, Sellars, and Eustis agreed that *Mother Courage* is their favorite among Brecht's plays. This feeling was shared by Richard Schechner, founder of the Performance Group, eminent performance theorist and editor of *The Drama Review*, who staged *Mother Courage* with his group in 1974, and also by Daniel Sullivan, former artistic director of the Seattle Repertory Theatre who also directed several Broadway hits – that is by two artists who have been working in profoundly different venues of the contemporary American theatre. Eustis, Kushner, and Sellars regard the text not only as Brecht's greatest but even one of the greatest plays of the century. According to Sellars, 'It is, along with *Waiting for Godot* and *Long Day's Journey into the Night*, one of the three Plays of the Century.' And Eustis calls it 'probably the greatest play ever written about people caught in history.' (Weber, 186)

In the repertory of the American regional nonprofit theaters, however, the two plays most often performed in the nineties were *The Caucasian Chalk Circle* and *Galileo*, plays that had been written or adapted by Brecht in America for America, with the viewing habits of the Broadway theatre public in mind. Whatever might be said about his probably all too optimistic assessment of that audience in the forties, he crafted two performance texts that were embraced by American audiences twenty years later and have remained enduring favorites. Tony Taccone, associate director of the Berkeley Repertory Theatre, who staged *Caucasian Chalk Circle* in 1994, when asked about the production's popular success explained: 'People are hungry for plays which speak to them intellectually, emotionally and aesthetically. Brecht's work satisfies many hungers.[14]'

In the present climate of financial duress and diminishing support for the arts by public and private founding agencies, it is remarkable that Brecht plays with their great demands in terms of personnel and production values are done at all. If one scrutinizes the plans for the 1995/97 seasons of the nonprofit theaters, the prevalence of plays with small casts, or even one character only, is conspicuous.[15] Robert Brustein, founder and artistic director of Yale Repertory Theatre as well as the American Repertory Theatre at Harvard, produced a notable number of Brecht plays in both his theaters but notes: 'Brecht plays are expensive to produce because of their cast size and production requirements.' (Weber, 187) Robert Falls, who directed an acclaimed *Galileo* at Chicago's Goodman Theatre, in 1986, explained: '*Galileo* isn't staged very often because it's a huge play in terms of costume demands and scenic demands.'[16] The more striking it is that four *Galileo* productions were announced for the 1995/97 seasons. Plays that closely comply with the audience's expectations and viewing habits are preferred in the American theatre system – as is to be expected since artistic success and economic survival both depend on box office sales.

It is no surprise, then, that critical voices denounce the lack of artistically challenging Brecht stagings in America. Most directors either follow what might be called a 'psychological-realist reading of the Berliner model' or, more frequently, try to 'modernize' Brecht at any cost in pursuit of the entertainment values audiences are supposed to be craving. Herbert Blau, the eminent critic and Brecht proponent in the fifties, observes: 'There isn't any theoretically very sophisticated work in the theatre. There are some efforts, like the Wooster Group's, which try to develop Brechtian ideas [...] but there hasn't been any real re-thinking of Brecht in the theatre that I could see.' (Weber, 190) Peter Sellars, who staged Brecht's *The Visions of Simone Machard* in 1983, complains: 'Brecht has been domesticated like a lapdog [...] Productions are at best showing the story but hardly much more [...]' (Weber, 184) And Richard Schechner, who named as 'the three classics of the Modern period: Chekhov, Brecht, and Genet,' points out: 'The political is what today's directors and actors put into the piece, not the mere text itself [...] it won't do the work, the performance has to do it [...] otherwise we arrive at lazy productions.' (Weber, 184) With good reason Robert Brustein proposes: ëWhat we need now are new versions which treat Brecht as freely and cavalierly as he used to treat his own sources.' (Weber, 185)

But what would be a feasible approach to create such new versions, and how would they function in the cultural/political landscape of America at the turn of the century? Tony Kushner speculated: 'In the process of re-imagining this refugee, in making him uneasily at home in America, we have no choice but to invent a new Brecht – or rather new Brechts – ready to apply the hard won lessons of the past to the tumultuous complexities of the present.'[17] The playwright Kushner put his tenet to the test and wrote *Angels in America* in the years following this comment. He already had tried his hand before: '[My] real, deliberate attempt to write a "Brecht play" was *A Bright Room Called Day* [...] I took a Brecht play that I have very little respect for, which is *Fear and Misery of the Third Reich*, and attempted when I started out to write *Bright Room* to do a sort of Reagan-era version of it.'[18] The result looked not at all like the Brecht text though it clearly displays the opinionated stance and sophisticated use of distancing devices that Kushner adopted from Brecht.

There have been other playwrights in the last decade who emulated a dramaturgy that might be called 'Brechtian'. For instance, Robert Schenkkan with a vast panorama covering two hundred years of history, *Kentucky Cycle*, or the African-American playwright/director George C.Wolfe who wrote and staged *The Colored Museum* and *Spunk* as well as the Broadway musical *Jelly's Last Jam*, the latter based on the life of early Jazz musician Jelly Roll Morton. All of Wolfe's work reveals aspects of a Brechtian dramaturgy, and it seems to be no accident that he also staged a noted *Caucasian Chalk Circle* at the New York Public Theatre whose Artistic Director he is and, on Broadway, Kushner's *Angels in America*. The African-American poet Rita Dove's play *The Darker Face of the Earth* follows a narrative pattern not unlike some of Brecht's, as it can also be seen in works by the Chinese-American playwright David H. Hwang, such as *M.Butterfly* and *Golden Child*. The Mexican-American playwright Cherie Moraga fashioned her plays about Chicano farm workers in California, *Heroes and Saints* and *Watsonville*, in the mold of epic theatre. 'I always keep reading Brecht again,' she said, 'his boldness, the willingness to take risks, always impressed me and, of course, his political commitment.'[19] Kushner's view that Brecht's 'hard won lessons' are of use-value for a theatre that wants to interact with 'the tumultuous complexities of the present' appears to be shared by a growing number of his contemporaries.

One striking example is the work of the African-American playwright/actor Anna Deavere Smith. Smith developed over a period of thirteen years a mode of performance that is coming remarkably close to the model Brecht proposed in his famous essay, 'The Street Scene'.[20] Smith called her project *On the Road*. She selects a particular theme or event and then audio-tapes interviews with a great number of people connected to the chosen topic, be it as active agents or marginal participants. The performance text is constructed from the transcripts and consists of a sequence of excerpted brief monologues by the individuals interviewed. In performing them, Smith employs carefully picked gestic signifiers that sharply define the portrayed individual while keeping her own personal gestus clearly recognizable. Her most acclaimed pieces, *Fires in the_Mirror* and *Twilight: Los Angeles,1992*, were presentations of two recent eruptions of the interracial violence that has become endemic in America's inner cities. Smith accomplished with her complex use of individual voices a multi-layered unfolding of the events that leaves it to the spectators to draw their conclusions, though she is far from concealing her own view. 'It was my goal to develop a kind of theater that could be more sensitive to the events of my time than traditional theater could [...] The challenge of creating *On the Road* works is to select the voices that best present the event I hope to portray.'[21] Smith arrived at her performance mode without being aware of Brecht's essay, she also was not particularly familiar with his writings on epic theatre. She explains: 'I want the audience to take sides. I want it to be a civic event.'[22] This sounds quite like a statement Brecht could have made. The fact that Smith arrived at an approach so close to Brecht's own not by way of his model but rather motivated by her personal response to the political realities of contemporary America, appears to support sentiments expressed by Kushner and others, namely that Brecht's theory and practice offer tools to the American theatre that are eminently useful at the end of the twentieth century.

It is not Brecht's political agenda – conditioned by and confined to his own historical moment as it was – that would provide the use-value, though there is no reason to dismiss his ideological texts without examining them for anything that might still, or again, be pertinent. It would be his keen eye for the paradox in human social interaction – his dialectics, if you will – and his ever inquisitive, eclectic exploration of all the aesthetic heritage from antiquity to his own century, a practice that anticipated much of what we have become used to call 'post-modern' in the arts. Most of the plays by Brecht and his collaborators were created in a complex process of de-constructing and re-constructing of what he called the fable, a process that involved countless re-writes and an avid scouring of literary and other sources for useful material to be incorporated into the text.

There is a contemporary American theatre group that developed a comparable practice, Cornerstone Theater, founded by Bill Rauch with fellow Harvard graduates in 1986, and devoted to the concept of a community-based theatre. The company travelled to towns and cities in many parts of the U.S. where they staged performances that involved the local community in all aspects of production. Usually, a text from the 'classic' repertoire was adapted to the particular circumstances of the community. Among the projects were several Shakespeare plays, the *Oresteia*, two plays by Chekhov and other texts. Brecht's *Good Person of Szechwan* was performed with the citizens of Long Creek, Oregon, as *The Good Person of Long Creek* in 1988. The group eventually took Los Angeles for its base where, in 1995, it collaborated with the residents of Watts, a district inhabited chiefly by an African-American and Latino populace, in staging *The Central Ave. Chalk Circle*, a version of the text Brecht wrote fifty-one years earlier in nearby Santa Monica. Lynn Manning's adaptation placed the fable in a California of the future when the state has proclaimed independence and is torn by civil war. Bill Rauch commented: 'We felt we could not set it in 1995 because of the events that happened in the play [...] We ended by setting the play in the very near future.' When asked if 'Brecht, Lynn Manning and Cornerstone all wanted to challenge our perceptions as an audience?,' Rauch confirmed: 'Exactly. I hope that any of our plays make people think as well as [they are] moving and entertaining people.'[23] While Cornerstone experimented with many other texts, it seems that plays by Brecht became especially effective when adapted to a contemporary American environment. Cornerstone's treatment of a Brecht text is as respectful as it is unorthodox and may be one feasible way to reclaim its use-value. A scholar who closely observed the work of Cornerstone during recent years, Sonja Kuftinec, noted: 'The fact that community performers are generally untrained in the "method" of psychological realism keeps them from "disappearing" into the characters that they play [...] By remaining outside the roles that they perform, these actors call forth the constructed nature of character and the instability of representation.'[24] Cornerstone's practice appears to come closer than that of any other contemporary group in the U.S. to a project Brecht developed in the early thirties and tried to revive in the mid-fifties, namely that of energizing a socially interactive theatre by combining the skills of professional actors with the useful attitude of amateur performers who identify strongly with their community.

The cited examples of artists who successfully adopted the theory and practice of Brecht in contemporary American drama and performance support the claim that a century after he was born Brecht remains to be – or is again? – a significant cultural force. Nevertheless, the voices who would vehemently disagree are numerous. Brecht has many detractors in academe as well as in the theatre who point out gleefully the obsolescence of opinions he voiced at one time or another and of the ideology he espoused. Some also keep questioning his authorship of texts that are credited to his name. As for the latter, those critics seem to be lacking factual knowledge of the way theatre is created in a collective process that utilizes the talents of a great number of participants. In his efforts to revitalize the theatre Brecht conceived a collaborative practice of playwriting in a manner that was deliberate and systematic. As for the obsolescence attributed to his work, it remains to be seen which of his views and projects will be invalidated by history and which may retain or regain their use-value. Few of his detractors seem to assess particular actions or failures of Brecht within the frame of their precise historical moment. Which only shows that these critics have neither closely read nor truly understood his writings. Many American theatre workers, however, have discovered the use-value in the texts Brecht left us and learned to understand his paradigm by applying it to their own work.

1. Bertolt Brecht, *Vergnügungstheater oder Lehrtheater?*, BFA, 22:1, p.106.

2. Stuart Little, W. *Off-Broadway: The Prophetic Theatre* (New York, Doubleday, 1976), pp.81-3.

3. See the bi-yearly *Theatre Profiles*, vol.1-12 (New York, Theatre Communications Group, 1974-95). This important and comprehensive publication lists all productions in the repertoire of regional companies that are members of T.C.G., the umbrella organization of the American nonprofit theatre movement. The listings document Brecht's firm position in the American repertoire but also the fluctuation in frequency of Brecht productions, which suggests a correlation to the shifts in the political climate of the United States. For a closer look at Brecht's reception in the U.S. and its history see: Carl Weber, 'Brecht auf den Bühnen der USA,' in *The Other Brecht II-The Brecht Yearbook*, 18 (1993), 166-99. Subsequent page references to this article will be cited in the main text of this essay.

4. For a study of the Brecht repertoire in the American academic theatre, see: Klaus M. Schmidt and Daniela Fromann, 'Survey on Brecht productions in the U.S. and Canada from 1975/76 to 1985/86 with Comparative Figues in the FRG, GDR and Austria,' in *Gestus: A Quarterly Journal of Brechtian Studies*, 2.3 (1987), 237-50.

5. For a widely noted example of the Anti-Brecht campaign during the Cold War years, see: Hannah Arendt, 'What is Permitted to Jove' in *New Yorker*, 5 November 1966. Arendt attacked Brecht for being a life long defender of Stalin's crimes.

6. Karl Marx, *Capital,* vol. 1, chapter I, section 1 (London, Lawrence and Wisehart, 1967), p.35.

7. Alan Bloom, *The Closing of the American Mind* (New York, Touchstone Book, 1987), p.154.

8. John Fuegi, *The Life and Lies of Bertolt Brecht* (London, Harper Collins, 1994)

9. John Fuegi, *Brecht and Company: Sex, Politics, and the Making of the Modern Drama,* (New York, Grove Press, 1994).

10. John Willett, James K.Lyon, Siegfried Mews, H.Ch.Norregaard, 'A Brechtbuster Goes Bust: Scholarly Mistakes, Misquotes, and Malpractices in John Fuegi's *Brecht and Company,* in *Brecht Then and Now/The Brecht Yearbook,* 20 (1995), 258-367.

11. Even fairly knowledgeable critics, such as Ronald Speirs of the influential *New York Times Book Review,* (New York, 7 August 1994), were impressed by what they apparently accepted as a meticulously researched book. Speirs wrote concerning Fuegi's assertions about Brecht's abuse of his female collaborators: 'The evidence certainly makes painful reading, but' Speirs mildly reprimands the author, 'Mr. Fuegi seems to me to lose his sense of proportion with the repeated parallels he draws between the careers of Brecht, Hitler and Stalin.' There were, of course, much better informed and consequently quite negative reviews as, for instance, the one by Erika Munk in *The Nation* (New York, 31 October 1994); she points out that '[Fuegi's] "Feminism" exists to serve another, much more conservative agenda. Brecht's politics are denounced from every side.'

12. See, for instance, a collection of statements and critical studies that reflect on feminist Brecht criticism as well as John Fuegi's book. Among the authors are Alisa Solomon, Gay Gibson Cima, Paula Hanssen and Liz Diamond, in *Theater,* vol.25, no.2 (New Haven, Yale School of Drama/Yale Repertory Theater,1994). For an earlier assessment of Brecht's use-value to feminist theory and practice by an American scholar, see Janelle Reinelt, 'Rethinking Brecht: Deconstruction, Feminism, and the Politics of Form' in *Essays on Brecht / The Brecht Yearbook,* 15 (1990), 99-107.

13. For the 1995/97 seasons, only nine productions of Brecht plays have been listed by the more than 250 resident professional theaters which are constituents of Theatre Communications Group. (In comparison, twelve other plays translated from the German were cited, texts by Büchner, Dürrenmatt, R.W.Fassbinder, Frisch, Lessing, Volker Ludwig, Heiner Müller, Oscar Panizza and Sternheim.) Of the nine announced productions, four were of *Galileo.* Seasonal planning is, of course, always tentative, and in the past the number of Brecht productions sometimes exceeded the one that had been announced.

14. Gudrun Tabbert-Jones, '*Chalk Circle* at the Berkeley Repertory Theatre,' in *Communications,* 24, 1 (May 1995), 46.

15. See '1995-96 Season Schedules,' in *American Theatre* 12/8 (1995), 43-72, and 13/8 (1996), 43-70.

16. Robert Falls Interview, *American Theatre* 6/7 (1989), 123.

17. Tony Kushner, 'American Brecht,' in *American Theatre*, 6/7 (1989), 123.

18. Carl Weber, 'I Always Go Back to Brecht: A Conversation with the Playwright Tony Kushner' in *Brecht Then and Now - The Brecht Yearbook,* 20 (1995), 74.

19. In an unpublished conversation, 22 May 1996.

20. Bertolt Brecht, *Brecht on Theatre,* ed.and transl. by John Willett (New York, Hill & Wang, 1964), pp.121-29.

21. Anna Deavere Smith, *Twilight: Los Angeles,1992* (New York, Anchor Books/Doubleday, 1994), p.xxii. The book's introduction illuminates Smith's creative process.

22. Carl Weber, 'Brecht's "Street Scene" – On Broadway of all Places? A Conversation with Anna Deavere Smith,' in *Brecht Then and Now,* 62.

23. All quotes cited are from: Sonja Kuftinec, 'Interview with Bill Rauch, Artistic Director of Cornerstone Theater. Conducted 18 November 1995.' (as yet unpublished).

24. Sonja Kuftinec, 'A Cornerstone for Rethinking Community Theatre,' in *Theatre Topics,* 6,1 (March 1996), 100-101.

MEG MUMFORD

'Dragging' Brecht's Gestus Onwards: A Feminist Challenge

One of the legacies of Brecht's subversive political theatre which has been given increasing attention in recent years is his concept and practice of Gestus. According to this concept the performer's main task is to provide an artistic critique of socio-economic and ideologically inscribed bearing by means of deictic gesture. Gestic acting is typified by a stress on comportment and positioning which serve to defamiliarize both cultural inscription and interhuman relations. Given the potential of gestic acting as a tool for exposing oppressive power relations, it is hardly surprising that since the 1970s it has attracted particular attention from the materialist feminist quarter. Characterized by their tendency to adopt a social constructivist approach to gender issues,[1] materialist feminists share with Brecht an emphasis on the way social behaviour and events are determined by historically specific material and ideological factors. Theatre critics aligned with this feminist group have responded positively to Brecht's theory of Gestus, regarding it as a useful method for deconstructing gender, sexuality and race systems and the dominant modes of representation in which they are embodied.[2]

My aim in this paper is to extend the discussion of the potential and limitations of both gestic theory and practice as a performance model for materialist feminist theatre. After outlining some of the main reasons for the interest in gestic theory expressed by feminist critics, I investigate the relevance to a materialist feminist project of the Marxist gist and the self-reflexive Gestus of showing in Brecht's post-1926 theatre work. One of the key and relatively neglected issues I open up for further investigation[3] is the extent to which Brecht's Marxist writings embody both the progressive and reactionary tendencies of Marx, Engels and Lenin's approach to sex-gender issues and ideology, an approach I will refer to as the 'classical' or 'traditional' Marxist position. The other main area of exploration is the Brecht Collective's utilization of Gestus to highlight gender issues in *practice*, the exploration of that practice being based not only on playscripts and theoretical writings but on performance work at the Berliner Ensemble during the 1950s. For the purpose of concise exemplification, I have chosen to orient my discussion around the Brecht Collective's manipulation of the female-to-male drag figure. Not only is the drag figure a striking instance of the Gestus of showing in Brecht's work, but it vividly illustrates the parameters of the Brecht Collective's presentation of gender construction. The two transvestite displays I have selected for examination, on the basis that they constitute the most sustained and developed instances of female drag in Brecht's theatre practice, are the Victoria/Squire Wilful figure in the Ensemble's 1955 production of *Trumpets and Drums* and the Shen Te/Shui Ta figure in the 1953 version of *The Good Person of Sezuan.*

A Feminist Appropriation of Brecht's Gestus Theory

Proclaiming their sensitivity to the sex-gender blind spots in Brecht's theatre practice,[4] Janelle Reinelt and Elin Diamond have nevertheless both upheld the radical potential of his performance *theory* for feminist theatre. Writing in the 1980s, both characterized Gestus as a method of making visible the material existence of gender ideology and the ensuing power relations which exist within the environment of the text or performance. While Reinelt tended to describe Gestus as merely one of several important techniques, Diamond characterized it as 'the explosive (and elusive) synthesis of alienation, historicization, and the "not, but."'[5] Diamond's description is more in keeping with Brecht's tendency to present Gestus as the synthesis of these aesthetic strategies.[6]

The elements of gestic theory that have been singled out by materialist feminists critics as of particular relevance to the performer are, firstly, the adoption of historically contextualized comportments and, secondly, the Gestus of showing. With regard to comportment, Diamond notes that Gestus constitutes the enactment of cultural inscription on the body and this, she suggests, makes it the ideal medium for highlighting gender, the mapping of ideology - of a system of beliefs and behaviour - across both male and female bodies.[7] Reinelt observes that Gestus is a means of demonstrating not only inscription but interaction in that it offers 'a physical correlative of relations between genders' (the strategy could just as well be applied to racial and ethnic interactions).[8] Drawing on Reinelt's discussion, Jill Dolan has also suggested that Gestus is an ideal tool for showing how these interactions and even theatrical representation itself are governed by ideology.[9]

Indeed, if there is one aspect of Brechtian acting theory which is retained and exploited in the feminist theatre it is the Gestus of showing. Diamond singles out this Gestus as a strategy of great importance in the struggle against what has been interpreted as 'the male gaze'. Drawing upon Laura Mulvey's feminist film theory of the 1970s, she describes this gaze as the product of representational forms which construct 'a specifically male viewing position by aligning or suturing the male's gaze to that of the fictional hero, and by inviting him thereby both to identify narcissistically with that hero and to fetishize the female (turning her into an object of sexual stimulation)'.[10] This gaze can be dismantled, Diamond suggests, by the creation of multiple subject positions generated by the Gestus of showing: an *historical subject* - Helene Weigel, for example, plays the role of an *actor/gestic demonstrator* who in turn narrates and embodies the behaviour and gestures of a *character* before a *spectator*. Conventional iconicity, which laminates the subject's body to the character, is broken. The female body on stage becomes difficult to fetishize as there is no longer a fixed and stable identity controlled by one authority. Furthermore, the female subject/actor is no longer merely the object of the gaze but asserts her own gaze as she looks back directly at the spectator. She connotes not 'to-be-looked-at-ness' (the perfect fetish) but 'looking-at-being-looked-at-ness'.[11] According to Diamond's theory, the one-way nature of the male gaze that specularizes the female body is replaced by several separate subject positions including that of the spectator.[12]

Diamond's claim that the gestic subject/actor-character-spectator triad is non-authoritarian is based on the argument that, while the actor is 'presumed to have superior knowledge in relation to an ignorant character from the past', the subject 'herself remains as divided and uncertain as the spectators to whom the play is addressed'.[13] Here Diamond is referring to the way the subject is divided into the roles of actor and character, both of which remain 'historical, processual and incomplete', rather than simply disappearing behind one or the other.[14] However, I would argue that in both theory and practice, Brecht's gestic triad tended to assert the gestic demonstrator as the figure of authority. In terms of theory, this positioning is manifest in the way Brecht emphasizes the importance of the actor's responsibility to society which, in turn, is embodied in the moment when the actor supplements the empathetic approach to the character with the *Haltung* [attitude/bearing] of social criticism, the *Haltung* the spectator is to learn.[15] In addition, Brecht has little to say about the subject's display of those aspects of self which contradict or are different from those of the socialist commentator. The discussion of empathy recorded by Brecht during the 1953 *Katzgraben* rehearsals exemplifies this point at the practical level. During the discussion Helene Weigel explained that when playing Mother Courage in the final scene, particularly on the line 'I must get back into business', her empathetic relationship with the character would be disrupted not simply by her awareness that she was a performer in a theatre but also by the fact that, personally, Weigel would be shocked that the human being she was depicting did not have the ability to learn.[16]   In this case Weigel's response as an historical subject neatly corresponds with that of a socialist commentator. At no other point in the discussion are subject positions incompatible with a socialist outlook raised.

Nevertheless, I agree with Diamond when she asserts that the Gestus of showing has the potential to provide a useful method for breaking down the remnants of conventional iconicity. The convention of iconic identity entails the practice of viewing the actor's body as a sign which represents its object - the character - through *innate* rather than *constructed* similarity.[17] In its lamination of the performer's body to that of a character of the same sex, traditional iconicity can perpetuate the naturalization and fixing of socially constructed gender roles. The gestic performer's historicizing display of comportment, most fully expressed in the configuration of the complexly split transvestite figure, not only opens up the possibility of multiple subject positions but facilitates the denaturalization of oppressive ideological systems.

A Materialist Feminist Critique of the Marxist Gist

Thus far the accommodation of Gestus into a social constructivist feminist theatre has been presented as relatively unproblematical. However, in actuality the appropriation process necessitates the readjustment of the gestic eye so that it focuses on a new *gist* in accordance with feminist interpretative strategies. The following discussion relates Brecht's writings on politics and gender issues to the classical Marxist position, indicating those areas where, from a materialist feminist perspective, his Marxist gist must be revised.

Brecht's presentation of female roles and relations cannot be reduced simply to a reflection of Marx and Engels's thoughts on the so-called 'woman's question'. However, after 1926 Brecht's writings and his application of Gestus to the presentation of women in performance are undeniably pervaded by Marxist notions about the subordination and emancipation of women. One noticeable feature of his theoretical and creative writings is the way they reveal a theoretical allegiance to Marx and Engels's pronouncements on the division of labour and to their presentation of capitalist production relations and ruling class ideology as the major determinants of contemporary human oppression. In *The German Ideology* (1845-46) Marx and Engels argued that the original sexual division of labour was nothing but the division of labour in the sexual act which in turn led to the 'natural' division of labour within the family, women being designated to household work and men to the gathering, hunting and cultivation of the means of subsistence.[18] In *The Origin of the Family, Private Property and the State* (1884) Engels reiterated the division of labour argument.[19] Upon this assumption he constructed a theory about the oppression of women, attributing it to changes in the mode of production which led to the usurpation of the dominant household means of subsistence and to the ascendancy of the male sphere of production, private property, class relations, patrilineal inheritance and the subordination of women within the patriarchal family.[20] Nineteenth-century naturalist assumptions about biological difference and heterosexuality pervade these explanations of the division of labour. In the 1980s feminists were still challenging the notion of a 'natural' division of labour, not only pointing to the anthropological inaccuracy of the description of gender roles and its heterosexual bias but criticizing the Marxist vision of history as exclusively oriented around production, the so-called male sphere of activity.[21]

Engels's argument that the patriarchal pairing marriage is the product of private property relations echoes throughout Brecht's negative portrayals of bourgeois wives, fiancés, weddings, marriages and family life.[22] In 1926 Brecht claimed that his main concern in the depiction of the 'love story' between Kragler and Anna in *Drums in the Night* had been the issue of property, a concern reiterated years later in his 1953 reference to the relation between Othello and Desdemona.[23] In his short pieces 'On the Art of Sexual Intercourse' and '[On the Wife's Adultery]', both written in the 1930s, he presents marriage as a contract for *mutual* exploitation of genital organs but stresses that women are in the more vulnerable position. Not only must poorly paid saleswomen and secretaries sell their sexuality in order to maintain their jobs, if not literally, then through the costume of sexuality, the painted lips and high-heeled shoes; even within marriage a woman must prostitute herself if she is to secure the means of subsistence.[24] That woman has been the sex most frequently reduced to a commodity is explained as the result of her position within property relations. Brecht's repeated use of the prostitute figure in his plays as an embodiment of exploitation is similar to Marx's treatment of prostitution as 'a specific expression of the general prostitution of the laborer'.[25] At the theoretical level, the alternative model Brecht offers is that of greater sexual freedom for both women and men and a non-possessive and productive partnership based on a shared interest.[26]

The essentialist assumptions behind the traditional notion of a 'natural' division of labour surface most obviously in Brecht's response to child-rearing and female homosexuality. While Brecht and his co-workers may have subverted the notion that the ability to nurture is pre-given in the female sex, most notably through the contrast of Grusche and the Governess in *The*

Caucasian Chalk Circle, their inability to question sexist arrangements of childcare has repeatedly drawn the attention of feminist critics.[27] Alisa Solomon has presented the counter-argument that it is ludicrous to look to Brecht for 'desirable behaviors modelled on stage' which the feminist spectator can identity with as his 'challenges to social arrangements come through epic process, not through traditional dramatic show-and-tell' or identification with heroes/heroines.[28] However, this argument does not account for the fact that Brecht *did* employ *reconstructive* strategies, exemplified, in its crudest form, in the depiction of the female tractor driver in the utopian prologue to the *Chalk Circle*, but simply did not apply them to the demonstration of male involvement in childcare. Brecht's tendency to regard childcare as a natural female role, pervades his suggestions for the world peace conference in 1954 which, in keeping with the stance of the Communist Party in the Soviet Union in the 1940s, contain the assumption that it is women who are responsible for ensuring the education of their children.[29] The association of women with the ability to nurture the future and the positive reinforcement of this ability is also manifest in the Brecht Collective's string of communitarian mothers, from Pelagea Vlassova and Señora Carrar, to Kattrin and Grusche.[30] With regard to sexuality in the theatre, while homoeroticism was briefly addressed in some of the plays and productions, the Brecht Collective tended to present female heterosexuality as given.[31]

Not only the essentialist assumptions but the economistic tendencies within the Marxist tradition leave their mark on Brecht's work, especially in the way he and his co-workers repeatedly subordinated gender issues to the class struggle and in their Leninist tendency to regard ideology as solely the reflection of class interests. In his writings on the base/superstructure model and economic determination, Brecht hovers between asserting reciprocal influence and a mechanical materialist notion of determination. Traces of the concept of reciprocity are to be found in his insistence that dialectical thinking should be regarded as part of technology and hence as a productive force.[32] However, in his eagerness to avoid the pitfalls of idealism, Brecht often went to the opposite extreme, upholding the notion that an individual's ideas were 'essentially determined by the economic situation and by the class he belongs to'[33] and maintaining that economic circumstances were the key to freedom, all aspects of culture, and even personal health.[34] In a statement of 1928 Brecht openly asserted the necessity of subordinating gender relations to class relations, proclaiming that the emphasis in bourgeois theatre on the contest between men over a woman was to be replaced by a more important conflict - the class struggle.[35] Brecht's subordination of gender conflicts to class struggle reflects the classical Marxist prioritization of forces and relations of *production* over the mode of *reproduction* of labour power,[36] a prioritization challenged by the materialist feminist emphasis on modes of reproduction and their importance as the site of the 'relatively autonomous' familial and sex-gender ideology so crucial to the maintenance of production relations.[37] As Jill Dolan puts it, materialist feminist performance criticism diverges from Brecht's theory when 'it focuses its analysis on material conditions of gender positioning, rather than privileging economic determinism'.[38]

Brecht's Gestic Drag Figure: Showing Economic Determination

Having explored some of the parameters of gestic performance with regard to its theory and gist from a materialist feminist perspective, I turn now to the female drag figure in Brecht's theatre work. My focus here is on those moments in their presentation of the cross-dressed female where the Brecht Collective anticipated the type of feminist employment of socio-historical comportments and the Gestus of showing encouraged by Diamond. The gestic cross-dressed female performer provides a vivid example of the synthesis of these two aesthetic strategies. Her theatrical masquerade and quotation of masculinity and femininity can be used to highlight gender as construct rather than 'natural', and to create a sense of the 'pastness' of the matter being re-presented.[39] The masquerade encourages the spectator to view gender conventions as 'man-made' and historical rather than eternal.

Transvestism is an intriguingly recurrent feature in the work of the Brecht Collective. As far as I am aware, the first instance of cross-gender play in Brecht's theatre was in the 1924 Munich production of his and Lion Feuchtwanger's adaptation of *The Life of Edward II of England* where, much to the horror of the Chamber Theatre's Management, he cast the Latvian Asja Lacis as young Edward. Lacis claims that the casting decision was based on her appearance.[40] After his immersion in Marxism, Brecht's employment of the drag or cross-gender figure is typified by a keen awareness of its potential as a defamiliarizing tool for highlighting gender as social construction. His post-1926 *oeuvre* contains a long string of female protagonists and performers who display the ability to mimic masculine comportment and skills. These characters include: the prostitute who assumes the persona of a male tobacco dealer and is given the status of the central protagonist in *The Good Person of Sezuan*;[41] the actress Helene Weigel dressed in jackboots and trousers for the role of Widow Begbick in the 1928 Berlin premiere of *Man Equals Man*; the woman who masquerades as her husband after he has died in order to take the job promised to him in Brecht's short story c. 1933 *The Job, In the sweat of thy brow shalt thou fail to earn thy bread*; the female member amongst the four Communist Agitators in *The Measures Taken* who is involved in re-enacting the behaviour of the male Young Comrade; and Victoria from the Berliner Ensemble's *Trumpets and Drums* production in 1955, who, when denied access to Captain Plume due to her father's financial concerns, dresses as a man and successfully gains entrance to the British army in order to be closer to her 'beloved'.

'Trumpets and Drums': The Gestus of the Colonizer

In addition to revealing gender as an artificial construct, Brecht and his co-workers often used the transvestite figure to expose the restrictive and undesirable nature of this construct, particularly with regard to conventional notions of masculinity. Carl Weber has pointed out that in the Ensemble's production of *Trumpets and Drums*, one of the drag role's main functions was to problematize habitual and 'customary' male behaviour. An aspect of this behaviour foregrounded in both the playtext and the production is the tendency of males, particularly those connected with the army and law, to treat women as exploitable commodities to be colonized. The sexual abuse of women by members of the army is comically defamiliarized when Victoria, dressed as Sergeant Wilful, fails to 'sleep' with the gullible peasant Rose she has 'ensnared'. That sexually aggressive masculinity is a socially acquired rather than innate trait was perhaps reinforced by the fact that the actress Regine Lutz played Squire (later to become Sergeant) Wilful as a 'quite attractive, slightly funny teenage boy'.[42] The comportment of the male teenager can be interpreted not only as a device for showing how Victoria gradually *acquires* male behaviour and gait but for illuminating how a young man, too, will *learn* this behaviour under the influence of a society which encourages male colonizing tendencies.

The transvestite figure in *Trumpets and Drums* not only exposes colonialist behaviour but contributes to the Brecht Collective's presentation of women as a group repressed by a society which empowers the colonizer. Instances of female cross-dressing in the Brecht *oeuvre* invariably demonstrate how women of different historical periods and classes require the status of an empowered male, either at the basic level of economic survival or in order to pursue their sexual desires. This function of the cross-dressed female becomes more apparent when compared with its male counterpart. In the case of Sergeant Kite in *Trumpets and Drums*, a rare instance of a male drag figure in Brecht's work, the transvestite 'disguise' does not unmask a gender-based vulnerability.[43] Sergeant Kite's decision to dress as a flower woman-cum-fortune teller is necessitated by his obligation to recruit soldiers for the British army rather than a need to escape sex-gender oppression. According to photos of the production held in the Berliner Ensemble archive, Kite constructed a comic pantomime figure of an obese ageing woman, clutching a walking stick, with her clothing billowing out in a grotesque fashion. His face was barely concealed by a large-brimmed hat. Weber points out that Kite's drag-role fails miserably 'not merely because it is clumsily performed but also because it isn't motivated by sexual or any other strong desire'.[44]

The radical potential of the Brecht Collective's female drag figures is somewhat tempered by an essentialist assumption of heterosexuality as the norm for women. This is not to say that Brecht as a playwright totally failed to question the sexual norm. In *Edward II*, for instance, the norm is estranged through the depiction of Edward and Gaveston's homosexuality, while in the performance of *Trumpets and Drums* a 'subtle homoerotic undercurrent' was generated in the early encounters between young Wilful (Victoria in disguise) and Plume, perhaps as a commentary on a male-centred imperialist society.[45] Yet while male homoeroticism is problematized, the same cannot be said for lesbian desire. Victoria as Wilful certainly has an opportunity to 'sleep' with Rose, but she never practises a sexual alternative herself, remaining instead steadfastly heterosexual.

Although the presentation of Victoria/Sergeant Wilful fails to defamiliarize female sexuality, it does exemplify how radical the Brecht Collective was in its attempt to subvert the traditional mode of representation, an attempt which anticipates Diamond's proposal for disrupting conventional iconicity. In her memoirs, Lutz provides a graphic illustration of how Brecht multiplied the subject positions she was to play through a costuming strategy. Initially she was instructed to consider four positions: that of Victoria, of the narrating actress, and Squire Wilful, and the young woman who plays Wilful. The split between Victoria and the actress was achieved, for example, by the alteration between Lutz showing Victoria behaving as the perfect innocent towards her father and then having Victoria, while remaining at her father's side, face the audience front on and silently express her real feelings. In similar fashion, Lutz would show the Squire listening appreciatively to Captain Plume's tales about his sexual exploits, and then turn aside to the audience in order to reveal Victoria's anger at her beloved's love affairs. In the early days of the rehearsal, the costume prepared for the Squire role consisted of a fitted suit in gleaming white with gold trim, a white rococo wig and tricorn, and tall top boots. When Brecht first saw Lutz in this carnival prince costume he was aghast, shocked by its fairytale *Rosenkavalier* overtones. His first criticism was that it was simply not realistic - how could a young woman in that period come by such a tailor-made costume?

Instead he suggested clothing which could feasibly be that of Victoria's brother, ill-fitting in all respects. Subsequently Lutz was given huge felt knickerbockers, an expansive coat and overly large buckled shoes, a broad-brimmed felt hat, and a comic pirate moustache.

Brecht's alteration was not based simply on the impulse towards realism. Rather, he saw the change as a productive opportunity to multiply the various subject positions. The costume not only enhanced the clumsy awkwardness of a woman who is learning to impersonate a male but demonstrated that the young Squire had not yet become a self-assured man of the world. When the Squire received the fitted uniform of the British army - depicted in the play as forcefully recruiting soldiers for their imperialist involvement in the American War of Independence - 'his' *Haltung* changed accordingly, shifting from clumsy to brash as he took on the new role of *Sergeant* Wilful. Victoria become increasingly skilled in the display of superior masculinity while the military costume had given the Squire the self-confidence of a dare-devil philanderer.[46] The multiple subjects contributed not only to the display of gender as social costume, but also to the linking of imperialist politics with male colonizing behaviour.

That Brecht was interested in disrupting the type of traditional performance iconicity which laminated gender to biological sex is also suggested by the fact that he regarded cross-gesturing as an important acting exercise. In one of *Der Messingkauf* dialogues from 1939-41, he upholds the efficacy of having a female performer play a man and vice versa so that behaviour which may appear common to all humans is revealed instead as typical of a certain gender. Brecht also adds that an actor who is *not* cross-dressed should incorporate the defamiliarized gender gestures of the cross-dressed performer into their presentation.[47] Brecht's development of his V-effect theory may in part be attributed to his own experience of cross-gesturing, for it was after he witnessed a performance in 1935 by the Chinese actor Mei Lan-fang, which involved the enactment of women's roles in male attire, that Brecht made his first reference to the theory in the seminal essay 'Defamiliarization Effects in Chinese Acting'.[48]

'The Good Person of Sezuan': Cross-Dressing and Capitalism

Perhaps traces of Mei Lan-fang's performance are to be found in the cross-dressed protagonist of *The Good Person of Sezuan*. Shen Te, a compassionate prostitute in the province of Sezuan, is forced periodically to adopt the persona and attire of a male businessman, the cousin Shui Ta, in order to ensure her survival in a capitalist market economy. Shen Te's act of cross-dressing shows that gender is a socially constructed costume. On the second occasion that Shen

Te must arm herself with the trappings of Shui Ta, the notion of artificial construction is emphasized when the change of clothing and gestural codes and the assumption of the cousin's mask is enacted before the audience. When disguised as Shui Ta, both the female character and the actress playing her role demonstrate their ability to embody a powerful businessman, the epitome of masculinity in capitalist society. While Shen Te is characterized by her lover, Sun, as 'thickheaded',[49] she also proves capable of being highly rational, calculating, and a stern figure of authority in matters of law and business. In keeping with Brecht's belief that humans are identities in flux rather than static entities, the text seems to open up the possibility that a female's destiny is *not* necessarily fixed by her anatomy. Moreover, gender polarization is disrupted through the presence of a double figure who simultaneously displays both masculine and feminine physical gestures and behavioural traits, a display which Brecht described as the 'continual fusion and dissolution of two characters'.[50]

Regine Lutz's description of the way she and Brecht approached the characterization of Shui Ta during private rehearsals (for a production which was never realised), demonstrates the manner in which Brecht approached the construction of gender. Lutz writes that both she and Brecht wanted to create a believable embodiment of a man rather then a comical ham version. As Lutz was of small stature she suggested that Shui Ta always be played seated. Inspired by her idea, Brecht began to envisage the *Haltung* of a male *Sitzriese*, a short man with a long body who uses the posture of sitting - which makes him appear taller - to bolster his sense of self-importance. Thanks to the Chinese setting, the posture and its implications could be heightened with the help of a sedan chair or rickshaw. The seated position also gave the actress many possibilities for using her lower body to create masculine *Haltungen* - stretching her legs out, casually crossing them, placing the right foot on the left thigh, bouncing and stamping the feet.[51] Most of Lutz's brief description focuses on the way she and Brecht used gestic devices to defamiliarize the masculine behaviour of a capitalist businessman. For example, they decided upon a Humphrey-Bogart hat and a pair of sun glasses in order to show how he masters the gaze by concealing his own. Shui's class status was suggested by the use of a cigarette which Lutz clamped in the corner of her mouth, never removing or lighting it. The cigarette prop not only helped Lutz to effect the transition, giving her voice a nasal and at times a staccato commandeering quality, but marked Shui Ta as the tobacco king. Attention was drawn to the wealth-determined nature of Shui's self-confidence through the possessive polishing and intermittent display of a large diamond ring worn on his little finger.[52] While the rehearsal of the role testifies that Brecht wished to expose gender as costume it also shows how, as in the case of

Victoria/Squire/Sergeant Wilful, Brecht tended to focus on the link between domineering masculine behaviour and capitalist ruling class ideology, rather than, say, the construction of femininity through relatively autonomous gender ideology.

The factor that limits the obviously radical potential of the gestic transvestite figure in *The Good Person of Sezuan* is the one-sided emphasis on economics and ruling class ideology as the paramount source of hierarchical gender polarization.   Indeed it is the capitalist system which generates the necessity of the split figure in the first place.   Shen Te creates the disguise of a male businessman so that in the dog-eat-dog world of the market economy she can successfully effect the transition from prostitute to petit-bourgeois small-time shop owner and maintain at least a subsistence level.   The play depicts the 'achievers' in capitalist society as dependent on character traits associated with masculinity, such as egoistic aggressivity and rationality.   These are traits displayed by the other successful businesswoman in the play, Mrs Mi Tzu.   The Gestus of the bipolar character in *The Good Person of Sezuan*, and of Mrs Mi Tzu, demonstrates how patriarchal behaviour is born of and therefore secondary to a capitalist economic system.

Alongside the tendency to present capitalist economics and capitalist ideology as the primary cause of female oppression, the use of the drag figure in *The Good Person of Sezuan* occasionally falls into the trap of affirming the essentialist argument that some aspects of gender behaviour are based on innate biological functions.   For example, Shen Te's gender behaviour and appearance is not subjected to the same sort of estrangement applied to her male counterpart. Where is the dress scene comparable to Shui Ta's in which *her* 'feminine' emotionally expressive and nurturing behaviour, gait and movements are *also* theatrically displayed as a construct rather than as 'natural'? Another technique that might have helped to defamiliarize the notion that femininity is 'natural' in a manner equivalent to the play's theatrical estrangement of masculinity, would have been the casting of a male - or a number of actors of different sexes - in the double role or, alternatively, to have given the female performer not only a Shui Ta but a Shen Te mask, options the Brecht Collective do not seem to have considered.   This is not to suggest that Shen Te's behaviour is never defamiliarized. Indeed, as Alisa Solomon argues, during the scene in which Shen Te changes on-stage into Shui Ta's costume, the actress creates an additional Gestus of showing by moving from the plane of speech to the more overtly artificial plane of song. In so doing the actress clearly demonstrates that she is impersonating *both* Shui Ta *and* the female Shen Te.[53] However, it would seem to me that while this defamiliarizing device may expose Shen Te as an historical and fictional construct, it does not fully disrupt essentialist assumptions about her gender. This is because an element of traditional iconicity is preserved: the resemblance between the actor's (female) body and the female character to which it refers is not as overtly interrupted. Furthermore, there is no indication in the text at this point that the estrangement of femininity itself is the focus of the display.

Generally speaking, whenever Gestus is employed in *The Good Person of Sezuan* to demystify roles and institutions oppressive to women, it tends to serve the illumination of their economic and class implications rather than relatively autonomous gender ideology. As the role and institution of motherhood has been repeatedly scrutinised elsewhere,[54] I will turn my attention to the way the play treats marriage and the concept of romantic love as the distorted products of capitalism.   The trick of juxtaposing the more romantically inclined and sentimental Shen Te with the competitive survivalist attitude of Shui Ta, reveals the type of marriage sanctioned by capitalist society as not only a business deal but one oppressive to women.   Wives are likened to prostitutes, saleable commodities. These themes are clarified by the Gestus of absence. That is, in a situation where one side of the split figure is not present, the true nature of such a marriage becomes particularly apparent. The episode in Scene 2, involving a discussion between Shui Ta and a Policeman about an arranged marriage for Shen Te, is one example of how the Gestus of absence functions throughout the play. According to the Policeman 'the authorities' have regarded the opening of the tobacco store with unease because they are concerned that a former prostitute may disrupt order. Prostitution is unacceptable, he explains, because sex is bought and sold. Marriage is respectable because sex is with the one you love. The Policeman then proceeds to suggest an arranged marriage and enthusiastically pulls out a notebook and pencil with which to map out the newspaper advertisement for a husband. To coax a 'buyer' he describes Shen Te as a profitable object: owner of a blooming business, attractive and pleasant. His actions negate all he has said about marriage: it is only to be differentiated from prostitution in that it is a socially sanctioned eternal slavery which more successfully veils the mechanics of property exchange and profit-oriented acquisition.[55] Shen Te's absence during the discussion of her marriage - she is obscured behind Shui Ta's mask - is noticeable and significant. It helps convey how in this exchange the woman is muted and manipulated by the power brokers. Yet while the episode with the Policeman serves to demonstrate how the bourgeois ideology of love conceals the profit motive behind marriage and the exploitation of women, at no stage is the historical development of the woman's position as the mute commodity addressed. As Elizabeth Wright puts it: 'What is missing from this analysis is an examination of the material conditions of gender behaviour outside its relation to class'.[56]

Conclusion

Although Gestus could in theory be applied to all forms of human relations, my investigation of the transvestite figure suggests that in practice the Brecht Collective tended to denaturalize comportment mainly in terms of economic determinants and class ideology, and that when the Collective did apply the historicizing Gestus to sex-gender relations the presentation sometimes contained the transgressive residue of essentialism, particularly in the case of female sexuality and the link between the female sex and the act of nurturing. I have posited Brecht's affinity with classical Marxist thinking - on the subject of the sexual division of labour, the relation between production and reproduction, and class ideology - as one factor which contributed to the sex-gender blindspots of the gestic eye in practice, especially the neglect of modes of reproduction and gender ideology. With regard to strategies of representation, I have suggested that while the theory of gestic acting implies a self-reflexive disruption of conventional iconicity, in practice this disruption was only partial, at least in the case of the drag figure. For example, when Regine Lutz presents Squire/Sergeant Wilful and the actress in *The Good Person of Sezuan* presents Shui Ta, the female performer remains clearly connected with the character of her own sex and ascribed gender, especially during her first entrance and the final 'unmasking' - the ultimate abandonment of the male 'disguise' and reassertion of female identity which occurs in both plays. Traces of the traditional lamination between actor's body and character prevail. Materialist feminist theatre has tended to opt for a more pronounced, wide-ranging and theatrical experimentation with representation than transitory cross-dressing, adding multiple forms of cross-casting and role doubling to its interruptive strategies.

However, in contrast to the tendency in feminist circles to emphasize the way Brecht's work was limited by a patriarchal discourse[57] I have also provided material that suggests Brecht was already starting to apply many of the strategies for problematizing gender construction which are outlined in Elin Diamond's proposal of 1988 for a gestic feminist criticism,[58] especially with regard to the reactionary codes of masculinity, homoeroticism and romantic love perpetuated under capitalism. While the authoritarian overtones of gestic demonstration may require further revision, the subject of that demonstration - the historicization of material and ideologically inscribed social bearing - continues to be of relevance to a contemporary materialist feminist theatre which seeks to challenge hegemonic modes of being.

[1.]   Rosemary Hennessy, *Materialist Feminism and the Politics of Discourse* (New York and London, Routledge, 1993), p.xxiv.

[2.]   See Janelle Reinelt, 'Beyond Brecht: Britain's New Feminist Drama', *Theatre Journal*, 38, 2 (1986), 154-163; Elin Diamond, 'Brechtian Theory/Feminist Theory: Toward a Gestic Feminist Criticism', *The Drama Review*, 32, 1 (1988), 82-94; Jill Dolan, *The Feminist Spectator as Critic* (Ann Arbor, University of Michigan Press, 1988), pp.14, 106-117.

[3.]   This issue has been referred to briefly by for example, Laureen Nussbaum, 'The Evolution of the Feminine Principle in Brecht's Work: Beyond the Feminist Critique', *German Studies Revue*, 8, 2 (1985), 217-244 and Darko Suvin, 'Brecht: Bearing, Pedagogy, Productivity', *Gestos*, 5, 10 (1990), 11-28.

[4.]   Reinelt, p.185; Diamond, pp.83-4.

[5.]   Reinelt, p.154; Diamond, p.89.

[6.]   See, for example, Bertolt Brecht, 'Kurze Beschreibung einer neuen Technik der Schauspielkunst, die einen Verfremdungseffekt hervorbringt', c. 1940, *BFA*, 22: 2, p.646.

[7.]   Diamond, p.85.

[8.]   Reinelt, p.158.

[9.]   Dolan, pp.108, 106, 112.

[10.]   Diamond, p.83. See also Laura Mulvey, 'Visual Pleasure and Narrative Cinema', *Screen*, 16, 3 (1975), 11-13.

[11.]   Diamond, p.89.

[12.]   Dolan, p.114.

[13.]   Diamond, pp.87-8.

[14.]   Diamond, p.88.

[15.]   Brecht, 'Stanislawski-Studien [3]', 1953, *BFA*, 23, pp.227-8; 'Einfühlung', 1953, *BFA*, 25 p.439.

[16.]   Brecht, 'Einfühlung', p.440.

[17.]   Michael Selmon, 'Reshuffling the Deck: Iconoclastic Dealings in Caryl Churchill's Early Plays', in Phyllis R. Randall (ed.), *Caryl Churchill: A Casebook* (New York and London, Garland, 1988), pp.59-60; Keir Elam, *The Semiotics of Theatre and Drama* (London and New York, Routledge, 1980), p.21.

[18.]   Marx and Engels, *Collected Works*, 5, pp.33, 43, 44, 46 as quoted in Lise Vogel, *Marxism and the Oppression of Women: Toward a Unitary Theory* (London, Pluto, 1983), p.50.

19. Frederick Engels, *The Origin of the Family, Private Property and the State*, trans. Alec West (London, Lawrence and Wishart, 1972), pp.113, 119. Engels combines a condemnation of female subordination in patriarchal marriage with an archaic and negative vision of homosexuality: ' ... but this degradation of the women was avenged on the men and degraded them also, till they fell into the abominable practice of sodomy and degraded alike their gods and themselves with the myth of Ganymede' (p.128).

20. Engels, pp.117-120. See also Vogel, pp.82-3.

21. Moira Maconachie, 'Engels, Sexual Divisions and the Family', University of Kent at Canterbury, Women's Studies Occasional Papers, 1 (1983), 10-12.

22. Laureen Nussbaum argues that while in the early plays such as *Baal, The Wedding* and *Drums in the Night* these negative portrayals of bourgeois fiancé, bride and wife figures reflect a 'horror of bourgeois family life', the criticism of bourgeois marriage and sex relations increasingly becomes sharpened by his Marxist perspective. See Nussbaum, pp.221-231.

23. Brecht, 'Vorwort zu "Trommeln"', c. 1926, *BFA*, 24, pp.18-9; 'Stanislawski-Studien [6]', c. 1953, *BFA*, 23, pp.230-1.

24. Brecht, 'B 47 Über die Kunst des Beischlafs', from the 'Tuitraktate', c. 1933-5, *BFA*, 17, pp.145-7; 'Über Kants Definition der Ehe in der "Metaphysik der Sitten"', c. 1938-40, *BFA*, 11, p.270; 'Me-Ti Wurde gefragt, ob es gegen die gute Sitte verstosse', from 'Buch der Wendungen', c. 1934-40, *BFA*, 18, pp.126-127; '[Bert Brechts Meinung über Eifersucht]', November/December 1928, *BFA*, 21, pp.258-9.

25. Marx and Engels, *Collected Works*, vol. 3, p.295, as quoted in Vogel, p.44.

26. Brecht, 'Die dritte Sache', c. 1937-8 in 'Buch der Wendungen', p.173; Brecht, 'An Ruth Berlau', 10 March 1950, in Brecht, *Briefe*, Hg. Günter Glaeser (Frankfurt aM, Suhrkamp, 1981), p.637.

27. Sarah Lennox, 'Women in Brecht's Works', *New German Critique*, 14 (1978), 92; Sue-Ellen Case, 'Brecht and Women: Homosexuality and the Mother', *The Brecht Yearbook. Brecht: Women and Politics*, 12 (1983), 66.

28. Solomon, pp.52-3. Sabine Keir argues in a similar vein that critics have ignored Brecht's use of the pedagogical technique of forceful negative examples. See Sabine Keir, 'Die feministische Brechtkritik', *Weimarer Beiträge*, 34, 2 (1988), 298.

29. Brecht, 'Gerede Brecht (gehalten auf dem Weltfriedenskongress in Berlin, am 28. Mai 1954) Ein Vorschlag', *BFA*, 23, p.280; *Women and Communism: Selections from the Writings of Marx, Engels, Lenin and Stalin* (Westport Conn., Greenwood Press, 1973), p.85.

30. Bernard Fenn, *Characterisation of Women in the Plays of Bertolt Brecht* (Frankfurt aM, Peter Lang, 1982), pp.140, 145, 149, 175; Case, p.73; Lennox, p.86. Lennox characterises the ability to nurture the future as a negative willingness to be instrumentalised.

31. For further discussion of this issue see Case, p.67. In an interview with John Fuegi, the lesbian actress Angelika Hurwicz reputedly stated that neither Brecht nor Weigel were able to deal openly with homosexuality. See John Fuegi, *The Life and Lies of Bertolt Brecht* (London, HarperCollins, 1994), p.539. Darko Suvin argues that the male relationships in Brecht's early plays cannot be interpreted as erotic, and hence they are not homosexual. For him erotics is bisexual in Brecht's works. Unfortunately Suvin states rather than supports his argument. See Suvin, 'Brecht: Bearing, Pedagogy, Productivity', 24.

32. Brecht, 'Thesen zur Theorie des Überbaus (Zweck: Die revolutionäre Bedeutung der Überbauarbeit)', c. 1932, *BFA*, 21, p.571.

[33.] Brecht, 'An Johannes R. Becher', early 1935, in Brecht, *Briefe*, p.232; Brecht, *Letters 1913-1956*, trans. Ralph Manheim, ed. John Willett (New York and London, Routledge and Methuen, 1990), p.192.

[34.] Brecht, '[Abhängigkeit der Kritik]', c. 1929, '[Verantwortlichkeit ökonomischer Zustände]', c. 1932 and 'Über die Freiheit', c. 1932, *BFA*, 21, pp.334, 569, 580; '[Der geistige Hunger]', c. 1937 and 'Der Faschismus und die Jugend', c. 1937, *BFA*, 22, pp.346, 349; 'An Karl Korsch', January 1934, in Brecht, *Briefe*, pp.195-6. Brecht's antipathy towards the psychoanalytic business generated his crudest polemics on economic determination, leading him to suggest that employment rather than psychoanalysis was the solution to the neuroses of the poorer classes. See 'Briefe an einen erwachsenen Amerikaner', c. 1944, *BFA*, 23, p.47.

[35.] Brecht, 'Für das Programmheft zur Heidelberger Aufführung', 24 July 1928, *BFA*, 24, pp.27-8. See also Brecht's comments to Sternberg in the Winter of 1926-7 as quoted in Fuegi, pp.171-2.

[36.] While Marx and Engels described social life as dependent both on production and procreation, they appear to have regarded procreation as a timeless natural process, totally subordinate to the mode of production, rather than a social structure subject to conscious intervention. See Engels, pp.71-2; Vogel, pp.63, 90; Susan Himmelweit, 'Reproduction', in Tom Bottomore (ed.), *A Dictionary of Marxist Thought*, 2nd ed. (Oxford, Blackwell, 1991), p.471.

[37.] Heidi Hartmann, 'Summary and Response: Continuing the Discussion', in Lydia Sargeant (ed.), *The Unhappy Marriage of Marxism and Feminism: A Debate on Class and Patriarchy* (London, Pluto, 1981), p.364; Michèle Barrett, *Women's Oppression Today: The Marxist/Feminist Encounter* (2nd ed.), (London and New York, Verso, 1988), p.97.

[38.] Dolan, p.14.

[39.] Dolan, p.116.

[40.] Heinz-Uwe Haus, 'In Memoriam Asja Lacis', *The Brecht Yearbook. Brecht: Women and Politics*, 12 (1983), 143. Unfortunately, Brecht does not seem to have recorded the reasons for his casting decision. Asja Lacis's autobiographical writings do not provide any further insights. See Asja Lacis, *Revolutionär im Beruf*, ed. Hildegard Brenner (Munich, Rogner and Bernhard, 1971), pp.37-40.

[41.] The prostitute figure is central to the earlier fragments upon which the play is thematically based - *'Fanny Kress'* or *'The Prostitutes' only Friend'*, c. 1927, and *Love is the Goods (Die Ware Liebe)*, c. 1930. See Brecht, *BFA*, 6, pp.280-1.

[42.] This was one of the descriptions Carl Weber offered me in his written response of 12 November 1995 to some of my questions about the cross-dressed figure in the production. I am grateful to Weber for drawing my attention to this much neglected instance of transvestism.

[43.] The same could be said for the cross-dressed male in the 1933 production of *The Seven Deadly Sins*, for which Brecht cast a bass in the singing part of the Mother. Klaus Völker, *Bertolt Brecht: Eine Biographie* (Reinbek, Rowohlt, 1976), p.197. See also Solomon, p.51. As the mother (along with the other members of the family, the father and two sons) is responsible for burdening Anna I and II with bourgeois morality and financial demands, the casting would seem to underline the patriarchal nature of the petit-bourgeoisie and their capitalist aspirations rather than emphasising male vulnerability.

[44.] Weber, 12 November 1995

45. Weber, 12 November 1995

46. Regine Lutz, *Schauspieler - der schönste Beruf* (Munich, Langen Müller, 1993), pp.259-261.

47. Brecht, 'B66' from 'Der Messingkauf', 1939-41, *BFA*, 22:2, pp.740-1. See also '[Wenn Kinder Erwachsene spielen]', c. 1936, *BFA*, 22:1, p.223.

48. Editorial notes in *BFA*, 22:2, p.959 and John Willett's editorial notes in Bertolt Brecht, *Brecht on Theatre*, ed. and trans. John Willett (London and New York, Methuen and Hill and Wang, 1964), p.99.

49. Brecht, Ruth Berlau, Margaret Steffin *Der gute Mensch von Sezuan*, 1938-40, *BFA*, 6, p.220. Henceforth, references to this playscript will be given in the body of the essay.

50. Brecht, 20 June 1940, in *BFA*, 26, p.392. Brecht, *Journals 1934-1955*, trans. Hugh Rorrison, ed. John Willett (London, Methuen, 1993), p.70.

51. Significantly, Lutz (p. 247) described the *Sitzriese* idea as a solution to what she regarded as the 'disastrous comic effect' that could arise from mimicking masculine gait and stance. Her attitude suggests that she was not totally confident about her ability to effect the transition convincingly.

52. Lutz, pp.247-8.

53. Solomon, p.45.

54. See for example, Solomon, p.48; Sieglinda Lug, 'The "Good" Woman Demystified', *Communications from the International Brecht Society*, 14, 1 (1984), 8; Elizabeth Wright, 'The Good Person of Szechwan: discourse of a masquerade', in Peter Thomson and Glendyr Sacks (eds.), *The Cambridge Companion to Brecht* (Cambridge, Cambridge University Press, 1994), p.122.

55. Helmut Jendreiek, *Bertolt Brecht: Drama der Veränderung* (Düsseldorf, Bagel, 1969), p.226; Peter Christian Giese, '"Der gute Mensch von Sezuan". Aspekte einer Brechtschen Komödie', in Jan Knopf (ed.), *Brechts 'Guter Mensch von Sezuan'* (Frankfurt aM, Suhrkamp, 1982), p.226.

56. Wright, p.121.

57. Janelle Reinelt, *After Brecht: British Epic Theater* (Ann Arbor, University of Michigan Press), p.82; Diamond, pp.83, 88-9.

58. Diamond, pp.82-94.

Notes on Contributors

Peter Davies is a Lektor in English at the University of Erlangen-Nürnberg. His doctorate (1997) deals with the early history of the German Academy of Arts and the GDR literary community in the context of Stalin's German policy. He is currently working on Johannes R. Becher.

Steve Giles is a Senior Lecturer in German and Critical Theory at the University of Nottingham. His publications include *Theorising Modernism* (1993) and *Bertolt Brecht and Critical Theory: Marxism, Modernity and the 'Threepenny Lawsuit'* (1997).

Katharina Hall studied German and English at the University of Southampton, and is in the process of completing a doctorate which presents a Lacanian approach to the novels of Günter Grass.

Astrid Herhoffer is Head of German in the Modern Languages Department at Staffordshire University. Her research interests and publications are in the field of contemporary German literature and society, and she specialises in East German literature.

Terry Holmes is a Lecturer in German at the University of Wales, Swansea. He has published many articles on Nineteenth Century German literature, a series of contributions to the *Georg Büchner Jahrbuch*, and a recent book on Büchner's *Dantons Tod*.

Tom Kuhn is a Faculty Lecturer in Twentieth Century German Literature at the University of Oxford and a Fellow of St Hugh's College. His publications include articles on modern German drama, and *The Young Brecht* (1992). He is a general editor of the Methuen Brecht edition.

Jonathan Long is a Lecturer in German at the University of Durham. He recently completed a doctorate (1997) at the University of Nottingham on Wolfgang Hildesheimer and Thomas Bernhard, and his research interests include narratology and contemporary German literature.

Rodney Livingstone is Professor of German at the University of Southampton. He has published English-language editions of works by Marx & Engels, Lukács, Benjamin and Adorno. His recent research has focused on topics connected with Jewish-German relations.

Anne Moss is a PhD candidate in German Studies at New York University. Her research focuses on the 1968 German Student Movement as seen in the press, student leaflets, and literature of the time. She has published six language textbooks, including *Der Spiegel*, a reader for students of German.

Meg Mumford is a Lecturer in the Department of Theatre, Film and Television Studies at the University of Glasgow. Her doctoral thesis (1997) dealt with the concept of gestus and gestic acting, and she has also published on Brecht and Stanislavski.

Stephen Parker is a Senior Lecturer in German at the University of Manchester. He co-edited *German Writers and the Cold War, 1945-1961* (1992), and recently completed a study of Peter Huchel. His main research interests are in cultural politics and literature in the GDR.

Julian Preece is a Lecturer in German at the University of Kent. His doctoral thesis (1991) dealt with uses of history in the prose works of Günter Grass, and he has published widely on contemporary German, Austrian and GDR literature.

Renate Rechtien is a Lecturer in the School of Modern Languages and European Studies at the University of Bath. Her doctoral thesis (1997) dealt with Christa Wolf, and her research interests include East and West German women's narratives, feminist appropriations of myth and fairy-tale, and the position of women in German society.

Mark W. Roche is the Rev. Edmund P. Joyce C.S.C. Professor of German Language and Literature at the University of Notre Dame. He has published books on Nineteenth Century German literature and philosophy and on Gottfried Benn, and has just completed a study of tragedy and comedy in Hegel.

Freddie Rokem is Professor in the Department of Theatre Arts at Tel Aviv University, Israel. He has published books on Swedish theatre at the beginning of the Twentieth Century, and on theatrical space in Ibsen, Chekhov and Strindberg. His research interests include performance theory, the theory of acting, and the theatre of Strindberg.

Martyn Saville is a postgraduate student at the University of Nottingham, currently researching the question of national identity in post-war Austrian theatre, especially in the plays of Thomas Bernhard.

Jürgen Thomaneck is Professor of German at Aberdeen University. He is the author and editor of numerous books, chapters and articles dealing with sociolinguistics and political and literary studies, particularly in the field of GDR studies.

Christina Ujma is a Lecturer in German at Loughborough University. She is the author of *Ernst Blochs Konstruktion der Moderne* (1995), and her research interests include Twentieth Century intellectual and artistic debates on Marxism and Modernism, and Nineteenth Century German writing on Italy.

Florian Vaßen is Professor of contemporary German Literature at the University of Hanover, and Head of the Educational Theatre section. He co-edits *Korrespondenzen. Zeitschrift für Theaterpädagogik*. His research interests include drama and theatre, the theory and practice of theatre in education, Brecht, GDR literature, satire, caricature, and the theory of laughter.

Carl Weber is Professor of Directing and Dramaturgy at Stanford University. He was an assistant director, actor and dramaturg with Brecht 1952-56, and one of the directors of the Berliner Ensemble until 1961. He has published numerous essays, and edited and translated three volumes of works by Heiner Müller, as well as the anthology *Drama Contemporary: Germany*.

John J. White is Professor of German and Comparative Literature at King's College London. His books include *Mythology and the Modern Novel* (1971) and *Literary Futurism* (1990). He has published a critical guide to Brecht's *Leben des Galilei*, as well as co-editing works on Grass, Kafka, Thomas Mann, Musil, Stramm and literary depictions of Berlin.

A Journal of Germanic Studies

seminar

Seminar wird seit 1965 im Auftrag des kanadischen Germanistenverbandes (CAUTG) unter Mitarbeit der Germanistenvereinigung von Australien und Neuseeland (German Section, AUMLLA) herausgegeben. Die Zeitschrift bringt Beiträge und Rezensionen zu allen Gebieten der deutschen Literatur und erscheint viermal im Jahr.

Manuskripte, die nach dem *MLA Style Manual* (1985) einzurichten sind, werden in je zwei Exemplaren in deutscher, englischer oder französischer Sprache erbeten an:

Professor Rodney Symington   oder
Editor, *Seminar*
Department of Germanic Studies
University of Victoria
Box 3045
Victoria, BC
Canada V8W 3P4

Professor Alan Corkhill
Associate Editor, *Seminar*
Department of German Studies
University of Queensland
Brisbane, Qld 4072
Australia

Bestellungen sind zu richten an:

University of Toronto Press, Journals Department
Downsview, Ontario, Canada M3H 5T8
Der Subskriptionspreis beträgt CAN $35.00 jährlich.
Einzelhefte $7.50.